SPIES AND COMMANDOS

SPIES AND COMMANDOS

How America Lost the Secret War in North Vietnam

Kenneth Conboy and Dale Andradé

UNIVERSITY PRESS OF KANSAS

Published by the University Press of Kansas (Lawrence, Kansas 66049), which was organized by the Kansas Board of Regents and is operated and funded by Emporia State University, Fort Hays State University, Kansas State University, Pittsburg State University, the University of Kansas, and Wichita State University.

Library of Congress Cataloging-in-Publication Data

Conboy, Kenneth J.
    Spies and commandos : How America lost the secret war in North
Vietnam / Kenneth Conboy and Dale Andradé.
      p.   cm. — (Modern war studies)
    Includes bibliographical references and index.
    ISBN 0-7006-1002-2 (cloth : alk. paper) ISBN 0-7006-1147-9 (pbk.)
    1. Vietnamese Conflict, 1961–1975—Military intellegence—United
States. 2. Vietnamese Conflict, 1961–1975—Commando operations—
Vietnam (Democratic Republic) I. Andradé, Dale. II. Title.
III. Series.
DS559.8.M44C66   2000
959.704'38—dc21   99-43457

British Library Cataloguing in Publication Data is available.

Printed in the United States of America
10 9 8 7 6 5 4 3 2

CONTENTS

v

PREFACE

During the fifteenth century, China ruled much of Vietnam. Burdened by taxes and an oppressive bureaucracy, the Vietnamese chafed under foreign rule. In Thanh Hoa Province, south of Hanoi, a revolt broke out, but badly outnumbered and outmatched by the Chinese army, the Vietnamese were quickly defeated. According to legend, the brave and futile battle was witnessed by Long Quan, the emperor of the water, and he decided to intervene.

At the time, there lived a fisherman named Le Than. One night, while casting his net under the twinkling stars, he noticed that it was heavier than usual. "A big fish," he thought, and was very pleased. But it was only an iron bar, which he threw back into the water. He cast his net again, dragged it back to the surface, and once more found the iron bar. This happened three times. Surprised by this uncanny coincidence, he looked closer at his catch. It was not an iron bar but rather a rough sword blade.

Some years later, rebellion rumbled again in Thanh Hoa, and Le Than joined a group of rebels commanded by a warrior named Le Loi. One day Le Loi called on Le Than, who was resting in his hut. It was dark inside, but in the corner was the blade, glowing with an unearthly light. Astonished by its brilliance, Le Loi took up the sword and studied it. "By the will of heaven" read an inscription engraved on the blade.

Once again the war went badly for the Vietnamese. Retreating from the battlefield, Le Loi entered a forest, where he saw a strange light gleaming from the swaying branches of a banyan tree. Climbing high, he found a sword hilt inlaid with jade. He remembered the blade he had seen in the fisherman's hut. Rushing back to the village, he found Le Than and asked for the sword. The hilt fit perfectly. "My prince, heaven must have sent it to you!" exclaimed Than. "We pledge to follow you and sacrifice our lives for the independence of our homeland."

Many died during the battles that followed, but Le Loi led his men unflinchingly against the Chinese, his arm strengthened tenfold by the magical sword in his grip. Soon the enemy was driven from Vietnam, and Le Loi became king.

One year later, Le Loi went boating on Luc Thuy Lake in the heart of Hanoi. Suddenly the royal boat rocked as waves rose up. In a frightening swirl of water and foam there appeared a golden tortoise. "Please be so kind as to return to my master, Long Quan, the emperor of the kingdom of waters, the sacred sword that he has entrusted to you," said the tortoise.

Standing in the boat, Le Loi felt the jade-handled sword at his side quiver in its scabbard. He drew the blade and flung it into the water. The golden tortoise swallowed it and disappeared beneath the surface. For a long time the glowing sword could be seen under the water as the tortoise journeyed back to his mystical world.

From that day on, the Vietnamese honored the sacred sword as a symbol of divine intervention against enemies.

Five hundred years later, the sacred sword returned to Vietnam, although the twentieth-century version was the brainchild of the U.S. Central Intelligence Agency. From its origins in the dying days of the First Indochina War, America's spy organization launched a covert operation against Hanoi that would have far-reaching effects on U.S. cold war policy, not just in Southeast Asia but throughout the world. By 1961, this program focused on the insertion of airborne commandos into the north. In all, twenty-seven CIA-sponsored teams were dropped—more than two hundred men. When the agency's mandate ended in 1964, the Defense Department took over, expanding the program and sending another two dozen teams into North Vietnam under the umbrella of the innocuously named Studies and Observations Group (SOG). The battle in Hanoi's backyard would at one time or another encompass just about every form of unconventional warfare: from stay-behind missions to resistance networks, sabotage and diversionary operations to intelligence collection, and the rescue of downed airmen. It continued until after the last American combat troops left Vietnam in 1972, making this one of the longest-running covert paramilitary operations in U.S. history.

All this occurred during turbulent times. The cold war was heating up; the superpowers sought influence in the Third World, but each feared nuclear war if brushfire conflicts burned too hot. President Dwight D. Eisenhower used covert operations in Iran and Guatemala as a cheap and quiet way of extending American interests without risking open war. In these instances, he was lucky. His successor, President John F. Kennedy, quickly found that such operators could be very costly. Within three months of Kennedy's inauguration, the CIA was humiliated at the Bay of Pigs in an attempt to overthrow Fidel Castro, Cuba's communist leader. The debacle shook the administration, and its effects rippled across the world. Nowhere were they felt more than in Southeast Asia, where the new administration was finding itself increasingly embroiled in a communist offensive in Laos and a burgeoning insurgency in neighboring South Vietnam.

The lessons of the Bay of Pigs caused a major reexamination of covert action as a tool of U.S. foreign policy. In a series of national security memorandums, Kennedy decided that the Defense Department would take over any operations that became too big for the CIA to keep completely secret. Vietnam was to be the proving ground for this new way of running covert operations, but the experiment presented many problems. Just what role should the CIA have in the escalating conflict? Was the Pentagon capable of running a secret war? Could it have a direct impact on Hanoi's ability to wage war in South Vietnam? How far would the United States go inside North Vietnam?

Enter the sword of Long Quan. Agency planners resurrected the ancient legend and incorporated it in their plan for a resistance movement in Hanoi's backyard. They called it the Sacred Sword Patriot's League, a name intended to invoke the Vietnamese peoples' historical memory of oppression at the hands of foreigners.

The new sacred sword was wielded by psychological warriors, men who fought with ideas instead of weapons, propaganda instead of bullets. Summoning the specter of China—Vietnam's timeless foe—was not lost on CIA planners. Updating the legend, they hoped to use it to convince the North Vietnamese people that their government was a lackey of China and the Soviet Union. The same disinformation also criticized the South Vietnamese reliance on the United States, a tactic designed to mask Washington's hand in the scheme and capitalize on Vietnam's historical distrust of any foreign intervention. The point of the sacred sword was to rid Vietnam of *all* foreigners—just as Le Loi had done centuries before.

Here was the root of the covert war inside North Vietnam, but, like much else during the war, implementation rarely mirrored planning. Washington waffled on what the Sacred Sword Patriot's League should accomplish. Would it be a "real" resistance front, one that would seek out converts, build an insurgency, and eventually threaten the communist rulers in Hanoi, or would it be a "notional" front, one that was meant to make Hanoi *think* there was a real revolution in its backyard? This debate over how to wield the sacred sword would go to the very heart of the covert operations against North Vietnam.

All the while, Washington found itself becoming more deeply involved in the escalating conflict. Troops shuffled in, casualties were carried out, and the Vietnam War became a fixture in the American public's daily life. Volumes have been published about the Vietnam "quagmire" and the soldiers who fought it. But little is known about the covert war waged behind the scenes, despite the fact that it was an important tool used by two U.S. presidents in the hopes that they could somehow stop Hanoi's assault on the south. How they wielded their "sacred sword" is the subject of this book.

We have many individuals to thank for helping us in our research and writing. First and foremost are the commandos themselves. These brave men parachuted into North Vietnam on missions they knew to be dangerous, then endured years—sometimes decades—of imprisonment and torture. All those we interviewed graciously answered questions and pointed us in new directions, but we would like to give individual recognition to Nguyen Van Vinh and Nguyen Nhu Anh, who helped us above and beyond our expectations. Former commandos still living in Vietnam also spoke with us despite constant surveillance by Hanoi's security police. Their courage will never die.

Special thanks goes to Robert Destatte, a talented Vietnamese linguist and an authority on the North Vietnamese side of the war. He shared his vast collection of Vietnamese sources and unstintingly gave of his time to translate them. Bob's knowledge of the war and his contacts in Hanoi opened doors and made sense of the many snippets of information we stumbled upon.

We received help from many people in Vietnam as well. In Ho Chi Minh City, Do Tuyet Huong helped procure books and tirelessly translated parts of them, despite her many more pressing tasks. In Hanoi, Le Hoai Phuong did the same. Both were unfailingly polite, even when our poor Vietnamese language skills seemed certain to get us into trouble.

Other people deserve our gratitude. James Morrison used his unique skills in seeking out sources and conducted several crucial interviews. Edwin Moise provided new documents on the Tonkin Gulf incident and on the Norwegian-made patrol boats that became an integral part of the maritime program. Richard Boylan at the National Archives pointed out the newly discovered (and declassified) MACSOG financial records and frequently altered his busy schedule to help with our bewildering requests. Professor David Elliott provided a fresh look at the psychological slant behind some of the covert operations and lent us his photographs. Many others also helped, some in the background. We remain in their debt.

Although all books are a collaborative effort, the authors take responsibility for everything in these pages. Any errors in fact or interpretation are our own, and none of the views expressed in this book reflect the official policy or position of the Department of Defense or the U.S. government.

1

TROJAN HORSES

The war was not going well for France. By early 1952, the Vietnamese communists—the Viet Minh—had seized most of the northern border region with China, leaving them free to make raids into northern Vietnam's rice bowl, the fertile Red River delta. Growing disillusionment on the home front only served to compound French woes. Hoping for a quick victory, French forces maneuvered into blocking positions at Hoa Binh, a provincial center west of Hanoi, where they planned to cut a key Viet Minh supply route running east toward the delta.

The Viet Minh responded by gathering three infantry divisions totaling some twenty-five thousand troops. Surprised and overwhelmed, the French began a gradual withdrawal toward the safety of the Red River, blowing up anything usable as a parting gesture. By the second week of March, Hoa Binh was deserted.

Halfway around the world in Washington, the Truman administration looked on with concern as the French position in Indochina eroded. The loss of any country in Southeast Asia to communism would have major psychological, political, and economic consequences for American interests.[1] Although the situation was grave, Harry Truman had few options. The United States was already supplying the bulk of France's military equipment for Indochina, and with American forces embroiled in Korea, greater involvement in a second Asian conflict was politically impossible.

But there was another option—covert operations. For the Central Intelligence Agency (CIA), now five years old, this was an inviting opportunity to get a foot in the Indochinese door. Combining the optimism and naïveté so prominent during those early days, the CIA selected one of its young case officers, Donald Gregg, and gave him a bold assignment: train a team of Vietnamese in small-unit tactics and prepare to parachute with them into rural northern Vietnam. Fresh from paramilitary training and yet to serve in an overseas post, Gregg readily agreed. Flying to Thailand, he picked up ten Vietnamese and escorted them to the CIA compound at the U.S. Navy base in Yokosuka, Japan, for a month of basic instruction. Two things quickly became apparent. First, Gregg saw little thought being given to what he and the trainees could possibly accomplish once they were back in the Vietnamese countryside. Second, and more disturbing, Gregg found that he knew about as much about Vietnam as his trainees. All ten had been recruited in Thailand by an agent who claimed they came from the pool of fifty thousand ethnic Vietnamese who had fled there immediately after World War II. But Gregg found that in reality his Vietnamese recruits had come from an earlier emigré wave that had left Vietnam more than 150 years before.[2] Even the CIA, with its chronic optimism, could not go forward with an operation based on such flimsy planning. "The Vietnamese were sent back to Thailand in April," Gregg recalled, "and my life expectancy increased."[3]

It would be another two years before the CIA would again toy with the idea of launching covert paramilitary operations inside Indochina. By then, the Viet Minh army—ranging from full-time regulars to village militia—had swelled to more than 350,000. Although withdrawal now seemed just a question of time, France would still accept only equipment and money from the United States, rebuffing any attempt to send advisers from either the military or the CIA.

President Dwight D. Eisenhower did not like the course France was taking in Vietnam. During a meeting with his National Security Council (NSC) on 21 January 1954, he insisted that Indochina not be allowed to fall to communism by default and asked his advisers what steps could be taken to bolster the French position. Besides material support, he was particularly interested in prospects for a guerrilla warfare program that could carry on the fight in the wake of the likely French departure.

Responding to the president, CIA director Allen Dulles told the council he had paramilitary experts ready to go to Southeast Asia, but France was stubbornly refusing permission. Guerrilla warfare, Dulles noted, was a long-term process requiring ample preparation. While sufficient time might no longer be available, he suggested a tough quid pro quo with the French: continued provision of American military equipment in exchange for agreement to the introduction of the CIA's paramilitary personnel. Eisenhower agreed.[4]

Eight days later, the president's top advisers reconvened. Picking up where Eisenhower left off, the CIA's Dulles introduced Edward Lansdale to those around the table and suggested he be the first to go to Vietnam. A U.S. Air Force colonel on extended duty with the CIA, Lansdale had a reputation as one of America's foremost experts on guerrilla and paramilitary operations. He had already made a mark in Southeast Asia, where, acting as a senior adviser to Filipino president Ramon Magsaysay, he had been instrumental in defeating the communist Hukbalahap rebel movement—accomplishments that had impressed Dulles and his equally influential brother, John Foster, the secretary of state. The NSC told Lansdale to pack his bags and head for Vietnam.[5]

Before Lansdale left, however, the war in Indochina entered its final stage. A French garrison in the Dien Bien Phu valley in northwestern Vietnam, under siege since late the previous year, was fast becoming France's last stand. As the Viet Minh noose tightened around Dien Bien Phu, the National Security Council upgraded Lansdale's lone advisory slot into an entire CIA team to be known as the Saigon Military Mission (SMM). The organization would work not with the French but rather with the anticommunist and nominally independent Vietnamese government headed by Emperor Bao Dai, a Paris-approved proxy.

Before anybody from the Saigon Military Mission had a chance to set foot in Vietnam, Dien Bien Phu fell to the Viet Minh in early May. Eisenhower did not particularly like the way the French had run their Indochinese colonies, but he liked the thought of a Viet Minh regime even less. As French soldiers were led away as prisoners from Dien Bien Phu, he considered the possibility of a major guerrilla operation in northern Vietnam to be supported through Thailand.[6] Very quickly, however, it became clear that there was no time for grandiose plans. In Geneva, an international conference was already negotiating France's withdrawal from Indochina. Fearful of a French sellout, Lansdale rushed to Saigon while the Geneva conference was still in session. Arriving on 1 June, he was ostensibly accredited as an assistant air attaché to the U.S. embassy.

There was no time to assemble additional members for his Saigon Military Mission, so Lansdale alone spent his first month forging contacts with Bao Dai's armed forces and working with its Armed Psychological Warfare Company in Hanoi. He met with less than complete success: on the company's first mission under Lansdale's tutelage, two team members defected to the communists.[7]

On 1 July, Lansdale was joined by a deputy, Major Lucien "Lou" Conein. A paramilitary specialist in his own right, Conein thrived on just this sort of mission. Known as "Black Luigi" to his fellow operators, Conein had infiltrated into northern Vietnam nine years earlier while serving in the Office of Strategic Services (OSS), the CIA's World War II predecessor. Unlike other OSS officers who had worked with the Viet Minh against the Japanese, Conein had linked up with French-led Vietnamese maquis. To Conein's advantage, several of those maquis were now senior Vietnamese military officers.

For the next three weeks, the two-man Saigon Military Mission continued to forge contacts among the Vietnamese. On 21 July, the Geneva conference concluded. According to the settlement, Vietnam faced a three-hundred-day period during which civilians were free to move about. After that, the country would be temporarily divided: all territory north of the seventeenth parallel would be turned over to the Viet Minh, while the zone south of that parallel would be governed by the pro-Western Bao Dai regime established earlier by the French. The capital of Viet Minh–controlled North Vietnam would be Hanoi, while Bao Dai's South Vietnam was to be run from Saigon. A nationwide election slated for 1956 would theoretically unite the country after two years. In addition, the number of foreign military personnel would be frozen after 11 August.

The Eisenhower administration considered the settlement in Geneva a disaster and immediately changed the Saigon Military Mission's mandate. With northern Vietnam soon to come under complete communist control, Lansdale's primary mission now became stay-behind resistance operations. For this, the CIA could turn to a precedent of sorts. Across Western Europe, the agency already had laid the groundwork for underground guerrilla networks ahead of a possible Soviet invasion. In Asia, too, the CIA had raised an elite Thai police unit to act as cadre for resistance against an expected Chinese push to the south. In neither case, however, had the stay-behind nets been put to the test.

In establishing a Vietnamese network, the Saigon Military Mission looked for help from the Dai Viet, a secretive, ultranationalist movement founded in 1939. The Dai Viet—literally Greater Vietnam—was born out of opposition to French colonial rule. This led to a brief alliance with other nationalists during World War II, including the Viet Minh. After the war the Viet Minh tricked the nationalist groups into a coalition and then turned against the noncommunists, killing or forcing most of them out of the country. The Dai Viet leadership fled to China. Returning to Vietnam in 1947, the movement toned down its anti-French rhetoric and attempted to shed its elitist image in order to broaden its appeal to the masses. It also began focusing on the threat from the Viet Minh. By 1951, the Dai Viet had begun armed opposition against the communists, forming a paramilitary civil guard in the north loosely allied with the French. By December 1953, this guard numbered some seventeen thousand.

The Geneva agreement spelled the end of the Dai Viet's northern power base, so Lansdale suspected a stay-behind scheme would appeal to them. With contacts facilitated by French intelligence, he ventured to Hanoi in July 1954 to sound them out. There he met with Minister of National Defense Phan Huy Quat, one of two senior Dai Viet officials who held cabinet positions in the Bao Dai government. Listening to the American colonel, Quat suggested he meet with another Dai Viet member and relative by marriage, Dr. Dang Van Sung.

The Dai Viet's unofficial secretary general, Sung was born into a wealthy landowning family in central Nghe An Province. Intelligent, courteous, and

People's Republic of China

Meng-tzu

Ching-hsi

Ha Giang

Ha Giang

Cao Bang

Cao Bang

Lao Cai

Viet Bac Autonomous Region

Lao Cai

Lai

Chau

Lai Chau

Yen

Bai

Nghia

Lo

Tuyen
Quang

Lang
Son

Ning-ming

Yen
Bai

Tuyen
Quang

Bac

Thai

Lang Son

Tay Bac

Son La

Autonomous Region

Son La

Nghia
Lo

Vinh
Phu

Thai
Nguyen

Pho
Tho

Hanoi
Municipality

HANOI

Ha Bac

Bac Giang

Quang
Ninh

Hon Gay

Laos

Samneua

Song   Ma

Ha Dong

Hoa
Binh

Ha
Tay

Hoa Binh

Hai Duong

Hai Hung

Nam
Ha

Thai
Binh

Haiphong
Haiphong
Municipality

Thai Binh

Song   River

Louangphrabang

Ninh
Binh

Nam
Dinh

Ninh
Binh

Thanh

Hoa

Thanh
Hoa

Xiangkhoang

Nghe
An

Song   Ca

Vinh

GULF

OF

TONKIN

Paksane

Ha Tinh

Ha Tinh

VIENTIANE

Thailand

Nakhon
Phanom

Quang
Binh

Dong Hoi

Laos

Vinh Linh
Special Zone

Vinh Linh
Demarcation Line

Savannakhet

Quang
Tri

South

Hue

Vietnam

501702 4-73

North Vietnam

serious, he earned a medical degree, but instead of becoming a doctor he joined the Dai Viet in 1940 and quickly became one of its most influential leaders. Following Viet Minh attacks against the movement after World War II, he briefly went into Chinese exile, returning in 1947 to play a major role in Dai Viet newspapers and youth organizations. One of the first in the party to advocate cooperation with Emperor Bao Dai, Sung was outspoken in his opposition to the Geneva agreement, particularly its call to partition Vietnam.[8]

Joined by Quat, Lansdale arrived at the Dai Viet headquarters in Hanoi. "Lansdale laid down his proposal for a stay-behind organization, and we ended up talking for two days," Sung recalled. "He pointed out that the Dai Viet was still a party of cadre, of intellectuals, not a party of the masses. He gave us a challenge: if we could prove we could work with the masses, he would support a network of stay-behinds in the north. I grabbed the opportunity to prove ourselves."[9]

Lansdale returned to Saigon, where he was met by ten more CIA officers, all experts in paramilitary and clandestine intelligence operations, who had been rushed in from Japan, Korea, and Okinawa to augment the Saigon Military Mission before Geneva's 11 August deadline. This made Vietnam unique in that it had two CIA stations within a single country: one under the station chief dealing with conventional espionage, and the Saigon Military Mission under Lansdale handling paramilitary activities. While the station chief and his spies were disguised as diplomats at the embassy, Lansdale's men were given cover slots in the Pentagon's Saigon-based Military Assistance and Advisory Group (MAAG) for Indochina, which had been providing military assistance to France.[10]

With his Saigon Military Mission up to strength, Lansdale assigned Conein to work with Sung on the details of the Dai Viet stay-behind program. Having just come off a tour in West Germany smuggling agents through the Iron Curtain, Conein had ample background in setting up spy nets. And with his detachment ostensibly assigned as MAAG supervisors for the nearly one million refugees who were expected to come south during the three-hundred-day grace period laid down in Geneva, he had a ready excuse for traveling between Hanoi and the port city of Haiphong.

The task would not be easy. Viet Minh agents already were beginning to take secret control of Hanoi. Racing against time, Sung chose Cao Xuan Tuyen, a senior Dai Viet officer and captain in the Bao Dai army, to begin recruitment. Tuyen's first agent candidate was Tran Minh Chau. A Catholic from the city of Nam Dinh, Chau had joined the Viet Minh during the closing days of World War II. Rising to the position of village chief, he led local militiamen against the French until his arrest in 1949. In prison he renounced ties to the communists and, with many fellow Catholics from Nam Dinh already gravitating toward the Dai Viet, eventually joined the sect.

For his next recruit, Tuyen settled on Nguyen Kim Xuyen. Also a Catholic from Nam Dinh, Xuyen was an established conservative and columnist for a Dai Viet newspaper. Two men for the budding stay-behind group was a good start, but Tuyen had only until the end of August to find another eighteen. He failed, ending up with only fourteen more Dai Viet recruits by month's end.

Code-named the "Binh" group, the Dai Viet—sixteen in total—assembled for Conein. According to Saigon Military Mission plans, CIA support for the Binh would be temporary, with control passed at some future date to the Bao Dai government in Saigon. These conditions were acceptable to the Dai Viet leadership, and the sixteen recruits were driven to Haiphong during early September, then secreted aboard a U.S. Navy vessel and taken to Okinawa. Subjected to a monthlong battery of physical and psychological tests, the group was reassembled in October and taken to the CIA's $28 million training complex on Saipan.[11]

Already in its fourth year of operation, the Saipan base—given the intentionally benign title of Naval Technical Training Unit—was by then the CIA's premier training center in the Far East. Previously host to trainees from Korea, Taiwan, and Thailand, the base was designed to handle numerous compartmentalized classes of foreign students. "The facilities on Saipan were really complete, like a miniature Fort Peary," said one officer, in reference to the CIA's main training facility near Williamsburg, Virginia.[12]

On Saipan, the Dai Viet recruits were whittled down to twelve. Those who went on with the training were assigned English and French aliases. Under the guidance of four American advisers, they were given a course in basic paramilitary and agent tradecraft. In a less-than-perfect arrangement, instruction was translated from English to French, then translated again by one of the students into Vietnamese.

Once this basic tutorial was finished, the recruits were divided in three subgroups. The first, which included Tran Minh Chau—now known as Leslie—and three others, was coached in weapons, demolitions, and sabotage. The second group, totaling five men, received an intensive espionage course. The last group of three recruits specialized in communications.[13]

The course on Saipan was supposed to last for six months, but the CIA decided that if the Binh group stayed for the entire duration it would not have enough time to infiltrate ahead of the Viet Minh takeover in northern Vietnam. So after only four months the three subgroups were gathered together and given a final test by a CIA polygraph expert. Pretending to be a Viet Minh police officer, he subjected the agents to a mock interrogation.

One agent was dropped when he was unmasked as a French informant; CIA officers were later told that he was beheaded upon his return to Saigon.[14]

Unknown to the Binh trainees, they were not the only Vietnamese on Saipan. Back in September, a second stay-behind network was taking shape under Saigon Military Mission auspices.[15] Called the "Hao" group, these agents were recruited from the Viet Nam Quoc Dan Dang (VNQDD), or Vietnam Nationalist Party. Established in 1927 as the Vietnamese arm of the Koumintang party in China, the VNQDD gained early prominence among nationalists after leading an anticolonial uprising in 1930. Brutally crushed by the French, its leaders were forced into Chinese exile until after World War II. Upon their return, they were decimated again, this time by the Viet Minh. Twice bloodied, the party remained a shadow of its former self through the early 1950s. Still, the group had members willing to volunteer for spy training, enabling the party leadership, with Lansdale's support, to select twenty-one members at the close of 1954 and send them to Saipan.[16]

While the stay-behind agents trained overseas, the Saigon Military Mission busied itself with other projects. As the new communist regime made last-minute preparations before the official turnover of power in Hanoi on 11 October, Lansdale spent much of his time waging a psychological campaign designed to stir up discontent with the new rulers before they were even settled. As refugees left their homes—fleeing overwhelmingly from north to south—during the Geneva-mandated grace period following the accords, Lansdale took steps to ensure that the flow would be as heavy as possible. Using propaganda to convince people that life was better in the south, Lansdale also spread rumors that the Chinese, traditionally disliked by the Vietnamese despite their communist alliance, were planning to take an active role in governing the country, and that many Vietnamese were to be sent to China as railroad laborers. Lansdale also exploited Catholic fears of godless communism, printing leaflets claiming that "the Virgin Mary is moving south" and promising a better life with fellow Catholics in the south. Tales of Viet Minh atrocities also fueled discontent. Some were probably true, but the Saigon Military Mission made up many more.[17]

Lansdale's biggest propaganda coup came when his men planted leaflets signed by Viet Minh officials instructing the Vietnamese on how to behave during the communist takeover of Hanoi in October, and hinted at how private property would be redistributed and the money system reformed. According to Lansdale, the campaign was a huge success. "The day following the distribution of these leaflets, refugee registration tripled," he wrote. "Two days later, Viet Minh currency was worth half the value prior to the leaflets. The Viet Minh took to the radio to denounce the leaflets; the leaflets were so authentic in appearance that even most of the rank and file Viet Minh were sure that the radio denunciations were a French trick." Even the French were fooled. They arrested one of Lansdale's Vietnamese team members while he was distributing leaflets late at night and charged him as a Viet Minh agent.[18]

During the first week of October, Conein's northern detachment prepared to vacate Hanoi just before the Viet Minh marched in. They spent their last days conducting acts of delayed sabotage in the city. Agents sneaked into the bus depot to contaminate gas tanks and smuggled high explosives—developed by a CIA technical team to look like lumps of coal—into the fuel supplies at the city's railroad yard. Both missions had their lighter moments, remembers Conein:

> The oil contaminant was delivered in canisters from Japan. When we opened them, the fumes nearly made us pass out while we were at the bus station, but we recovered long enough to fill the tanks and leave. The lumps of coal were also delivered from Japan. The idea was to plant them at railheads and wait for a bang. We were afraid that some guy would come by, steal some coal to heat his home, and get blown to hell. We later got word that some of it exploded inside locomotives.[19]

Finishing their sabotage, Conein and his men shifted to Haiphong—which was not to be turned over to the Viet Minh until May 1955—to select secret sites to hide arms and equipment for the Binh group. Supplies began arriving from Saigon in January 1955 aboard planes belonging to Civil Air Transport, the CIA's proprietary airline, and the teams moved into action. Arms and ammunition were concealed inside building foundations; other supplies were brought to cemeteries and buried during phony funeral ceremonies orchestrated by the Saigon Military Mission.[20] By month's end, everything had been cached.

On 8 February, the Binh agents finished their polygraph session and were returned to Saigon, where they underwent a month of political indoctrination before infiltration. According to plan, the twelve agents would be split among three locales. Leslie, given the rank of lieutenant, was placed in overall command. He and five other agents were to operate in Hanoi, three others in Haiphong, and the last three in Nam Dinh.

In early March, the twelve agents were taken to Haiphong by ship. There Conein gave them a final briefing and provided each with forged identity cards. New occupations and residences had also been arranged by the Saigon Military Mission. Most were disguised as fishermen. By month's end, each had successfully slipped into northern society. The Binh network was in place.

Infiltration of the VNQDD's Hao group was a more ambitious undertaking. Eight and a half tons of supplies—to include 14 radios, 300 carbines, 50 pistols, and 300 pounds of explosives—were quietly brought north aboard American planes and ships during February and March. The bulk was hidden in caches along the Red River. Much of the remainder was stashed in Haiphong, some of it concealed within building foundations.[21]

Other supplies were diverted for the VNQDD network. Bui Van Ninh, a member of that party and an officer in Bao Dai's Government Information Office, was one of those solicited to help hide supplies: "A law professor who had taught at the Hanoi University and whom I had known for some time asked me to hide two radios supplied by the Americans. They were packed inside large containers. I dug a hole two meters deep at my house on Son Lam Road in Haiphong and placed one of the radios there. I took the second to a relative's house two kilometers away and put it down a hole, also two meters deep."[22]

During April, the Hao students finished their Saipan course and were taken to Clark Air Force Base in the Philippines for a final briefing. Once finished, the agents boarded a U.S. Navy vessel and sailed straight to Haiphong. In small groups under cover of darkness, they slipped ashore and divided into four groups, one each to the cities of Ha Dong, Haiphong, Hanoi, and Son Tay.[23]

One month later, in compliance with the Geneva Accords, the Viet Minh marched into Haiphong and the other residual French coastal sanctuaries in North Vietnam. With both agent networks in place, Conein's detachment retreated south to Saigon.

Now behind communist lines, the Binh agents put their training into practice. The heaviest burden fell on the Haiphong detachment, which set about unearthing the buried supplies. In short order, they had recovered their entire allotment of radios and weapons. Also among their supplies was a batch of explosive coal like that used by the Saigon Military Mission against the Hanoi railroad yard. One of the Haiphong agents, Bui Manh Ha, alias Bosco, then purchased a Citroen taxi and began shuttling portions of the supplies to the other Binh sites.

Trouble was brewing down in Saigon, the result of the earlier verbal pact between Lansdale and the Dai Viet leadership. Lansdale had stipulated that the stay-behind network would eventually come under the control of the central government in Saigon. The Dai Viet had agreed. At the time the pact made sense because the Bao Dai government was heavily represented by Dai Viet officials, including two cabinet ministers. But by early 1955 the government had changed considerably. The new prime minister, Ngo Dinh Diem, was a

Catholic mandarin from Hue and intolerant of competition. Immediately upon gaining power, he set about purging the Dai Viet.

While Diem was seen as a threat by the Dai Viet, he was embraced by Lansdale. Just as with Magsaysay in the Philippines, Lansdale chose to place his support behind a single political figure, a charismatic personality. Very quickly, he assumed a personal stake in Diem's success. As part of this close relationship, Lansdale briefed Diem on the existence of the Dai Viet agents in North Vietnam.

Hearing of this, Diem demanded a hand in administering the spy network. Dr. Dang Van Sung, the movement's secretary general, protested, arguing that the northern agents were a long-term means of promoting the Dai Viet cause, not a personal tool for the president. From Sung's perspective, Diem would misuse the spies: "They were supposed to work against the communists as underground agents. Their main task was recruitment. For this purpose we had even sent a second group of Dai Viet, chosen from northern refugees settled around Saigon, for training in Saipan. This second group included minorities, and was supposed to go north and reinforce the original network. Diem's people didn't want agents, they wanted commandos."[24]

In the end a compromise was reached. Sung was allowed to keep control of the second group of Dai Viet agents trained in Saipan, who would be retained in Saigon as party cadre. The first group of spies, however, were to be taken over by Diem—with Sung completely excluded from the program.

Sung was replaced by General Nguyen Ngoc Le, Diem's new chief of the National Police. Le had earlier worked with the Saigon Military Mission while organizing a Vietnam Veterans League and was already acquainted with Lansdale. With General Le nominally in charge, Cao Xuan Tuyen, the Dai Viet official responsible for recruiting the agents, informed the Binh via radio of the new command arrangement in Saigon. Leslie, speaking on behalf of the other spies, pledged loyalty to Diem.

As Dr. Sung feared, the change was more than just semantics. Prompted by their new handlers, the stay-behind agents were directed to accomplish two seemingly incompatible missions. On the one hand, they were encouraged to conduct commando operations such as sabotage, actions that would invariably draw the attention of the authorities. On the other hand, they were expected to expand their spy network, a mission that could be accomplished only by drawing as little attention to themselves as possible.

The Binh spies were naturally reluctant to commit sabotage—with one exception. Using the CIA's exploding coal, Binh agents were able to plant a lump in the Haiphong railyard. Later reports from the Hanoi's official news agency claimed that the suspect anthracite was discovered by a vigilant worker before damage was done.

Slightly more effort was given to recruiting new agents. Operating under cover as a bicycle repairman, Leslie reported that he had enlisted two supporters, both Dai Viet members.

Sitting in Saigon, General Le and his American counterparts were unimpressed with the limited results to date. Worse, some CIA officers at the embassy thought they detected signs that the agents had been doubled. To test their fears, they wanted to bring one of the agents south for a debriefing. Lansdale strongly opposed this plan, fearing it would blow the agent's cover and make it impossible to get him back north, but by that time he was set to rotate home and his former Saigon Military Mission paramilitary responsibilities were being assumed by the regular CIA station. Because relations between the Saigon Military Mission and the CIA station had never been good, Lansdale's advice was ignored.[25]

Volunteering to make the trek south was a member of the Nam Dinh subnet going by the name of André. On 6 September 1956, André stole south along the North Vietnamese panhandle and crossed the border. Once in Saigon, he was subjected to two days of polygraphing. After the CIA was satisfied that André had not been doubled, he was debriefed for nine more days, then sent back north laden with a generous supply of money for distribution to the other Binh members.

André restored the CIA's confidence in the Binh network, perhaps even blinding the agency to the reality of the situation in North Vietnam. For over a year, communist authorities had been closing in on the agent net, ever since three pieces of exploding coal were discovered during a police crackdown on illegal coal peddlers. When an investigation traced the source of the explosives to a Binh agent, North Vietnamese intelligence managed to infiltrate part of the network. Among those captured and doubled was André.

For a short time, Hanoi refrained from closing down the entire Dai Viet operation, hoping to turn it to their advantage. At least one agent in each of the three Binh locales was allowed to operate under Saigon's control through the fall of 1958. Together, they managed to recruit at least seven more subagents, including one woman.[26]

Then, on 12 November 1958, North Vietnamese security forces snapped up all the remaining Binh operatives. Bosco, the Saipan-trained commander in Haiphong, was arrested while one of his subordinates was sending a message to Saigon in a radio set hidden inside a table. In Hanoi, Leslie, the overall commander, was seized, while a third Saipan graduate, going by the alias Philip, was captured in Nam Dinh.[27]

On 4 April 1959, the Binh trial opened in Hanoi. Ten suspects were identified at the highly publicized spectacle. Next to the courtroom, Hanoi au-

A Haiphong court sentences ten agents from the VNQDD stay-behind network, April 1965. (Vietnam News Agency)

thorities showed off an exhibit of captured Binh equipment. On display were silenced submachine guns, explosives, small spring-loaded pistols hidden inside toothpaste tubes, and radio sets. (The CIA had not been too careful in providing plausible deniability. While the weapons were sterile, the radios were clearly marked with U.S. Army Signal Corps plates.) In their typically heavy-handed approach toward propaganda, the Hanoi authorities also included photos of one agent reading a pornographic magazine with pinups visible on the walls.[28]

After twenty-four hours of testimony, verdicts were returned. Seven men received sentences of up to ten years in prison. Philip, the Nam Dinh agent, faced twenty years. Bosco, from Haiphong, got a life sentence. Leslie, the commander in Hanoi, was to meet a firing squad. According to Hanoi radio, a crowd of ten thousand outside the courtroom cheered the decision.

The Binh agents were unmasked, but the Hao network remained in place—barely. Starting on a bad note, the group's leader, Nguyen Tien Thanh,

Weapons and other supplies unearthed from VNQDD caches on display at the Haiphong trial, April 1965. (Vietnam News Agency)

immediately lost contact with most of his network. As a result, many of the group's supplies were never recovered. Worse, it took months for him to get an initial response from Saigon over the radio.

According to accounts later published by Hanoi, a desperate Thanh ordered two agents "in early August"—they left the exact date unstated—to make their way to South Vietnam via the Demilitarized Zone that separated the two countries at the seventeenth parallel. Apparently Hanoi was embarrassed to reveal that this occurred in August 1963: for eight years, the VN-QDD agents had operated undetected inside North Vietnam.

Both agents who tried to reach the Demilitarized Zone in 1963 panicked and returned to Haiphong after covering only half the distance. Shortly afterward, another group of VNQDD agents tried to make their way west toward the highlands along the Laos border, join a commune, and plan resistance activity. Like the first pair, however, this group also cut short its journey and returned.

It was not until 1964 that their collective luck came to an end. That year, a North Vietnamese construction crew clearing an old cemetery in Haiphong uncovered an arms cache. Hanoi launched an investigation, and ten VN-

QDD agents were eventually rolled up and put on trial the following year. Two members were executed, the rest given prison sentences.[29]

Curiously, no mention was ever made of the eleven other members of the Hao network. Not until 1977 did the likely answer slip during a statement by the minister of interior at a closed conference in Hanoi. Speaking about the investigation of political subjects, the minister made reference to a stay-behind network still operational until the mid-1970s: "In 1974, [the Ministry] deployed special agents to make contact [with the stay-behinds], using the password and recognition signals to establish communication. They communicated immediately."[30]

Two decades after the Saigon Military Mission's ambitious plan to spy on North Vietnam, it was all over. There were no more Trojan horses.

2

SINGLETONS

At the beginning of 1955, the list of threats to Prime Minister Ngo Dinh Diem's nascent regime was long and growing. Throughout South Vietnam a combination of religious sects, nationalists, and gangsters were all trying to topple Diem in order to protect their individual fiefdoms. By midyear, however, he shocked domestic and foreign observers alike by sweeping aside opponents in and around Saigon. Winning firm support from Washington in the aftermath, Diem staged a rigged election in October, tore down the imperial facade of the aging Emperor Bao Dai, and assumed the mantle of president of the Republic of Vietnam.

Although his strong-arming eliminated serious opposition, Diem still pressed ahead to insulate himself against foes both real and imagined. He did this through not one but four separate intelligence agencies. The first of these was the Office of Political and Social Studies. Behind this benign title, Dr. Tran Kim Tuyen, a devout Catholic and Diem confidant, built a spy agency tasked with domestic intelligence gathering against Diem's opponents, communists or otherwise.

The second, the Military Security Service (MSS), was created with Lansdale's help as an intelligence and interrogation organization. It was headed by General Mai Huu Xuan, previously the highest ranking Vietnamese in the colonial Sûreté, who was soon co-opted by Diem to spy on the armed forces and preempt any military coup attempts.

The third intelligence organ came under General Nguyen Ngoc Le's National Police. A trusted Diem loyalist, Le was chosen to assume control over the stay-behind spies in the north. This northern venture never amounted to more than a sideshow, however, as Le's police conglomerate had its hands full in the south running everything from the former Sûreté, to municipal police, to customs.

Finally, Diem's Army of the Republic of Vietnam—now known by its French acronym, ARVN—got into the spying act by revamping Office Six within its General Staff. Formerly a counterespionage unit under the French, Office Six had some early trouble when its chief, a Bao Dai appointee, fled to France in October 1954. In his place, Diem elevated a loyalist and changed the office's name to the General Studies Department of the Ministry of Defense.[1] Like the other three organizations, this army unit focused

16

on gathering intelligence about domestic political opponents, regardless of their political persuasion.

With four organizations all concerned with domestic intelligence, there was clearly a duplication of effort. This did not bother Diem, who used the various offices to spy on each other. While such misuse might have kept the president abreast of palace intrigue, it did little to foster government control in the countryside, an area where Diem's hold was slipping. Things became worse in 1956 after the president, under the pretext of a "Denunciation of the Communists" campaign, arrested thousands. Many opponents, including communist sympathizers who had illegally remained in the south in violation of the 1954 Geneva Accords, struck back, assassinating government officials.

Diem was quick to blame the rise in rural violence on clandestine support from North Vietnam. In hindsight, he was partially correct. After reunification elections set for 1956 failed to materialize, Hanoi indeed flirted with more militant ways of taking over the south, including support for southern communist insurgents (later popularly known as the Viet Cong). Added to this was growing dissatisfaction among noncommunists who opposed Diem's dictatorial methods and blatant Catholic favoritism among a predominantly Buddhist population.

While there was no smoking gun confirming Hanoi's interference, Washington shared Saigon's suspicion of the north. For the United States, North Vietnam posed additional threat as conduit for an invasion by the People's Republic of China south across mainland Southeast Asia, a contingency deemed possible, even probable, at the height of the cold war.

Adding to these dark scenarios was the fact that Washington knew next to nothing about what was going on inside North Vietnam. Since 1955, the CIA had tried to fill this vacuum by encouraging the Diem regime to launch spy operations into the north. Agency officials wanted the job to go to their Vietnamese civilian counterpart, Dr. Tuyen's Office of Political and Social Sciences.

While prone to xenophobia, Tuyen was willing to work with the United States. By 1956 he claimed to be running nine agent nets in the North Vietnamese panhandle. While the CIA was not privy to the mechanics of the operation, it was allowed to read radio messages allegedly coming from these agents. Washington was impressed and provided funds for Tuyen to build a motorized junk to spirit spies in and out of North Vietnam.[2]

Besides working with Tuyen's office, the Eisenhower administration in 1957 initiated a covert assistance program—jointly administered by the CIA and the Department of Defense—to create a South Vietnamese special forces unit. As with the elite Thai police cadre the agency had raised in the early 1950s, this Vietnamese formation, given the innocuous title of 1st

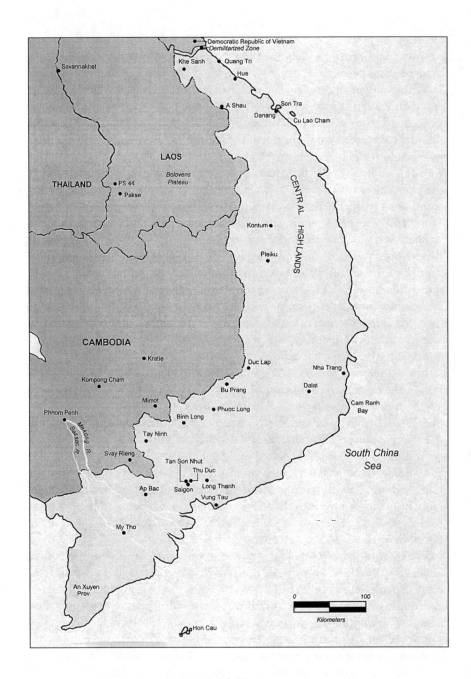

South Vietnam

Observation Group, had a defensive role: to act as a guerrilla cadre behind communist lines in the wake of a Chinese-led invasion.[3]

To shield the 1st Observation Group from publicity, it was placed under the Ministry of Defense's intelligence organ, the General Studies Department, which itself underwent two important changes that year. First, it changed its name to the Presidential Liaison Office (PLO), indicating a shift from the Ministry of Defense to Diem's direct control. Second, command of the liaison office was transferred to Lieutenant Colonel Le Quang Tung. A Catholic native of Hue, the soft-spoken, professorial Tung had previously been posted to the Military Security Service. Gaining the president's favor by virtue of his religion and hometown, he jumped rank from lieutenant to lieutenant colonel in just two years.[4]

With the creation of the 1st Observation Group, the Presidential Liaison Office suddenly had a stay-behind role beyond its mandate of domestic spying. Hoping for further assignments—and no doubt looking to compete with Tuyen's operation—Tung's 1st Observation Group looked northward. Lacking experience with North Vietnamese operations, Tung turned for assistance to a staunchly anticommunist priest, Father Nguyen Viet Khai, who had fled south in 1954. With Catholic recruits provided by Father Khai, these early efforts bore little fruit. One Presidential Liaison Office official, Tran Gia Loc, remembers:

> We had almost no information about conditions inside North Vietnam, so we wanted to send agents who would act like pigeons. At the time, North Vietnam allowed letters to pass back and forth across the DMZ, provided that they didn't have any political content. We worked out a code system where our agents could send us information through normal letters. The first man was trained and he walked north across the DMZ to his hometown of Nam Dinh, a Catholic stronghold. The first month we received nothing, but we got one letter during the second and another during the third month. After that, silence. We canceled the program.[5]

While the Presidential Liaison Office's letter-writing scheme amounted to nothing, it came at an opportune time. By 1957, the CIA had begun to suspect that Dr. Tuyen's northern agent nets were largely fabrications. "We were getting the same generic reports month after month," said David Zogbaum, an agency official assigned to South Vietnam at the time. A Yale graduate with a French wife, Zogbaum noticed some irregularities in Tuyen's reports. "I told headquarters that I thought they were manufacturing them in Saigon." Zogbaum eventually found a smoking gun when Tuyen's people handed over an agent radio transcript on which they had inadvertently matched the agent's call sign heading to the wrong reporting location. With a little more digging, the CIA found that its motorized junk, which Tuyen claimed was operating in North Vietnamese waters, had actually been leased to a Japanese fishing company.[6]

The agency immediately reduced ties with Tuyen and turned to Tung and the Presidential Liaison Office. According to one CIA officer who was there:

> [We were looking] to establish basic information about and (hopefully) contact with Catholic villages, and surviving knots of dissident anti-regime groups . . . and potentially anti-regime minorities that had been strongly influenced by the French. . . . No one that I know of was naive enough to anticipate the acquisition of strategic data (plans and intents) from the regime leaders from initial cross-border efforts; only low-level data on social, economic and political conditions in general and more precise data on the "operational environment" in which we would subsequently revise and refine objectives.[7]

With these modest goals, in 1958 the CIA's Saigon station created an external operations branch that would be matched up with a similar bureau in the Presidential Liaison Office. Heading the American side was veteran case officer Russell Miller. Fresh off an assignment near the rugged Khyber Pass in Pakistan, Miller operated under light diplomatic cover as he watched Tung choose twelve trainees for the new unit. Eleven of them were young and eager army lieutenants. The commander of the group was Captain Ngo The Linh, a native of Ha Tinh Province in southern North Vietnam who had spent five years at a staff position in Danang.[8] Like Diem and Tung, he was a Catholic.

In November, the twelve prospects were flown to Saipan. There they were put through the CIA's Special Intelligence Training Course, a two-month primer that touched on everything from combat intelligence to sabotage techniques to running an agent network. Returning to Saigon by year's end, Captain Linh was officially placed in charge of the Presidential Liaison Office's new North Vietnam bureau, code-named Office 45.[9]

Only a dozen strong, Office 45 spent the next few months training more men. By mid-1959 a second class of five young officers was sent to Saipan for an abbreviated six weeks of instruction. Shortly thereafter, the CIA dispatched a training officer to Saigon, where he began the first of two twelve-week cycles.[10] For these latest trainees, a premium was placed on junior army officers born in northern Vietnam, to include some from key ethnic minorities.

As training continued into late 1959, Office 45 drew up plans for its first operation. In this, the problems confronting the fledgling bureau were considerably greater than those encountered by Lansdale in 1954. The Saigon Military Mission had the benefit of establishing caches and creating aliases for its agents before a communist takeover. Office 45, by contrast, faced the prospect of penetrating a closed society whose government and omnipresent security apparatus had been under tight control for nearly five years.

As the CIA well knew, doing this successfully was one of the most challenging assignments to confront a spy organization. Even with vast resources at its disposal, its own track record of infiltrating single agents—singletons in agency parlance—into any Asian communist nation was fraught with frustration and failure. Of the 212 agents infiltrated into the Chinese mainland during 1951–53, for example, it is believed half were killed and the other half captured. Even attempts to penetrate North Korea had fallen woefully short. According to one case officer on Korean operations, "We had no record of success putting long-term agents into North Korea by boat or by parachute. Getting an agent into a closed society was hard enough, but sometimes it was as simple as them tracking the footprints in the snow coming off the beach."[11]

The task of launching the Presidential Liaison Office's first singleton was handed to Lieutenant Do Van Tien. Urbane and sophisticated, Tien, who went by the call sign François (case officers were given French or American names, primarily to overcome language difficulties with their American counterparts), had begun his military career as an interpreter for French intelligence, then as a noncommissioned officer in a colonial artillery regiment. Set to rotate to Algeria with his unit, he instead resigned and entered the army as a staff officer in Saigon. Possessing the two pedigrees favored by Diem—he was Catholic and a native of Hue, the ancient imperial capital ninety kilometers southeast of the Demilitarized Zone—François was soon posted to Office 45.[12]

François's first prospective singleton was a North Vietnamese defector named Pham Chuyen. Once a ranking Communist Party member from Quang Ninh Province, Chuyen had become profoundly disillusioned in 1958 after his wife jilted him for an officer in the North Vietnamese security service. Brooding, he fled south.[13]

Holed up in a government refugee camp in Gia Dinh Province not far from Saigon, Chuyen's political background came to the attention of southern authorities. Because communist officials of any stature were rare among the pool of northern refugees, interest in him quickly grew. Eager to recruit an asset, Dr. Tuyen, Diem's discredited spymaster from the Office of Political and Social Research, dangled an offer. Chuyen did not bite. Viewing the Diem regime with as much contempt as he had for his former northern comrades, he chose to remain among the refugees.

Hoping to best Dr. Tuyen, Lieutenant Colonel Tung joined in the competition to recruit the sulking ex-communist. He sent a young Presidential Liaison Office lieutenant to dog Chuyen for six months, but still Chuyen refused the offer to work for Saigon.

Unwilling to concede defeat, Tung gave François the job of hooking Chuyen. Fresh from training and with no field experience, François was paired with a CIA case officer named Edward Regan. Regan had already spent a year in South Vietnam before being transferred to Miller's northern project. Using the French he learned on the streets of Saigon, he quickly developed a close working relationship with François. But Regan's presence actually hurt the chances of recruiting Chuyen, who made no secret of his contempt for Americans. So François went on his own to the Gia Dinh camp.

"Chuyen was a small man, very cold, very hard," recalled François. "He did not speak much." After a few meetings, François talked his superiors into allowing him to take Chuyen out of the camp to see a movie. On another occasion they went to Saigon, Chuyen's first time in the bustling city. "Finally, after six months he offered no protest when I came to see him," said François, "and following that he agreed to work for us, to go back north for revenge. But I still faced the problem of his dislike for Americans. I told him frankly that somebody had to pay for him to go back north."[14]

Reluctantly, Chuyen agreed to meet Regan. During a rendezvous in a Saigon hotel room, François introduced the CIA officer. To everyone's relief, the initial contact went well. Chuyen was then whisked to Nha Trang, where he underwent a battery of psychological tests. Receiving an excellent score, he took more tests in Saigon, then a third set in Nha Trang. Finally, Chuyen began six months of communications training.

While Chuyen was in the classroom, François and Regan were busy planning the insertion of their new agent into North Vietnam. Because Chuyen would be going back as a long-term agent to his hometown in the coastal province of Quang Ninh, in the far northeastern corner of the country, the logical means of getting him there was by sea. To secretly dispatch a boat, the Presidential Liaison Office needed a launch site in Danang, the northernmost port in South Vietnam. Taking a flight from Saigon, the two case officers scouted facilities and rented a small walled villa. All subsequent operations from this modest locale were code-named PACIFIC.

Just as the CIA had earlier done for Dr. Tuyen, a fishing junk seemed the most inconspicuous way to infiltrate Chuyen. But the choice came with problems. In Asia, the design of fishing junks varied from one fishing community to the next. To the trained eye they were as distinctive as a fingerprint. For this very reason, CIA maritime operators during the Korean War had altogether shunned the use of native junks. But this time there were few alternatives, so the Presidential Liaison Office sent an officer to the coastal town of Vung Tau to make contact with a community of ethnic Nung fishermen. The Nung, a minority group that emigrated south from China in the sixteenth century, had settled in pockets along Vietnam's border with China, especially the northern seaside province of Quang Ninh. Given semiautonomous status by the French, they had strongly resisted Viet Minh encroachment. With the 1954 Geneva Accords, an estimated fifteen thousand fled to South Vietnam, many of them settling in coastal villages and resuming their livelihoods as fishermen.

Using funds from the Presidential Liaison Office, a team of Nung craftsmen built a single junk to the exact specifications used in Quang Ninh Province. It was then outfitted with two silenced Gray Marine outboards and a pair of machine guns, one fore and one aft.[15]

As these preparations were under way, an undercurrent of paranoia was slowly building inside North Vietnam. There were at least two reasons for Hanoi's concern. First, North Vietnamese security officials at the time were busy exposing the stay-behind spy rings and were no doubt concerned that others remained hidden. Second, Hanoi had learned of the creation of the 1st Observation Group and was convinced that the unit's true mission was to carry fighting into the north. Two internal warnings to this effect had already been issued in 1958.[16]

By 1959 North Vietnamese authorities were even more concerned. On 3 March, a coastal antiaircraft position in Thanh Hoa Province reported a C-47 "with quisling troops" encroaching on North Vietnamese airspace.[17] After this unsubstantiated intrusion, Hanoi formed three new radar-guided antiaircraft regiments, joining the seven regiments already in its order of battle.[18] In addition, on 22 September North Vietnam issued a directive calling on its border defense units to conduct sweeps after foreign aircraft were spotted overhead.[19] Given the fact that no agents had been infiltrated by air, the efforts showed that while Hanoi knew something was going on, it was still only stabbing in the dark.

North Vietnam was also spooked by the Demilitarized Zone. Its claim of capturing twenty southern spies going north during 1959 came without a single person offered as evidence.[20] If anybody was indeed captured, they more likely were smugglers than agents.

Although short on proof, Hanoi became increasingly convinced of the growing menace posed by Saigon's covert operations. The end result was a February 1960 directive outlining counterrevolutionary threats, specifically defined as spies launched by the American and South Vietnamese governments. On the heels of this document, some 1,993 suspected reactionaries were reportedly questioned.[21]

Office 45 continued preparing Chuyen for his mission. Before he was inserted, however, the office decided to launch a short-term agent for a quick foray across the Demilitarized Zone. The candidate for this mission, a Catholic native of Ha Tinh Province named Vu Cong Hong, was given a brief training stint and sent to a safe house in the city of Hue.

Joining Hong at the safe house were two Presidential Liaison Office lieutenants, Pham Van Minh and Tran Ba Tuan, both Saipan graduates. Now going by the names Michel and Brad, the two were matched up with a single CIA case officer, David Zogbaum, the man partially responsible for exposing Dr. Tuyen's fraudulent operations. In keeping with the oceanic precedent set by Regan and François at Danang, he and his Hue-based counterparts code-named their cross-border operations ATLANTIC.

Unlike the denuded no-man's-land of later years, in 1960 the Demilitarized Zone was a tranquil five-kilometer-deep ribbon of hills and forests stretching from the Tonkin Gulf to the Laos border. Along part of the southern edge ran a natural barrier, the Ben Hai River. Little more than a trickling stream at its western extreme, by the time it flowed down from the mountains and toward the ocean, it became a wide and imposing barrier.

At the eleventh hour Hong revealed that he could not swim. With no time for lessons, Brad took Hong to the Perfume River on the outskirts of Hue and had him practice paddling with both hands while floating inside a rubber tire tube. Satisfied he could make the short trip, Hong, now going by the code name HIRONDELLE, was declared mission-ready that December.

Major Tran Khac Kinh, the Presidential Liaison Office's deputy commander, went along for this first insertion. "We reached the river at midnight and watched him row across slowly," he said. "Then we heard a clear noise above the flat, calm surface of the river: air was escaping from the tire, as our agent had cut it with a razor." HIRONDELLE hid the tube and disappeared into the night.[22]

A few weeks later, the agent reappeared inside South Vietnam. While only able to provide general information on travel and security controls in the north, his successful recovery provided a boost of confidence to the fledgling Office 45.

Two months after the HIRONDELLE mission, Chuyen emerged from a year's worth of training. He would need all the skills he learned. Unlike HIRONDELLE's brief foray across the border, Chuyen's mission was both to collect information and to begin recruiting subagents over a period of several

years. As cover, he was to become a fisherman near Cam Pha, a town adjacent to Ha Long Bay. Since this had been his hometown before 1958, there
was concern that Chuyen's sudden reappearance might raise some eyebrows.
However, these fears were offset by the fact that Chuyen's brother and other
relatives still lived in the area—and could potentially be recruited as willing
accomplices.

His cover rehearsed, Chuyen was ready. Now code-named ARES, he
boarded the CIA's motorized junk, *Nautilus 1,* in early April 1961 and departed Danang for the two-day voyage north. But the weather quickly
turned foul, and *Nautilus 1* returned to port. A few days later, the skies
cleared, and the mission resumed. François and Regan went to the dock to
bid their agent farewell. "I wished him good success," remembers François.
Characteristically, ARES said nothing in reply.[23]

With clear skies and calm seas, *Nautilus 1* approached the coast of Quang
Ninh Province. Taking care to avoid detection, the junk crept toward the
edge of Ha Long Bay. Striking karst pillars dotted the bay, formed, according
to legend, when a dragon spit jade into the water. Giving the bay the beauty
of a Chinese watercolor, the jagged limestone also provided ARES sufficient
cover to paddle toward shore aboard a rattan skiff. Landing near Cam Pha,
he removed two RS-1 long-distance radios and other supplies, then pulled
the boat into a sewage runoff. The radios were cached in a nearby hole.

Leaving the beach, ARES looked for shelter. His first order of business was
to recruit at least one assistant who could help him operate the hand-cranked
generator on his radio. Office 45 had taken this into account, and did not
expect radio contact for several weeks, if not months.

Without being seen, the agent stole into his former commune and went
straight to his mother's house. Reunited with his family, he made a pitch to
his younger brother, Pham Do. Reluctantly he agreed, so ARES retrieved the
radios from the beach and hid them under the dirt floor, covered with a
bamboo mat.

While the infiltration of ARES may have appeared flawless, a single oversight proved to be his undoing. On 9 April, fellow fishermen discovered his
undamaged skiff floating in the sewage culvert. After the fishermen reported
the suspicious boat to the local authorities, armed patrols began canvassing
the local fishing community. After it was determined that the boat was not
owned by any locals, the search spread along the beach. Soon after, police
found the hole where the radios had been hidden.[24]

Suspecting the infiltration of a spy, the chief of police in Quang Ninh
Province planned a door-to-door search along the coast. Special attention
would be given to families who had members living in the south, and those
who had ties to the previous colonial government.

Unaware of the impending police dragnet, ARES spent much of his time hidden in a nearby forest. One of the radios was hauled into the woods and, while his brother cranked the generator, the agent sent his first message. To avoid signal interference, it beamed from the North Vietnamese shore across the South China Sea to BUGS, the code name for a CIA radio facility in the Philippines. From there the message was relayed to the CIA office in Saigon. When it arrived, Robert Kennedy, an officer assigned to Miller's team, walked into Office 45 waving the transcript and beaming. "Victory! Success!" he shouted to his surprised compatriots.[25]

With this initial radio contact, ARES sent a rush of enthusiasm through the American and South Vietnamese case officers in Saigon. A copy of the transcript was even handed to President Diem. While another twenty-two messages quickly followed, however, the end was fast approaching. Up in Quang Ninh, North Vietnamese counterintelligence officials scanning the airwaves intercepted some of the cryptic radio messages. At the same time, an elderly resident tipped police to a stranger living in a beachfront house who had tried to hide his face when seen by the informant. He also pointed out that someone from the same house was showing off a new ballpoint pen, a rarely seen commodity in the north.[26]

With these leads, the police focused on the Pham household. On 11 June, authorities arrested Pham Do as he was heading toward the forest with supplies for his brother. Six days later, ARES was in custody. A search of their house uncovered radio gear under the mat and codes in a basket of rice.[27]

Hanoi had two options. It could announce the capture, publicize the subsequent trial, and milk the event for propaganda value as it had done during the Dai Viet court hearings. Or it could "double" ARES, enticing or coercing him into continuing normal radio contact with Saigon. That way, the North Vietnamese could gain better insights into the budding South Vietnamese agent operation, and perhaps even use ARES as a diversion to feed disinformation to the south.

Hanoi chose the second option. At 0900 hours on 8 August, the agent's RS-1 radio came back to life. There had been a lapse of nearly two months, but ARES—with North Vietnamese security officials at his side—had a ready explanation. His mother and sister had been arrested after not paying agricultural taxes, he tapped out in Morse code. Frightened, he had briefly fled to Hanoi.[28]

To those in Saigon, the explanation sounded plausible. They also took at face value his request for more supplies, and they agreed to send *Nautilus 1* back to Ha Long. ARES was informed of the time frame and the general location where the supplies would be cached. The junk left Danang on 12 January 1962, arriving at Ha Long without incident. Then radio contact from the vessel mysteriously ceased.[29]

Office 45 was naturally concerned by the disappearance of its sole boat and entire crew. But while some suspicion fell on ARES, his handlers preferred to believe that the junk had more likely fallen prey to a routine North Vietnamese patrol when it approached the coast.

Short one junk and with ARES still radioing for supplies, Office 45 commissioned the Nung fishermen in Vung Tau to construct another vessel. Dubbed *Nautilus 2,* this second boat was ready by April. Meanwhile, a second junk crew, recruited from among northern refugees, was quickly trained at Danang.

On 11 April, *Nautilus 2* departed for Ha Long. While the CIA still believed ARES to be uncompromised, the agency hedged its bets by not informing its agent about the time or location of the resupply. Two days later, the junk was positioned just off Quang Ninh. Six of the fourteen crewmen transferred to a rubber boat laden with seven metal canisters and twenty-three cardboard boxes encased in plastic. "We paddled to a small island in the middle of Ha Long," recounted one member of the shore party. "Nobody saw us and we were able to unload all of the supplies and camouflage them with rocks and brush."[30]

Once *Nautilus 2* was safely back in Danang, Office 45 celebrated. "This first successful resupply of ARES was almost as memorable as infiltrating ARES himself," recalled François.[31] A message was then sent to ARES on 2 May informing him of the cache's location. Shortly thereafter, a return message stated that the agent had recovered all the boxes, which included radio gear and a 35mm camera.[32]

Despite the "success" of ARES, Saigon's track record for infiltrating singleton agents was not good. In September 1961, Office 45's third singleton, code-named HERO, was landed by junk along the North Vietnamese coast in an attempt to contact family members. He failed and was immediately exfiltrated. That same month, the original singleton, HIRONDELLE, was reinserted by junk along the coast of Ha Tinh Province. He promptly disappeared.[33]

During 1962 the list of missing singletons continued to grow. An agent known as TRITON, inserted by boat into Ha Tinh Province during May, vanished without a trace.[34] Later that month, a singleton code-named ATHENA was sent into the same province. That agent, whose real name was Dang Chi Binh, disguised himself as a student and managed to take a bus to the city of Vinh. The charade did not work for long, however, and he quickly aroused police attention. By the time he took another bus to Hanoi, he noticed two men were shadowing his every move. The end came a few days later on the way to Sunday church services.

"I saw in the distance two policemen with rather familiar faces walking toward me," recalls Binh. "My heart started to pound. They were the ones that followed me to the Lang pagoda!" The first time they had been wearing civilian clothes; this time they were in uniform. Binh knew he was in trouble. One of the men asked for Binh's papers. "Saying nothing, I gave them my identification papers," said Binh. "He glanced at it and said, 'This one's not correct. Please go with us to the police station.'"[35]

Despite these repeated failures, the CIA remained committed to the singleton program. During the spring of 1962, operations took on a new twist. The idea was Ed Regan's:

> [Following an attempted coup in November 1960,] it was deemed politic for me to be recalled to Washington briefly. While in Washington, I retrieved and reviewed documents as to Dai Viet and VNQDD activities in North Vietnam prior to the communist takeover in 1954. I became interested in the question of any possibility of some survival of anticommunist assets in the north. From this sprang the idea of infiltrating Dai Viet and VNQDD cadres to reestablish contact with any still active cells and determine if this avenue offered any opportunity for obtaining intelligence on North Vietnam.[36]

Two separate plans were formed. The first involved a singleton agent sent to recover some of the VNQDD radios still thought to be cached in Haiphong since 1955. To carry this out, the CIA's Robert Kennedy located Bui Van Ninh, the VNQDD member who had hidden two radios in Haiphong prior to fleeing south in 1955. Kennedy asked Ninh for details on where the radios were hidden, as well as help with suggestions for possible agents to go and retrieve them.[37]

Ninh directed Kennedy to Nguyen Van Hong, a close friend and northerner by birth. Hong immediately left his carpentry job and began agent training. Given the code name NESTOR, he departed Danang aboard a junk on 6 June. Inserted in Quang Binh, he was to make his way to his family in Hanoi, then eventually seek out the radios in Haiphong. Using forged papers, NESTOR took a car to Hanoi. After sending seven postcards with secret messages for Office 45—which apparently never arrived in the south—he arrived at his parents' house. After he had been home just one day, his frightened family persuaded him to turn himself in.[38]

A more elaborate plan was hatched for the Dai Viet.[39] Lou Conein, the Saigon Military Mission agent who had helped insert the stay-behinds just after Vietnam's partition, returned to Saigon in 1960 for another CIA tour. Using Conein as an intermediary, senior Dai Viet officials were asked for their blessing. Understandably, they were cautious about further covert ventures with the Diem regime. Ed Regan shared their concerns: "Remembering the internal security function of the Presidential Liaison Office, surfacing Dai Viet cadre to them certainly presented high risks. There was always the risk that [Presidential Liaison Office] agreement to the operational plan was more concerned with obtaining inroads into Dai Viet activity in South Vietnam than any true interest in northern operations. Both Conein and I stressed this risk repeatedly to our own service."[40]

Despite the dangers, the Dai Viet agreed—with one stipulation. They insisted that the mission be completely staffed with their own cadre. Saigon concurred, and a full team, code-named THERA, was trained and deployed to Danang for seaborne infiltration. Before it left, however, problems arose. Reneging on its earlier commitment, the Presidential Liaison Office insisted on inserting two agents on the team to control communications. Considering this a betrayal of their prior understanding, the Dai Viet agents took matters into their own hands: both radiomen were soon found murdered at their safe house. The team leader was subsequently sent to prison, and THERA disbanded.[41]

By 1963, the idea of infiltrating long-term singletons by boat into a closed society such as North Vietnam was largely discredited. Apart from ARES, a total of four maritime agents were missing and presumed dead. Even operations across the Demilitarized Zone were growing more hazardous: whereas HIRONDELLE had earlier been able to make five shallow penetrations prior to September 1961, a second overland agent, code-named WOLF, went missing on his first foray in February 1963.[42]

Against all this, ARES stood apart. Literally hundreds of short messages had been radioed from his set in Quang Ninh. While the intelligence haul was minimal—mostly general observations about the nearby port at Haiphong—it was better than anything else coming out of North Vietnam. On occasion, ARES went farther afield, such as to the Uong Bi power plant outside Haiphong, and sent back his findings.

In the summer of 1963, Office 45 began planning another resupply. Hoping to repeat the previous year's success, it planned to send a junk to Ha Long and dispatch a rubber boat to one of the unpopulated karst islands in the bay. On 11 August, the junk left Danang. Two days later it was near Ha Long. Six of the crew boarded a rubber raft and headed to the beach. They were never seen again. When the shore party failed to return, the remaining crewmen on the junk panicked. Their worst fears were confirmed when a North Vietnamese vessel was seen heading in their direction. Gunning the twin Gray Marines, the junk dodged machine-gun fire and sped back to Danang.[43]

Suspicion again fell on ARES. But just as with the first incident, Office 45 concluded that the second loss was due to the hazards inherent in approaching close to the North Vietnamese coast. As if to prove his bona fides, ARES sent flowery Republic Day greetings to Diem that October. The following month, when Diem was killed in a bloody coup d'état, ARES sent multiple messages of mourning.[44] Convinced of his sincerity, Saigon radioed ARES with news that he had been awarded the Cross of Gallantry.[45]

3

AIRBORNE AGENTS

Although Office 45's earliest efforts focused on the infiltration of singleton agents by land and sea, the backbone of its North Vietnam program came from the sky. Airborne insertion was not an original idea. In fact, Saigon intentionally borrowed a page from one of the most successful French-led units in Indochina, the Groupes de Commandos Mixtes Aeroportes (Mixed Airborne Commando Group, or GCMA).

First fielded in 1951, the GCMA was an effort by French intelligence to harness the historical animosity between hill tribesmen and the ethnic Vietnamese of the lowlands. Using small teams of French airborne advisers as cadre, ethnic tribesmen were given the opportunity to take up arms against the Viet Minh, which was dominated by lowlanders. Thousands accepted the offer and were organized into tribal guerrilla bands. For the French, the GCMA was an economical means of denying the rugged countryside to the communists. For the minorities, the concept gave them the hope of defending themselves after centuries of domination and prejudice.

The GCMA never amounted to more than 9,500 partisans in northern Vietnam, but these guerrillas struck a nerve with the Viet Minh. Referring to the tribesmen by the Vietnamese name Biet Kich (commandos), the Viet Minh in December 1953 issued a resolution calling on field units to "surround and arrest the [GCMA], root them up from their social bases, and isolate and wipe them out." Three months later, another Viet Minh decree called on its armed forces to launch a "prolonged struggle" to wipe out the GCMA by "leaning on the public, persevering to the end, and killing off the root." Even after the withdrawal of French advisers from North Vietnam in early 1955, the GCMA threat refused to die. By Hanoi's own admission, it was not until the end of 1956 that the last of these tribal commandos was subdued.[1]

Hoping to repeat this success, the CIA organized a similar project within Office 45. In fact, some of those involved with the new venture had been Biet Kich during the French war. Prominent among them was Se Co Tin, a village chieftain from Lao Cai near the Chinese border. From the Tho ethnic group, Se Co Tin had been instrumental in helping the French organize twenty-five hundred GCMA partisans around Lao Cai, which had then been used in October 1953 on a spectacular guerrilla attack against communist forces along the Chinese frontier.

By the early 1960s, Se Co Tin was in Saigon as a key adviser to Office 45. "He was a canton chief and had respect, so he could introduce our case officers to recruits from his province and ethnic group," recalled Ngo The Linh, the office commander.[2] One of those Se Co Tin brought forward was his nephew, Lo Ngan Dung, himself a GCMA guerrilla from Lao Cai. Dung had come south after the French withdrawal, joined the South Vietnamese army, and was posted to the General Studies Department, the forerunner of the Presidential Liaison Office.[3] Following his introduction to Linh, Dung, by then a lieutenant, underwent intelligence training in 1960. Given the call sign Jacques, he was assigned in early 1961 as the first case officer for the airborne agent teams.

Paired with a young CIA counterpart named David Thoenen, Jacques began forming the first hill tribe team. Just like the GCMA, this team was to operate along the border highlands where North Vietnamese security, the CIA believed, had "less control . . . due primarily to poor access and to the traditional animosity of the tribal groups there to the lowland Vietnamese." Unlike the GCMA, which had run sabotage operations and recruited tribal partisans, the team would be tasked just with reconnaissance and intelligence—observing roads and establishing only limited contact with the local population.[4]

In opting for such a limited mandate for its initial team, the CIA and Office 45 appeared to be building a cautious, though perhaps flawed, foundation. While it was true that the highlands could offer the best chance of concealment, the harsh topography and thin population in those areas meant that there was little information for an intelligence-gathering team to collect. Mountainous terrain also meant that it would be difficult to find food. And since the team was forbidden from organizing local guerrillas, the fact that those locals might harbor an exploitable dislike for the ethnic Vietnamese would probably not help its mission.

Still, selection of the first team began in early February. Given the need to find northern tribesmen with solid political credentials and military experience, Jacques was given permission to scour the ranks of the Presidential Liaison Office's own 1st Observation Group. Because it had been conceived as a stay-behind force in the event of a Chinese invasion, the 1st Observation Group was composed mainly of northerners. It had also begun accepting South Vietnamese army volunteers of Tai, Muong, and Nung origin—all natives of northern Vietnam—in anticipation of upcoming forays into the Lao panhandle.[5] From among these, Jacques found three suitable Muong and a Tai.

Whisked off to a Saigon safe house, the four began instruction on the RS-1 radio. Airborne and jungle warfare training had already been completed under the auspices of the 1st Observation Group, sparing Office 45 the trouble. And unlike ARES, who had been trained for an entire year to lead a double life as a full-time spy within Vietnamese society, the four trainees were to live isolated in the hills, so they were not required to learn any spycraft techniques. After three months, they graduated.

As its first airborne team was being readied for deployment, the CIA needed to decide on a form of air transport into North Vietnam that was both reliable and deniable. The agency had performed dozens of similar parachute missions into China since 1952, using a variety of airframes: C-47 and C-54 transports, converted bombers like the B-17 and B-26, and even refitted P-2V submarine chasers. In the case of North Vietnam, it was not so much the aircraft that caused concern as the pilots. The need for "deniability"—hiding the American hand in the operations—meant that the U.S. Air Force was out of the question. And the CIA was adamant that Air America, its proprietary airline in Asia, not be used because of its high profile in neighboring Laos.[6]

By the process of elimination, this left the Vietnamese to do the flying. But while the South Vietnamese air force had suitably qualified pilots, it, too, needed to operate under a veneer of deniability. So the CIA created a shell company by initiating a paper exercise between the Delaware Corporation—which was affiliated with Air America—and a Vietnamese partner. Called Vietnamese Air Transport, or VIAT, the new "airline" had only a single unmarked C-47 aircraft.

To pilot the VIAT plane, the CIA approached Major Nguyen Cao Ky, commander of Tan Son Nhut airport on the outskirts of Saigon. The young officer—only thirty at the time—had originally been trained as a transport pilot by the French in Morocco. Known for his flamboyance and charisma, Ky put out the word among the Vietnamese air force's two transport squadrons that volunteers were being sought for a special unit. Twenty Vietnamese, led by Ky himself, were quickly rounded up for the northern assignment, which was code-named HAYLIFT.

While the volunteers had sufficient experience with conventional transport flights, the missions to the north required special instruction. Specifically, the crews would be required to fly extremely long missions at very low altitudes to precise drop zones—all without the aid of advanced navigational equipment. And if that was not enough, North Vietnam's heavy rainfall and rugged terrain combined to create some of the worst flying conditions in the world.

To help coach the Vietnamese aviators, the CIA arranged for the loan of one pilot instructor and one navigator from Air America. The pilot, Captain Al Judkins, had spent the previous months on a CIA assignment parachuting Khampa guerrillas into Tibet. The navigator, Jim Keck, was also a Tibet veteran. Beginning with daylight low-level sorties, Judkins and Keck soon had the Vietnamese flying their C-47 at treetop level at night. Many dropped out of the difficult training, eventually leaving a five-man primary crew under the command of Major Ky and a backup crew under Lieutenant Phan Thanh Van.[7]

For a final rehearsal run, Ky took the C-47 for a night flight over the Tonkin Gulf. Aboard for the ride was the CIA Saigon station chief, William E. Colby, long a proponent of action operations. Colby's own military career had more than its share of derring-do. In August 1944, he led an OSS team into occupied France, establishing a flank guard for General George Patton's advancing tank columns. The following March, he parachuted with another OSS team into Norway. At the time, the Germans were redeploying 150,000 troops into northern Norway. They were using the Nordland rail line, moving their men at a rate of one battalion per day. Armed with demolition charges, Colby and his guerrillas cut a bridge and a large section of track, slowing the redeployment to one battalion per month. The mission was rated a major success.[8]

At the controls, Ky tried to impress his CIA passenger with his ability to infiltrate at low levels. The plane dipped toward the sea until it barely cleared the wave tops. Colby was impressed. "Ky, the next time you fly me like that so close to the water," he quipped, "let me know beforehand and I'll bring my fishing rod."[9]

Half a world away, President John F. Kennedy's new administration was talking tough behind closed doors. The war in Indochina was rising to the top of a growing number of foreign policy crises, and the young president wanted to send Hanoi a message. North Vietnam, after all, was not only infiltrating arms and personnel into South Vietnam but also intervening against the pro-Western royalist government in Laos. Edward Lansdale, the CIA's roving expert on both covert operations and counterinsurgency, finished a fact-finding trip in January 1961 and returned to Washington to brief the National Security Council. Kennedy later told his advisers that "for the first time [it] gave him a sense of the danger and urgency of the problem in Vietnam."[10]

Kennedy wanted to act without igniting a superpower rivalry in Southeast Asia, so he turned to the CIA. On 9 March 1961, during another meeting with his National Security Council, the president said that he wanted to "make every possible effort to launch guerrilla operations in Viet Minh territory at the earliest possible date," and he asked both the CIA and the Defense Department to present "views on what actions might be undertaken in the near future and what steps might be taken to expand operations in the longer future."[11]

Kennedy also approved several covert operations already on the table. The first of these, infiltrating agents into North Vietnam, was currently in progress. The CIA told the president that it had teams "allocated to working on a series of guerrilla pockets" near the Lao–North Vietnam border." But Kennedy felt that this was insufficient; "he want[ed] guerrillas to operate in the North."[12] So further plans, such as sabotaging northern ports and recruiting North Vietnamese living elsewhere in Asia and in Europe, were put on the fast track.[13] Two months later, however, the president again checked on the progress of his covert plan and found that the CIA was not acting fast enough, so in early March he issued National Security Action Memorandum No. 28 (NSAM 28) ordering the agency to "make every possible effort to launch guerrilla operations in North Vietnamese territory."[14]

Before these measures could be fully implemented, Washington suffered a pair of policy setbacks. On 19 April a CIA-sponsored paramilitary operation by Cuban exiles at the Bay of Pigs went terribly wrong. This was followed immediately by a series of reversals for the American-backed Royal Lao army, leaving them on the ropes after a North Vietnamese-led communist land grab.

Gathering his National Security Council on 29 April, Kennedy again hoped to turn the tables by using the CIA. William Colby had traveled back to Washington to help make the pitch for an increase in covert operations.[15] These actions, far more broad than those outlined the previous month, included propaganda leaflet drops, clandestine radio broadcasts, and sabotage raids into North Vietnam and Laos by the 1st Observation Group. It also called on agent teams in North Vietnam not only to conduct reconnaissance and gather intelligence but also "to form networks of resistance, covert bases and teams for sabotage and light harassment."[16]

This latest Kennedy action plan was extremely ambitious—and very confusing. In the space of a month, Washington had expanded the mandate of its untested Vietnamese agent teams to include the full gamut of unconventional warfare. Whereas the original CIA plan had its agents focused on low-profile intelligence collection, they were now approaching a full-fledged GCMA concept, but without any additional training.[17]

The effect of the National Security Council decision had yet to filter down to Saigon. As the council was meeting in the White House, the first airborne team had just finished its brief training. In mid-May, it underwent final fitting and was given the code name CASTOR, referring to the Greek god who aided Hercules. Ironically, CASTOR had also been the name for France's November 1953 airborne operation to retake the Dien Bien Phu valley—an operation that led to France's final defeat in Indochina.

CASTOR would face an increasingly hostile environment in North Vietnam. Already paranoid about penetration by counterrevolutionaries, Hanoi became more concerned in February with the discovery of ARES's boat along the beach near Ha Long Bay. On 1 March the Vietnamese communist party issued secret instructions ordering its security forces to redouble efforts at combating undercover agents, a measure no doubt driven home when ARES was captured three weeks later.[18]

South Vietnam played into Hanoi's hand by telegraphing its next move with two violations of northern airspace in early May.[19] Already fearful about aerial insertions—which had prompted a 1959 directive calling on border defense forces to search the terrain under the flight path of intruding planes—Hanoi undoubtedly saw these probes as clear evidence that an airborne threat would soon materialize.

As if not to disappoint, CASTOR was scheduled to go north on 27 May. A full moon and favorable weather were forecast for that night. Unlike maritime infiltrations, which used moonless nights to approach the coast, the Vietnamese air force crews needed something approaching a full moon that was at least thirty degrees over the horizon—usually only four nights a month—to navigate to the drop zone. In addition, the agents needed the moonlight to get a visual fix on the drop zone and on each other during descent.

As planned, the four CASTOR members boarded the unmarked VIAT C-47 at Tan Son Nhut. In the cockpit was Major Ky. The entire crew was dressed in sterile flight suits with no identification or connection to the military. If they went down over the north, their thin cover story was that they were a civilian outfit smuggling illegal goods. Each member also carried one hundred dollars, to be used during an escape.

The plane left Tan Son Nhut and flew north to Danang for refueling. At 2200 hours, Ky lifted off and headed low over the Gulf of Tonkin on a direct course for Ninh Binh Province in central North Vietnam. The two navigators remained busy: one gave a ground fix every two minutes, the other plotted the route to the target.

Coming upon the Ninh Binh coast, Ky banked the plane on a northwest heading across Hoa Binh Province, then veered north toward Son La. Crossing the Da River, the two navigators called corrections. Below, a forested high point—marked on the maps as Hill 828—shone in the moonlight. As Ky activated the green jump light, parachute delivery officers in the cabin pushed palleted supply bundles through the rear door, with the four members of CASTOR following quickly behind. The aircraft then reversed course and headed home.

On Hill 828, Sergeant Ha Van Chap, the CASTOR team leader, stripped off his parachute harness and assembled his men. They had landed one kilometer from a nearby village. Nine kilometers farther south was the Da River, and another ten kilometers south of that was Route 6. By North Vietnamese standards, Route 6 was a major road. Leading across the neighboring district, it then veered southwest into the Lao province of Sam Neua. Given the Kennedy administration's preoccupation with Laos and the fact that Sam Neua was the communist stronghold in Laos, CASTOR's ability to provide an accurate accounting of movement down Route 6 gave the team's mission a strategic dimension. Moreover, CASTOR's ethnic composition—which included two minority groups indigenous to the area—would hopefully enable the team members to supplement their observations with information from local contacts.

Even before they could move off the mountain, however, CASTOR was doomed to failure. The CIA had counted on the ability of a low-flying aircraft to successfully skirt the North Vietnamese heartland without detection. This meant avoiding Hanoi's already robust antiaircraft defenses. By early 1961, North Vietnam had ten antiaircraft regiments in its order of battle, three of which were equipped with radar. Unfortunately for the commandos, a company from one of these regiments was in Son La's Moc Chau District, which had been overflown during CASTOR's infiltration.

Even if the VIAT aircraft managed to evade North Vietnamese radar, much of the flight path was over provinces dotted with small villages. The sound of a twin-engine aircraft, especially in the dead of night, was certain to draw the attention of the rural population. Even in the remote interior, villages were connected through a security network, the Cong An Vu Trang Nhan Dan (People's Armed Security Force, or PASF). Created in March 1959 within the Ministry of the Interior, the PASF was a combination of gendarmerie and border defense force deployed in rural areas as the vanguard in Hanoi's defense against counterrevolution. Decidedly low-tech but highly effective, the PASF provided a coherent, well-armed network that enforced party control down to the district, and in some cases village, level.

When CASTOR jumped over Hill 828, villagers were within earshot. They reported what they heard, and by the morning of 28 May the North Vietnamese authorities had a good idea of the plane's likely drop zone. Immediately, three local PASF formations converged around the commune closest to Hill 828. After three days of hunting, they came upon the team. CASTOR surrendered without a fight.[20]

Even as CASTOR was being pursued, the PASF headquarters issued a classified set of instructions ordering its field units to "heighten vigilance to cope with, prevent, and defeat the enemy plot." This plot, explained the directive, involved new commando teams being sent by Saigon to the north.

Significantly, the name Hanoi used for the commandos was Biet Kich, the same term it had used in relation to the GCMA.[21]

While privately ordering its security forces to deal with the Biet Kich threat, publicly North Vietnam made no mention of CASTOR's arrest or the associated airspace violation. Just as with the capture of ARES back in April, Hanoi chose to secretly exploit its captive commandos.

Meanwhile, the CIA and Office 45, as yet unaware of CASTOR's fate, were busy preparing more intelligence teams for infiltration. Just as before, they were allowed to scour the ranks of the 1st Observation Group for candidates. Helping in the selection was Father Nguyen Viet Khai, the same Catholic priest who had helped Lieutenant Colonel Tung find agent recruits in 1957.[22]

Khai's participation was necessary because the next team was set to parachute into central Quang Binh, North Vietnam's southernmost province, and contact a specific Catholic priest assigned to the village of Trooc. It was hoped that the Trooc priest, when shown a photo and letter of introduction from Khai, would offer food and shelter to the commandos. Using the church as cover, the agents were then to watch Route 15, a major artery running west into the Lao panhandle, which Hanoi used to transport supplies to South Vietnam. The agents were also tasked with confirming the presence of a North Vietnamese infantry division and an artillery unit, both believed to be located just north of the Demilitarized Zone.

On 2 June, this second airborne team of three commandos, code-named ECHO, headed north from Danang aboard the VIAT C-47. Making a shallow arc over the seventeenth parallel, the plane crossed into Quang Binh Province, and the team parachuted into the hills five kilometers north of Trooc.

The team's timing could not have been worse. As the paratroopers exited the plane, two nearby hamlets were in the midst of a late-night ideology session. Hearing the aircraft engine, they rushed outside in time to see the C-47 silhouetted against the moon. It took only a few hours to round up a search party using PASF militia, a dog platoon, and an infantry company. Coordinating along three fronts, they began to work their way up the hills.

ECHO was in bad shape from the start. One of the commandos had drifted three kilometers and landed in a tree. Cutting loose from his harness, he fell to the ground and injured his leg. The other two commandos managed to link up, but they were nervous wrecks, well aware that their drop had been spotted by nearby villagers. With survival foremost on their minds, they contacted Saigon by radio to say they intended to run toward the border. Before they could make any progress, however, North Vietnamese search parties tightened the noose. The next day all three were captured.[23]

Again, the CIA was unaware that its team had been captured. Twelve days later, a third team, code-named DIDO and consisting of four Black Tai agents, departed Danang. The agents' target was the heart of the Black Tai minority, Lai Chau Province in extreme northwestern North Vietnam.[24] There they were to parachute near Route 6 midway between the provincial capital and the crossroads village of Tuan Giao. Once more, the connection to the war in Laos was prominent. From their vantage point, DIDO could observe traffic heading toward Tuan Giao, where a prominent road artery forked southwest through the Dien Bien Phu valley—now being used as a base for the North Vietnamese 316th Brigade—and into northern Laos.

Overflying the Gulf of Tonkin toward the Chinese border, Major Ky steered the C-47 across northernmost North Vietnam. Pausing to drop propaganda leaflets over Cao Bang Province near the Chinese border, the plane headed west toward the designated drop zone in Lai Chau. When the green light flashed, the four commandos leaped into the void, while the C-47, linking up with the same return flight path used by CASTOR, turned southeast toward the coastal province of Ninh Binh.

Landing in a mountain clearing, the four DIDO commandos hid their parachutes and assembled. Unlike ECHO, all had escaped injury. But their main supply bundle—containing clothes, ammunition, food, and their radio—was nowhere to be found. For over three weeks, the parachutists, by now very hungry, combed the hills to no avail. Then one morning they ran into a PASF patrol, which for the previous ten days had been sweeping four neighboring districts after receiving villager reports of a parachute drop. The weakened commandos ran for Laos, only to be captured at the border.[25]

By the second week of July, Hanoi had all three airborne teams in custody. Publicly, not a word had been uttered. Privately, its security services were working overtime. Fearful that more airborne teams would follow, on 22 June party officials issued a directive underscoring the need for swift searches when commandos were dropped.[26] This was followed by publication of a classified PASF booklet outlining how to counter airborne teams.

Even at that early date, the PASF booklet showed a remarkably complete understanding of the CIA's unfolding operation. Written with strong assistance from Beijing, it drew several lessons from China's long experience with CIA airborne teams and revealed an intimate understanding of the agency's methodology. For example, the publication noted that in both China and North Vietnam, teams jumped between 2200 and 0100 hours. The booklet also noted that teams usually parachuted into mountainous areas or along district boundaries, where the jurisdiction between local security forces was often confused. It also correctly pointed out that agent teams would normally move from the drop zone to a nearby area to regroup.[27]

Of course, Hanoi knew very well that whenever agent teams were parachuted into North Vietnam they would soon be followed by supply drops. It was these follow-on drops that convinced the Ministry of the Interior to launch a "counterespionage operation." The plan was to double the Biet Kich radio operators, "persuade" them to establish controlled contact with Saigon, and convince their former masters that the teams were safe. In doing so, North Vietnam's intelligence officials hoped they could not only channel disinformation but also lure supplies—or even future teams—into drop zones of their choosing.

At 1200 hours, 29 June—just over a month after insertion—CASTOR flashed its first message to BUGS, the CIA's radio relay station in the Philippines. Saigon was apparently not overly concerned about the delay in establishing contact because it immediately sent back words of encouragement, followed by a promise to send supplies in four days. To Hanoi's satisfaction, the ploy appeared to be working.

On the afternoon of 1 July, one day before the promised resupply, pallets were packed at Tan Son Nhut and loaded on the VIAT C-47. Major Ky was scheduled to fly the plane, but at the last moment handed off the mission to the backup crew headed by Lieutenant Phan Thanh Van. Joining Van's men would be three noncommissioned officers seconded from the 1st Observation Group to help kick the supplies out the rear door to CASTOR's position.

After a final CIA briefing, Lieutenant Van lifted off for Danang late that afternoon. This would be the first attempted resupply of an in-place team, an extremely challenging mission. Using nothing more sophisticated than a navigator looking out the window and following the terrain in the moonlight, the team was expected to work its way through the mountains and find CASTOR's small drop zone.

Following the customary refuel at Danang, the VIAT crew took off near midnight and, traveling along the same air corridor used by CASTOR and DIDO, made a direct line for Ninh Binh Province. Up in Son La Province, meanwhile, PASF officials had hiked to the mountain clearing where, according to their radio play with Saigon, CASTOR would be awaiting the drop. Joining them at the scene was Ha Van Chap, the CASTOR team leader, who had been coerced into providing assistance.[28] A signal fire blazed nearby as the North Vietnamese waited for the plane.[29]

On Hon Ne, a small island six kilometers off the coast of Ninh Binh Province, North Vietnamese soldiers heard the C-47 as it approached the mainland. The garrison on the island had been augmented in mid-June after Hanoi deduced that Ninh Binh was the primary infiltration point used

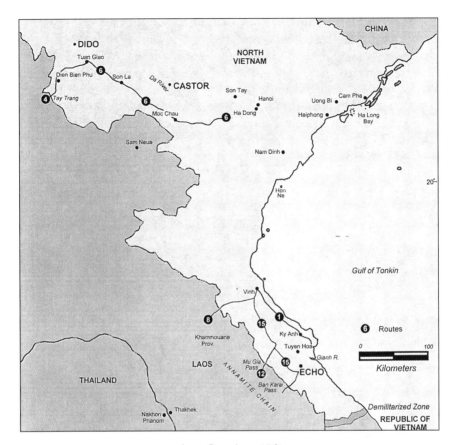

Agent Insertions, 1961

during the commando flights. By overflying Ninh Binh, Hanoi correctly reasoned, the planes could skirt the antiaircraft ring around Hanoi and take the most direct path to the mountainous northwestern portion of the country where rough terrain and sparse population played against the security forces.

The soldiers on Hon Me—which included both PASF and an antiaircraft platoon—had failed to react during two previous VIAT overflights. This time, the gunners were alert as the drone of the low-flying C-47's engines grew louder. As the plane came into view, the gunners opened fire, riddling the bottom of the aircraft with bullets. Seriously damaged, it dropped from the sky and crashed in a plantation twenty kilometers inland.[30]

Word of the shootdown raced through official Saigon. The U.S. ambassador, Fritz Nolting, was livid over the potential for diplomatic embarrassment.[31] Within the CIA and Office 45, there was a sinking feeling that

CASTOR was under North Vietnamese control and that the resupply plane had been lured into an ambush.

Strangely enough, the mood in Hanoi was restrained. While the North Vietnamese media converged on the crash site and reported outrage at the obvious purpose of the flight, the Ministry of the Interior was probably less than pleased. The shootdown, after all, jeopardized its long-term plans because CASTOR would now fall under intense scrutiny. Unless it could placate the CIA's suspicions, Hanoi's first counterespionage operation would likely end prematurely.

4

SECOND WIND

Hanoi guessed right. CIA radio messages reaching CASTOR during the third quarter of 1961 were seething with suspicion. Saigon repeatedly challenged the agents, trying to find some error, some anomaly in their response. It listened carefully to the radioman's "fist"—his unique cadence and style of typing out words in Morse code—for some signal that the team was turned.

By adhering to their own *bo nao* (master plan), North Vietnamese counterintelligence agents carefully won back Saigon's trust. Part of this involved "moving" CASTOR south to the Song Da River in accordance with CIA radio instructions. Once it appeared to be maneuvering along the riverbanks, CASTOR then appeased Saigon with a slow stream of low-level information.[1]

A more complicated part of the *bo nao* involved the July C-47 crash in Ninh Binh. Seven crew members, including the pilot, had survived that fiery wreck. This Hanoi could not deny, since it had been widely reported by the media soon after the shootdown. At the very least, the pilot—if not the entire crew—would have known that the supplies on the C-47 were destined for CASTOR. If this were admitted during the trial, however, Hanoi would have to acknowledge it knew about a team in Son La Province. Saigon would then have no doubt that CASTOR had been captured and doubled.

But Hanoi devised a cover story by the time three crewmen (four others had since died of their wounds) were put on trial in November. According to their testimony in court, these men admitted to being involved in commando operations. But rather than resupplying a team in Son La, they claimed they were headed for a remote location in Hoa Binh Province.[2]

In order for Saigon to accept this tale, it needed to believe that all three crew members had withstood North Vietnamese interrogation and managed to keep their true mission from their captors. Saigon also had to believe that Hanoi had swallowed the lie. Taken together, it seems impossible for the CIA to have concluded CASTOR was still a viable team. Yet that is exactly what happened. By year's end, CASTOR was again considered one of Saigon's "good" assets.[3]

Satisfied that its team had not been doubled, Lieutenant Colonel Tung's outfit (which had since been renamed the Presidential Survey Office because the earlier title, Presidential Liaison Office, was compromised during the Hanoi trial) was ready to dispatch more agents.[4] But with VIAT's sole plane gone, there was no way to get them into North Vietnam. The CIA did not want another C-47 for two reasons. First, the C-47's limited range meant that the plane was forced to take direct routes to the drop zones. Second, the C-47 had to refuel in Danang on each mission, leading some planners to speculate that the July shootdown might have been the result of a North Vietnamese spy having infiltrated Danang to radio a warning each time a plane left that airport at night. (In fact, the reason for the shootdown had nothing to do with a spy in Danang but instead had come about after the C-47 repeatedly used the same entry point over Ninh Binh.) This time, the agency wanted an aircraft with greater range that could avoid Danang and its suspected resident spy.[5]

It turned to the 1045th Operations, Evaluation and Training (OE&T) Group. Jointly managed by the CIA and the U.S. Air Force, this small unit specialized in managing unconventional aviation support for some of the agency's far-flung covert operations. In Tibet, for example, the group had arranged for Air America to borrow the U.S. Air Force's new C-130 transports in order to parachute guerrillas and supplies over the Himalayas. In Laos, the group had helped coordinate air force and Air America support for the fledgling guerrilla army taking shape there.[6]

Due to its heavy involvement in Laos, the 1045th could spare just two of its officers, Captain Edward Smith and Lieutenant David Clarke, for the Saigon operation. Both were on hand when it was decided that VIAT's new aircraft would be a C-54 transport. In use with several civilian airlines—which would provide a veneer of plausible deniability—the C-54 more than doubled the operating range of the C-47, eliminating the need to refuel in Danang and allowing the crews to approach drop zones via a more circuitous route.[7]

Not everything changed, however. Nguyen Cao Ky, by this time promoted to lieutenant colonel, remained commander of the South Vietnamese pilots. Once again he looked for volunteers, while the same Air America team of Al Judkins and Jim Keck returned to train the prospective crews in low-level flying and navigation.[8]

Flight training on the C-54 ended in early 1962. Upon graduation, Ky piled his aviators aboard the new plane and flew to Singapore. There he purchased a black flight suit, purple scarf, cigarette lighters, and distinctive insignia for each member. The American advisers were mortified. Ky and his men were supposed to blend in with the rest of the Vietnamese air force, but their new flamboyant attire screamed for attention. William Colby, the CIA station chief, noted in dour resignation, "When you get a gift, you need to accept the paper it's wrapped in."[9]

As the C-54 was being readied for VIAT service, Office 45 turned out half a dozen new agent teams. To manage these new trainees, Jacques was augmented by a second case officer, an ethnic Tai named Dao Vinh Loc who went by the call sign Maurice. Together, the two officers readied the next team to head north. Composed of five ethnic Muong going by the code name EUROPA, it underwent final fitting on 20 February. Taking off from Tan Son Nhut that night, Lieutenant Colonel Ky bypassed Danang and headed toward the North Vietnamese coast. Taking a roundabout flight path, he arrived over Hoa Binh in central North Vietnam, a province heavily populated by the Muong minority.

As Ky hit the green light, the five commandos disappeared out the rear door. Their drop zone, Tan Lac District, was a poor choice. Route 6 wound across the middle of the district, which was laced with feeder roads and dotted with villages. Once again the paratroopers were spotted during descent. The next morning, in what was becoming an effective routine, the PASF, together with militia and students from the nearby border guard school, converged on the Muong agents. All were captured alive by the following day.[10]

In captivity, the EUROPA radio operator was soon transmitting over the airwaves to Saigon. Thinking it had another successful insertion, Office 45 decided that its next mission would be another attempt at resupplying CASTOR. According to its radio messages, the team had been living off the land for nearly ten months. It was hoped that the new plane would have better luck.

Because Ky's crew had flown the EUROPA mission, a second string of aviators, headed by Captain Hoi, took their turn in the cockpit. Lifting off from Tan Son Nhut, they cut a winding path toward Son La. Shortly before reaching the designated drop zone, misfortune struck again. Caught in an unexpected rainstorm, the pilot lost his bearings and slammed into a mountain.[11]

Back in Saigon, the CIA planners were beyond frustration. This was the second aircraft loss in seven months. If there was any good news, it was that, after reviewing transcripts of North Vietnamese communications, they knew that pilot error had caused the crash and that Hanoi was unaware of the loss. Because of this, they could still cling to their misplaced belief that CASTOR had not been doubled.

Once more without an airplane, the CIA again asked the 1045th OE&T Group for another C-54. However, the Vietnamese air force crews now had such a bad flying record that Saigon decided to look for alternatives. The CIA turned to a familiar source—the Republic of China on Taiwan, where it had been mounting airborne infiltrations into mainland China almost continuously since 1952. Beginning in 1955, many of these covert flights were flown by pilots from the Chinese air force. With seven years of experience in secret operations, most of it deep penetration work, the Nationalist Chinese were well qualified for the North Vietnam missions. Better still, they were already involved in covert operations in Southeast Asia: the previous year the CIA had arranged for Chinese pilots to fly resupply missions for government-backed guerrillas in Laos.[12]

For the North Vietnam assignment, the CIA sought volunteers from the Republic of China's commercial flagship, China Airlines. Established in late 1959, China Airlines was staffed almost entirely by seasoned pilots from the Chinese air force, and they were quite willing to fly classified operations. Since earlier resupply missions into Laos had been code-named NORTHERN STAR, the North Vietnam project was dubbed SOUTHERN STAR.

The CIA also arranged for Air America to dispatch two navigators to Taiwan, where they would train ten candidates in low-level flying techniques. Ken Rockwell, one of the navigators, recalled the training. "We were flying at two hundred feet or less, primarily around the off-shore islands," he said. "The C-54 had an old radar installed, and we wanted to teach them what it looked like to come upon a hill feature higher than their flying altitude. To do this, we would approach a two-thousand-foot peak from the sea, and show them how it looked on the scope. We had a language problem with the students, but they soon came up to speed."[13]

While the Chinese navigators were still undergoing training, the CIA was anxious to launch its next team. Just as with the previous year's ECHO agents, Office 45 again looked to persecuted Catholics as a way into North Vietnam. Father Khai had already identified four Catholic farmers from Nghe An Province who, in protest of communist agrarian policy, had walked to Laos in 1959 and been relocated to the south. With Khai acting as intermediary, the four were approached by the chief of Office 45, Captain Linh, and successfully recruited.[14]

Shifted to a Saigon safe house, the former farmers, now going by the code name ATLAS, were to be reinserted into Nghe An near Route 7. Like ECHO, they were to watch road traffic into Laos. Also like ECHO, they were to make contact with two Catholic priests and seek their assistance in providing cover.[15]

During the first week of March 1962, ATLAS was flown to Laos. Since the Chinese C-54 crews were still not ready, the CIA arranged for the one-time use of Air America helicopters to insert the team along the Laos border with Nghe An. From there, the agents would hike into North Vietnam.

Late in the afternoon of 12 March, the team and its supplies were loaded aboard a pair of American-piloted H-34 helicopters. They were to be escorted by a third chopper, which would act as a rescue bird in case one of the other two was downed. Since much of the flight would be over unfamiliar territory, the crews were to be guided to their target by a Helio Courier plane piloted by Captain Ron Sutphin, one of the most experienced light aircraft pilots in the Air America roster.[16]

Following Sutphin's lead, the helicopters deposited ATLAS at last light on a mountain clearing near the border. Dressed in black pajamas and armed with Sten submachine guns (favored by the CIA because of its non-American manufacture), the team headed east. For three days the agents moved without incident. On the fourth day, however, they came upon a young boy.

"He disappeared into the forest," said one of the agents. "After that, local militia came. We started running toward the Laos border. One member was shot and killed; another one stepped on a mine and died. We assembled our radio and sent a message to Saigon saying that we were being chased, but the transmission got cut off due to bad weather. After that, we were surrounded and taken prisoner."[17]

Here was an outright failure that could not be explained away, but the CIA elected to press ahead. Because the Chinese aircrews were still not ready, the CIA again turned to Air America. This time, the airline offered use of a C-46 from Takhli air base, Thailand. Ron Sutphin, the same pilot who had helped lead ATLAS to its drop zone, would be in the cockpit, along with Captain M. D. "Doc" Johnson.

The team they were to drop, code-named REMUS, consisted of six Black Tai. Just like the earlier Team DIDO, which also consisted of Black Tai, REMUS's target was Lai Chau Province near the Dien Bien Phu valley. Not only was Dien Bien Phu the largest military complex in northwestern North Vietnam, but its resident infantry unit, the 316th Brigade, had been intervening in neighboring Laos since early in the year.

Like the ATLAS agents, REMUS would try to avoid detection by inserting inside the Laos border and walking to its target. On 16 April, the six men jumped onto a rugged drop zone fifteen kilometers northwest of Dien Bien Phu. For once, the jump was not spotted, and the team reassembled without incident. Five days later, the agents established contact with Saigon and moved into North Vietnam.

With REMUS crossing the border undetected, Office 45 returned once more to its original set of agents, CASTOR. In late April, CASTOR was ordered to move south from the banks of the Song Da River into Moc Chau District. From there, they were to await a much-needed resupply drop. In addition to fresh supplies, they would also be joined by a new team. These agents, code-named TOURBILLON, were different in several respects. Where most previous teams had each been recruited from a single ethnic group, which in turn had been matched with the ethnicity of its target province, TOURBILLON's members were a mix of four different minorities, at least two of which were not indigenous to the team's target. And while most of the earlier agents had been given low-profile intelligence-gathering missions, TOURBILLON was wholly dedicated to hit-and-run sabotage.

Although TOURBILLON's sabotage agenda was a departure for Office 45, the mandate for such a team was not new. Since the previous May, President Kennedy had repeatedly called for harassment measures to be undertaken by agent teams inside North Vietnam. Much of this was born out of frustration with events in neighboring Laos, where the conflict had gone sour for the American-backed royalist government. A showdown had been building since March in the northwestern provincial capital of Nam Tha, with the royalist army on the ropes at the hands of a communist opponent stiffened by several battalions of North Vietnamese infantry.

With a climax looming at Nam Tha, TOURBILLON was to parachute into the unpopulated hills in northern Moc Chau District and make its way eight kilometers south to Route 6. The team would then blow several of the bridges along that road, a move expected to inhibit traffic heading west via Dien Bien Phu into Laos. While at first glance such a limited sabotage venture would be expected to have an equally limited effect, in that part of North Vietnam it might actually be quite devastating. Rugged mountains, seasonal monsoons, and a shortage of roads meant that most traffic had to converge at only a few bridges. If TOURBILLON could blow some of them, it could substantially slow North Vietnamese aid to the Lao communists.

But using a long-term agent team to accomplish this mission was doomed to failure. These teams were trained and equipped to shun attention. Acts of sabotage, by contrast, grabbed headlines. As the earlier experience of Lansdale's stay-behind networks had shown, surviving in a closed society like North Vietnam was difficult enough without attracting attention. At the very least, the concept of a long-term sabotage team expected too much from a group of young agents. It also showed a profound lack of appreciation for the depth and skill of North Vietnamese security forces.

Perhaps in partial recognition of the serious challenges confronting such a team, Office 45 was again given permission to recruit from the more experienced ranks of the former 1st Observation Group, since renamed Group 77.[18] Seven soldiers were chosen, all with prior airborne and ranger training. In addition, the radio operator was a veteran of two reconnaissance missions into Laos.[19]

By May, Royal Lao troops were falling apart before the communist offensive in Nam Tha. During the first week of the month, TOURBILLON made four attempts to insert, but each time the mission was aborted due to either poor weather or, given the primitive navigation techniques, the pilot's inability to spot CASTOR's ground signal made from a series of flame pots. So TOURBILLON was still waiting at Tan Son Nhut when Nam Tha fell to communist forces on 9 May. A third of the Lao government's frontline units were cut to shreds, the remainder too demoralized to fight on. Regarding the

Nam Tha fight as a deliberate action to test American resolve, President Kennedy quickly sent sixty-four hundred U.S. serviceman to Thailand.

One week later, TOURBILLON prepared again for insertion. This time the Chinese crews were ready for their maiden mission. As part of a very weak cover story, they had been issued identification cards from Saigon and were to pose as South Vietnamese commercial pilots if shot down—this despite the fact that none of them could speak Vietnamese.

As the plane arrived over the drop zone, the pilot spotted the flame pots on the ground and signaled the team to jump. Ten minutes before midnight, the seven agents were floating toward the ground.[20]

Of course, CASTOR was not waiting at the drop zone. In its place was at least one company of PASF militiamen and several police dogs concealed around the mountain clearing.[21] But the joke was also on the North Vietnamese because TOURBILLON ran into unexpectedly strong winds as the commandos descended and missed the drop zone. As they drifted into the distance, the PASF set off in pursuit.

Floating down, the TOURBILLON agents saw the flame pots pass underneath them and knew they were off target. As the jungle rushed up to meet them, the commandos prepared for a rough landing. It was worse than they expected. "Landing in the forest, the assistant team leader got caught in a tree, and he was shot in his harness when he resisted," said one team member. "The rest of us ran as soon as we landed, but we were captured over the next two days."[22]

Isolating the radio operator, Ministry of the Interior officials ordered him to establish contact with Saigon. Since Office 45 believed that the drop zone was secured by CASTOR, it had ordered TOURBILLON to get on the air within two days; any delay longer than forty-eight hours meant Saigon would assume TOURBILLON—and CASTOR—had been compromised. But the team did not send its first message for a full eleven days. Incredibly, Office 45 chose to ignore its own safety precaution and decided TOURBILLON was safe. Once again, Saigon believed it had pulled off a perfect insertion.[23]

Four days after TOURBILLON jumped at Moc Chau, the next agent team, code-named EROS, boarded a C-54 at Tan Son Nhut and flew in a clockwise arc over Laos. Arriving near the border with Thanh Hoa Province in the northern panhandle, the plane briefly penetrated North Vietnam's airspace, dropped its commandos, and headed home. Because the intrusion was so short, North Vietnamese border guards remained unaware that an insertion had taken place.[24]

On the ground, the five members of EROS assembled without incident. Ethnically, they were a mix of Muong and Red Tai, both indigenous to western Thanh Hoa. EROS was also a family affair: two of the Muong were brothers and the third was a cousin, while the two Tai were uncle and nephew. Office 45 hoped the tight familial bond between the EROS members would make it easier for the team to establish links with some of its tribal brethren. In fact, the drop zone was only eight kilometers from the home village of one of the team members. Also, there was a history of commando operations in western Thanh Hoa dating back to 1953 when the French successfully tapped Red Tai support and built a two-thousand-strong GCMA formation in the very district where EROS jumped.[25]

Once on the ground, however, the commandos were reluctant to leave the forest. After two weeks, some Tai villagers approached the bivouac site where they had been hiding. The frightened agents fled north. At the abandoned campsite, the locals discovered several empty food cans, none of them with brand names sold inside North Vietnam. They immediately told authorities about the suspicious garbage, and a manhunt was launched using an infantry regiment, a local army battalion, and a reinforced company of PASF. But they found nothing, and after beating the bush for two weeks, the infantry were withdrawn at the end of June.

Meanwhile, EROS had nearly exhausted its supplies. The team requested a resupply drop, which Saigon promised would come in July. When it failed to arrive, Saigon blamed poor weather. Left to fend for themselves, the agents set out to find food. On 2 August, they were again spotted by villagers, and the manhunt resumed. A quick radio message from EROS let Saigon know they were being pursued. Finally, on 29 September the PASF surrounded the team. One member was killed and a second captured. Three others escaped to the border and joined a band of Lao hunters; they were eventually betrayed and turned over to the North Vietnamese.[26]

Despite problems with EROS, the CIA was satisfied with its record of inserting airborne agents. Of the eight long-term teams dispatched by the summer of 1962, the agency believed that half—CASTOR, EUROPA, REMUS, and TOURBILLON—were operational. Also cause for celebration was a report on 29 July that TOURBILLON had succeeded in blowing up a bridge. Of course, CASTOR, EUROPA, and TOURBILLON were actually under Hanoi's control. Even the sabotage mission was a sham, a false report sent out by the team's North Vietnamese handlers. The CIA would never know it, but TOURBILLON's explosives and other demolition supplies were sent south to the Viet Cong, who used them in attacks on Bien Hoa and Tan Son Nhut airfields and in a terrorist bombing of a hotel in Saigon.[27]

But as far as the CIA was concerned, it was on the right track. At long last, after the failure of similar paramilitary missions on cold war battlefields in Eastern Europe, North Korea, and China, the agency thought it had found a formula for success.

5

VULCAN

As the sun rose over the Tonkin Gulf, fishing boats ventured out onto the sparkling sea. Behind them lay the verdant coast, sharply outlined in the clear morning light. Fishermen came here regularly to cast their nets, taking advantage of the rich waters near the mouth of the Gianh River, about forty kilometers north of Dong Hoi, North Vietnam's southernmost town of any note. But this was wartime, and the peaceful appearance was merely a facade. A kilometer upriver, on the south bank, lay Quang Khe naval base, home to part of Hanoi's fledgling coastal defense fleet.

On 16 May 1962, the scene looked much the same as on any other day. No one suspected that just below the surface lurked an American submarine, the USS *Catfish,* carefully watching the naval base. A few days earlier, the submarine had sailed from the Philippines toward the mouth of the Gianh River on a mission code-named WISE TIGER. Remaining in international waters, the *Catfish* was collecting data on North Vietnam's gunboats.

The *Catfish* was an old sub, commissioned near the end of World War II and hurried into the Pacific theater with the mission of locating mines near the Japanese island of Kyushu. After the war, it had been extensively modified for greater submerged speed and endurance. When the Korean conflict broke out in June 1950, the *Catfish* was on another Far East cruise. Rushed to the Korean peninsula, it was assigned an impromptu reconnaissance mission. The operation was a success, and for the next fifteen years the *Catfish* continued quiet snooping throughout Asian waters.[1]

On this trip the submarine was interested in Swatow gunboats, a Chinese-made vessel that formed the backbone of the North Vietnamese navy. Hanoi had acquired two dozen of these boats three years earlier.[2] Measuring eighty-three feet long, they packed up to three 37mm guns, two twin 14.5mm guns, and eight depth charges. With a crew of thirty, a Swatow could travel at twenty-eight knots and use its surface-search radar to detect incoming boats. While the boats were potentially deadly, the North Vietnamese kept them mostly in port and had yet to use them against the CIA's motorized junks.[3]

A trio of Swatows was thought to be harbored at Quang Khe. After patient monitoring, the *Catfish* confirmed the presence of all three and sent word back to Manila.[4] This was then relayed to Saigon, where the CIA was finalizing plans for a bold maritime strike against the gunboats.

51

This mission was long in coming. Back in March 1961, the CIA had first proposed sabotaging North Vietnamese ports as part of a diverse covert warfare menu forwarded to President Kennedy. The scheme lay dormant until the early spring of 1962, when Hanoi's increasing aggressiveness in both South Vietnam and neighboring Laos prompted Washington to reexamine its options. Frustrated by North Vietnamese involvement in the burgeoning southern insurgency, especially its expansion of the Ho Chi Minh Trail, the Kennedy administration groped for some way to react. There was little the president could do except express his displeasure to Hanoi. Using covert action to send signals would become an increasingly common tool as the war escalated.

In April 1962, Admiral Harry D. Felt, commander in chief, Pacific (CINCPAC), echoed the president's sentiment when he called for a "direct cause-and-effect relationship" between communist actions in South Vietnam and American retaliation in the north. "A [Viet Cong] mining of Dong Ha–Saigon railroad would be followed within a week by slightly larger [U.S.] destruction of the DRV [Democratic Republic of Vietnam, or North Vietnam] Lao Kay–Hanoi railroad." Of course, Admiral Felt envisioned overt bombing of North Vietnamese targets, but he knew that was impossible. So as an alternative he also advocated a "commando raid on some DRV coastal facility."[5] In response, the CIA was ordered to launch its airborne sabotage campaign—beginning with Team TOURBILLON—and, as an additional prod to Hanoi, given the green light to plan a maritime strike against the Quang Khe naval base.

Maritime operations were nothing new to the CIA. Beginning in 1951, the agency had frequently used motorized junks and commandos from Taiwan to strike at the Chinese mainland. "We used them as mother-ships to launch smaller boats with hit-and-run teams," said Jack Mathews, an officer who helped run these missions. "The teams hit coastal targets, and on a few occasions managed to burn down some warehouses with thermite grenades."[6] During the Korean War, the CIA had shunned junks, instead using Soviet-style trawlers to deploy sabotage teams along the northern half of the peninsula.[7]

Adapting this to a North Vietnamese setting, the CIA case officers in Saigon envisioned a motorized junk making its way up the Quang Binh coast and from there deploying a team of commandos to steal up the Gianh River and set charges against the Swatows. But while the CIA already had a junk and qualified crew to perform the job, Office 45 lacked any commandos versed in maritime operations. Fortunately for them, two years earlier a contingent of eighteen select trainees from the South Vietnamese army, navy, and marines had been sent to Taiwan for four months of combat swimmer instruction.[8] While not originally intended for covert operations in North Vietnam, they were qualified for the Quang Khe mission.

In April 1962, Office 45 secured loan of four Taiwan-trained commandos. Code-named Team VULCAN, they were brought to Danang and coached in planting limpet mines on the hulls of boats. The following month, after receiving confirmation of the gunboats' presence from the *Catfish,* the CIA decided to make a trial run. VULCAN and ten crewmen loaded into the *Nautilus 2,* the agency's lone motorized junk, and headed up the coast. Anchoring off the mouth of the Gianh River, the commandos sneaked to shore in a raft for a beach reconnaissance. After looking around for signs of activity, they returned to the junk. No one had seen them.[9]

Captain Ha Ngoc Oanh, a two-year veteran of Office 45 known by his call sign, Antoine, looked around the table at the four VULCAN commandos. This was the first team under his direct supervision. When the final order to attack the Swatows came on 28 June, he scheduled this final briefing. Joined by a pair of CIA officers, Antoine translated instructions into Vietnamese, aided by aerial photos of Quang Khe taken just a few days earlier. On the wall behind him was a map of the naval base marked with avenues of approach and retreat.[10]

The commandos listened closely. From the junk, they would switch to a smaller wooden boat and head to the river mouth. The aerial photos showed only three Swatows at Quang Khe, so only three frogmen would enter the water and swim the rest of the way using scuba gear. The fourth combat swimmer, Nguyen Chuyen, would remain on the boat as backup. They would target one boat apiece, planting a limpet mine below the waterline near the engine, then swim back to the boat.[11]

It was past midnight when the briefing ended. Joining their American advisers for a farewell party, they ate and drank into the new day. The team then went into isolation, spending the next afternoon gathering gear and rehearsing the mission among themselves. For operational security, no one was allowed to contact their families.

At 2030 hours on 29 June, VULCAN was taken to the Danang piers. Boarding *Nautilus 2* along with a dozen crewmen, the team prepared to cast off. Antoine handed the junk captain a bundle of colored flags. "If you see any boats flying a pennant," he said, "you raise one of the same." The North Vietnamese often ordered fishermen to fly different flags on different days as a way of spotting interlopers. Antoine then shook the captain's hand. "Be careful," he warned. "I wish you good luck and success."[12]

Sailing through the night and all the next day, *Nautilus 2* blended with the other junks at sea. The following night the team closed on its objective. Darkness cloaked the coastline. Just before midnight on 30 June, the junk cut both engines. Two crewmen lowered a small motorized launch into the gentle swells, then climbed in. The VULCAN commandos, dressed in scuba gear and each clutching a limpet mine, joined them. As its small outboard coughed to life, the skiff slowly parted from the junk.

Fifteen minutes later, Le Van Kinh, one of the commandos, could clearly see the shores of the Gianh River. In the darkness, the VULCAN members set their mines to detonate in two hours—sufficient time for them to swim in, plant the charges, and get back to the skiff. Kinh put on his mask, cleared his mouthpiece, and slipped into the water. He was soon joined by a second commando, Nguyen Van Tam.

Nguyen Huu Thao, the last of the three, went through the same motions in a daze. A devout Catholic, Thao had been denied permission to return home and attend the burial of his father, who had died a few days earlier. Still visibly grieving, he quietly adjusted his mouthpiece and entered the sea.

On the deck of Swatow 185, a guard heard faint splashing in the water under the stern. Peering into the darkness, he saw nothing, although he felt compelled to report the noise to the boat's skipper, Captain Ho Ngoc Minh. Taking a group of sailors with him, Minh walked back to the stern and leaned forward for a closer look.[13]

In the oily water, Nguyen Huu Thao was in the process of fixing his limpet mine to the Swatow's hull. Hearing the commotion above, he apparently panicked. The North Vietnamese navy would later claim that "the commando, who was planning to lay the mine, got startled by the noise on the ship; the mine exploded prematurely and killed him immediately." But Le Van Kinh recalled Thao's depression over his father's death and speculated that his mind was just not on the mission.[14] Whatever the truth, it no longer mattered because what had been a stealthy raid was now a race for survival.

Kinh, the first commando in the water, had managed to place his mine without incident. Twenty meters from the Swatow, he surfaced to get his bearings. At that same moment, Thao's limpet detonated in a blinding flash. The shock wave hit Kinh on the back of the skull, then slammed into the rest of his body. As his limbs went numb, he floated helplessly on the surface. Kinh saw that the Swatow was badly damaged, but he also knew that the North Vietnamese would soon be swarming about the base.

In the skiff, Nguyen Chuyen and the two crewmen watched as the explosion lit up the night. It took only minutes for the North Vietnamese to spot the bobbing boat silhouetted in the smoke and flames. Frightened by the sound of revving Swatow engines and fearing the worst, the men did not wait around to see what would happen next. Their own engine coughed to life, and the little boat turned tail for the open sea. In the stern, Chuyen raised a submachine gun and fired long bursts toward his pursuers. The North Vietnamese fired back, and by the time the little boat reached the junk, Chuyen was hit and bleeding.

Alone in the water, Kinh had little time to think. In pain, he kicked toward shore and rolled out of the water into a bush. Peeling off his tanks and wet suit, he planned to hide until the commotion subsided, then try to swim south. It was not to be. Within an hour, North Vietnamese patrols found him. Beating him almost senseless, they marched him off for interrogation. Blindfolded, he managed a smile as the sound of a second limpet detonation rumbled in the distance.[15]

Nguyen Van Tam, the third swimmer, had only slightly better luck. After placing his limpet, he headed back toward the skiff. Then the first mine detonated prematurely, and he suddenly found himself abandoned in the middle of the river. As his mind raced for alternatives, Tam spied a boat lying at anchor nearby and silently swam alongside. Hoping to creep out to sea unnoticed, he climbed over the gunwale—and into the arms of some North Vietnamese militamen.

Quang Khe erupted into action. Holed by the first limpet, Swatow 185 was taking on water fast. In the confusion, one gunboat, Swatow 161, took to sea after the escaping skiff. Throttling up its engines, the gunboat surged into the bay looking for the culprits and soon spotted the little wooden boat. Tailing it back to the junk, the Swatow bore down on its quarry with guns blazing.

Far from helpless, the crew of the *Nautilus 2* aimed machine-gun fire at the gunboat in their wake. For the next three hours they kept the Swatow at bay as they ran south along the coast. At 0600 hours, however, gunfire from the North Vietnamese vessel struck the junk's engine compartment. With *Nautilus 2* dead in the water, the circling Swatow pummeled it to matchwood. Nguyen Chuyen, the frogman who had earlier escaped in the skiff, and one other crewman died in the exchange.[16]

As the Swatow picked its way among the flotsam, ten surviving South Vietnamese were plucked from the water and blindfolded. Unknown to the gunboat crew, an eleventh crew member, Nguyen Van Ngoc, was hiding in the junk's partially submerged cabin. Clinging to the wreckage, he floated south toward the seventeenth parallel, where he was spotted by a patrolling aircraft and rescued.

On 21 July, Hanoi placed the captured commandos and crew before a jury, the second publicized Biet Kich trial in as many years. Receiving sentences of up to life in prison, the somber South Vietnamese agents headed for their cells.[17] Burned by the ordeal, it would be another year before the CIA again tried its hand at sabotage in the Tonkin Gulf.[18]

6

BANG AND BURN

Events on the diplomatic front quickly overshadowed the failure of the VULCAN operation. The Geneva Declaration and Protocol on the Neutrality of Laos went into full effect on 6 October 1962, prompting the Kennedy administration to suspend all "provocative acts" in the theater. This meant that the substantial U.S. military advisory group in the kingdom could do no more than maintain the Royal Lao army in a defensive posture against communist forces. Similarly, the CIA's agent teams already in North Vietnam were ordered to lie low and refrain from further sabotage attacks.

But only one month later, CIA analysts were crying foul. Of the nine thousand North Vietnamese troops and advisers believed to be in Laos before the accord, only forty self-described "technicians" officially withdrew by the proscribed deadline. This paltry number, combined with some other rear units that were secretly taken home, left an estimated 6,000 Vietnamese soldiers illegally inside Laos.[1]

The peace agreement was further frayed on 22 November when a Lao antiaircraft battery shot down an Air America C-123 aircraft loaded with humanitarian supplies. Two American crew members died in the crash. An investigation determined the gunners were openly sympathetic to the Pathet Lao, the communist liberation movement in Laos closely allied with Hanoi.

As peace in Laos drifted away, the situation in South Vietnam also deteriorated. After a strong counterinsurgency performance in the summer of 1962, the South Vietnamese army began to falter during the fall, and, by December, few observers were optimistic about Saigon's long-term chances.

Policy makers in Washington were openly frustrated. Since the unspoken moratorium on offensive military operations in Laos garnered no similar goodwill from Hanoi, the CIA and Office 45 were authorized to restart covert operations against the north. First they rekindled the veteran TOURBILLON saboteurs. According to its radio transmissions, the team had been keeping a low profile after demolishing a bridge in July. Having already proved their ability, the agents in early December were ordered on another "bang and burn" mission—the CIA's slang for sabotage—against a bridge two dozen kilometers west of the first. On 8 December, they reported success.

Had Saigon bothered to order aerial reconnaissance to corroborate TOURBILLON's claim, it would have found the Ta Vai bridge over Route

6 was indeed damaged. So great was Hanoi's desire to demonstrate the bona fides of its doubled teams that it had ordered the destruction of one of its own bridges.[2]

TOURBILLON's dramatic string of successes appeared to vindicate the long-term sabotage team concept. As a variation on this theme, Saigon's next group of agents, code-named LYRE, combined both sabotage and intelligence gathering. According to this marriage of opposites, LYRE would divide its time between interdicting roads and soliciting information from locals.

As had already twice been the case, LYRE took its members from the refugee population of northern Catholics. Both previous attempts—ECHO and ATLAS—had failed, but this time it was hoped that LYRE's longevity could be improved by infiltrating near Deo Ngang, a gorge twenty-six kilometers up the coast from the Swatow base targeted by VULCAN. While nobody lived in the gorge itself, the surrounding area was, in Hanoi's words, a hotbed of "Catholic reactionaries."[3]

Since Deo Ngang was on the coast, the CIA decided to insert the team by motorized junk from Danang. The switch from the less-successful airborne insertion method made no difference: when the team infiltrated on the night of 29 December, it was spotted by a coastal outpost almost immediately. Five members were captured within a day; the final two, attempting to flee south toward the Demilitarized Zone, were picked up by week's end.[4]

For Saigon, the failure of LYRE was compounded by bad news on the home front. On 2 January 1963, a three-battalion South Vietnamese army pincer attack against a badly outnumbered Viet Cong unit near the southern village of Ap Bac went awry. The South Vietnamese were smashed, along with a company of armored personnel carriers and five American helicopters. Eighty South Vietnamese troops and three American advisers were killed.

In Washington, the Ap Bac debacle put the lie to any claims that the insurgency in South Vietnam was under control. Worse, the bad news came just as the fragile peace in Laos was coming unraveled, threatening to throw the kingdom back into a state of war.

In response to these worsening developments, the CIA's covert program against North Vietnam underwent major restructuring. Unlike the earlier effort, which focused on intelligence with an occasional act of sabotage, the new schedule relied almost exclusively on sabotage teams in the hopes of turning up the pressure on Hanoi. And with Washington now paying more attention to its South Vietnamese ally rather than Laos, the sabotage effort in North Vietnam shifted away from targets directly linked to the Lao conflict, such as the bridges central to TOURBILLON's mission, and more toward economic targets and lines of communication thought to be crucial to Hanoi's war machine.

The first sabotage team of the new year was TARZAN. Five strong, the agents were targeted against Tuyen Hoa District in Quang Binh Province, the same general area where ECHO had parachuted two years earlier. On the night of 6 January they boarded a Chinese-piloted C-54 at Tan Son Nhut and headed north. Dropped without incident, TARZAN was soon on the air with Saigon.[5]

Following this apparent success, the CIA began a wholesale retraining of all its airborne teams. Coincidentally, the agency's impending sabotage campaign against North Vietnam was being repeated half a world away in Cuba. There, as part of the settlement to the October 1962 missile crisis, Kennedy had pledged not to use American military might to overthrow Fidel Castro. But while keeping to the letter of this promise, Washington flouted the underlying spirit by starting up a harassment campaign against Cuba, set to begin by mid-July. Desmond FitzGerald, a ranking CIA officer on the Cuban task force, let it be known he wanted a "major act of sabotage every month."[6]

Just as in Cuba, the CIA campaign in North Vietnam expanded to include a monthly act of sabotage. On 12 April, six ethnic Tho agents, codenamed PEGASUS, parachuted into Lang Son Province. Their target was one of the two critical rail lines that ran from the Chinese border to Hanoi.[7] Down in Saigon, the CIA waited for word from its saboteurs. None came.

The following month, another team flew north. No contact was ever established.[8]

Undeterred by these twin losses, Saigon began a full-scale blitz on 4 June. A record three teams were ready for insertion that night. Because the sole C-54 piloted by China Airlines could not handle the trio, a second unmarked C-54 arrived from Taiwan for one month of temporary duty. Manning the plane was a crew seconded directly from the Republic of China air force. Dividing the loads, the military crew took one team; the China Airlines C-54 boarded the remaining two. By the morning of 5 June, both aircraft had returned safely to Tan Son Nhut. Up in North Vietnam, however, only one of the three teams—code-named BELL—came on the air; the other two had disappeared.[9]

Three days later, the CIA tried again. Packing two teams in one C-54, agents were dropped over Ninh Binh and Thanh Hoa. Neither established contact. Two days after that, another pair of teams loaded into a single C-54 and were dropped over Ha Tinh and Nghe An. Again, no radio contact.[10]

With only two apparent successes in ten missions, the CIA took pause. Fortunately, at about the same time, a new piece of equipment appeared in Saigon that might change the situation—a new airplane to deliver the agent teams. Since the previous September, the agency had been looking to replace its C-54s. They had adequate range, but the small side door hindered a fast exit for the commandos and their supplies, dispersing the drops. A better alternative was the C-123, with its wide rear ramp, which allowed for the ejection of cargo and paratroopers in a matter of seconds.[11]

The benefits were obvious, but so was the drawback: the C-123 offered no plausible deniability. Unlike the C-47 or C-54, the new plane was not in use with any civilian airlines, nor were any available on the commercial market. In fact, it was exclusively in the inventory of the U.S. military. As a result, while the CIA could say that the C-54 was a commercial Vietnamese aircraft engaged in smuggling, this cover story would not hold up for the C-123. Should one crash in North Vietnam, the plane's true sponsor would be undeniable.

Despite this danger, the CIA elected to go ahead with the C-123. To man the new plane, it again turned to the Republic of China. This time the new covert pilots came from the 34th Squadron of the Chinese air force, which under different names had flown dozens of agents into mainland China dating back to 1955. Fifteen pilots, ten navigators, and five flight engineers from the squadron were taken to Pope Air Force Base in North Carolina and given three months of conversion training. Returning to Taiwan in December, they waited until February 1963 before five gray, unmarked C-123s were delivered to the island.

Continuing with low-level flight training for the next three months, the crews paid special attention to the sophisticated electronic countermeasures (ECM) package designed to identify and jam North Vietnam's formidable antiaircraft network. After perfecting this, they were declared mission-ready. On 15 June, they departed for Tan Son Nhut.[12]

Seventeen days later, the C-123 was scheduled for its maiden mission. The next team—eight ethnic Vietnamese agents code-named GIANT—boarded one of the unmarked planes that night. "We headed over the Gulf of Tonkin until we got to Vinh," recalled the pilot. "I could see the lights of the city as we cut in to the north. We then went west until I could see a mountain range. The team went out the back and we turned around, exited just below Vinh, and headed south over the water."[13]

Back in Saigon, the CIA scanned the airwaves for word from GIANT. No contact was ever established.[14]

Two days later, another pair of teams was readied in Saigon. The first, an ethnic mix named PACKER, was scheduled to infiltrate Yen Bai Province in the north central part of North Vietnam. There it hoped to repeat the success of BELL—the only team to come on the air that summer—which had dropped into the same vicinity. Like BELL, PACKER's five agents were targeted against the rail line that ran through the province. The team leader, Ngo Quoc Chung, relished the idea of wreaking havoc in the north. An ethnic Tai, Chung had fought at the battle of Dien Bien Phu, losing an eye and most of one hand in the process. Violently anticommunist, he dismissed his handicap with bravado: "I fight them with one hand," he promised.[15] The second of the two scheduled teams was a three-man reinforcement group for EUROPA, the Muong agents who had supposedly been living off the land in Hoa Binh for the past seventeen months.

By this time, however, the first contingent of pilots from China Airlines was fast approaching the end of its contracted deployment to South Vietnam. The pilots' presence was now made redundant by the arrival of the C-123s and Chinese air force crews, but it was decided to let them fly one last mission in their C-54. Onloading both teams, the lone plane first headed for Yen Bai. Arriving over the drop zone, PACKER jumped. With the team on its way, the plane cut a counterclockwise arc toward Hoa Binh, hugging the ground to escape a bank of threatening clouds. They vanished before arriving over the second target.[16]

Mortified over their third aircraft loss, CIA officers in Saigon desperately tried to establish the fate of the missing C-54 and its Chinese crew. Presumably they hit a mountain, but no wreckage was ever found. To add insult to injury, PACKER—the first team to jump from the plane—never made radio contact.

Still unwilling to call its sabotage campaign a bust, Saigon prepared one more team to go north. Code-named DRAGON, the unit had been recruited from among the Nung ethnic group. The same independent-minded minority that had earlier helped with building infiltration junks, the Nung had long shown an eagerness to take up arms against communism. This had previously been recognized by both the French and Chiang Kai-shek's anticommunist Koumintang regime. As early as 1946, the Koumintang had secretly begun supporting the Nung White Star resistance movement in the hope that it would create a southern diversion against communist Chinese forces.[17] After the end of French colonial rule, thousands of Nung combatants, including most of the White Star movement, fled to South Vietnam. Many subsequently joined the South Vietnamese army, in particular the 5th Infantry Division, which was stationed northwest of Saigon.

As the first all-Nung agent team, DRAGON was targeted against the traditional Nung heartland in easternmost Quang Ninh Province near the Chinese border. Infiltration was to be by motorized junk, but the weather was proving most uncooperative. Five times they tried, and five times they aborted. Finally, on 15 July, the commandos entered North Vietnamese waters. Transferring to a smaller boat, the seven Nung headed for shore. They were not heard from again.[18]

Including DRAGON, the CIA had now sent thirteen teams into North Vietnam in just seven months. Of these, just one was still in radio contact by July.[19] The other twelve were presumed captured. Any doubt was erased on 9 July when Hanoi announced a trial for PEGASUS. Five more commando trials were publicized over the next three months.[20]

Clearly, the CIA's campaign was not working. Even its blitz strategy—inserting multiple teams on a single night—had come up painfully short. In hindsight, there were several reasons for this. First, several of the drop zones had been poorly chosen. In some cases, the teams were jumping too close to villages and were immediately detected. For example, TELLUS, which jumped on 8 June into Ninh Binh Province, was spotted on descent and landed next to a collective farm. All four of its members were captured within twenty-five minutes.[21] Even worse was the case of PACKER, which landed directly on a village. The team's radioman crashed through the roof of a hut packed with villagers midway through a town meeting.[22]

A second reason for the teams' repeated failures was the gradual expansion in the program during 1961 and 1962, which had given the North Vietnamese security service ample opportunity to fine-tune its ability to detect infiltrations. By the time the CIA started its concerted sabotage campaign in April 1963, Hanoi had a proven formula that could easily keep pace with the increased number of teams. As proof of North Vietnam's efficiency, of the eleven teams dropped through July, ten had been captured in two days or less.[23]

Despite its successes, not all had gone Hanoi's way. Behind the scenes, mounting frustration over the CIA campaign clearly rankled communist officials, partly because of the more aggressive nature of the sabotage agents. Previously, most of the intelligence teams had surrendered without a fight. By contrast, the well-armed saboteurs were staging deadly gun battles before capture. In many cases, North Vietnamese troops were killed or wounded. Hanoi responded by executing commandos who took a life while resisting arrest.[24]

North Vietnamese officials were also deeply concerned about the Catholic connection to the commandos. After five teams tapped this religious vein (TELLUS and BART, both of which jumped in June, were the most recent), Hanoi began to repeatedly rail against the Catholic link, including a shrill English-language diatribe read over North Vietnamese radio in December 1963.[25]

On the surface it might seem that the biggest embarrassment to the North Vietnamese was their continuing impotence in the face of repeated airspace violations. True, they were capturing teams on the ground, but aside from the July 1961 shootdown of the C-47, CIA aircraft had been plying the northern skies for two years without retribution. Despite fielding ten antiaircraft regiments, none had been mobilized with the specific intent of downing one of the commando planes. While Washington could take comfort from this small victory, the reality was that Hanoi, not wanting to risk its radio play by raising Saigon's suspicions, purposely allowed the planes a free ride in the skies over North Vietnam.

By December 1962, however, North Vietnam's patience had worn thin. Using the doubled EUROPA as bait, four platoons of 14.5mm antiaircraft guns were moved into position in the hills near Hoa Binh. For two weeks they waited, scanning the skies. Unknown to Hanoi, however, Washington's moratorium on commando flights in the wake of the Lao peace accords was still in effect, and there were no flights into North Vietnam.[26]

Following the surge in airborne infiltrations during mid-1963, Hanoi again decided to down a commando flight. Once again, EUROPA was the bait. Bigger this time, some ten antiaircraft companies were prepositioned in the hills around Hoa Binh.

Unaware of the awaiting gauntlet, a Chinese-piloted C-123 loaded with supplies and a reinforcement team headed for EUROPA on the evening of 10 August. "We were flying in a northwestern direction; the drop zone was on a parallel heading off to the east," recalled the first officer. "Our ECM operator began picking up some faint, distant radar signals from near the drop zone, but we didn't think this was reason to abort." The plane flew on, then banked toward the drop zone. Moments later the pilot spotted a lighted "T" signal on the ground. "Normally the signal was made with three fire-barrels across and three down," said the first officer. "This one had four across and three down. It was really bright, and almost looked like electric lights."

About ten seconds after seeing this ground signal, the electronic counter-measures operator yelled, "Radar guns: twelve o'clock . . . one-thirty . . . three o'clock!"

The first shell exploded directly under the plane at a lower altitude. The second burst near the right wing, the third off the left wing. Tracers flashed in front of the cockpit, and the smell of gunpowder filled the cabin.

"Before we could do any evasive maneuvers, we needed to secure the pallets on the ramp or else the heavy weight would slide and make control difficult," recalled the first officer.

Because we were so close to the drop zone, the loadmasters had already lined the six pallets on rollers near the ramp. They began pushing the pallets back toward the front of the plane, and the Vietnamese paratroopers, who had on their chutes, were also trying to help. One of the boxes went off the track and blocked the others behind it. All the men in the back had to lift up that pallet and get it back on the rollers. As soon as the pallets were secure, we entered into a dive.

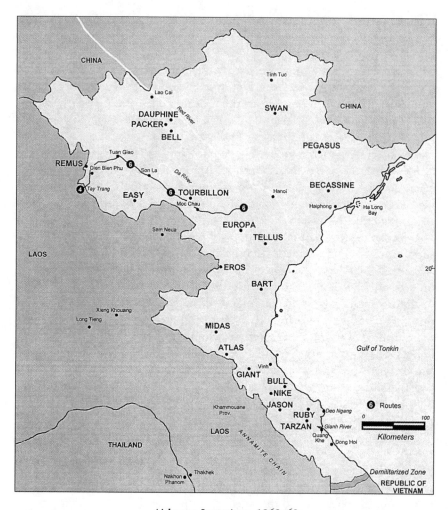

Airborne Insertions, 1962–63

The bright moonlight helped the North Vietnamese gunners lock onto their target, but it also allowed the pilot to see where he was diving. Mountains rose on both sides of the plane, leaving no choice but to nose down the valley directly ahead. The C-123 gained speed as it dropped; then suddenly more bullets flashed up from the ground. Amazingly, the North Vietnamese gunners hit everything but the plane. The electronic countermeasures operator had managed to jam their radar-controlled guns by giving off a false signal.[27]

Safely back in Saigon, the Chinese crew was still badly shaken. The captain of the flight immediately quit the program and took the next plane back to Taiwan. The other aviators, while remaining at Tan Son Nhut, strongly suspected the attack was not a chance encounter. To confirm their suspicions, they sent a back-channel message to the 34th Squadron headquarters, which then dispatched one of its RB-69 electronics aircraft for a single overflight of North Vietnam. A sophisticated modification of the P-2V submarine-chaser, the RB-69 had been developed by the CIA in 1955 specifically to penetrate communist airspace. Several had been provided to the 34th Squadron, which had used them to infiltrate agents and plot antiaircraft grids in mainland China.

Making a pass over Hoa Binh Province, the RB-69 crew aimed its instruments at the EUROPA drop zone. The gauges went wild with traces from at least four antiaircraft positions lining the target valley. This information was quickly channeled to the Chinese aircrews in Saigon, confirming their suspicions they had been dispatched to supply a bad team.

One week later, EUROPA reestablished radio contact. Repeating their request for supplies and reinforcements, the agents claimed not to have heard the resupply plane pass overhead. Learning of this, the Chinese aircrews refused to fly further missions to Hoa Binh. For them, Hanoi's hand was obvious.

But not everybody was so quick to condemn EUROPA. In a stunning underestimation of the North Vietnamese security services and a blatant disregard for the telltale signs of compromise, the CIA refused to write off its Hoa Binh team. EUROPA, they insisted, would remain on the active rolls.

7

NASTY BOATS

While the CIA's airborne program might have been short on success, in terms of tempo it had reached new highs. Not true for maritime operations, which had been conspicuously absent since the abortive Swatow attack of June 1962. The agency's reticence was understandable. VULCAN had been caught in the act, leaving the U.S. government little wiggle room to deflect blame. Photos of the team's captured equipment were splashed across English-language publications coming out of Hanoi, and one of the commandos was even enticed into making a public condemnation of the program.[1]

Although an embarrassing episode, the VULCAN failure had the indirect result of giving CIA operators in South Vietnam a better appreciation for the complexity of seaborne operations, especially those involving coordination between boat crews and combat swimmers. The next time around, the agency knew, there needed to be better planning and preparation.

And there would be a next time. Back when the CIA began preparations for its airborne sabotage campaign, plans were also advanced for a complementary maritime effort. Chosen to head this portion of the program was a seasoned paramilitary operative named Tucker Gougleman. A U.S. Marine veteran of the World War II Pacific campaign, Gougleman walked with a permanent limp courtesy of a Japanese bullet. This handicap had not prevented him from transferring to the CIA, where, running small-boat operations from the Yellow Sea, he spent the Korean War conducting strikes along the embattled peninsula.

From Korea, Gougleman eventually made his way to Afghanistan, where he opened the CIA station in the Kabul embassy. Many from those days remembered him for his gruff demeanor and salty language. All of this, however, belied a sharp, calculating mind. "He had a greater intellectual capacity than more than half the people in the organization," recalled one of his fellow CIA officers. "In later years, he could walk to an empty blackboard and start diagraming the local communist party and infrastructure from memory."[2]

After Afghanistan, Gougleman appeared in South Vietnam. His first assignment was to Hoa Cam, the CIA's primary paramilitary training base three kilometers southwest of Danang. When word went out that the agency's maritime program was about to expand, Gougleman, citing his previous experience in Korea, volunteered to run the show, although in late

1962 there was little to run. Half a dozen motorized junks were on hand, but, spooked by the VULCAN fiasco, the CIA had used them on only one team infiltration since June.

The commando situation was even worse. After losing the four VULCAN commandos it borrowed from the armed forces, the CIA decided to raise its own pool of combat swimmers. By November 1962, over four dozen volunteers had been assembled at makeshift camps strung along the Danang waterfront. But without qualified teachers and training facilities, instruction proceeded at glacial speed.

Gougleman's arrival quickly improved things. Shortly after he took over, a team of U.S. Navy Sea, Air, Land (SEAL) commandos were detailed to Danang for support, making Gougleman's job much easier. Formed in 1961 as the U.S. Navy's answer to the U.S. Army Special Forces, the SEALs had first come to South Vietnam in January 1962 for a survey of that country's new coastal defense force. This force, known as the Biet Hai (Vietnamese for "sea commandos"), was envisioned as a paramilitary guard deployed along the entire South Vietnamese coast. By year's end, two cycles of Biet Hai students were trained under SEAL auspices. The program, however, failed to live up to expectations and was subsequently dropped.

Freed from the Biet Hai training obligation, two SEAL officers and ten enlisted men were transferred to Gougleman's program at Danang. For the next six months, the SEALs put their South Vietnamese subjects through the paces. By late summer of 1963, four action teams had emerged.[3] To camouflage their true purpose, they were collectively dubbed Biet Hai, taking their name from the now-defunct coastal defense group. Each Biet Hai team was composed of civilian agents combined with a handful of former South Vietnamese army sergeants. One of them, NEPTUNE, was qualified in scuba. Another, CANCER, consisted entirely of ethnic Nung who had earlier served in the predominantly Nung South Vietnamese 5th Division.

Gougleman now had a wealth of commandos on hand, but he still had a problem with his boats. Although the North Vietnamese navy paled in comparison to its South Vietnamese enemy, Hanoi's gunboats both outgunned and outpaced the CIA's motorized junks, leading the agency to conclude that "junks and rubber boats for MAROPS [maritime operations] against NVN involved an unacceptable degree of risk." Clearly, Gougleman needed a better vessel to get his men to and from their target.[4]

The search for such a boat was not new. In fact, it dated back to 1959. At that time, U.S. Navy officials wanted to replace their aging fleet of World War II–vintage torpedo boats and at the same time provide allies in Asia with suitable craft to use in "preventing overt or covert communist infiltration or even actual aggression." In their search, many came away impressed with the

Admiral Arleigh A. Burke, U.S. Navy chief of naval operations (center foreground), and Royal Norwegian Navy commander, Vice Admiral Erling Hostvedt, inspect a Nasty-class patrol boat at Haakonsvern, Norway, in May 1960. (U.S. Navy)

Norwegian Nasty-class patrol boat. Built by Westermoen in Mandel, Norway, the Nasty was considered one of the fastest and most reliable patrol boats of its day. Its superior performance came from two diesel Napier engines, which could propel the twenty-four meter, eighty-ton mahogany and fiberglass hull at speeds of more than forty knots. Packing a wide range of light weapons, the boat could cover sixteen hundred kilometers without refueling. Best of all, its foreign manufacture afforded plausible deniability.[5]

Because development of a new patrol boat was a low priority in the U.S. Navy, procurement of the Nasty was put on hold for three years. Only after the failed VULCAN raid in June 1962, resulting in the CIA's second loss of a motorized junk, did the subject get renewed attention. In September, Admiral Harry D. Felt, CINCPAC, prodded American officials in Saigon to move faster toward developing an effective maritime operations program, complaining that "the program should have been under full steam a long time ago." Felt believed that the CIA was not equipped to run maritime operations under any circumstances, but its inadequate boats compounded the problem.[6]

As it turned out, the American military in Vietnam (represented by the newly formed Military Advisory Command, Vietnam [MACV]) had the same complaint. One month earlier, General Paul D. Harkins, the MACV commander, had suggested that U.S. motor torpedo patrol (PT) boats be used for missions north. His proposal had already been sent for review by President Kennedy's top national security advisers. President Kennedy, himself a PT boat commander during World War II, liked the idea. On 27 September, Washington cabled back approval for the scheme, along with the suggestion that covert maritime operations be assisted by the U.S. Navy's SEAL commandos.

Acting on this mandate, the U.S. Navy looked on its rosters for anything immediately available. One week later, it ordered two 1950-vintage aluminum-hulled torpedo boats, PT-810 and PT-811, out of mothballs at the Philadelphia Naval Shipyard. Assistant Secretary of Defense Roswell Gilpatric called the move a "step in the right direction," but he also ordered that "priority attention be given to the procurement of foreign-made craft of the PT category." Specifically, Gilpatric had his eye on the Nasty, and he ordered immediate action to procure two boats.[7] Selected to head the entire PT effort was Edward Lansdale, the same officer who had established the original stay-behind network in North Vietnam. Now sporting general's stars after returning to the Pentagon following his extended service with the CIA, he was one of Kennedy's most prominent unconventional warfare specialists.

The two aluminum boats, nicknamed "gassers" because their antiquated engines burned gasoline rather than more efficient diesel, took a couple of months to refurbish. Each was given a 40mm gun on the bow, a .50-caliber machine gun amidship, and engine muffling to run more quietly. They were also renamed: PTF-1 and PTF-2 (patrol torpedo boat, fast, in navy nomenclature). Despite these improvements, both boats experienced serious mechanical troubles during sea trials, and further tests were delayed as ice clogged the Delaware River in late 1962.

While the gassers went back for repairs, the CIA bypassed the Pentagon's bureaucracy and ordered two Nastys. In early 1963, at the same time that Gougleman arrived in Danang, the agency passed both boats to the U.S. Navy for comprehensive testing. Designated PTF-3 and PTF-4, they were refitted that spring with U.S. equipment for familiarization drills at Little Creek, Virginia.[8]

Even though the Nastys were intended for covert duty in Vietnam, the U.S. Navy did not keep them a secret. In fact, it put on a publicity show. On 30 April, PTF-3 raced from Little Creek through the Chesapeake Bay, then up the Potomac River to the Washington Navy Yard for a three-day promotional visit. The press was told only that the vessels were "designed to perform amphibious support and coastal operations," but the fact that the Norwegian boats were in U.S. service was completely in the open. Then, on 15 May, the secretary of the navy and high-ranking naval officers rode aboard the boat for a thirty-minute demonstration on the Potomac. The *Washington Post* carried the story the next day.[9]

Less than a month later, plans were made to deploy the Nastys to Vietnam. On 28 June, Admiral George W. Anderson, the chief of naval operations, assigned the boats to the Pacific Fleet's Amphibious Group 1, to occur immediately following modifications to their armament. Technicians added two 40mm and two 20mm guns, plus two 3.5-inch rocket launchers and provisions for up to three flamethrowers. Work was completed by the end of August, and the boats were then loaded aboard the transport ship *Vancouver* for the journey to San Diego via the Panama Canal.

The layover in California was short, just enough time for U.S. Navy SEALs based at Coronado to swarm over the Nastys and check out their ability to perform special warfare operations. The SEALs liked the boats, especially the small armory of weapons that each carried. Problems were beginning to emerge, however. Specifically, the Nastys needed frequent screw replacements and engine overhauls, which, because spares came only from Europe, demanded dedicated repair facilities. Moreover, their wooden hulls required a spell in drydock once every six months.

Such a sophisticated support regimen would tax even an experienced logistical base, yet the CIA's maritime operation at Danang consisted of a pier and little else. Without a more sophisticated training and repair base in South Vietnam, observed Vice Admiral Ephraim P. Holmes, commander of the Pacific Fleet's amphibious force, "this operation will soon come apart."[10]

Plans were drawn up for the U.S. Navy to deploy mobile training teams to South Vietnam to assist with engine repair, weapons maintenance, and electronics. However, all this took time—and the CIA was getting edgy. Washington-level talks were then under way for the impending transition of covert operations to Department of Defense control. According to William Colby, then the agency's head of Far East operations, there was some feeling within the CIA that the operational tempo had to rise under the agency's watch so that the Pentagon could not claim bragging rights for single-handedly bringing maritime operations up to speed.[11]

With one eye on the calender, the CIA looked for an interim boat to put into immediate operation before the arrival of the Nastys. The answer came from one of its other covert operations, this one in Cuba. As part of President Kennedy's campaign to maintain pressure on Fidel Castro after the 1961 Bay of Pigs fiasco, the CIA was authorized to conduct a maritime harassment campaign inside Cuban territorial waters. To do this, the agency turned to a

A Nasty patrol boat performs high-speed tests off Pearl Harbor in October 1963. (U.S. Navy)

boat known as the Swift. Already a common sight on the Gulf of Mexico, it was made by Seward Seacraft in Burwick, Louisiana. Originally designed for oil companies operating in the Gulf's far-flung drilling platforms, it was fifteen meters long, displaced twenty tons, and had two diesel engines.

CIA maritime officers liked the Swift, but Cuban operatives wanted something else. "The guys in Miami had their own idea about boats," said one former CIA official. "It should look more like something tourists and fishermen would use, and it had to go faster. The Swift could do thirty knots if it was lucky. Still, it was a solid boat; it could go all day."[12]

The CIA bought a few Swifts, modifying them with bigger engines and extra fuel tanks, machine guns, rocket launchers, and electronic gear to detect radar surveillance. Testing was completed in late 1962, and the Swifts were then shipped to San Diego by rail for further trials under U.S. Navy auspices the following spring.

The Swifts were still in California when the call came for some boats to handle North Vietnam missions. While they did not offer much plausible deniability, as an interim measure they sufficed. Three were immediately crated and sent to the Philippines. From there, they were ferried to Saigon. Sailing up the coast to Danang, they were ready for action by October 1963.[13]

While the Swifts were a welcome addition to Gougleman's clandestine maritime force, they had one drawback. Although easier to maintain than the temperamental Nastys, they represented an insurmountable leap in technology for the CIA's existing roster of junk crewmen. This put the agency in a fix. Forbidden from recruiting experienced sailors from the South Vietnamese navy, and also unable to use Americans in order to uphold plausible deniability, there was nobody on hand to operate the ships.

To solve this dilemma, the CIA turned to foreign experts. Because they already had developed good contacts in Oslo during the Nasty purchase, they arranged for three Norwegian civilians to be hired on six-month contracts. Arriving in Danang, these men were given the barely disguised code name "Viking" and were assigned as skippers, one per Swift.

Young and aggressive, the Norwegians got along well with the South Vietnamese. "They were *real* Vikings," remembers Captain Truong Duy Tai, a maritime case officer. "They knew about navigation so well."[14]

Now with boats as well as crews, the CIA looked to stage its first maritime hit-and-run since the VULCAN debacle. Showing little imagination, their plans called for essentially a repeat of the failed strike against the Swatows at Quang Khe. The only difference was that the team would ride a Swift instead of a junk.

On 15 December, one of the new powerboats headed north. Aboard was Team NEPTUNE—the lone scuba-qualified team—with a supply of limpet mines. Short of their target, however, the skipper became lost, forcing an abort.

Returning to Danang, the CIA waited out the New Year. Finally, on 14 January 1964 it launched an ambitious doubleheader. Plans called for two Swifts to leave their berths shortly before midnight. They would stay together until they crossed the seventeenth parallel, then continue to their objectives alone. One would head for a coastal desalinization plant near the town of Dong Hoi, the southernmost town of note in the North Vietnamese panhandle. The other would go to the Ron River, eighteen kilometers farther up the Quang Binh coast from the Swatows on the Gianh. One kilometer inland along the Ron was a ferry that connected North Vietnam's major north-south logistical artery, Route 1.

The Dong Hoi team, code-named ZEUS, had no problems. The Norwegian skipper approached his designated target just before dawn, throttling back on the engines as he neared shore. Unlike the earlier scuba attacks, the

ZEUS commandos took a rubber boat to shore. There they off-loaded a makeshift weapons package devised by CIA technicians. Consisting of six 3.5-inch "flat-firing" rockets, the cluster was affixed to a central battery pack. Pointing it in the general direction of the desalinization plant, the agents set a timer, slipping back into their rafts, and reached the Swift without incident. Before leaving, they threw several boxes of propaganda leaflets into the sea and watched as the pamphlets dispersed in their wake.[15]

The second team, code-named CHARON, was not as lucky. When the Swift was less than nineteen kilometers from its target, the Norwegian skipper spotted a boat heading toward them from the north. Although the boat was not moving fast enough to pose a threat, the Viking reversed course, taking evasive turns until he lost his pursuer. Hugging the coast, the team then doubled back north. It was now more than an hour behind schedule.

Electing to proceed with the mission, the team leader ordered CHARON into a rubber raft. As it neared the mouth of the Ron, the team donned flippers and entered the water. One pair of swimmers headed along the north bank, while the other pushed along the south. Quickly, things began to fall apart. One pair soon encountered a junk coming downriver. With heavy silt clogging the entrance of the Ron, the agents feared that the water was not deep enough to clear the passing hull without being seen. Panicking, they turned tail and swam back to the rubber raft.

The second pair was nowhere to be found. After exceeding their proscribed wait, the first two swimmers headed back to the Swift alone. With dawn fast approaching, the Norwegian captain reluctantly decided it was time to leave. But as the engines throttled up, he spotted a flashlight blinking near shore. Taking an enormous risk, he turned the Swift inland. To his relief, bobbing in the water were the two missing swimmers. With a full complement, the team headed south.

Back at Danang, the CIA had mixed emotions about the missions. CHARON had failed to reach its objective, and ZEUS, while claiming it was sure the rockets went off, had not actually been there to witness the event. On the other hand, both teams had returned safely, marking the first time any of the agency's saboteurs had managed to return home intact. Best of all, the CIA had succeeded in creating a tested program of maritime teams, boats, and crews. For the purposes of interservice rivalry, it had at least managed to steal some of the Pentagon's thunder.

8

SACRED SWORD PATRIOT'S LEAGUE

Winston Churchill described the invisible wall that both shielded and contained the Soviet empire as an "Iron Curtain." As the CIA could attest, the name was aptly chosen. Try as it might, nearly every team it infiltrated into the Soviet bloc during the early 1950s was quickly captured. These failures persisted for so long that one internal CIA history concluded that, although there was "little likelihood of ever influencing Soviet policy," running such operations made case officers feel like they were at least accomplishing something.[1]

By the late summer of 1963, the wall around North Vietnamese society was proving just as difficult to penetrate. Despite changing missions (from intelligence to sabotage) and exploring various means of infiltration (parachute drops, boat inserts, walking across the border), the CIA had yet to arrive at a successful formula.

At the heart of the CIA's troubles was the fact that it was running an agent operation in name only. "They were more of an overt introduction of a commando team or the overt introduction of a group of people who had to hide," one U.S. Army officer assigned to the program later lamented.[2] Parachuted blind into the forests of North Vietnam, the teams were relegated to living off the land and avoiding the general population. None of the teams tried to blend into North Vietnamese society. Even on the rare occasions when members were authorized to seek out a local contact—such as a priest or family member—interaction was to be kept to a minimum. And they were expected to do this for years on end, remaining undetected in the hills until the next aerial resupply.

Even for the uninitiated, such a formula sounded unrealistic. If the CIA wanted to have an impact on North Vietnamese society, it needed to forge a resistance movement that would act as a support structure. Just as the North Vietnamese troops infiltrating through Laos could lean on Viet Cong comrades once they arrived in South Vietnam, theoretically the CIA's agents could rely on a network of northern sympathizers. They could turn to the locals for basic necessities like food and water, thereby spending less time foraging for meals or relying on airdrops. A resistance movement could also help agents escape if they were pursued by the authorities and could form a pipeline for the infiltration of further reinforcements.[3]

From the beginning, just such a scenario was in the cards. In April 1961, President Kennedy unequivocally called for "networks of resistance" inside North Vietnam.[4] But strong words were not enough, and the concept had failed to gather steam, mainly because the CIA's small staff already had its hands full launching the initial round of intelligence-gathering teams.

It would be another year—after its intelligence agents had fallen flat—before the agency found time to revisit the idea. Once again, it was the war in neighboring Laos that prompted another look at the situation in North Vietnam. While Vientiane's regular army had proved itself one of the most ineffectual in Southeast Asia, a CIA-backed guerrilla force in the northeastern part of that kingdom was proving troublesome to the encroaching communists. Recruited primarily from the Hmong hill tribe, the CIA's partisans were operating as local raiding parties reminiscent of the French GCMA. Significantly, the Hmong military chieftain for the CIA, Colonel Vang Pao, had earlier been the premier Hmong officer in the GCMA.[5]

Proving themselves equal to the North Vietnamese infantry they confronted, the CIA's unconventional Hmong warriors effectively raised an anticommunist resistance umbrella extending from Xieng Khouang north and east into Sam Neua Province. While Sam Neua was headquarters for the communist Pathet Lao, the province was also pockmarked with Hmong villages, some of whom, thanks to strong clan allegiance, were throwing their support behind Vang Pao and the government. And many of their fellow clansmen populated an arc extending across the North Vietnamese border into Son La.

This last dimension—the Hmong living in Son La—struck a chord with CIA planners in Saigon. For them, the presence of the fiercely independent Hmong inside North Vietnam was an attractive recruitment target. Moreover, the CIA managers in Laos—who no doubt welcomed the idea of an intelligence screen extending into North Vietnam—were willing to act as supportive intermediaries. On 21 June 1962, a team of South Vietnamese recruiters, code-named ZEUS, was escorted from Xieng Khouang north to the North Vietnamese border. Crossing into Son La, three Hmong, all from Vang Pao's own clan, were selected and quickly sent to a Saigon safe house.[6]

With this modest core of three tribesmen, the seeds for a limited resistance movement took shape. Training in Saigon continued through the fall, only to be delayed by the moratorium on North Vietnamese operations in the wake of the Geneva agreement on Laos. Not until late in the spring of 1963, with the Geneva agreement in tatters and the CIA's sabotage program showing early signs of strain, did the resistance concept regain momentum.

By that time, the pilot resistance team, code-named EASY, had grown. Besides the original three Hmong exfiltrated the previous June, it was augmented by four Tai tribesmen from Lai Chau and a single Eurasian of French and Hmong parentage named Vang Cha.[7]

All eight agents would have their work cut out for them. From previous experience, the CIA knew that the concept of resistance movements was a dangerous one. Indeed, few successful precedents existed. Some CIA case officers wrongly drew comparisons with OSS airborne teams during World War II, which had jumped into occupied Europe to help organize and expand anti-Nazi resistance movements. But these OSS teams, to include the famed Jedburghs, had linked up with local partisans who were already active and widespread. Moreover, they were battling a foreign occupying army. In cases where agents landed blind in Germany itself—where no resistance existed—success was far more fleeting. Of the twenty-one American radio teams that jumped, only one established contact.[8]

More recently, the CIA's experience in closed communist societies underscored the difficulty of resistance efforts. According to one of the agency's experienced Soviet hands, in a resistance cell of just ten persons, the chance of penetration by the enemy was 50 percent. Extrapolating from this, the chances were almost 100 percent that a fledgling resistance network would be penetrated before it could expand to a size that would make a difference.[9]

In spite of these long odds, EASY was given a robust menu of resistance-type goals to accomplish once back in Son La. Besides making contact with Hmong and Tai villagers, the agents were to establish a safe area, selectively arm tribesmen, and recruit leaders to be spirited out of North Vietnam for training. They were supplied with ten French MAS bolt-action rifles for later distribution to local recruits.[10]

Laden with this ambitious—and unrealistic—agenda, on 11 August 1963, EASY boarded a Chinese-piloted C-123 along with two agents who would reinforce Team REMUS in Lai Chau. Crossing southern Son La Province, EASY leaped from the plane over Song Ma District near the Laos border. Shortly after, the team established radio contact.

While EASY was off to a good start, it did not foreshadow things to come. This was because EASY was a CIA initiative, and in a few short months the agency would no longer be calling the shots. Back in May, talks had been initiated at the Washington level to have the entire covert program against North Vietnam turned over to the Department of Defense. As CIA and Pentagon planners sat down to work out the mechanics of the transfer, a major point of contention proved to be the question of a resistance movement in North Vietnam.

In principle, the CIA believed that creation of a resistance front was a key part of a successful covert program. But agency officials doubted that the plan under way would work. During discussions with the Defense Department in late May, the CIA argued that "this 'Liberation Front' will not be firmly enough established in the near future to provide a plausible basis for either the SVN or US governments to deny responsibility."[11]

It seemed hard to believe that there could ever be any question of who was behind such plans, but even when proof seemed irrefutable—like after the July 1961 C-47 shootdown—Washington maintained its innocence. Despite its reputation for covering its tracks, the CIA had actually done little to mask its role. For example, weapons used by the teams were sterile, but radios were not. Similarly, aircraft crews were not American, but the planes were.[12]

From the Pentagon's perspective, the agency's half measures needed shoring up. Plausible deniability was "rather weak," the military felt. In order to have any credibility, cover stories had to be strong enough to allow both the Americans and the South Vietnamese to feign innocence.[13] While such claims might not stand up to prolonged scrutiny, the semantics—coming prior to the overt military escalation of later years—were considered sufficiently important to warrant the effort.

To provide a bigger fig leaf, on 14 August the Joint Chiefs of Staff approved preliminary CINCPAC plans for the creation of a notional liberation front in North Vietnam that would ostensibly claim responsibility for future covert attacks carried out by airborne and maritime teams.[14] Notional fronts were not exactly new to Vietnam. Besides dabbling with a real resistance organization to be spearheaded by EASY, the CIA had also been quietly laying a parallel foundation for a fake movement. Groundwork had started back in March 1963 with the arrival of CIA officer Herbert Weisshart. Brooklyn-born and Harvard-educated, Weisshart brought with him nearly a decade of psychological warfare experience from the China theater. Part of a six-man psychological warfare team dispatched to Taiwan in 1952, he had been instrumental in coordinating leaflet drops and radio play against mainland China in support of one of the agency's first notional resistance campaigns.

With hindsight, it is clear that Weisshart and his Taiwan-based team had reinvented the wheel. Most of their concepts, it turned out, dated to World War II. For example, just as they portrayed a shadowy resistance group of dissatisfied cadre broadcasting from somewhere inside China, the OSS and British intelligence had run German-language radio stations purportedly operated by Nazi dissidents inside the Rhineland. And just as the CIA salted its programs with criticism of the United States to hide its true origins, one British station had included venomous tirades against England, like repeated references to Churchill as a "flat-footed bastard of a drunken old Jew."[15]

While perhaps not original, the CIA's fake Chinese front broke new ground for the postwar period. Still in operation as late as 1963, it stood as the agency's longest-running notional campaign. As its author, Weisshart arrived in Saigon with orders to initiate a similar program against North Vietnam. Quickly, he put out the call for the rest of his Taiwan team. In short order, all six were on hand.[16] As they reassembled, Weisshart studied the psychological campaign to date. There was not much to review. Leaflets and radio broadcasts had started back in 1961, but the effort was overly simplistic. Leaflets, for example, carried little more than crude antigovernment messages, like "Kill Communists."

Not only was there little foundation to build on, but Weisshart immediately assessed the environment in North Vietnam to be more difficult than that faced in China. First, the Hanoi regime was still basking in an extended honeymoon after having defeated a foreign colonial power. Because of this, many of its political and military leaders were widely deified as heroes. Second, while communist economic policy was harsh (some fifty thousand North Vietnamese had died during brutal land reforms in the latter half of the 1950s), alternatives like capitalism had yet to demonstrate clear advantages in Southeast Asia. Third, Hanoi had imposed strict controls on personal movement and closed the border, sharply cutting the flow of refugees who could be recruited or debriefed. Fourth, the North Vietnamese economy featured little international commerce, further limiting opportunities for intelligence gathering. Finally, corruption and human rights abuses in South Vietnam strongly undercut Saigon's appeal as a political alternative.[17]

Despite such challenges, the CIA's psychological experts dusted off their Chinese template and decided to adapt it for North Vietnam. As with other notional fronts, their purpose was twofold. First, they wanted to instill the idea among the North Vietnamese people that there was already a resistance movement secretly operating in their midst, and that it was possible for them to express resentment against Hanoi's edicts and actions. Second, it sought to make Hanoi expend personnel, assets, time, and energy investigating and countering a nonexistent front. From its past experience against dictatorial regimes, the CIA knew that any hint of a resistance represented a potential breach of, and threat to, the North Vietnamese government's need for absolute control over the people and their thoughts. A notional front, they knew, all but guaranteed an overreaction on the part of Hanoi.

For its resistance movement to be effective, the CIA needed a rallying symbol. After casually interviewing some of its Vietnamese counterparts, the agency learned of the fifteenth-century legend of the Sacred Sword. The tale's hero was Le Loi, a historical figure who had formed a resistance movement in northern Vietnam to confront waves of Chinese invaders. At a critical point in the fighting, Le Loi had gone to a lake in central Hanoi. There a giant turtle rose from the depths and gave him a magic sword. With this saber, he defeated the Chinese hordes in 1428 and ascended the Vietnamese throne. Victory attained, Le Loi returned to the lake, where the turtle rose once more, snatched the sword from his hand, and disappeared forever.

Making reference to this Vietnamese version of Excalibur, the agency's psychological warfare experts named their liberation front the Sacred Sword Patriot's League (SSPL). To bring the SSPL to life, a simple logo was devised depicting an arm holding a golden sword on a red background. In time, the CIA had leaflets and gift kits—comprising simple items like soap, pencils, pens, writing pads, towels, cloth, and candles—emblazoned with this sword and dropped from aircraft. "We wanted useful things that would favorably influence the attitude of the recipients toward the SSPL," recalled Weisshart. "It sought to inspire them to discuss the SSPL with trusted friends and neighbors."[18]

The SSPL even got its own radio station. Purportedly beamed from a secret location inside North Vietnam, the Voice of the SSPL (which, after delays, did not begin broadcasting until April 1965) was actually recorded at a CIA studio in downtown Saigon, allowed the front to expound on its values and beliefs.[19] Targeting various audiences such as fishermen, Catholics, farmers, and junior cadre, it called for carefully planned and executed actions, most of which were passive, like spreading news of the SSPL, using its recognition symbol, and awaiting contact from other SSPL members. It also offered the SSPL viewpoint on happenings in different parts of North Vietnam, most of which were gleaned from Hanoi's own broadcasts.

Significantly, SSPL commentaries were almost completely devoid of political ideology. Indeed, in its zeal to present an independent line, Voice of the SSPL was equally harsh toward all major foreign powers—Soviet and Chinese, as well as American. Rather than making a stand along conventional political lines, the SSPL lauded traditional Vietnamese values, which were then contrasted to the excesses of Hanoi's communism and the corruption of Diem's Saigon. From this script—meant to thoroughly disguise American sponsorship—the SSPL hoped to make the North Vietnamese population long for the simple times of the past. It even went so far as to seek a halt to the U.S. bombing and ask for payment from the world's major powers in order to rebuild their war-torn country.[20]

Another step in bringing the SSPL to life involved cooperation with the airborne sabotage teams. "We won permission to piggyback our mission on a pair of teams," explained Weisshart. "For this we gave them some elementary psychological training and SSPL orientation."

Besides receiving an SSPL primer, the teams were trained on specialized gear. CIA technicians, for example, developed a crude printing press for making SSPL leaflets. "We warned them to move often," said Weisshart, "and use the presses sparingly."[21] The CIA also crafted a leaflet round that could be fired from disposable mortars with delayed fuses; these could be used to shower an area with SSPL propaganda long after a team had fled.

The first of the SSPL's psychological warfare teams was a six-man unit code-named SWAN. Composed of ethnic minorities from Cao Bang in northernmost North Vietnam, the team, laden with a canister of SSPL leaflets and banners, boarded a C-123 on 4 September and headed north toward its home province. Crossing the Tonkin Gulf, the aircraft cut inland near Haiphong, then traced a northwest path parallel to the Chinese border. Arriving over the boundary between Cao Bang and Bac Thai, SWAN exited the plane over a section of sparsely populated hills southwest of the provincial capital. In Saigon, the CIA waited for radio contact. None came.[22]

Exactly three months later, the SSPL's second psychological warfare team, code-named RUBY and consisting of eight ethnic Vietnamese, departed Tan Son Nhut. Its target was northern Quang Binh Province at the southern end of North Vietnam. Again the team exited over forested mountains, and again no radio contact was ever established.

With 1963 fast coming to a close, the CIA's airborne program had recorded its worst annual performance to date. Stymied on the sabotage front during the first half of the year, its psychological warfare effort had faltered during the second. But the CIA was out of chances. Beginning in early 1964, it would be the Pentagon's turn to try.

9

SWITCHBACK

On 20 November 1963, the men who would decide how to fight the Vietnam War were meeting in Honolulu. As they assembled around a long oak table inside a command center at CINCPAC headquarters in Camp Smith, their mood was dour. President Diem was dead, killed by his own generals at the beginning of the month, and it seemed that internal instability was becoming more dangerous than the Viet Cong to the faltering South Vietnamese government. These men were trying to form a plan to put it all back together again.

At the head of the table sat Robert S. McNamara, the secretary of defense. At his arm was Admiral Felt, CINCPAC, commander of all U.S. forces in the entire Pacific region. Any orders from McNamara would pass through him on the way to Saigon. The others around the table were the "best and brightest" of Kennedy's cabinet: Secretary of State Dean Rusk; his assistant, Undersecretary of State George Ball; National Security Advisor McGeorge Bundy; the CIA's director, John McCone. Joining them were two officials from Saigon, Ambassador Henry Cabot Lodge and MACV commander General Paul Harkins. In a secondary ring sat a bevy of aides, ready to step forward with clarifications or explanations.

High on the agenda at Camp Smith was the faltering CIA covert program against North Vietnam.[1] Already, the decision had been made to switch these operations from the CIA to Pentagon control, part of a broader move to transfer all CIA paramilitary programs in Vietnam to the Defense Department. The move came to be known as Operation SWITCHBACK.

McNamara grilled the CIA's McCone on this issue. The director, in turn, handed the floor to William Colby, the agency's Far East Division chief. Looking professorial in a gray suit and bow tie, Colby stood before the group.

The moment was nothing short of cathartic. For years, Colby had been pushing the covert agenda against North Vietnam, first as deputy station chief in 1959, then as station chief in 1960 and deputy in the Far East Division in 1962. This support remained uninterrupted through January 1963, when he was elevated to division head. By that summer, however, it was increasingly difficult to disguise the agency's history of failure with agent operations in Asian communist countries. These setbacks were not limited to

Vietnam. As early as 1959, in fact, questions were voiced about the useless-ness of similar airborne missions into China. Peter Sichel, then Hong Kong chief of station, pleaded that the missions be stopped. "It was a complete waste of life," Sichel argued at a conference of Asian station chiefs. "We may as well just shoot them."[2]

Colby was getting similar counsel from his new deputy at the Far East Di-vision, Robert J. Myers. A longtime OSS and CIA Asia hand, Myers had held posts in China, Indochina, Indonesia, Japan, and Taiwan. Most re-cently, he had finished a tour as station chief in Phnom Penh, Cambodia. While in Cambodia, one particular episode had served to poison his view of agent operations run by South Vietnam. It occurred in 1962, near the end of his tour, when a back-channel message arrived from Saigon telling him that a South Vietnamese agent would be arriving shortly.

The agent in question was a South Vietnamese army sergeant named Le Cong Hoa. Born in Phnom Penh, Hoa spoke fluent Cambodian and French. Although technically out of its jurisdiction, Lieutenant Colonel Tung gave Office 45, the unit responsible for North Vietnam operations, the job of running one source inside the Cambodian capital. On account of his back-ground, Hoa was selected and given the code name ADONIS.

When informed of ADONIS, Myers protested sharply. He suspected that the Presidential Security Office, the unconventional warfare group that acted as counterpart for all CIA paramilitary programs in Vietnam, leaked like a sieve and it was only a matter of time before the mission came to an embar-rassing end. Despite Myers's concerns, ADONIS was allowed to slip into Phnom Penh. In short order he was exposed and thrown in jail. Prince Norodom Sihanouk, the kingdom's mercurial monarch, was already con-vinced of CIA plots against him. ADONIS only served to stoke his fears.[3]

Myers viewed the notion of infiltrating agents into communist societies with even deeper suspicion. During his OSS days in China, he had helped run teams across the northern half of that country and into Korea. "We were successful," he later recounted, "because Japanese control had been within cities and military bases. This left a fair amount of latitude outside the pop-ulation centers."[4]

In May 1950, however, Myers found a radically new landscape. Return-ing to the Far East as one of the original group of paramilitary advisers based in Taiwan, he was charged with running OSS-style missions into China. For three years he tried—and failed. Postwar communist societies, Myers con-ceded, were a different ball game. "The totality of communist control mea-sures made such operations impossible," said Myers. "The reason for our failure lay in the thinking of our superiors that it was World War II all over again." North Vietnam, Myers told Colby, was no different.

The argument was compelling, and Colby had little choice but to agree. But it is not clear exactly when he came to this belief. In fact, during a meeting with CINCPAC on 5 June, one of Colby's key subordinates, the CIA's Saigon station chief, had complained that his operations were "gravely hampered" by, among other things, restrictions on the use of sabotage teams inside North Vietnam. The station chief acknowledged that the CIA "had little productive activity in NVN then [spring 1963]" but asserted that, "if permitted to do so," the agency could insert "assorted sabotage and intelligence teams into Vietnam by the end of 1963."[5]

This aggressive plan could only have been put forth with the approval of the Far East Division chief—William Colby. And in the seven months leading up to the Honolulu Conference, the CIA sent fifteen teams into North Vietnam—nine of them during June and July alone, and another four in August, September, and October. This represented a little more than half the total number of teams inserted by the CIA during the entire three years that it ran the agent program. The furious pace of insertions belied Colby's contention that the CIA wanted to stop sending teams north, yet the precise reasoning behind the sudden explosion of operations against Hanoi in the last half of 1963 is not clear. Perhaps the agency just wanted to put in as many teams as possible in order to show up the military, which it knew was about to take over the program. Or perhaps there was disagreement within the CIA over just how effective they were. But if Colby really did doubt the value of the teams—or if he believed they were all captured or turned—then the huge jump in the number of teams going into North Vietnam on the eve of Operation SWITCHBACK becomes even more puzzling.

Standing before McNamara, Colby spoke frankly of his newfound doubts. He ticked off agent teams for the gathered officials: most were either captured or killed. When the military took over, Colby predicted, it could only count on five CIA teams and one singleton active inside North Vietnam. "It isn't working," he concluded, "and it won't work any better with the military in charge." What's more, Colby informed his audience, the CIA was already planning to shut down agent insertions and sabotage operations by 1965. In their place, he suggested the emphasis be shifted to psychological operations—black radio stations, leaflet drops, and the like—which he believed were "better ways of infiltrating ideas, rather than agents and explosives."[6]

McNamara was not impressed. The atmosphere at the conference was decidedly proactive; Colby's suggestion for more passive psychological means did little to satisfy the secretary's desire to "do to them in North Vietnam to match what they are doing to us in the South." For McNamara, Colby's skepticism was not a warning, but rather proof that the agency just was not big enough to do the job right.[7]

The secretary made his desires very clear. MACV and the CIA would proceed with the plan for covert action against North Vietnam.[8] Already well under development in Washington, it would include a psychological warfare element, as Colby suggested, but the main focus would remain on escalating agent and commando operations.

The transfer of covert paramilitary operations to the Defense Department was precipitated by events far away from Vietnam. After the Bay of Pigs debacle of 1961, discussions at the highest level of government concluded that the resources of the CIA, while adequate for agent recruitment and other small-scale covert operations, were insufficient for larger paramilitary programs, which were, in reality, small wars. In those formative years of the cold war, this was new and untested ground, but the general consensus was that the military was best at fighting, and the CIA best at spying.

This mind-set spawned a series of National Security Action Memorandums. The first of these, NSAM 55, was issued on 28 June 1961. Entitled "Relations of the Joint Chiefs of Staff (JCS) to the President in Cold War Operations," it charged the chiefs with "defense of the nation in the Cold War." This seemingly obvious statement was actually quite revolutionary because it handed both military and paramilitary aspects of cold war programs over to the Pentagon. For the past decade the CIA, not the military, had handled paramilitary programs.[9]

Two other memorandums followed—NSAM 56 and NSAM 57. The first called for the Defense Department to assess its paramilitary capabilities, outline the requirements for such operations throughout the world, and then make plans for meeting them. This task was given to General Edward Lansdale, who prepared three reports for the president, all of them pointing toward Southeast Asia as a prime testing ground for the Pentagon's opening paramilitary gambit.

NSAM 57 was a more comprehensive document. Addressed to the State and Defense Departments as well as the CIA, it outlined general responsibilities for planning and executing paramilitary operations. In this, the State Department would have oversight, while the Pentagon would take over operational control of paramilitary projects requiring military specialties "peculiar to the Armed Services." The CIA was relegated to a supporting role except for those operations that were "wholly covert or disavowable."[10]

Uncomfortable with its new mandate, the military stonewalled. Privately, the generals derided Kennedy's "counterinsurgency kick." By the end of 1961, the resultant lack of progress had thoroughly irritated the president, who went straight to the Joint Chiefs with his displeasure. In response, in

January 1962 the chiefs created the office of the Special Assistant for Counterinsurgency and Special Activities (SACSA) and appointed U.S. Marine Corps Major General Victor H. "Brute" Krulak as its first head. Consumed by Vietnam, Krulak divided his time between advising the president and the Joint Chiefs of Staff on the ongoing counterinsurgency effort against the Viet Cong and planning the covert campaign inside North Vietnam.

Nine months later, the Joint Chiefs had a new chairman, General Maxwell D. Taylor. Since July 1961, Taylor had been the military representative to the president, a special position invented because Kennedy had lost faith in the advice he received earlier from the chiefs. Now at the pinnacle of military command, Taylor embraced paramilitary operations as an opportunity to enhance the influence of the military in general and his office in particular. He quickly formed and personally chaired a series of special Paramilitary Study Groups to expedite the transition.

Under Taylor's lead, the Pentagon by early 1963 was finally coming around to the idea of running paramilitary campaigns, particularly as they might be applied in Southeast Asia. That spring, General Taylor ordered CINCPAC and SACSA to cooperate in preparing a plan for South Vietnamese "hit-and-run" operations against North Vietnam. They were to be "nonattributable," yet carried out with U.S. military material, training, and advisory assistance.

On 23 May, General Krulak answered Taylor's request with a memo entitled "Military Operations in North Vietnam." In nearly every respect, it mirrored what the CIA was already doing in its newly launched sabotage campaign. The only difference was that the SACSA plan had roles reversed: the Pentagon would run the show, with the CIA dropped to a second tier.[11]

When CIA headquarters at Langley was informed of the plan, it hit a raw nerve. The agency did not like being associated with a paramilitary plan it did not control, remembers William Colby, and expressed its concerns to the president.[12] Undaunted, the Joint Chiefs went ahead anyway, assigning CINCPAC responsibility for fleshing out Krulak's concept. This was completed by midsummer and forwarded to the Joint Chiefs. The chiefs endorsed CINCPAC's scheme in principle on 14 August and formally approved it on 9 September as Operational Plan (Oplan) 34-63. Full implementation, date unspecified, was set to come near year's end, after the conference in Honolulu.[13]

On the ground in Vietnam, the CIA and the Pentagon were cooperating long before Washington approved Oplan 34-63. As far back as 1957, in fact, U.S. Army Special Forces advisers—popularly known as Green Berets because of their distinctive headgear—were on hand to advise the 1st Observation Group, the elite South Vietnamese unit jointly funded by the agency and the Defense Department.

In 1961, the Green Beret connection deepened. That year, the CIA opened a training center at Thu Duc, on the outskirts of Saigon, and another at Hoa Cam, near Danang. The first housed four airborne ranger companies intended for cross-border operations into Laos. The second was a training base for border scouts, trail watchers, Republican Youth, and other CIA-backed irregular forces. While the agency paid all the bills, Green Berets formed the instructor cadre at both sites.

Early the following year, the CIA initiated its Civilian Irregular Defense Group (CIDG) program. Enlisting hill tribesmen into lightly armed militia companies along the western South Vietnamese border, the agency intended the CIDG as a means of harnessing ethnic minorities against Viet Cong encroachment. To train and live alongside these irregulars, the CIA used Green Berets by the dozens. South Vietnamese support, meanwhile, was provided by the Presidential Survey Office.

In July 1962, as the first major test of the Kennedy administration's new paramilitary policy, the CIA agreed to begin turning over control of the CIDG. This was the beginning of Operation SWITCHBACK, and it was completed in exactly twelve months. Few complications resulted, primarily because the reality on the ground was that Special Forces already were running the program with limited CIA involvement.

North Vietnam operations—the subject of Oplan 34-63—were a wholly different matter. In this, the Pentagon was very much in the backseat. Cooperation existed, but on a limited scale. Back in January 1963, for example, the U.S. Navy had dispatched a dozen SEALs to assist with maritime training at Danang. Two months later, a team of twelve U.S. Special Forces advisers from Okinawa was given a six-month temporary duty assignment to a new CIA complex at Long Thanh, twenty-two kilometers east of Saigon.

Officially known as Camp Quyet Thanh (Determined to Win), Long Thanh was intended as a replacement for the small Thu Duc complex. Little more than an old Japanese-built airstrip before the CIA moved in, the site soon grew to include a few simple barracks and a security wall. Most of these quarters were quickly occupied by the airborne rangers previously housed at Thu Duc. In addition, a small isolation area was set aside in the back of the camp for the teams destined for North Vietnam.

Prior to the establishment of Long Thanh, all northern agents had been trained by CIA advisers in safe houses spread across Saigon. While theoretically good for operational security, this cramped arrangement taxed nerves among the commandos.[14] Moreover, with dozens of new agents needed for

Overhead view of Camp Long Thanh. (Conboy collection)

the sabotage campaign to be initiated that spring, segregated instruction inside the capital was not efficient. The larger facilities at Long Thanh allowed for a demolitions range to be established alongside the main compound, affording the trainees a convenient location to practice with their explosives.

The first dozen Green Beret advisers at Long Thanh—team A-413, headed by Captain Clinton Hayes—trained both the agents and airborne rangers. For the rangers they devised a textbook bloc of instruction entitled Combined Military Operations Studies. Consisting primarily of drills in reconnaissance techniques, the course was similar to that given by previous Special Forces teams rotated through Thu Duc.

The North Vietnam agents, by contrast, were to receive a course in Combined External Operations Studies. In theory, this consisted of parachuting, small-unit tactics, and survival techniques. In reality, the CIA kept a tight hold over the training regimen for its sabotage teams, rarely calling on the Special Forces other than to act as jumpmasters during occasional parachute practice.

In October, one month after the Joint Chiefs endorsed Oplan 34-63, Captain Hayes's A-413 was replaced by a new Okinawa team, A-211, commanded by Captain Lawrence White. As before, most of the team members' interaction with the North Vietnam trainees involved parachute training. What they did see of the covert agents did not impress them. "These Vietnamese were going north and apparently getting captured in one or two days," observed Sergeant Charles Gutensohn, a member of the training detachment. "We had experienced guys on our team who I think could have lasted longer on the ground than these agents."[15]

In Saigon, Operation SWITCHBACK was being matched by changes in the South Vietnamese military. On 1 April 1963, the Presidential Survey Office was renamed the Luc Luong Dac Biet (Special Forces) and made part of the South Vietnamese army. The change was more than just semantics. Previously, the Presidential Survey Office had remained under President Diem's direct control, outside the normal military chain of command. Pressured by his American patrons, Diem ostensibly relinquished his grip by handing the Special Forces over to the army.

Despite its new name, however, the Special Forces retained Lieutenant Colonel Tung as commander and continued to enjoy a privileged position close to the president. As domestic unrest against Diem built over the summer, the president's brother used the airborne rangers at Long Thanh to suppress demonstrators.

Thus tainted, the Special Forces were seen as an integral part of Diem's corrupt establishment. As a result, when several key military commanders conspired to topple the president on 1 November, the Special Forces were also targeted. Diem was ultimately murdered by his officers, as was Lieutenant Colonel Tung and the Special Forces deputy chief of staff, who happened to be Tung's brother. Moreover, the airborne rangers, because of their earlier suppressive tactics, were summarily disarmed and partially disbanded. More insulated because of its external orientation, the Special Branch (formerly known as Office 45) was left untouched.

In Washington, too, there was turmoil. On 22 November, just two days after McNamara's gathering in Honolulu, an assassin's bullet struck down President Kennedy. Vice President Lyndon B. Johnson was sworn in as the new president that day. His job would be an uphill battle. Kennedy had not shared his Vietnam policy plans with his vice president, and Johnson was forced to wrestle with the political problems of a burgeoning war from the outset. One of those problems was what to do with the covert war against North Vietnam. Kennedy never had a chance to read the final deliberations of the Honolulu Conference or the draft of the covert plan headed for his signature, so a new plan was drawn up. On 24 November Johnson was briefed on the program.

The new memo, NSAM 273, differed little from what was intended for Kennedy. Still based on McNamara's recommendations from the CINCPAC meeting earlier in the week, the document dealt in part with the secret war against Hanoi. The Joint Chiefs, according to the NSAM, were to immediately order MACV and the CIA station in Saigon to jointly pen a twelve-month graduated schedule of covert operations in the north.

On 15 December, the plan was completed. Officially called Oplan 34A-64 by the military and Oplan Tiger by the CIA, it listed some 2,062 separate missions. CINCPAC approved of the scheme and forwarded it to the Joint Chiefs in Washington. Four day later, the chiefs added their concurrence.[16] All that remained was Johnson's signature.

The very next day, 20 December, McNamara flew to Saigon. Having been briefed on Oplan 34A, the secretary "showed great interest in developing full capability for early implementation" of the program, according to one Pentagon memo. In person, he was much more blunt, demanding that planners get the job done immediately.[17]

In Washington, those closest to the president were painting a favorable picture that was difficult to resist. Walt Rostow, one of Johnson's most trusted advisers, called Oplan 34A "a well reasoned plan of gradual escalation." McNamara was of a like mind. On 21 December he informed the president that the transfer plans presented by MACV and the CIA were "an excellent job. They present a wide variety of sabotage and psychological operations against North Vietnam from which I believe we should aim to select those that provide maximum pressure with minimum risk."[18]

With Washington's national security establishment generally reflecting McNamara's optimism, Johnson was swayed. Four days before Christmas, he appointed an interdepartmental committee headed by General Krulak to review the plan before final implementation. The Pentagon would be getting its war.

10

NEW MANAGEMENT

On 2 January 1964, Krulak's interdepartmental committee came back with its review of Oplan 34A. The general liked the plan, calling it an "excellent military-CIA study" that would allow Washington to signal Hanoi that "their support of the Viet Cong insurgency was about to bring down direct punishment."[1]

But even for a proponent of covert measures like Krulak, doubts about the proposal were apparent. The North Vietnamese were "toughened . . . by long years of hardships and struggle," he explained. "[T]hey will not easily be persuaded by a punitive program to halt their support of the Viet Cong insurgency, unless the damage visited upon them is of great magnitude."[2]

The official language of the committee reflected Krulak's waffling. On the one hand, it said "progressively escalating pressure" would "inflict increasing punishment upon North Vietnam . . . which may convince the North Vietnamese leadership, in its own self-interest, to desist from its aggressive policies." On the other hand, the review noted that it was "far from clear whether even the successful conduct of the operations . . . would induce Hanoi's leaders to cease and desist."[3]

President Johnson's Board of National Estimates, consisting of representatives from the CIA, Pentagon, and State Department, was more blunt. Reviewing thirteen of the proposed operations in the plan, the board concluded that even if all were successful, they would not convince Hanoi to change its policy. North Vietnam's leaders might view the operations "as representing a significant increase in the vigor of U.S. policy, potentially dangerous to them," but that was about all.[4]

Despite such eleventh-hour criticism, the plan—now abbreviated simply as Op 34A—went ahead. On 19 January, it was formally implemented through a joint message from the State Department, Pentagon, and CIA. Of the 2,062 actions in the original plan, General Krulak's committee selected those entailing the least risk and shaped them into a twelve-month, three-phase program. The primary purpose of these actions was to send a signal to Hanoi—symbolic acts meant to show American determination to resist North Vietnamese aggression rather than any tough measures to actually force them to stop.

At this stage, the South Vietnamese were still in the dark about the expanding covert operation. In fact, as MACV commander General Harkins pointed out, "whether or not the plan is acceptable to the GVN has yet to be determined." Since the proposal required the "covert use of the best of their regular forces, as well as their military resources," there was no choice but to read Saigon into the plan on a "discreet basis."[5]

On 21 January, Ambassador Henry Cabot Lodge presented Saigon officials with a "sanitized" version of the plan. In further meetings with military officials held two days later, Lodge discussed "certain military details of the plan," but he refused to reveal the "tactical plan" or specific targets in North Vietnam, except for two: a commando operation against dredges and a buoy tender in the Haiphong channel, and an attack on the nearby Ben Thuy petroleum storage facility.[6]

Although the secrecy may have seemed self-defeating in view of the fact that Washington could go no further without Saigon's cooperation, Lodge's cloak-and-dagger approach was rewarded less than a week later. On 30 January, General Nguyen Khanh, the South Vietnamese army I Corps commander, overthrew General Duong Van Minh in a bloodless coup. Briefings continued with the new rulers, and Op 34A remained on schedule pending General Khanh's approval. But CINCPAC was concerned that "information possessed by these deposed officials could cause serious repercussions if it were passed to neutralists or communists" and recommended that all operations be postponed pending a "complete assessment." CINCPAC decided that the two missions briefed to South Vietnamese officials on 21 January should be "held in abeyance," but the others—those not yet revealed to the South Vietnamese—could proceed as planned.

General Khanh was briefed on Op 34A on 3 February and promised his support—with reservations. Covert action, Khanh realized, would exert increased pressure on Hanoi, although he knew full well that such operations were not a substitute for victories on the ground against the Viet Cong. In fact, Khanh questioned whether the assets used in the North might not be better used against the Viet Cong in South Vietnam. There were other concerns as well: how would China react to the covert operations, and, if they intervened, would the United States retaliate? On the other side of the coin, if 34A was successful in gutting North Vietnam's fragile economy, could it trigger a mass flight of refugees to South Vietnam?[7] In the end, Khanh told Ambassador Lodge and Secretary McNamara that his "base in SVN was not strong enough for overt operations against NVN but that he would like to 'redouble' covert operations right away."[8]

In reality, Op 34A planning continued despite Saigon's turbulent political scene. On 24 January, a joint-services coordinating body, dubbed the Special

Operations Group (SOG), was formed under the direct supervision of the chief of staff, MACV. On paper, SOG had an all-inclusive unconventional warfare mandate. Designed to result in "substantial destruction, economic loss, and harassment" against North Vietnam, SOG's broad marching orders included fomenting political pressure, capturing prisoners, physical destruction, acquisition of intelligence, generation of propaganda, and diversion of resources.[9]

Translated into actual operations, SOG was to implement twelve months of covert actions "under conditions short of limited war." These actions fell into four categories, each designed to be more damaging than the last. The first category included "small unspectacular raids" not unlike the CIA's sabotage program of the previous year. "The expected reaction," surmised the Pentagon, "was to cause awareness of opposition, embarrassing irritation, possible interruption to movement of material, and increased readiness of [North Vietnamese] forces." Washington predicted that Hanoi would absorb such harassment with no major retaliation.

The second category encompassed "attritional" acts. This included small-scale resistance operations, raids against military and civilian installations, and demolition of important facilities. In theory, this would pose a "clear threat" to the North Vietnamese leadership. Planners expected that reaction from Hanoi would still be limited, most likely "retaliation by Viet Cong forces in South Vietnam and requests for aid from Communist China."

The next notch in the Op 34A ratchet was "punitive" operations. Under this, commandos operating in company- and battalion-sized forces would strike into the heart of North Vietnam, destroying large strategic facilities such as factories and military bases. Such actions, reasoned the Pentagon's planners, would cause large-scale internal redeployment of resources by Hanoi to deal with the threat.

The final category was nothing short of conventional efforts designed to have a "crippling effect on [North Vietnamese] potential to maintain a stable economy and progress in industrial development." Specifically, the Pentagon had airstrikes in mind. This would certainly provoke a strong reaction from Hanoi, warned the planners, and might well "escalate the conflict rather than convince the [North Vietnamese that] continuance of the war was unprofitable."[10]

From this broad menu, SOG was to implement Phase One from February to May 1964. Totaling thirty-three missions drawn primarily from the first category, it included some twenty sabotage raids. While further phases were tentatively scheduled for later in the year, planners optimistically felt there might be no need for taking 34A past Phase Two.

While SOG's birth attracted attention all the way up to the White House, on the ground in Saigon the fledgling group, with an initial authorized strength of just six officers and two enlisted men, commanded little clout or respect. Its headquarters, set in a colonial villa in Saigon's Chinatown district of Cholon, came furnished with only a few bare desks. Running SOG was U.S. Army Colonel Clyde R. Russell, a former regimental commander in the 82nd Airborne Division and group commander in the Special Forces. Despite his small team and a dearth of resources, Russell had less than two weeks to begin Op 34A's first four-month phase.

Although it was a daunting task, Russell would not be starting completely from scratch: SOG inherited the existing CIA programs built over the previous three years. Maritime operations, for example, had the Swift boats, mercenary boat crews, and a mix of Biet Hai naval commandos. Air operations took control over the CIA's C-123 transports and Chinese crews. The Airborne Operations Section, meanwhile, received control over the Long Thanh facility, as well as the twelve-man U.S. Special Forces detachment acting as instructor cadre at the camp and six long-term agent teams already inside North Vietnam.[11]

The CIA had also agreed to a six-month phased withdrawal from operations. Until June, one case officer and two training officers would remain at Long Thanh to help SOG come up to speed with airborne missions.[12] Similarly, Tucker Gougleman would remain at Danang until midyear to assist with the transfer of the maritime program, while an Air America officer would act as liaison between the military and the Chinese aircrews. For black psychological operations, an area where the Pentagon had little expertise, the CIA would maintain de facto control over SOG's program.

Given such continuity in assets, it came as no surprise that SOG's initial agenda differed little from the earlier CIA operations.[13] Many, however, gave SOG a better chance of success. On the eve of its implementation, Ambassador Lodge predicted real results. "I welcome exerting increased pressure on North Vietnam with the double aims of bringing about a ceasefire by Viet Cong and Pathet Lao and neutralizing North Vietnam, turning it into an oriental Yugoslavia," he wrote to Krulak a few weeks after SOG's formation.[14]

Lodge had some reason for optimism. The Pentagon, after all, was taking on North Vietnam with a stronger mandate than had been afforded the CIA. Later phases in the SOG plan even included tentative plans for unmarked South Vietnamese air force planes to bomb targets in the north, while another contingency called for Haiphong's harbor to be closed with dummy mines.[15] Other schemes were just plain silly, such as the proposal by the U.S. Air Force chief of staff, General Curtis LeMay, to use SOG teams to destroy crops in the Red River Valley with herbicides—this despite the fact that a handful of agents could only be expected to carry the smallest fraction of herbicides needed for even the most modest crop eradication program.[16]

Despite these inevitable flights of fancy, there was no denying that the Defense Department planned to tackle the covert war against North Vietnam with more advanced assets than ever before. For instance, the Nasty boats, which were still en route to Danang, would revolutionize maritime operations. And in the air, SOG intended to have the CIA's four C-123s (only two of which were in South Vietnam at any one time) replaced by six C-123s modified with both an improved electronics countermeasures package and advanced Doppler navigation. Known as Project DUCK HOOK, these new planes, capable of more precise low-level navigation in bad weather, were to be flown by seven fresh crews seconded from the Chinese air force's elite 34th Squadron and three more from the South Vietnamese air force, all sent for intensive instruction at Eglin Air Base in Florida. Meanwhile, different South Vietnamese aviators were being trained to fly sanitized fighter aircraft off U.S. Navy aircraft carriers, part of yet another SOG contingency plan to close North Vietnam's harbors, this time using real mines.[17]

Such training took time. Until then, SOG began the airborne portion of its campaign where the CIA left off. The first drop was a three-man reinforcement team for REMUS. On 23 April, a Chinese C-123 crew, using one of the four original aircraft inherited from the CIA, headed north toward the hills near Dien Bien Phu. The crew sighted the proper fire signal on the ground, and the commandos exited the aircraft without incident. Shortly thereafter, the REMUS radio operator reported that the new members had arrived safely. SOG's first airborne infiltration was an apparent success.[18]

Two days later, SOG prepared for its second insertion. ATTILA, consisting of six ethnic Vietnamese, jumped from a C-123 over southern Nghe An Province. This time, SOG was not as lucky. In an all-too-familiar refrain from years past, the team never established radio contact.[19]

By late summer, SOG had dispatched eight more airborne teams. Among them, three were reinforcements for teams previously established under the CIA's watch. According to subsequent radio reports, all three were successful. The five remaining teams, meanwhile, were jumping blind into new locales. Of these, just one came on the air.

Washington was watching closely, and as the failures mounted, officials who were once optimistic about the operations became much more critical. After some nine months in operation, they pointed out, SOG could boast little improvement over the agency's effort. Michael V. Forrestal, a ranking staffer on the National Security Council, reported to the president that "despite considerable effort . . . very little has come of these operations." Even the military was becoming impatient. Lukewarm in their support in the first place, the Joint Chiefs reminded Secretary of Defense McNamara that "it would be idle to conclude that these efforts will have a decisive effect" on Hanoi's will to continue the war in South Vietnam.[20]

SOG's airborne woes were symptomatic of larger problems. By 1 June, it had completed just one-third of its scheduled operations. Blame for this poor showing was dumped onto everyone. The CIA, lamented Colonel Russell, had left them with inferior goods. Camp Long Thanh, he noted, had an inadequate demolitions and firing range. In addition, the agent pool in training was of exceedingly poor quality.[21] At the same time, of those teams already inserted into North Vietnam, many were critically short of food.[22] One team, BELL in Yen Bai Province, had gone for over a year without a resupply. Before a drop was eventually made that July, the team's radioman grimly reported three members had died of starvation.[23]

Equally problematic for SOG was the group's convoluted, micromanaged system of command and control. According to its 19 January implementation message, Op 34A effectively had two bosses: political control in the hands of the U.S. ambassador in Saigon and military control wielded by the MACV commander. Further complicating the picture, SOG also answered to SACSA in Washington. Basically, SOG needed permission for each and every mission—a complex process. At a minimum, Russell had to submit proposals to CINCPAC for comment, notify the Joint Chiefs of Staff of his intent, and get final clearance from the ambassador twenty-four hours in advance. Many missions had to be cleared by President Johnson himself. Any officer at any level could veto a SOG proposal without stating a reason.[24]

Partly because of the heavy red tape and partly for reasons of their own, the South Vietnamese remained guarded in their support of the program. Only after much prompting did they agree to expand the Special Branch, previously headed by Major Ngo The Linh, into a larger Special Exploitation Service (SES) that would act as direct counterpart to SOG. Commanded by Colonel Tran Van Ho, an airborne officer with no special forces background, the Special Exploitation Service headquarters was not formally instituted until 12 February, while some of its subordinate components did not take shape until April.[25]

Another problem for SOG was the lukewarm cooperation it was receiving from the CIA. What had begun—on paper at least—as a smooth transition became strained when the agency balked at permanently assigning a high-ranking officer as the group's deputy chief. Instead, the CIA opted to place a more junior officer in the vague position of "SOG special assistant."[26] Then in June, partly because of the questions surrounding responsibilities within the growing covert program, Director of Central Intelligence John McCone suggested in a letter to the secretary of defense that the CIA should play a role only in "covert psychological activity." McCone inferred that this should be a separate activity, with little or no input from SOG. "As Oplan 34A unfolds," wrote the CIA director, "there will be less and less need for covertness. Since it appears feasible to do so, CIA would prefer to resume its traditional covert operations posture." McCone believed that "the continuing covert operations, for which CIA would continue its independent and peculiar responsibility, would then be serviced and controlled outside of MACSOG, but with appropriate coordination."[27]

Alarm bells sounded in the Pentagon. The CIA appeared to be washing its hands of the program, leaving SOG with a big job that it was not yet prepared to handle alone. General Krulak, SACSA, saw the CIA suggestion as "a segmented, independent (though coordinated) charter for 34A-type operations" with the agency running its own show. This "fragmentation of direction" would harm the overall program, Krulak concluded, and it "was contrary to the doctrine of central control and responsibility for an operation, and violated the President's decision of 16 January 1964." In other words, SACSA did not want different agencies running around with similar—but independent—missions. The joint chiefs agreed, ruling that the military would retain "full operational control" of the program, and that the CIA "should continue to support 34A with all SEAsia assets."[28] Deputy Secretary of State Cyrus Vance also argued for "no changes in the CIA support for MACVSOG," but the agency began to reduce its numbers anyway.[29]

This high-level bickering trickled down to the men executing the operations. For example, SOG complained that the Air America pilot acting as link with the Chinese C-123 crews was uncooperative.[30] One of the pilots recalled, "There was a definite conflict when SOG took over. After SOG would brief us before a mission, the [Air America] officer would tell us not to believe what we just heard. He would tell us that there were anti-aircraft guns waiting in the area where we were going."[31]

Colonel Russell charged that, as a rule, CIA personnel were "uncooperative," and he got no help "without demanding it." Other military officers within SOG noticed the same thing. "They were reluctant to provide us with any information and help," noted Colonel William Becker, one of the air force's top SOG representatives. He believed that part of this uncooperativeness stemmed from a feeling that the CIA "had to turn the job over to the military because of failure and [was] less than enthusiastic to see the military take over the job."[32]

But SOG itself was not without blame for the poor start to Op 34A. For one thing, its initial increment of American personnel was woefully short on unconventional warfare experience. For instance, the first head of maritime operations at Danang, Commander Albert Thomas, was a submarine officer. Similarly, none of the officers in the Air Operations Section had any background in special warfare. And while Colonel Russell loaded the Airborne Operations Section with Green Berets, having Special Forces experience—with its focus on guerrilla warfare—did not necessarily equate with an understanding of covert long-term agent operations.

In addition, SOG's military men did little to endear themselves to the former CIA assets they inherited. A case in point was SOG's sour relationship with the Chinese C-123 pilots. When the CIA was in charge, airborne missions were paramount, but when SOG took over, priorities changed. According to one pilot:

> The U.S. military was planning to start its bombing campaign, and they wanted all the information they could get on the radar in North Vietnam so they could penetrate the anti-aircraft coverage. SOG would tell us to do our drops, then circle to collect information on the radar. Our electronic countermeasures officer would monitor and plot all the signals. Our planes were very vulnerable, and we started getting tracers all the time. We told the SOG planners, "Collect the information on the anti-aircraft guns by other means, then send us to do the drops." But they wanted it the other way.[33]

Already angry, the Chinese were further alienated by a string of risky resupply missions. Following the antiaircraft ambush near Team EUROPA the previous August, the C-123 crews were already wary about revisiting any of the existing teams. These fears were underscored in November 1964, when a resupply flight to TOURBILLON met with heavy fire. After SOG planners ordered the aborted mission to be reflown, the aircrews conveniently became sick.[34]

Besides mishandling ties with the plane crews, SOG also showed a disturbing lack of imagination when targeting its airborne teams. Quick to blame better North Vietnamese defenses for its initial failures, SOG had made it easier for Hanoi by repeatedly running the same basic missions into the same areas.[35] For example, ATTILA was parachuted during April into Nghe An Province; the following team to go north, LOTUS, landed in the same province. The next team making a blind drop, SCORPION, went to the same general location used by earlier teams BELL and PACKER.[36] BUFFALO, the next to head north, jumped into almost the exact target area as RUBY.[37] North Vietnamese security forces were no doubt on alert from the previous jumps. Not surprisingly, every one of these SOG teams failed to make radio contact.

Despite these early problems, by late summer SOG had some reason for optimism. As of August, the group was brimming with agents in various states of readiness. Some sixteen teams, ranging in size from one to fifteen members, were crowded into Long Thanh.[38] Moreover, SOG's counterpart, the Special Exploitation Service, had managed to salt nearly all of these teams with volunteers from the South Vietnamese army, thereby raising the overall quality of trainees.[39]

Things were also looking up for the perennial problem of insertion into North Vietnam. By August, the first of the six modified C-123s had arrived in South Vietnam for evaluation. Arriving, too, were the seven Chinese and three Vietnamese aircrews—together called the First Flight Detachment—that had trained in low-level flying in Florida and were now posted to a new SOG air support base in Nha Trang. Replacing the earlier group of disgruntled Chinese air force crews, the fresh contingent quickly proved its mettle. On 14 November, the crews headed north with a reinforcement team for BELL in Yen Bai Province. Successfully dropping their agents on target, they returned without incident.[40]

Hopes were high for the Vietnamese C-123 crews, code-named Co Trang, or White Crane. Nguyen Cao Ky, now a colonel, had chosen three of his more experienced crews for the project. Their skill would soon be on trial. Despite the fact that Vietnamese air force crews had not flown a northern drop mission in over two years, their initial flight was to be among the most risky to date. The mission involved parachuting a sabotage team along the North Vietnamese coast north of the city of Vinh to set demolition charges on the Cam bridge, a critical link feeding both truck and railroad traffic to the North Vietnamese panhandle. When the mission was completed, the raiders would paddle rafts out to sea and rendezvous with waiting Nasty boats.

Destroying the Cam bridge made sense. An attack on such an important logistical artery stood a better chance of inflicting economic pressure than any of Op 34A's prior acts of sabotage. But this mission would be far more sophisticated than anything SOG had ever attempted. To make up for any possible weakness in planning, SOG's airborne section beefed up the strike force with extra personnel. The resulting thirty-three-man unit, code-named CENTAUR, was more than triple the size of any previous sabotage team.

Training for CENTAUR began on 26 July, with two full dress rehearsals planned over the following month. Quickly, however, scheduling bogged down. Particularly bothersome was the scanty intelligence on the target area, as well as logistical problems associated with dropping the commandos, their demolition charges, and escape boats. By 19 August, with SOG operations placed on temporary hold following skirmishes between Swatows and U.S. Navy destroyers in the Gulf of Tonkin, the ambitious attack was called off.

Three months passed before CENTAUR was resurrected, this time with a reconfigured mission. Instead of the Cam bridge, the team would now hit a coastal radar site near Dong Hoi. At first, thought was given to infiltrating CENTAUR by boat—until a familiarization run in rough seas sent the team into a panicked frenzy. So it was decided that two Nastys would take a pathfinder team of Biet Hai commandos north and let them sneak ashore in rubber boats. These commandos would then light flares near the beach to guide in a South Vietnamese–piloted C-123. CENTAUR would parachute onto the signal, then move with the Biet Hai commandos to the radar and destroy it. This done, they would make their way back to the beach and take rubber boats out to the waiting Nastys.

Just as with the proposed attack on the Cam bridge, CENTAUR's new orders expected far too much from novice raiders. This was not lost on some of those involved with the mission's planning: SOG maritime officers at Danang argued in vain that Biet Hai commandos alone could just as easily blow the radar, forgoing the difficulty of coordinating an airborne drop. However, the group's airborne chief, Lieutenant Colonel Edward Partain, insisted on keeping the complex mix of parachutes and boats.[41]

The likely risks outweighed any expected benefits. By substituting a target of true economic importance (a key bridge) for one of limited military value (a small radar post) it looked like SOG was simply searching for any excuse to showcase its skills. Noted one senior SACSA official sarcastically, "Damn it, we've got to do something up there, so let's do something. Let's conduct some unconventional operations."[42]

Justified or not, CENTAUR was set to parachute into North Vietnam on 22 December. Before that, the team traveled to Danang to conduct three night rehearsals. The first took place on 10 December. Two Nastys left the dock and headed for an isolated stretch of beach north of the city. While the boats idled on the dark water, the Biet Hai went ashore and waited to light their signal.

Back at Danang, twenty-eight members of CENTAUR boarded one of SOG's modified C-123 transports. Joining them in the rear was a SOG airborne instructor, Sergeant Dominick Sansone, and a Vietnamese jumpmaster. Major Woodrow Vaden, a U.S. Air Force adviser for the Doppler navigational system, took a seat in the cockpit to assist the Vietnamese crew with the new radar.

At 2100 hours, the plane rolled down the Danang runway and took to stormy skies. The aircraft commander, Ho Van Kiet, had orders to follow the coast north, locate the combat swimmers, and drop the commandos from 120 meters, the same altitude to be used on the actual mission. The combination of rain and darkness, however, proved to be a deadly combination.

Ten kilometers from the airport, the C-123 entered a cloud bank and slammed into Monkey Mountain, a massive karst outcropping rising from the tip of the Son Tra peninsula. There were no survivors.[43]

With the loss of CENTAUR, SOG painfully finished out its first year of airborne operations. The Joint Chiefs of Staff tried hard to put a positive spin on the previous twelve months. "Quite apart from the military objectives of these actions," wrote the Joint Chiefs in a year-end evaluation report, "they have served a very useful psychological purpose by keeping [North Vietnam] on alert through harassment and by maintaining pressure on defense forces."[44]

Despite such meaningless platitudes, SOG could not help but feel more frustration than satisfaction with its performance to date. For its airborne operations in particular, the stark truth was that, despite the major investment in more sophisticated aircraft and enhanced aircrew training in Florida, SOG had managed to establish only one new long-term agent team in North Vietnam over the previous twelve months—the worst annual tally since the CIA had started the program in 1961. If expectations had been for the Pentagon to transform a modest agency project into a powerful covert lever against Hanoi, SOG had yet to deliver.

11

SEA COMMANDOS

Airborne operations were not the only source of early frustration for SOG. At sea, the Pentagon had taken over a CIA maritime project short on experience and even shorter on success. Between June 1962 and January 1964, only four hit-and-run missions had been launched by the agency. Just one had accomplished its task without incurring friendly losses.

Looking to do better, the Pentagon dispatched some of its best unconventional warfare operators to Danang. First to arrive in early January 1964 was a twelve-man U.S. Navy SEAL training team, replacing a similar-sized SEAL unit that had been instructing the Biet Hai under CIA auspices for the past year. Also arriving at Danang was a four-man detachment drawn from the elite 1st Force Reconnaissance Company of the U.S. Marine Corps. Together, these SEALs and Marines constituted the training backbone for SOG's Maritime Operations Group, better known by its more benign cover designation, the Naval Advisory Detachment (NAD).[1]

Overseeing the detachment was Commander Albert Thomas. A naval officer with prior experience in submarines, Thomas was strangely out of place in a setting of Swift boats, Norwegian mercenaries, and Asian frogmen.[2] For the time, however, his role was limited to liaison with the CIA's Tucker Gougleman, who, scheduled to remain until June to help with the transition, was still very much in control of the entire operation.

On 15 February, in the midst of the month's moonless phase, Gougleman decided to flex some maritime muscle. That morning, he gathered the Naval Advisory Detachment at the "White Elephant," a two-story whitewashed compound in downtown Danang that for the past year had served as operations center for the CIA's PACIFIC project.

The Naval Advisory Detachment advisers were at the beginning of their learning curves, and Gougleman's strong hand was evident. Their debut, he revealed, would involve a Swift boat taking a team of combat swimmers to the mouth of the Gianh River, from where they would swim upriver and plant magnetic limpet mines to the hulls of some Swatow gunboats.

For those with any institutional memory, the plan showed precious little imagination. It was an exact rehash of the abortive attack the previous December, which in turn was recycled from the 1962 VULCAN disaster. Still, while it lacked originality, at least it was a plan with which the

Combat swimmer Truong Van Le poses for North Vietnamese authorities after attempting to destroy a bridge along Route 1 in Quang Binh Province, March 1964. (Vietnam News Agency)

boat crew and South Vietnamese commandos were by now familiar and comfortable.

That noon, four combat swimmers from Team NEPTUNE rechecked their gear at the pier and boarded a Swift. Heading northward through the blue Tonkin Gulf, they stayed far enough from the coast to avoid radar detection. An hour before midnight, the Norwegian skipper throttled back and the boat eased to a stop, bobbing in the gentle swell.

The Biet Hai worked quietly in the velvet darkness. One of them, Vu Duc Guong, was already a two-year veteran of the program. A northern Catholic, Guong fled south in 1954 and made his living as a carpenter. In late 1962, answering a recruiter's pitch to become "the first arrow" in the fight against communism, he made his way to Danang and joined the initial class of CIA swimmers. Eventually selected for advanced scuba training and posted to Team NEPTUNE, Guong had been on the December 1963 mission when the team's Swift became lost en route to the Swatows.

This time it was on target. When the Swift stopped off the coast, the NEPTUNE swimmers climbed over the gunwale and into a rubber raft. Three men from the boat crew went with them. Just as with the earlier VUL-CAN mission, it was their job to take the raft to the mouth of the Gianh, drop the frogmen off for the swim upriver, then pick them up after the operation. One member was also to stay in radio contact with the Swift in case something went awry.

It did. No sooner had they left the side of the Swift than a brisk wind blew in from the sea, chopping the water's surface into dangerous whitecaps. The operation briefing had not mentioned big waves, and rubber boats make notoriously poor surfboards. As the raft slowed to let the frogmen into the water, a wave loomed over the side. Before the crew could adjust, it smashed down, throwing men and supplies into the water. Scuba gear and mines intended for the Swatow attack sank to the bottom.

After several terrifying moments in the churning sea, the commandos righted their raft and climbed back aboard. But the outboard motor was dead and the radio useless. There was no way to contact the Swift and report their problem. Using a pair of emergency oars, the crew retraced their path, looking to find the mother ship before dawn broke. If not, a North Vietnamese coastal patrol would be sure to spot them.

For hours they paddled, hoping to hear the sound of the Swift in the darkness. But there was only the hiss of wind churning the water's surface. Exhausted and near panic, the commandos watched as a ribbon of light appeared on the horizon, followed by an arc of sun.

Suddenly a boat appeared in the distance—and it was heading straight for them. Was it the Swift or a Swatow? The Biet Hai stared in silence. No one dared wave at the onrushing shape. Then one of the commandos shouted. He recognized the bow of the Swift and knew they were saved.

Safely aboard and heading south, the Norwegian skipper explained that when the team had missed the rendezvous, he had begun circling in an ever-widening spiral hoping to find them. Since he heard no gunfire from shore, he figured there was a good chance they had not been discovered. The commandos sank gratefully down on the deck and slept all the way back to Danang.

The Naval Advisory Detachment waited for the next moonless period before trying again. On the afternoon of 11 March, the team was again summoned to the White Elephant for a briefing by Gougleman. The mission was to be more of the same. Four combat swimmers drawn from NEPTUNE would again be heading north on a Swift, and they would again be targeted against the Swatows on the Gianh River.

The following afternoon, the NEPTUNE swimmers left Danang. The team leader was a hard-core commando named Nguyen Van Nhu. Nurtured by his hatred of Hanoi, Nhu had tattooed the words *Sat Cong* (Kill Communists) across his heart. Also on the mission was Vu Duc Guong—the same swimmer from the last aborted mission—and two others named Pham Van Ly and Vu Van Gioi.[3]

In a trip that was becoming routine for the Swift crew, the boat raced north and arrived offshore from its target. A rubber boat went into the water, and a boat crew plus four combat swimmers climbed in. This time the sea was calm as they approached a buoy marking the mouth of the Gianh. Donning scuba tanks, masks, and flippers, the NEPTUNE swimmers slipped overboard in teams of two. One man in each pair carried two limpets stored in a styrofoam bucket to lend buoyancy. The other man carried a compass board for navigation. Both pairs were to rendezvous at a Swatow pier.

Avoiding all contact, the swimmers approached their objective. Cautiously, two of the commandos, Guong and Ly, surfaced to eye their target. To their shock, the pier was empty. Missing, too, was the other pair of swimmers.

Recalling their mission briefing, Guong and Ly immediately headed farther upriver toward a second pier thought to be an alternate mooring for the Swatows. As they kicked against the current with the bulky limpets, however, Guong grew concerned. They were running low on oxygen and might not have enough for the return swim to the rubber boat. He signaled Ly, and they headed for shore, stowed their tanks in the bushes, and then began picking their way through the jungle toward their objective.

Before they made much progress, a voice rang from the darkness. "Halt!" For a second, Guong debated going back to the riverbank to retrieve his scuba. But more voices and the light of flickering torches between him and the water quickly canceled that option. With bullets snapping branches behind them, the two commandos raced deeper into the jungle. Eventually, the shouts faded. But because dawn would surely bring methodical search parties, the pair crashed on.

Back at the rubber boat, the crewmen kept vigil. With the sun slowly edging above the horizon, they had no choice but to retreat back to the Swift, short four swimmers.[4]

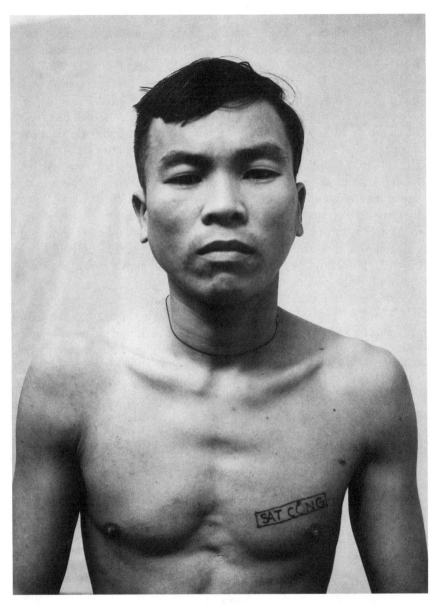

Nguyen Van Nhu, leader of Team NEPTUNE, was photographed in detention following his failed attempt to destroy North Vietnamese gunboats on the Gianh River, March 1964. The tattoo over his heart reads "Kill Communists." (Vietnam News Agency)

At the White Elephant, the mood was somber. As a new entity, the Naval Advisory Detachment had just suffered its first casualties, and the advisers were determined to do better next time. The first step was to make a clean break from the CIA's prior obsession with scuba operations and the Swatows on the Gianh. This time they planned to focus on cross-beach amphibious raids against some of the coastal bridges along Route 1.

Approaching the missions with a military mind-set, the Naval Advisory Detachment's SEAL and marine instructors prepared highly detailed team briefings. According to plan, the first raid would take place well north of the Gianh River, in southern Ha Tinh Province, on 15 March. A nine-man team would launch from a Swift at 2200 hours, proceeding via rubber boat to the edge of the surf zone. Four scout swimmers, wearing life jackets and flippers and carrying silenced submachine guns, would enter the water. Two of them would proceed to the beach and check for North Vietnamese patrols; the other two would remain in the surf and observe the actions of the first two. If no patrols were sighted, the scouts would give a safety signal to the rubber boat using flashes from an infrared metascope.

Once cleared by the scout swimmers, the remainder of the team would take the rubber boat up to the beach and hide it in the brush. Leaving one man behind to guard the boat, they would then patrol inland past a series of streams and paddies to the targeted Route 1 bridge. If it was too heavily guarded, an alternate bridge was located three hundred meters to the north.

Once under the bridge, the commandos would place their explosives using two pencil timers per charge. After pulling the pins, they would set up two propaganda mortars on either side of the bridge. Developed by the CIA to support the notional resistance front concept, the mortars, using delayed fuses, would shower the site with SSPL leaflets claiming credit for the attack.

Patrolling back to the rubber boat, the team would then make contact with the boat guard and ensure no North Vietnamese patrols were in the area. Launching from the beach, the commandos would paddle through the surf zone before restarting the engine. They would then use the metascope to search for the infrared beacon on the Swift, while at the same time activating a beacon transmitter and monitoring their radio for course corrections from the Swift. The final rendezvous with the mother ship was expected by 0200 hours the next morning.[5]

From this detailed script, the first bridge raid began as planned. The commandos for the mission, ethnic Nung drawn from Team CANCER, piled onto a rubber boat on the side of the Swift and headed for Ha Tinh's Ky Anh District. At the edge of the surf zone, the rubber boat dropped anchor, and

An abandoned rubber boat and 57mm recoilless rifle after the cross-beach attack near Dong Hoi, 30 June 1964. (Vietnam News Agency)

four swimmers took to the water. With two remaining in the surf, the other two swimmers, Voong A Cau and Chau Henh Xuong, stepped onto the sand.

As his eyes strained to adjust in the darkness, Xuong's heart jumped. A North Vietnamese foot patrol was on the same stretch of beach, heading in his direction. Keeping low, Xuong pointed the metascope in the direction of the rubber boat and gave two flashes—the danger signal. He and Cau then ran across the sand and into the jungle in the hope that the patrol would pass and they could then bring in the boat.

It was not to be. As the patrol came even with their position, the men saw the twin trail of footprints across the desolate beach and immediately launched a manhunt. The Swift was ultimately forced to return to Danang, short two swimmers.[6]

Two days later, the Naval Advisory Detachment launched a second Route 1 bridge mission, this time inside Quang Binh Province. Using the exact same mission plan, the nine-man team took a rubber boat to the surf zone, dropped anchor, and deployed swimmers. Two of them walked onto the beach—and promptly ran into a party of fishermen. As the alarm went up, the pair of commandos fled into the jungle. Again the Swift was forced to return to Danang minus its swimmers.[7]

After four failures in four outings, policy makers in Washington began to take notice. Few had expected SOG to be an unqualified success, but now many wondered if it was worth any effort at all. Henry Cabot Lodge, the American ambassador in Saigon, reported to the White House that Op 34A missions "might be good training but were certainly having no effect on Hanoi."[8]

Military leaders were also critical. Admiral Felt, nearing the end of his tour as CINCPAC, had never been fond of the covert operations, which he regarded as a poor stopgap for stepping up military action. Now events seemed to be bearing this out. Felt believed that "lack of adequate intelligence is a prime factor in the failure of maritime operations." He also pointed out the new Swatow threat and North Vietnam's "increased state of alert and mobilization" as additional hurdles, concluding that "the odds against pulling operations under present conditions are high."[9]

Pacific Fleet commander Admiral Ulysses S. G. Sharp, who would take over as CINCPAC on 30 June, echoed these sentiments. "I have been watching this [covert maritime] program closely," wrote Sharp, "and see . . . some of our early reservations on the PTF concept becoming reality." He also admitted that Hanoi's increased vigilance was "more extensive and effective than originally thought."[10]

Still hopeful that the president might approve a bombing campaign against North Vietnam, the Joint Chiefs also voiced their concerns. "While we are wholly in favor of executing the covert actions against North Vietnam," wrote General Taylor, "it would be idle to conclude that these efforts will have a decisive effect" on the communist leadership. Even Secretary of Defense McNamara began to suspect that "this program will not amount to very much."[11]

Well aware of the watching eyes in Washington, SOG took immediate steps to revamp its maritime wing. One of the biggest involved the Naval Advisory Detachment's South Vietnamese counterparts. On 1 April, the Coastal Security Service (CSS) was officially formed at Danang under Major Ngo The Linh, previously commander of the Special Branch. Linh had been out of a job since January, when the Special Branch was expanded into the Special Exploitation Service and the commander's slot given to a full colonel. As chief of the Coastal Security Service, Linh would now command the boat crews, the Biet Hai, and all other South Vietnamese maritime support and advisory personnel.

Together with the Naval Advisory Detachment, the Coastal Security Service spent the next few months training new cross-beach teams. Each of the teams numbered up to thirty members, roughly equivalent to a small platoon. Unlike the CIA, SOG was able to directly solicit various units of the South Vietnamese military for recruits. These recruits were then kept segregated according to their original units. One of the resultant teams, code-named ROMULUS, consisted entirely of South Vietnamese marines. Team NIMBUS was drawn from South Vietnamese army ranger and airborne battalions. Two more came from the South Vietnamese navy: Team VEGA, recruited from the navy's paramilitary Junk Force, and Team ATHENA, from sailors in the regular fleet.[12]

Bigger changes involved the boats and boat crews. In March, PTFs 1 and 2—the gassers that had been undergoing slow modification since the winter of 1962—finally arrived at Danang. Two months earlier, Saigon had agreed to provide full crews from the South Vietnamese navy for the two gassers. While already experienced seamen, these sailors needed conversion training for the torpedo boats. For this, SOG once again turned to European mercenaries. Instead of Norwegians, however, it allowed the CIA's Bonn station to help select five West Germans.

It was a bad choice. Incompetent as navigators and demeaning to their Vietnamese students, the Germans offended almost everyone. "They drank a lot of cognac and their tactics were not too good," summed up Captain Truong Duy Tai, one of Linh's deputies in the Coastal Security Service.[13] Added a SOG officer, "[They] were difficult to control and caused all sorts of problems while on liberty. They were getting in trouble in Danang and there were definite fears in the Washington circle that the whole program would be blown because these people were getting involved with Vietnamese girls and the police in Danang."[14]

In the end, there was little for the Germans to do. Only a few weeks after the gassers arrived, one of them ruptured a gas tank during sea trials.[15] After this problem was determined to be the result of a serious structural flaw, both boats were sent to U.S. Navy facilities at Subic Bay, the Philippines, for repairs. Seizing the opportunity, SOG terminated its contract with the Germans and sent them packing after just one month.

Fortunately there were other new boats arriving in theater. By late 1963, the two Nastys—PTFs 3 and 4—had made their way from California to Subic Bay. There they underwent further modifications, including having their 40mm guns stripped from the deck to make room for extra fuel tanks. Also gone were the flamethrowers, which had proved useless during trials.[16]

That December, Secretary of Defense McNamara asked about the Nastys during a fact-finding tour to South Vietnam. Admiral Felt, the CINCPAC, pointed out that the two Norwegian-made boats, plus the gassers and Swifts, would be able to manage only small-scale raids. No problem, countered McNamara, simply order more boats. Accordingly, the U.S. Navy approached the Norwegian government to have another four vessels made available "for maximum readiness."[17]

By February 1964, four more Nastys were en route to Subic. For these, as well as the two Nastys already there, Saigon had agreed to provide six crews directly from the South Vietnamese navy. Like the gassers, they would need conversion training. Unlike the gassers, however, SOG would not have to rely on foreign training expertise. Instead, the U.S. Navy had agreed to provide a Mobile Support Team (MST) to bring the Vietnamese up to speed. Composed of the U.S. Navy crews that had ferried the Nastys to Southeast Asia, plus some additional personnel versed in the Nasty's Napier engine system, the Mobile Support Team was subdivided into Boat Training Teams that would coach the Vietnamese in boat handling and gunnery, and a separate Maintenance Training Team responsible for engineering and maintenance instruction.[18] These teams, all based at Subic, would be matched with pairs of South Vietnamese crews for between three and seven weeks.

With the U.S. Navy's helping hand, the first two Nasty crews graduated in April. Two more headed to Subic in May, and the final two were expected to arrive later in the summer.

Back at Danang, the Naval Advisory Detachment was restarting its northern operations after a two-month hiatus. On hand in May was a growing fleet of three Swifts, two Nastys, and, after a brief repair spell at Subic, the two gassers.[19] The highly regarded Norwegians were in the last weeks of their contracts and were scheduled to return home, but SOG intended to use their expertise during the Nasty's baptism of fire.

Because cross-beach missions had been unsuccessful, the Naval Advisory Detachment planners conjured up an entirely new kind of maritime operation. Code-named LOKI, it involved kidnapping the crews of North Vietnamese fishing junks and spiriting them down to Cu Lao Cham, an island twenty-two kilometers off the coast of Danang. There SOG had built a small base in the island's mountainous interior to serve as notional headquarters for the SSPL resistance. Populated only by monkeys and a handful of locals, the site—code-named Paradise Island—was far enough from Danang to let SOG operate in secrecy, yet close enough for land-based reinforcements if they were needed.

On Paradise Island, the SSPL compound was festooned with banners and other propaganda from the notional front. South Vietnamese personnel, all dressed in SSPL "uniforms," acted as the camp's cadre. According to plan, captured junk crews would be taken to the island while blindfolded, then marched up to the mountain redoubt. There they would be interrogated by the SSPL for up to two days.

The purpose of the interrogation was twofold. First, the captives would be milked of low-level intelligence on coastal defense arrangements, the fishing industry, and the North Vietnamese economy in general. On a more subtle level, they would be exposed to the fact that a resistance movement was allegedly operating in their midst, information they would spread among their peers when they were released back north. As a parting act of good faith, the SSPL would give toys, radios, and other gifts to the returning fishermen.

On 27 May, the first junk capture mission—called LOKI 1—was launched off the Quang Binh coast near Dong Hoi. Spying a fishing flotilla, the Swift closed in on one medium-sized junk. The crew, ostensibly members of the SSPL, led six fishermen aboard at gunpoint. Behind them, a Nasty moved in and hooked the junk to a towrope. Together, they sped back south.

Aboard the Swift, the kidnapped fishermen were blindfolded and huddled in a corner of the patrol boat. As they crossed the seventeenth parallel, the skipper brought the vessel to a stop as the detainees were transferred to a motorized junk for the rest of the voyage to Cu Lao Cham.

Sergeant David Elliott, a linguist with MACV's small translation section, was in Saigon when he received an emergency call from Danang. Without going into details, the Naval Advisory Detachment said it needed an American translator in a hurry. Flying north, Elliott was picked up by three case officers and taken to a CIA safe house on the waterfront. There he was given a set of black pajamas and a Swedish K submachine gun, and together with the similarly garbed CIA men, went to the Naval Advisory Detachment pier and boarded a Swift bound for Cu Lao Cham.

The island, Elliott found, was a tropical backwater. There were no signs of civilization, only a single tent erected near the beach. Reflecting on the serenity, it made him wonder why they had gone through the charade of dressing in the pajamas. As he and the case officers relaxed on lounge chairs, a Vietnamese dressed in identical black garb materialized from the jungle. He carried a set of interrogation reports from the fishermen being held at the SSPL compound in the island's interior. Elliott immediately translated them for the case officers.

"This continued for two days," Elliott recalled. "We slept in the tent near the beach, and the Vietnamese, who was an ARVN captain originally from the north—a Catholic—would bring down the reports and I would translate them. It was mostly questions about targets, especially around Dong Hoi."[20]

His mission over, Elliott was taken back to Danang and then on to Saigon. The fishermen, meanwhile, were taken aboard a junk to the seventeenth parallel, then transferred to a Swift and shuttled further up the Quang Binh

U.S. Army interrogator and Vietnamese linguist David Elliott poses with a submachine gun on Cu Lao Cham, the SSPL's "secret" base. (Courtesy David Elliott)

coast. A Nasty, junk in tow, followed behind. Once near Dong Hoi, the captives, gifts in hand, were given their boat and a fast farewell.

With its first success in five tries, the Naval Advisory Detachment could not help but be pleased. The Nastys' baptism had gone without a hitch. Before further missions could be contemplated, however, they had to deal with major changes taking hold at Danang. First, the Norwegians had finished their contracts and departed for Europe. While they had been highly competent, it was risky using them on kidnapping missions because the SSPL was supposed to be an indigenous resistance movement. Deniability would go out the window if one of the captured fishermen were to catch a glimpse of a white face on the boats. Looking for replacements, SOG turned to a familiar source of assistance: Taiwan. In short order, eight Nationalist Chinese skippers were sent to Danang in June to begin a transition course for the Swifts.

Meanwhile, a third Nasty crew graduated from training on 7 June and returned to Danang with another boat. Curiously, despite the fact that the Norwegian-made vessels had been chosen in large part because of the plausible deniability they afforded, the Nasty was not shaping up to be very covert. Just as with the SOG C-123 aircraft, much of the sophisticated internal hardware, like radars, was American issue. So were the weapons mounted on deck. And while phony contracts were being drawn up showing that the boats were turned over to South Vietnamese possession for unilateral operations, they remained under U.S. Navy register.[21] "Theoretically, this boat would have been sanitized," said Captain Bruce Dunning, a U.S. Navy officer assigned to Danang. "However, one can refer to *Jane's Fighting Ships* and see that, in 1964, the United States Navy procured 13 Norwegian Nasty-class PTFs and that a certain number of them [were] later transferred for use in Southeast Asia."[22]

Such details aside, SOG was excited about its new boats. Not only did they have the range to wreak havoc along the entire North Vietnamese coast (the Swifts could only get as far as southern Ha Tinh Province), but their added capacity allowed them to carry triple the number of raiders onboard. Best of all, a Nasty could outrun anything in the North Vietnamese navy.

Five days later, the Naval Advisory Detachment had a chance to explore the Nasty's full potential. Its target was a coastal depot in Ha Tinh's Ky Anh District, near the scene of one of the failed March bridge missions. As the commandos arrived off Ky Anh, rubber boats went into the water. Previously, cross-beach raids had relied on stealth. Teams had been small, lightly armed, and ordered to avoid contact if possible. This was reflected in their main armament, such as flat-firing rocket pods with delayed timers that gave them time to escape.

But with the Nasty, cross-beach raids were an entirely different game. Teams were big, heavily armed, and looking for a fight. Instead of the flat-firing rockets—which often malfunctioned—they were equipped with recoilless rifles and conventional rocket launchers.[23] What these gave away in stealth, they made up in accuracy.

Storming the beach in a trio of rubber boats, twenty-six Biet Hai approached the combination storage facility and barracks. For ten minutes, they poured machine-gun fire and recoilless rifle rounds into the target. There was no return fire. With the depot in flames, they withdrew to the Nasty.[24]

SOG made quick plans for an encore. A fourth Nasty crew had returned from Subic on 24 June, and it was chosen to transport the team. The target this time was a Route 1 bridge all the way in Thanh Hoa Province, farther north than any previous mission. Emboldened by their added firepower, the SOG planners decided not to wait for optimal lunar conditions and instead strike during the moonlit phase.

On the night of 26 June, the commandos struck. Seven were assigned the demolition mission; another two dozen would provide security. Killing two guards, they set charges under the wooden bridge and activated pencil timers. They then backtracked toward the rubber boats, wiping out a four-man North Vietnamese patrol they encountered. Without suffering any casualties of their own, the commandos headed into the surf toward the Nasty.[25]

Figuring it had a winning formula, the Naval Advisory Detachment decided to stage an even bigger cross-beach raid. This one would involve two Nastys—one to transport the team, the other to act as escort. They would be paying a repeat visit to Dong Hoi, specifically the pumping station near the water reservoir just north of the town. Perhaps becoming overconfident, or perhaps because it perceived pressure from Washington to meet mission quotas, Danang decided to again strike under the light of the moon.

At midnight on 30 June, the two Nastys approached Dong Hoi. With PTF-6 waiting at a distance, rubber boats went over the side of PTF-5 and thirty commandos climbed in. Muffled outboards came alive as the Biet Hai raced for shore.

This time, the North Vietnamese were ready. Burned twice over the previous two weeks, Hanoi had its coastal security forces on heightened alert. This was especially true for Dong Hoi, which had been hit the previous December. As the commandos landed on the beach, they were greeted with a hail of tracers. PTF-5 saw the fiery streaks, moved closer to shore, and returned fire from its deck guns. They were joined by the Biet Hai, who struck back with their own weapons. Some of the commandos hauled 57mm recoilless rifles within sight of the pumping station and fired off eighteen rounds.[26]

Instead of withering, the North Vietnamese defenders pushed forward. Under pressure, the commandos retreated toward the beach, and confusion reigned as both sides traded automatic weapons fire, then engaged in hand-to-hand fighting. Fearing they would be left behind, the commandos who had hit the pumping station spiked their recoilless rifles with grenades and fled toward shore. In the end, twenty-eight managed to escape; two were left behind.[27]

The Naval Advisory Detachment spent little time mourning its losses. Two weeks later, this time during the moonless phase, it struck again. The darkness made little difference. When the team went ashore near the Ron River on the night of 15 July, the North Vietnamese were again waiting. The commandos withdraw before finishing their attack, again leaving two of their own behind.[28]

Clearly, the Tonkin Gulf was becoming increasingly perilous. As if to underscore the point, MACV received intelligence that ten Swatows were being deployed to Dong Hoi, and four more to the Gianh River naval base. Hanoi was rising to the maritime challenge.

12

TONKIN GULF

The Swift skipped across the waves, its crew scanning the waters off northern Quang Binh for the low silhouette of a fishing junk. Spying prey, the Chinese skipper circled close, then brought the Swift alongside his target. Barking orders, the crew herded the fishermen aboard and blindfolded them. As fast as it began, the LOKI snatch was over, and the Swift was heading south with its captives.

But it was not alone. Appearing on the horizon were two Swatow patrol boats. Reacting quickly, the skipper opened the throttle and threw the Swift into a series of evasive turns. Losing the Swatows in the night sea, the crew was back at Danang the following morning, 26 July 1964.[1]

While they had not been a factor earlier, the Swatows were suddenly beginning to make life difficult for the Naval Advisory Detachment. As SOG commander Colonel Clyde Russell pointed out, before July "the Vietnamese gave us no trouble with regard to chasing our boats with Swatows. We had access to the entire coast and could have done anything along that coast that was required." Of course, Russell was ignoring the fact that North Vietnamese shore defenders were routinely thwarting cross-beach missions, leaving SOG with few maritime options.[2]

Washington had little sympathy for delays. Worried about keeping his Op 34A program on schedule, the secretary of defense feared the "tempo of attack was not building up in consonance with improving capabilities."[3] Rather than continue to call off missions when there was danger of North Vietnamese opposition, McNamara asked his military advisers if it might make more sense to switch from cross-beach raids to standing offshore and bombarding coastal targets with ship-based heavy weapons.

McNamara's recommendation soon found its way to Saigon and the desk of the new MACV commander, General William C. Westmoreland. Briefed by SOG, Westmoreland replied that the U.S. Navy already was having 81mm mortars placed on the last two Nastys scheduled for delivery from Subic. He also diplomatically reminded the secretary that such missions were technically forbidden. The rules of engagement imposed by the Joint Chiefs stated that SOG boats could not fire into North Vietnam unless the North Vietnamese fired first.

Within hours, the entire essence of maritime operations was transformed.

From Washington came word that the restriction on offshore bombardment no longer stood. In response, on 30 July Westmoreland revised the Op 34A maritime schedule for August, increasing the number of missions by 283 percent over the July program and 566 percent over June. Nearly all of these would involve offshore bombardment.[4]

That very night the idea was put to the test. By that time, six torpedo boats—four Nastys and two gassers—had been delivered to SOG at Danang. The last two Nastys—the ones with 81mm mortars—were not yet ready, so it was decided to initiate the bombardment concept using 57mm recoilless rifles already on the decks of the existing six vessels.

Leaving Danang late that afternoon, four boats headed north. Just before midnight, they slowed off the coast of Thanh Hoa north of Vinh. Splitting up, two of the Nastys veered northwest toward the island of Hon Me. The other boats—one gasser and one Nasty—turned southwest toward the island of Hon Nieu. Both islands were significant because they held radar outposts used for detecting waterborne intruders.

Twenty minutes into the new day, 31 July, the two Nastys closed on Hon Me. The officer in command of the pair, Lieutenant Son, was considered the best of the Nasty skippers during their training stint at Subic. But before he could give the order to fire, a Swatow appeared from a cove on the island, guns ablaze. Bullets peppered the port bow of the lead Nasty, wounding four South Vietnamese, including Son.[5]

To illuminate the scene for their Swatow, the island defenders fired flares into the air. It proved a bad decision; the entire military outpost was now bathed in flickering light. Maneuvering away from the Swatow, the two Nastys rushed in and directed their weapons toward shore.

In less than twenty-five minutes, the attack was over. After destroying a gun emplacement and a number of buildings, both Nastys streaked south for safety. Although the crews did not know it, the Swatow was still giving chase, but the slower craft could not keep up and eventually broke off pursuit.[6]

At Hon Nieu, the attack was equally successful. Just after midnight on 31 July, the two SOG boats, under the overall command of Lieutenant Huyet, arrived undetected off the island. Moving closer, the crew could see a communications tower in the moonlight. Both vessels opened fire, scoring hits on the tower, then moved their sights to some nearby buildings. Machine guns rattled from shore but did no damage. Forty-five minutes later, the two boats headed south.

Back in Danang, the American advisers waited at the pier for the boats to come in. When Lieutenant Son's Nasty arrived, jaws dropped. "The whole port bow from the water-tight panel just below the bridge was shot up," recalled Lieutenant James Hawes, a SEAL training officer. "I'm surprised it made it back."[7]

Lieutenant Son was also in bad shape. Fragments from a 14.5mm round had hit him during the attack, shredding flesh from elbow to fingers. "We were sad to see him go," said Hawes. "He was a real gutsy guy."

SOG was not the only outfit running secret operations in the Tonkin Gulf that night. For years, special U.S. Navy patrols, code-named DESOTO, had been making regular runs off mainland Asia to eavesdrop on shore-based communications in China and North Korea. Typically the missions were carried out by a destroyer fitted with portable vans welded to the ship's deck. These vans were manned by communications technicians from the National Security Agency whose job was so sensitive that they were kept separate from the crew.

Until 1964, DESOTO patrols were authorized no closer than thirty-two kilometers from communist shores. But on 7 January, restrictions were eased, allowing the destroyers to within less than seven kilometers of the coastline. The following month, the first such close-range DESOTO mission was run along North Vietnam, with others scheduled for later in the spring.

Now that U.S. Navy electronics ships were frequenting the Tonkin Gulf, there was obvious opportunity for cooperation with SOG maritime operations. The first to recognize this was Admiral Ulysses S. G. Sharp, CINC-PAC, who in May suggested that SOG raids be coordinated "with the operation of a shipboard radar to reduce the possibility of North Vietnamese radar detection of the delivery vehicle." CINCPAC said that a U.S. destroyer could be made available for this purpose—an obvious reference to the DE-SOTO patrols—and also suggested a U.S. Navy ship could be used to vector SOG boats to their target.[8]

Given SOG's lack of success during the first half of 1964, the proposals looked attractive. But now General Westmoreland felt that coordination between the two would be too much trouble. The complex communications needed to coordinate SOG actions with a state-of-the-art destroyer, he argued, were beyond the capabilities of the South Vietnamese crews. In addition, close coordination between SOG and the DESOTO patrols would destroy the thin veneer of deniability surrounding covert operations against North Vietnam's coast.

For these reasons, in mid-July Westmoreland called for a total split between MACV and DESOTO. A MACV liaison officer, who had accompanied the most recent DESOTO patrol in March, would no longer be made available for the next one scheduled later that month. SOG, for its part, was told to adjust its operations so as not to interfere with the eavesdropping missions.[9]

While Westmoreland did not want his covert raids tainted by a U.S. Navy operation, he soon eased his calls for a total divorce. Provided it remained a one-way street, he was still more than willing to continue receiving DE-SOTO intelligence. Saigon was even prepared to request DESOTO to conduct specific missions that could benefit SOG. This is exactly what happened in late July when Westmoreland asked the U.S. Navy to focus its DESOTO coverage along Ha Tinh and Thanh Hoa Provinces, especially toward some of the radar outposts located on offshore islands. These radar stations, combined with Hanoi's recent move to shift some of its Swatows to southern ports, were of understandable concern to the SOG planners in Danang.

On 28 July, the destroyer *Maddox* set out from Taiwan to begin its scheduled DESOTO run. Three days later, the ship rendezvoused with a tanker in the Tonkin Gulf just east of the Demilitarized Zone. While refueling, the *Maddox* sighted two torpedo boats streaking south, followed half an hour later by two more. Although the crew did not know it at the time, they had seen SOG boats returning from the first offshore bombardment mission.

The *Maddox* planned to sail to sixteen points along the North Vietnamese coast ranging from the Demilitarized Zone north to the Chinese border, including the targets requested by Westmoreland. At each point the ship would stop and circle, picking up electronics signals before moving on to the next orbit.

For the next four days, the *Maddox* stuck to this schedule without incident. During the early hours of 2 August, however, things began to go sour. That morning, American intelligence picked up indications that Hanoi had moved additional Swatows to the vicinity of Hon Me and Hon Nieu—the two islands shelled by SOG two days earlier—and instructed them to prepare for battle. Warned of this, at 0354 hours Captain John Herrick, the DESOTO task group commander, ordered the *Maddox* farther out to sea to avoid a night confrontation.

Six hours later, after the North Vietnamese attack failed to materialize, the destroyer was back near the coast, this time north of Hon Me. Unknown to Herrick, CINCPAC and the Seventh Fleet were receiving further intelligence that the North Vietnamese were preparing to repulse a possible repeat raid on Hon Me.[10] To Hanoi, it made little difference if the encroaching foreign warship was a Nasty or a destroyer—both were a threat. That noon, it dispatched three Soviet-made gunboats toward the *Maddox*. Radioing in the clear, Herrick sent a message to the Seventh Fleet that his vessel was "being approached by high-speed craft with apparent intention of torpedo attack. Intend to open fire if necessary self defense."[11]

When the North Vietnamese boats had closed to less than ten thousand yards, the destroyer fired three shots across the bow of the lead vessel, which responded with a torpedo. The *Maddox* fired again, this time to kill, hitting the second boat just as it launched two torpedoes. Badly damaged, the boat limped home. Changing course just in time to evade the torpedoes, the destroyer was again attacked, this time by a boat that fired yet another torpedo as well as its 14.5mm machine guns. The bullets struck the *Maddox,* but the torpedo missed. As the boat passed astern, it was raked by gunfire, which killed the commander.

In twenty-two minutes, the battle was over. Breaking contact, the North Vietnamese vessels turned for shore with the *Maddox* in pursuit. Aircraft from the carrier *Ticonderoga* appeared on the scene, strafing the fleeing boats and sinking one that had been damaged earlier by the *Maddox.* The others escaped. Unfazed by the encounter, Admiral Thomas H. Moorer, the Pacific Fleet commander, ordered the *Maddox,* this time accompanied by another destroyer, the *Turner Joy,* to resume DESOTO coverage up the North Vietnamese coast.

Back at Danang, the Naval Advisory Detachment was eager to run its second offshore bombardment raid. During the afternoon of 3 August, one day after the attack on the *Maddox,* another four boats headed north. Arriving off southern Ha Tinh Province, they again split up, with two boats—a gasser and a Nasty—heading toward the Vinh Son radar station, while a single Nasty (the fourth boat, a gasser, had developed engine trouble) made a solo run toward a coastal security post on the Ron River.

At Vinh Son, the SOG boats fired 57mm rounds for twenty-five minutes, setting the radar ablaze. The Ron outpost, which had been the scene of an earlier failed cross-beach raid, got a similar 57mm hosing. With the outpost in flames, the Nasty raced south, easily outpacing a pursuing North Vietnamese patrol boat.

On the morning after this second offshore bombardment, the DESOTO task force was positioned off Thanh Hoa. Over the previous night there had been a long-distance debate as to whether the mission should continue. Captain Herrick, for his part, was in favor of terminating the patrol. Admiral Roy Johnson, the new Seventh Fleet commander, agreed. Admiral Moorer, however, was against cancellation. The DESOTO mission, reasoned Moorer, could act as a decoy for SOG bombardment raids farther south. That SOG was now being used as a rationale for DESOTO was a surprising twist, especially given MACV's earlier feelings about distancing the two operations.

In the end, Moorer's views carried the day and the patrol steamed north. Late that afternoon, however, U.S. intelligence again began to receive indications of an impending North Vietnamese attack. Over the next few hours, during a period of inclement weather, edgy crews in the *Maddox* and *Turner Joy* detected—and engaged—what they believed were no less than four hostile gunboats. Some sixteen carrier-based aircraft responded to the perceived attack, though no North Vietnamese vessels were ever spotted.[12]

Since the attacks were now front-page news, SOG assumed the worst—that an investigation would expose its operations against the north. It was also worried that Hanoi would launch reprisal attacks against Danang. To avert this, a flash message was sent to the Naval Advisory Detachment: hide the eight torpedo boats until further notice.

Carrying out these orders, Lieutenant Hawes, the SEAL training officer, led the Nastys and two gassers out of the Danang docks on 5 August. Turning south, they traveled 480 kilometers to the more discrete setting of Cam Ranh Bay. Far from the sprawling logistical center of later years, at that early date Cam Ranh was home to a junk force training base and little else. Ordering water buffalo steaks and Ba Muoi Ba beer, Hawes and the South Vietnamese crews settled back to ride out the unfolding crisis.[13]

Reverberations from the Tonkin Gulf skirmishes quickly circled the globe. Hanoi denied the second attack took place while at the same time publicly blasting Washington for the multiple commando raids being conducted along its coast. It could not have come at a worse time. The Johnson administration had just made the first of several secret diplomatic attempts to convince the North Vietnamese to stop warring on South Vietnam, using the chief Canadian delegate to the International Control Commission (ICC, the implementing body for the Geneva Accords), J. Blair Seaborn, to open a channel to Hanoi. After the Tonkin Gulf incident, as it came to be called, the U.S. State Department sent Seaborn a cable instructing him to tell the North Vietnamese that "neither the *Maddox* [nor] any other destroyer was in any way associated with any attack on the DRV islands." This was the first of several carefully worded official statements aimed at separating Op 34A and DESOTO and at the same time leaving the impression that the United States was not involved in the covert operations.[14]

Among the president's advisers, however, there was little disagreement that Hanoi was bound to see the covert raids and the DESOTO mission as linked. The State Department noted that "the action against the *Maddox* took place within the same 60-hour period as an OPLAN 34A harassing action. . . . It seems likely that the North Vietnamese and perhaps the Chicoms [Chinese communists] have assumed that the destroyer was part of this operation."[15]

President Johnson was less sanguine. American warships, after all, had been attacked in international waters, an affront that begged a forceful response. "Do they want a war by attacking our ships in the middle of the Gulf of Tonkin?" he asked CIA director McCone on the evening of 4 August.

Of course, McCone knew about the SOG bombardment operations earlier in the week, and he assumed Hanoi connected them with the DESOTO patrol. "No," answered the CIA chief truthfully. "The North Vietnamese are reacting defensively to our attacks on their off-shore islands. They are responding out of pride and on the basis of defense considerations."[16]

Hanoi's perception was only part of the equation. International opinion mattered much more, and Johnson was concerned about the publicity shining on his covert program. The president immediately halted all Op 34A operations "in order to avoid sending confusing signals associated with recent events in the Gulf of Tonkin."[17]

But there was no such candor two days later when Secretary of Defense McNamara and Secretary of State Rusk were called before a secret joint session of the Senate Foreign Relations Committee and the Armed Services Committee. Taking the offense, McNamara opened by explaining the attacks on the American destroyers were not isolated events but rather "part and parcel of a continuing communist drive to conquer South Vietnam."[18] He made no mention of the SOG raids.

Senator Wayne Morse, the Oregon Democrat, immediately challenged this account. He specifically mentioned the raids, correctly noting that Hanoi could only have concluded that the maritime attacks and the DESOTO patrols were linked. "I think we are kidding the world if you try to give the impression that when the South Vietnamese naval boats bombarded two islands a short distance off the coast of North Vietnam we were not implicated," he chided McNamara.[19]

The senator's account, though more accurate than that offered by the secretary, had a fatal flaw. Like the other committee members, Morse had not been officially briefed about SOG's existence. His limited knowledge of the raids came from sketchy accusations made over North Vietnamese radio. Hanoi, also unaware of the details behind SOG, had incorrectly assumed the raids were conducted by South Vietnamese naval units. Morse simply repeated this assumption, charging the South Vietnamese navy with complicity.

Morse's imprecision gave McNamara his opening. Looking to shift the finger of blame squarely onto Saigon, the secretary suggested that the raids were probably part of a South Vietnamese anti-infiltration operation being conducted by their fleet of coastal junks. The diversion worked. Taking up this line of questioning, the senators asked what role, if any, the U.S. Navy had with junk operations. "Our naval personnel afford no cover whatsoever," said the secretary. "Our naval personnel do not participate in junk operations." McNamara was being truthful on this last issue, though he knew full well that it was SOG Nasty boats—not South Vietnamese junks—that had done the deeds in question.

The perfidy continued later that day during debate on the Senate floor. George McGovern, Democrat from South Dakota, again called attention to the raids, only to be told by his colleague J. William Fulbright, chairman of the Senate Foreign Relations Committee, that the Pentagon assured him "our boats did not convoy or support or back up any South Vietnamese naval vessels." Fulbright also repeated the White House bromide that the DESOTO patrol was "entirely unconnected or unassociated with any coastal forays the South Vietnamese themselves may have conducted."[20]

The fig leaf of plausible deniability had served the administration in this case, but it was scant cover. Here was a covert action that was barely covert: Hanoi was more than willing to tell the world about the attacks, and it took either a fool or an innocent to believe that the U.S. government knew nothing about the raids.

Despite this, congressional reaction fell in behind the president's men, and the question of secret operations was overtaken by the bigger issue of punishing North Vietnam for its blatant attacks on American warships in international waters. On 7 August, one day after McNamara's appearance on Capitol Hill, the Senate passed the Tonkin Gulf Resolution by a margin of 88 to 2. Senator Morse was one of the dissenters. The House of Representatives passed it unanimously. President Johnson, read the resolution, was now authorized to take "all necessary steps, including the use of armed force" to assist South Vietnam.

SOG, conceived as a means of showing American resolve short of war, had instead helped precipitate one.

13

MARITIME OPTIONS

President Johnson emerged from the Tonkin Gulf incident with a stronger mandate to pressure Hanoi, but there were no coattails for SOG to ride. For the present, missions into North Vietnam were on hold as disagreement over the continued role of covert operations roiled the administration. The halt itself was a bone of contention. If there had been any doubt about whose hand was behind the raids before the Tonkin Gulf incident, surely there was none now.

For this reason, some administration officials—even those who had questioned the program only a few months earlier—argued that there should be no break in the Op 34A operations. In Saigon, Ambassador Maxwell Taylor said, "It is my conviction that we must resume these operations and continue the pressure on North Vietnam as soon as possible, leaving no impression that we or the South Vietnamese have been deterred from our operations because of the Tonkin Gulf incidents."[1]

In the State Department, sentiment was also against halting the program. "We believe that present Oplan 34A activities are beginning to rattle Hanoi and [the] *Maddox* incident is directly related to their effort to resist these activities," wrote Secretary of State Dean Rusk. "We have no intention of yielding to pressure." Assistant Secretary of State for Far Eastern Affairs William Bundy went even further, arguing that the incident radically changed the situation in South Vietnam. He argued that "34A operations could be overtly acknowledged and justified by the GVN [government of Vietnam]. Marine [maritime] operations could be strongly defended on the basis of continued DRV sea infiltration, and successes should be publicized."[2]

The Joint Chiefs summed up the military view by pointing out that the 34A operational timetable was being thrown off track by the mission halt. They argued that if the program was to have any hope of attaining its goals, maritime operations would have to be resumed by August 10, and air operations, which depended on the moon phases, should begin one week later.[3]

But the administration dithered, and for the time being the Naval Advisory Detachment kept a low profile. After a decent interval of five days, its fleet of Nastys and gassers returned from Cam Ranh Bay to Danang. There they were joined by two more Nastys, these being the first to be outfitted with 81mm mortars. The ensuing weeks were spent testing these boats, as well as other newly arrived equipment like the T-14 Swimmer Propulsion Unit—a James Bond–type contraption used for pulling frogmen through the water—and 106mm recoilless rifles, to be fitted atop the Nastys for reaching shore targets beyond the range of 81mm mortars.[4]

After a full two months, the operational stand-down was rescinded. Just as before, bombardment missions were to remain the focus. But things were not the same. The earlier concept of bombardment attacks was shown to be largely ineffective. For one thing, it put the Nastys within range of shore fire. Even if the boats could avoid North Vietnamese guns, the Nasty's weaponry could reach only a limited number of lucrative targets.

Actually, none of this really mattered much anymore. With the escalation of hostilities following the Tonkin Gulf incident, MACV now had a much more effective means of punishing Hanoi—air strikes. On 5 August, in a tit-for-tat retaliation for the gunboat attack on the DESOTO patrol, the U.S. Navy flew fifty-nine sorties against five North Vietnamese naval bases, including the Swatow port at Quang Khe. A total of eight torpedo boats were destroyed and another nineteen damaged in a single day's work.[5] By contrast, maritime commandos had been able to destroy just two of the Quang Khe Swatows in four attempts over two years.

While airpower clearly held greater promise, for the time being Nasty bombardments resumed on a select basis and were set to continue into early 1965.[6] But following a second American air strike against North Vietnam that February, this one in reprisal for a mortar attack on a South Vietnamese air base, covert maritime bombardments looked more passé than ever. Forced to search for a better way to employ its resources, the Naval Advisory Detachment scrounged for alternatives. Its options were limited. Cross-beach raids had minimal returns and high risk. Scuba missions, too, were dangerous and had been abandoned the previous spring.[7]

The LOKI junk capture missions were the only bright spot. During the second half of 1964, a series of LOKI snatches had been successfully performed by the Chinese-skippered Swift boats. The concept had changed little since its inception: captured fishermen were blindfolded and taken to Cu Lao Cham for a couple of days, then released to return north with gifts. The only difference was that, instead of towing the junks south, they were now booby-trapped and left behind.[8]

At the end of 1964, the Nationalist Chinese finished their contracts and left Vietnam. By that time, there were enough experienced South Vietnamese crews on hand to make further foreign skippers unnecessary. There were also more than enough Nastys to handle all northern operations; the less-capable Swifts, as a result, were relegated to logistical work around Danang.[9]

Picking up the LOKI assignment where the Swifts left off, Nastys were soon at work ferrying fishermen down to Cu Lao Cham. Deeming the operation a success, the Naval Advisory Detachment began to consider variations on the same theme. In the spring of 1965, it authorized LANCE missions, which involved capturing North Vietnamese seamen from vessels other than junks. It even began to flirt with the idea of seizing a Swatow and its crew.

Until this time, the emphasis had been on snatching North Vietnamese for the purpose of interrogation, with the destruction of the northern fishing fleet being an added bonus. It suddenly occurred to SOG that, given the firepower available on two or three Nastys, it should switch its focus to interdicting North Vietnamese maritime traffic and make the interrogations secondary. The idea was passed back to the Joint Chiefs, who granted approval in July. Under this concept of maritime interdiction—MINT for short—Nastys were authorized to make wide coastal sweeps, stopping and searching any small-tonnage vessels encountered on the way. Innocent boats were to be set free; those carrying military cargo would be sunk and their crews taken to Cu Lao Cham.[10]

MINT proved profitable. Together with the ongoing LOKI fishing junk snatches, half of all attempted missions during the first four months were considered successful. These statistics led MACV in September to rank maritime operations as the "most productive of all 34A programs" and the only one worth stepping up.[11]

Hanoi's reaction seemed to verify SOG's optimism. That same month, intelligence sources reported that North Vietnam had heightened its coastal alert to such a level that fishermen were often fired on when they returned home with their catches.[12]

Not everybody, however, was happy with the newfound emphasis on MINT raids and LOKI snatches. Both of these missions were conducted by the Nasty boat crews themselves, meaning that the six Biet Hai action teams languishing in Danang had been without hazardous duty pay since the summer of 1964. To partially compensate, the Naval Advisory Detachment began rotating the Biet Hai as gunners aboard the Nastys.

With the success of its waterborne snatches, SOG decided to try its hand at kidnapping ashore. This was especially timely because the intelligence haul from kidnapped fishermen was becoming repetitive; shore snatches, by contrast, might open the door to sources other than those from the limited world of fishing crews. Code-named SWALLOW, the first shore kidnaps were scheduled for June 1965. As in the earlier cross-beach missions, an action team would land by rubber boat and look for anybody unlucky enough to be walking along the beach. If any were found, they would be bundled back to the Nasty and taken down to Cu Lao Cham.

This was easier said than done. Of eighteen attempts during the second half of 1965, most were aborted. Unfazed, SOG persisted into early 1966. On 22 February, Team ATHENA tried its hand at a shore snatch. Stopping off the Quang Binh coast, two rubber boats were dropped overboard. Using a formula dating back to the cross-beach raids of March 1964, they stopped at the surf line, and two combat swimmers slipped into the water. With silenced Thompson submachine guns and infrared metascopes in hand, they headed to shore for a beach reconnaissance.

Immediately, things went wrong. Peering into the darkness, the two commandos saw a group of fishermen staring back at them. Startled, they turned on their heels for the rubber boats. But while they had easily been able to ride the waves into shore, going back out through the high surf proved impossible. Beaten back on every attempt, the exhausted pair had no choice but to run across the beach and hide in the coastal jungle. By morning, militia were scouring the brush, capturing them two days later.[13]

Problems continued into spring. During May, Team ROMULUS returned to the shores of Quang Binh in search of a prisoner. But like the earlier ATHENA snatch, the team was surprised on the beach, and beat a hasty retreat. Two commandos were left behind and eventually captured.[14]

That June, it was Team CANCER's turn to try. As the Biet Hai's only ethnic Nung team, CANCER stood apart in the Coastal Security Service. Many of its members had been born in China, and several had difficulty speaking the Vietnamese language. This had raised eyebrows within the South Vietnamese military, which questioned the need to keep a team of non-Vietnamese commandos under arms. For the time, however, CANCER's solid performance allayed Saigon's fears.

On 7 June, four combat swimmers from CANCER paddled their rubber boats toward the shore near Nghi Son, an island off the coast of southernmost Thanh Hoa Province. Dividing into pairs, they disappeared into the blackness.[15] Hours passed as the remaining Nung commandos waited for a metascope flash from shore. Finally, with dawn about to break, they were forced to retreat to their mother ship.

In Danang, Major Bernard Trainor, the Naval Advisory Detachment's chief of operations and training, reported the missing CANCER swimmers to SOG headquarters. Referring to the pressure from Saigon to dissolve the team, his message concluded on a sarcastic note: "I think we may have found a solution to the Nung problem." Though SOG headquarters did not appreciate the humor, it disbanded CANCER a few weeks later.[16]

As it turned out, CANCER was lucky to get anywhere near the North Vietnamese coast. Unwilling to let SOG act with impunity, Hanoi was becoming increasingly determined to stop the Nastys before they reached their targets. Sometimes they responded with gunboats; during 1966, six such naval engagements were recorded.[17]

Of greater concern to SOG was the use of coastal gun batteries. In late 1964, Hanoi ordered its artillery forces to begin deploying units along the beach and to strategic islands. Special attention was given to Deo Ngang, the coastal gorge north of the Ron ferry that Saigon had used as a clandestine infiltration point since 1962. Employing one battalion from the 165th Artillery Regiment, guns were placed around Deo Ngang as part of a coordinated fan reaching out to sea. For several months they waited, but no Nastys came. Finally, on the night of 5 January 1965, a trio of SOG boats wandered into the trap.

Waiting until the Nastys were within two kilometers of their 85mm guns, the North Vietnamese let loose a ferocious barrage. Luckily for the Nastys, the North Vietnamese gunners were new at their jobs. After the first volley, recoil from the firing pushed several of the heavy artillery pieces back into the soft earth, causing them to fall over and collapse some of the trenches. Communications lines were severed, turning the coordinated ambush into a mismanaged embarrassment. The three Nastys easily escaped, unaware of the concerted effort that had gone into the abortive ambush.[18]

Despite this early failure, coastal gunfire became more frequent in the months that followed. By 1966, there were thirty-nine instances of SOG boats being attacked by shore-based artillery. While no boats were sunk, in some cases Nastys were driven off by accurate fire reaching as far as sixteen kilometers out to sea.[19]

Coastal guns and patrol boats were not the only way Hanoi was countering SOG at sea. By far the most bizarre engagement took place on 7 March 1966 when three Nastys were returning from Thanh Hoa. Over the previous month, there had been radar evidence that slow-moving North Vietnamese aircraft were trying to intercept them over the gulf. None of the attempts to date had been successful. That night would be different.

As the three boats raced across the water, a spotlight suddenly danced across their wake. As it moved closer, the two rear boats in the formation veered to the sides. The lead boat, however, could not shake the light. Finally, the Nasty was bathed in its glare. Overhead, a Soviet-made An-2 Colt biplane dropped bombs from makeshift wing pylons, breaching the boat's hull and stopping it dead in the water.

By chance, a U.S. Navy patrol was off Thanh Hoa that night and was following the engagement on its radio and radar scope. Just after the An-2 engaged the Nasty, one of the patrolling vessels, a guided missile frigate, fired on the plane. The plodding Antonov dropped from the sky.[20]

The thought of SOG being stymied by an antiquated biplane would have been comical had it not been so successful. As it was, the Naval Advisory Detachment was seriously shaken by the incident and scrambled to develop countermeasures. Exercises were held with a Danang-based U.S. Marine Corps helicopter unit, with the choppers using spotlights and playing the role of aggressors. Evasive maneuvers were practiced, and there was some thought given to outfitting the Nastys with Redeye surface-to-air missiles.[21] In the end, the panic proved unnecessary; Hanoi kept its biplanes confined to base, apparently figuring that further bombings were not worth the loss of another aircraft.

Sometimes the sharp edge of nature was just as dangerous to the Nastys as were the North Vietnamese. At midnight on 20 November 1965, three Nastys carrying a cross-beach team ran into bad weather off the coast of Ha Tinh Province. A steady rain fell, and thick fog clung to the waves; there was no choice but to abort the mission.

Skippering the middle Nasty was Hiep Hoa Trinh. Starting his military career as a frogman, Trinh had transferred to the Coastal Security Service in 1964 as the original case officer for VEGA, the action team recruited from the navy. After a year in that slot, he transferred again, this time to the Coastal Security Service boat crews. Six months later he was in command of his own Nasty.

The Nastys ran with no lights, and in the rain and fog the sea was jet-black in all directions. Unable to see, Trinh was forced to rely on the boat's temperamental radar, which was not working well in the rain.

Without warning, the Nasty was thrown violently from the sea. Trinh hit the console; the rest of the crew spilled across the deck. The boat started taking on water. Regaining his senses, Trinh looked out the front window. They had run into a sandbar, and the Nasty was settling onto its side.

Crawling to the upper edge of the sinking boat were the members of VEGA, Trinh's old team. Nobody was seriously injured, but they knew they were in grave trouble. The boat was hopelessly grounded, and from the sound of nearby breakers the commandos knew they were close to shore. Worse, neither of the other Nastys was answering distress calls over the radio.

Trinh tried to get an approximate fix on their location. The sandbar ran in a long finger toward shore, so two of the VEGA commandos were chosen to conduct a beach reconnaissance. As the pair of Biet Hai departed, the rest of the crew waited impatiently on the crippled boat.

Less than an hour later, the VEGA members ran back to the Nasty. North Vietnamese troops were on the beach, they reported, and were searching with flashlights. The news was made worse by the improving weather. The rain had stopped and the fog was lifting, bringing the strip of shoreline into partial focus. Trinh saw the lights reported by his men, but they were much too dim to be flashlights. They were probably fireflies, he decided.

With daylight fast approaching, the crew's collective anxiety was nearing the breaking point. Finally, at 0400 hours, their radio crackled to life—the lead boat had returned and was in the area. When the Nasty came into view, Trinh and his men jumped into the sea and swam for a rendezvous. Exhausted, they sprawled across the deck for the trip back to Danang. Before they arrived, American jets raced north and bombed the grounded Nasty into oblivion.[22]

On 22 May 1966, a similar situation unfolded near Hon Me, the island garrison off Thanh Hoa that had figured during the very first Nasty bombardment in July 1964. This time, three Nastys were to land a combined commando team drawn from VEGA and NIMBUS for a snatch.[23]

Without incident, the trio of Nastys neared the island, and rubber boats went into the water. From the middle vessel, Major Truong Duy Tai supervised. As the overall Coastal Security Service commander for Biet Hai teams, Tai was technically too senior to go north. For morale purposes, though, his superiors frequently waived this restriction and let him escort his commandos to the target area.[24]

Before the Biet Hai could push off from the Nastys, geysers exploded all around. Heavy weapons fire poured from Hon Me, bracketing the boats on all sides. Scrambling, the commandos jumped aboard their mother ships. The Nastys then turned broadside to deliver return fire. In the ensuing battle between cannons and mortars, the Nastys were outgunned and outranged. Breaking contact, the three ships turned south.

They did not get far. In the confusion, the lead boat veered toward a shallow reef. Plowing into the coral heads, the vessel ground to a halt. Throwing the Napiers into reverse, the skipper tried to disengage his vessel, but the Nasty refused to budge.

On Hon Me, the North Vietnamese gunners were blind under the moonless sky. But their ears told them the Biet Hai boats were still offshore. Correctly concluding that one was grounded, they kept up a steady—though inaccurate—rain of shells. On the receiving end, a second Nasty ignored the coastal fire while maneuvering close to its crippled mate. But without charts, sonar, or lights, the skipper had little to go by. Soon he, too, was wedged atop the reef.

With two crews now in need of a rescue, the third Nasty approached the coral. Looking to avoid the same fate at all costs, the skipper stopped well short of the reef. Stripping their boats of classified communications gear, the stranded crewmen, including Major Tai, then used rubber boats to paddle to the third vessel. Airstrikes were called the next morning to destroy the evidence.[25]

Sometimes the Nastys were their own worst enemy. On 16 June, a pack of SOG boats raced up the Ha Tinh coastline on a MINT patrol. Getting a radar return on two targets, they moved in for the kill. Just before they had a chance to board the suspect vessels, however, North Vietnamese gunners opened up from shore. Spotlights snapped on, and the Nastys were suddenly bathed in an unwelcome glare.

Speeding away in line formation, the boat crews suspected an ambush. Spooked, they were on alert for any marauding Swatows that might be part of the trap. Their vigil for North Vietnamese gunboats, however, was hampered by the lack of moonlight. Worse, the Nastys themselves were painted black and ran without lights, making identification of friend and foe largely a matter of luck.

That night, everything went wrong. As the lead boat throttled into an evasive turn, the Nasty behind picked up a radar signal for what it thought was an approaching Swatow. Panicking, the skipper ordered his crew to open fire. Deck cannons went into action, smashing the target. Frantic radio calls quickly informed them of their error, but by then it was too late.

Rushing to the scene, the third Nasty picked its way through the flotsam. Survivors were plucked to safety, and most of the bodies, including that of the skipper, were retrieved. During the return trip to Danang, tempers remained high. By the time they got to dock, those from the sunken ship wanted revenge. Naval Advisory Detachment advisers were forced to intervene, bundling the guilty skipper aboard a flight to Saigon.[26]

In the end, it was not friendly fire or coral reefs or even the North Vietnamese military that proved the biggest threat to SOG maritime operations. It was the Pentagon. In October 1966, the U.S. Navy was authorized to initiate Operation SEA DRAGON. According to the concept, an armada of up to four destroyers and one cruiser would prowl the North Vietnamese coast. Targets—shipping, coastal batteries, radar sites—would be selected by carrier-based aircraft, which would then pass them to the destroyers for immediate interdiction.

During the time MINT operations were in vogue, the Nastys had achieved respectable numbers. In all of 1965, for example, a total of fifty-two MINT patrols were launched, accounting for over fifty junks sunk and nineteen others damaged, including three patrol boats. By the following year, some 106 missions were launched, during which eighty-six North Vietnamese vessels were destroyed and sixteen more damaged.[27]

SEA DRAGON, however, made SOG look impotent. On a good day, an armada of destroyers could sink what the Naval Advisory Detachment could only hope to do over the course of several months. As with so much else in the SOG agenda, the escalating war had given President Johnson more effective overt means that eclipsed his earlier covert options. As the war changed, Danang was left scrambling for relevance.

14

FRUSTRATION SYNDROME

On 20 January 1965, a gray C-123 cut across the moonlit sky of western Lai Chau Province. Circling north of Dien Bien Phu, the Chinese crew spotted the prearranged pattern of flame pots glowing from the forest below. Signaling the rear cabin, four Vietnamese paratroopers stepped off the ramp, static lines jerking open their canopies. The C-123 then banked toward Laos for the return trip to Danang.[1]

These latest commandos—SOG's first for 1965—were reinforcements for REMUS, the agent team with the longest and most successful history. Perhaps more than any other team, REMUS mirrored SOG's evolving mission, which in turn reflected the escalation of the Vietnam conflict. When it had first infiltrated in April 1962, the insurgency in South Vietnam was still only simmering. The civil war in neighboring Laos, by contrast, was a serious foreign policy crisis for the Kennedy administration. With Laos in mind, it made sense to plant an intelligence-gathering team near Dien Bien Phu, where the North Vietnamese had a rear base for troops heading into northern Laos. REMUS's ethnic Tai composition also gave the agents the potential for forging contacts with the local populace.

By early 1963, a weak international settlement had given Laos the facade of a neutral tripartite government. Below the surface, however, North Vietnam was intervening on behalf of communist guerrillas in the countryside. This violation was compounded by Hanoi's apparent hand in stoking South Vietnam's insurgency. Doubly frustrated, Washington groped for ways to make Hanoi feel the pinch on the home front. Suddenly REMUS found its mission switched from intelligence collection to sabotage.

Because REMUS had neither the equipment nor the expertise to handle such missions, two specially trained sabotage agents were inserted by parachute on 10 August 1963. Both men were ethnic Tai, which allowed REMUS to expand its capabilities while keeping ethnic integrity, and thus its potential to interact with locals. Three months later, the augmentation team reported that it mined the main route southwest of Dien Bien Phu leading into Laos.

After SOG took over the team in January 1964, sabotage remained the focus of Oplan 34A. So prominent was this mission, in fact, that the CIA's earlier sensitivity to the ethnic composition of the teams fell by the wayside.

When the next three REMUS reinforcements were parachuted in on 23 April, all were ethnic Muong, a hill tribe minority, but not one indigenous to western Lai Chau.

Just as it had during the CIA's tenure, SOG's sabotage agenda seemed to pay dividends. In August, REMUS claimed to have blown up two bridges on the north side of the Dien Bien Phu valley. Satisfied by these results, SOG dropped four more agents to the team in October. Like the previous reinforcements, three of the four were Muong from outside of Lai Chau.

REMUS's two downed bridges were the best results of any long-term team in 1964. But they were hardly noticed as President Johnson, Tonkin Gulf Resolution in hand, escalated the pressure on Hanoi with air strikes and an increasing American ground presence in South Vietnam. Under pressure to make a bigger impact, SOG spent the final weeks of the year considering ways to give its teams sharper teeth. The solution: arm the commandos with rockets.

The idea of outfitting SOG commandos with rockets was not new; maritime teams had been using them since 1963 without much success. This time, SOG intended to use larger, 4.5-inch projectiles. A light fiberglass, disposable launcher was specially designed and sent to South Vietnam for testing. The SOG instructors at Long Thanh found the launcher to be too cumbersome and had better luck using sandbags to prop up the rockets in their cardboard packing tubes. Hooked to a six-volt battery, the missiles had satisfactory accuracy against big targets over four kilometers away.

After familiarizing a pilot team of nine agents on the system, the group was ready for deployment in January 1965. All its members were ethnic Vietnamese lowlanders, and all were slated to augment REMUS. This marked a significant turning point in the program. Previously, historical animosity against ethnic Vietnamese lowlanders had been a key motivating factor for SOG's hill tribe agents; both SOG and the CIA had actively encouraged such hatred. Now SOG was reversing itself and expecting these same hill tribesmen to welcome ethnic Vietnamese into their midst.

Their target would be the Dien Bien Phu airfield, then being used as a forward base by the North Vietnamese air force. On 20 January, four of the rocket-trained saboteurs parachuted to REMUS; the remaining five had balked before boarding the aircraft, feigning illness. Word soon came back to Saigon that of the four new commandos on the ground, one had broken a leg and another died from a fractured skull.[2] The two surviving agents, together with their cargo of rockets and batteries, joined the rest of REMUS, walked to the northern edge of Dien Bien Phu, and fired into the valley below. They reported destroying a handful of aircraft, a claim corroborated when American aerial reconnaissance showed damaged planes on the tarmac.[3]

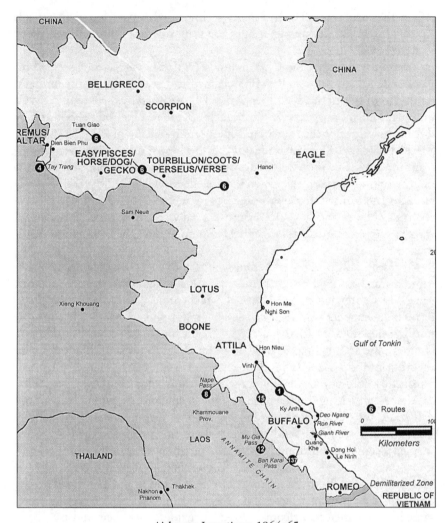

Airborne Insertions, 1964–65

Following the airport attack, SOG hailed REMUS as the best of the long-term teams. Yet there was growing sentiment inside the Pentagon that SOG's physical harassment campaign was not living up to expectations. The first signs of a full-scale reevaluation came during the second week of March, when the U.S. Army chief of staff, General Harold K. Johnson, made a fact-finding tour to South Vietnam. Johnson's posttrip assessment made no secret of his disappointment with the scope and tempo of SOG's activities.[4]

Such criticism was understandable. Since the Tonkin Gulf incident, SOG operations—especially those involving airborne teams—were barely moving forward. Only four long-term teams had been inserted over the previous six months, far short of the breakneck pace established by the CIA in 1963.[5] In fact, if the reinforcements to teams previously established by the CIA were excluded, SOG had managed to infiltrate just one new long-term team since taking over in January 1964.

In accepting the army chief of staff's findings, President Johnson approved an escalation in SOG operations. CINCPAC was ordered to present concrete proposals, and on 27 March it responded with three policy recommendations. First, long-term teams were to expand activities to include support for resistance operations, intelligence gathering, guerrilla warfare, and escape nets for downed American pilots. Second, submarines were to be used to infiltrate agents. And third, SOG's modified C-123s were to be replaced by more sophisticated C-130 transports. While the Joint Chiefs approved the three proposals on 29 March, the State Department in June vetoed all but the first idea.[6]

Given the green light to expand northern agent operations, SOG planned to tackle a wider array of unconventional activities, even though past performances had shown that the teams were hard-pressed to accomplish even a single task. Clearly there was some underlying confusion within the Pentagon regarding just what its SOG assets could or should do. It was, in the words of U.S. Navy Captain Bruce B. Dunning, a senior SACSA official, the first sign of a "frustration syndrome." Dunning traced the problem to a lack of specific goals. "I am not convinced," he concluded, "that the real objectives of this program were adequately spelled out by Washington and that the program was backed by a really well-thought-out concept."[7]

Perhaps nothing was more confusing than the rebirth of the resistance effort. First raised by Kennedy in 1961, the idea had always hovered around the periphery of CIA contingency plans. In 1963, the agency had even taken limited steps toward forming a resistance movement inside North Vietnam with Team EASY acting as cadre. But that went almost nowhere.

When SOG took over, the resistance concept received an initial boost. According to the original January 1964 charter, one of its key objectives was to build organized resistance groups inside North Vietnam under the mantle of a "liberation party."[8] To fulfill this ambiguously worded mandate, the notional SSPL kept up the resistance facade over the airwaves and through leaflets. On a more substantive basis, Team EASY, the quasi-resistance unit inherited from the CIA, contacted relatives that January, handed out two rifles to local recruits in June, and received six more agent reinforcements in July. Apart from these minimal actions, however, Washington—particularly the State Department— was unwilling to allow SOG to make more serious efforts.[9]

Foggy Bottom's rejection of a wider resistance plan sprung from its conventional diplomatic mind-set. Washington did not advocate overthrowing Ho Chi Minh, State Department policy makers reasoned, so a resistance network theoretically aimed at displacing him flew in the face of American objectives. Further opposition to the idea came on the grounds that support for a resistance movement entailed a moral obligation for prolonged and consistent assistance from Washington, assistance that could not be guaranteed if resupply overflights were suddenly halted. This second objection held particular resonance following events in Laos two years earlier. At that time, members of the U.S. Army Special Forces had built a guerrilla network of hill tribe partisans on the Bolovens Plateau in southern Laos. When the Geneva Accords were signed, however, they had been forced to quickly vacate Laos and leave their guerrillas out on a limb.[10]

But as much as the State Department loathed the idea of a resistance movement, SOG tried hard to show the Pentagon that there was merit in the concept. Colonel Russell, the SOG commander, was adamant that early establishment of resistance cells inside North Vietnam would have had a devastating effect on Hanoi:

> One of my biggest disappointments was that we could not start a [resistance movement] in North Vietnam. I feel that had we been able to do that, get it started in 1964, . . . we could have had a counter organization for the NLF [the Viet Cong]. . . . I am quite confident we could have quite a guerrilla effort going in [North Vietnam] today [1969] and it would have put us in a real good position from a bargaining standpoint. I can't understand why, as a nation, we take such a dim view of guerrilla warfare that we run and yet it's one of the best operations that the communists have been running against us.[11]

Defense Department supporters of the resistance movement concept made no secret of their belief that harassment operations in and of themselves were never going to be effective. In fact, since 1963, those involved with planning SOG's initial agenda conceded that North Vietnam, which was 90 percent underdeveloped, was not susceptible to economic ruin from raids alone. The country simply did not have the quantity or quality of sabotage targets that would hinder planned economic development to more than a limited degree.[12] And even if SOG had found some factory or other site whose loss might have caused severe economic discomfort, it was expressly forbidden from hitting well-defended targets so as not to provoke military intervention by China.[13]

SOG planners also noted that full-fledged unconventional warfare inside

North Vietnam would not be possible without some form of cooperation from the native populace. In Mao Tse-tung's famous analogy, guerrillas had to operate like fish in the sea, but SOG's agents were more like fish out of water. Unconventional operations, SOG reasoned, could not be developed in a short time for immediate effect; they needed an indigenous base of support, which could only be realized over the longer term. By building indigenous support through a resistance movement, other types of unconventional warfare operations—which could put real pressure on Hanoi—then became possible.[14]

Another argument was that SOG's recruitment efforts were suffering because no resistance was permitted. There were plenty of anticommunist hill tribe leaders willing to return north and contact people who they felt certain were still loyal to them. However, they were prepared to do this only if given some assurance that they would be permitted to organize a resistance movement with the ultimate goal of creating an autonomous area inside North Vietnam. When no such guarantee was forthcoming, the leaders scoffed at the idea of going north themselves. Worse, they began retaining their smarter personnel and family members in the south, unwilling to nominate them for one-way road-watch or sabotage missions.[15]

Finally, SOG claimed that it never really entertained the thought of overthrowing the North Vietnamese government, making State Department concerns about the fall of Ho Chi Minh moot. Rather than backing an upheaval against Hanoi, said one SOG officer, planners merely wanted to "create the impression in North Vietnam that the dissidents in North Vietnam were doing so."[16]

As Colonel John K. Singlaub, a future SOG commander, pointed out: "The purpose of SOG was to permit the government to pressure the enemy outside official public pronouncements of policy toward North Vietnam. . . . But with constraints tied to overt policy, this subvert[ed] the original purpose and made the mission more difficult to accomplish."[17]

This reasoning must have had some effect, because during the summer of 1965, with CINCPAC's rehashed proposal, serious resistance activities were apparently back on the table. However, that September, both the State Department and the CIA came together to veto the concept.[18]

A few short months later, SOG tried again. Spearheading the drive was Colonel Donald D. Blackburn, who had replaced Clyde Russell as SOG chief in June 1965. During World War II, Blackburn had led a regiment of Filipino guerrillas—affectionately dubbed Blackburn's Headhunters—and developed a solid appreciation for unconventional warfare. Now, as chief of SOG, one of his first orders of business was to apply his Filipino resistance experience to North Vietnam.

Unlike SOG's earlier support for the SSPL, Blackburn wanted the real thing. For starters, he envisioned creation of an international front that could spread resistance viewpoints overseas. A prime example of this was before their very eyes—the National Liberation Front, or Viet Cong. It claimed to be the independent voice for all opposition to Saigon, regardless of political persuasion, but in reality was controlled from Hanoi. In the same vein, Blackburn saw his front as a way of packaging an alternative message by a group of overseas anticommunist Vietnamese nationalists with no direct links to the American or South Vietnamese governments. A specially designated staff member was assigned to SOG to flesh out this idea.[19]

In short order, a blueprint for creating the front took shape. In the first phase, a control group—composed of members of the State Department, CIA, and Defense Department—would identify target audiences in South Vietnam and other third countries that would be susceptible to the front's message of stopping North Vietnamese aggression and bringing peace to a free Vietnam. These target audiences would include ethnic hill tribesmen, Catholics, Buddhists, businessmen, farmers, fishermen, and members of the VNQDD.[20]

Blackburn's second phase involved organizing these target audiences into political action groups whose ultimate purpose would be to exert political influence. While they would resemble political parties in a sense, they would be more similar to religious organizations and labor groups. Each of these action groups would have an American and a South Vietnamese case officer, who, in turn, would deal with the groups through a third South Vietnamese—a handler.

As soon as two or more action groups became viable, the third step would be to activate the front. To do this, the American and South Vietnamese case officers would exert influence to bring the groups together under a coalition. Once this was done, the front could develop its own identity and political program. For example, the front could organize demonstrations with sample slogans like "Stop the fratricidal war" and "Return freedom of worship to the people of North Vietnam."

A key element of the front concept was its relationship to the SSPL. Because the organization was the denial mechanism for disclaiming American and South Vietnamese sponsorship of paramilitary activities inside North Vietnam, an SSPL action group was to be among the most important in the front. The cover story for this group was that it was the action arm of the front and that it received funds from the front. While this action group would not publicly claim responsibility for acts of sabotage inside North Vietnam, it would acknowledge that it had agents in the north, and that it was in contact with them via a system of clandestine couriers and radio nets.

A Biet Hai team prepares for parachute training, 1966. (Courtesy Ho Van Ky Thoai)

Significantly, the SSPL action group would also be used for the purpose of motivating agent teams and boat crews. These agents and sailors would be told that they had been hired by the SSPL for specific missions. At the end of their training, these agents would be sworn in as members of the SSPL and would be told to recruit new members in the north.

As a corollary to the external front, Blackburn also wanted to build a solid resistance foundation inside northwestern North Vietnam. Only by making an actual resistance with actual people, argued Blackburn, could they create a rallying point more credible than the existing SSPL. This strong base structure—in effect a sanctuary—would straddle the Laos border. As Blackburn later explained, "I wanted to walk them in from Laos—let them feel their way in, like the Philippines."[21]

From these rear bases, resistance cells could be resupplied and reinforced, and from there cross the border into North Vietnam. Just as communist forces were using sanctuaries in Cambodia while fighting in South Vietnam, sanctuaries in Laos would also allow the SOG teams to retreat when pursued. More important, direct links via a Lao sanctuary would give SOG a means of verification other than radio messages, something that could not be done, for example, with the alleged resistance activities conducted by EASY inside Son La Province.[22]

In previous years, given the delicate neutrality of Laos, such a sanctuary might have been unthinkable. By mid-1965, however, Laos had been thrown open by a bitter civil war in which anticommunist guerrillas held numerous pockets of territory, in some cases extending right up to the North Vietnamese border. The leader of these guerrillas, General Vang Pao, was sympathetic to Saigon, and had even met with Colonel Tran Van Ho, the South Vietnamese chief of the Special Exploitation Service, to brainstorm ways of jointly opposing Hanoi.[23]

Not only was Vang Pao willing to help, but Blackburn could count on critical support from Se Co Tin, the ethnic Tho chieftain and recruiter first used by the CIA. Eleven years earlier, Se Co Tin had been intimately involved in another resistance scheme, this one hatched by French GCMA officers in the final months before the 1954 Geneva agreement. Planning what they called the "Liberation Committee of the Upper Red River," French commandos and Tho tribal leaders sought to convert their GCMA partisans into an anticommunist pocket along the Chinese frontier. From a logistical standpoint it was suicidal, and the concept was quickly dismissed by French military commanders in Hanoi.[24]

Now a recruiter for SOG, Se Co Tin had just returned from northern Laos. Invited to participate in Blackburn's unfolding resistance concept, he quickly agreed to help establish cells and contacts.[25]

Wrapping these elements into a coherent plan, Blackburn sent his proposal to Henry Cabot Lodge, the U.S. ambassador in Saigon. Lodge had earlier been hostile to resistance activities when SOG first pushed them in 1964, but this time around he saw enough advantages in Blackburn's scheme to offer agreement.[26]

Clearing that critical hurdle, the SOG chief forwarded the plan in July 1966 for what he thought was easy CINCPAC approval. To his dismay, CINCPAC rejected the idea and passed its disapproval on to the Joint Chiefs of Staff.[27]

CINCPAC, it turned out, was not alone in its opposition. Once again, the U.S. ambassador to Laos, William Sullivan, a quintessential pinstriper who demanded strong control over all American activities within his domain, was opposed to any encroachment by MACV, to include use of Laos as a sanctuary for North Vietnamese penetrations.[28] In this, Sullivan was backed by the CIA station in Laos. Like Sullivan, the agency saw SOG through the prism of its territorial dispute with the Defense Department. The CIA's paramilitary operations in Laos had escaped the 1963 switch to Pentagon control. Wanting to keep it that way, the agency consistently rebuffed encroachment on its monopoly. Both the CIA and Sullivan had vetoed SOG's resistance plans in mid-1965, and Blackburn's proposal one year later, seen as a renewed attempt to capture a piece of the Lao paramilitary pie, was considered equally objectionable.[29]

Like any good soldier, Blackburn saluted and carried on. But he would always believe that an opportunity had been missed. With no resistance movement on the ground inside North Vietnam, SOG had to rely on what Blackburn called "blind drops," which were, in his mind, never very productive. "To put teams in the north by means of blind drop, to collect intelligence, and to conduct certain harassment, leaves a lot to be desired," he recalled after the war. "This type of operation often proved to be a one-way street."[30]

The rejection of the resistance concept could not have come at a worse time for SOG. By 1965, the Vietnam conflict was escalating by the month, and SOG was slowly being sidelined as irrelevant. When Operation ROLLING THUNDER, the American bombing campaign over North Vietnam, began on 3 March, there was even less reason for SOG's pinpricks. Rather than spending months to prepare for the insertion of a sabotage team armed with a few rockets, American planes could now rain down thousands of times more explosives during a single afternoon. If a bridge needed to be downed, it was much more efficient to request an air strike than stage a complex commando infiltration. SOG's airborne sabotage mission, like its maritime counterpart, had become both redundant and antiquated.

Deprived of a resistance mission and superseded in the sabotage role, SOG spent mid-1965 desperately looking for new direction. To its rescue came MACV, which was itching to improve interdiction against North Vietnamese forces and supplies crossing Laos en route to battlefields inside South Vietnam. During the spring, Ambassador Sullivan had been forced to give ground in his turf war with Saigon and allow MACV to coordinate American bombing down the length of the Ho Chi Minh Trail in the eastern Lao panhandle. To complement this bombing, MACV also wanted American-led commando teams to run reconnaissance along the trail from staging bases inside South Vietnam.

Theoretically, Laos was still a neutral country. MACV's reconnaissance program, therefore, needed to be secret and deniable. Because SOG had the mandate for deniable external operations, it landed the assignment. But strategic ground reconnaissance was a new venture for which SOG had neither the personnel nor the experience. As a result, it was forced to spend the second half of 1965 bringing in dozens of Green Berets to Long Thanh and matching them with South Vietnamese teammates. SHINING BRASS, the name for the new mission, kicked off on 8 October with the insertion of the first mixed reconnaissance team into Laos. By the time these agents completed this maiden jungle foray later in the week, they had called in four air strikes and destroyed eleven North Vietnamese "structures," a confirmed tally higher than any previous SOG mission. If SOG had needed a new and, bureaucratically speaking, prosperous niche, SHINING BRASS was clearly a godsend.

This new lease on life did not, however, extend to its long-term airborne operations into North Vietnam. Still hoping to ensure their continued existence, SOG had been unofficially reorientating its Airborne Operations Section since summer. This revision was aimed at pleasing Washington on three counts. First, since early 1965 both the Joint Chiefs of Staff and the Defense Intelligence Agency (DIA) had shown concern over the possibility of communist Chinese intervention in Vietnam. To better prepare for this, they wanted early warning teams in the north to provide advance notice. Second, existing Defense Department collection assets were not providing sufficiently broad coverage, particularly detailed information regarding Hanoi's military buildup, including the new SA-2 surface-to-air missiles shipped from the Soviet Union that spring.[31] Third, with the onset of the American bombing campaign, the DIA needed help gathering target information.[32]

Matching these Pentagon requirements with Op 34A, in early October CINCPAC devised a new SOG mission statement overriding the one issued just seven months earlier. According to this new blueprint, SOG's priority in North Vietnam was now road watching along the major routes leading into Laos. This would allow its agents to fulfill the DIA's wish for targeting information as well as providing some idea of Hanoi's military buildup by reporting on matériel moving toward the Ho Chi Minh Trail and into South Vietnam. While a bit of a stretch, the agents could also relay advance notice of Chinese military intervention. Wrapping all of these assignments into a neat package, the new mission was given the acronym EWOT, for Early Warning Observation Team.

To put EWOT into practice, on 16 October SOG proposed that all long-term teams in the North Vietnamese panhandle be given road watching as a priority assignment. Meanwhile, all teams in northern North Vietnam, including those already in place, would take on EWOT as a secondary assignment. As an added duty, all teams were also to help in establishing escape nets for downed pilots, which included the recruitment of locals. Sabotage missions were only to be performed if and when they did not jeopardize road-watching or escape and evasion assignments. Resistance plans were also placed on the back burner.[33]

Approved on 30 October, EWOT officially went into effect during November. Almost from the start, however, problems arose. First, by transforming the northern teams into road watchers, SOG had effectively come full circle. Observing the trails leading into Laos, after all, had been one of the CIA's original objectives in 1961. Back then, the idea of having covert teams radio infrequent messages via the Philippines had failed to spark imaginations. That the concept would be successful in 1965—with SOG teams using the same antiquated radios and still relaying information through the Philippines—was just as unlikely.

Second, the Pentagon now intended to use the same pool of agents for a fundamentally different mission. In the words of future SOG chief Singlaub, such thinking was a "basic error." Agents recruited as saboteurs were now expected to count trucks, not taking into consideration the vastly different mind-set needed for the two assignments. A saboteur, said Singlaub, was likely to be very different from a person willing to sit passively on a mountain perch for months on end. As he later noted, "The new mission of intelligence collection and the establishment of intelligence-collection nets was not feasible with the type of people who have already been infiltrated into North Vietnam."[34]

Third, EWOT agents were again being expected to perform contradictory missions. On the one hand, they were tasked with missions that demanded contact with locals—organizing escape nets for American pilots, for example—yet on the other hand, they were prevented from blending into society at large. According to one officer close to the project, "Our experience has shown that the stringent and effective controls the North Vietnamese exercise over the population have caused such a fear in the people that they are quick to detect and report our agent teams once they make an overt act."[35]

Overcoming such fear was difficult in the best of circumstances. Resistance activity, which entailed a continuous armed presence by the agents, offered frightened locals at least some chance of resisting the communist government. But with a resistance program once again off the table, fear of the central authorities would almost certainly thwart any attempt to raise an effective evasion network.

Fourth, with the new emphasis on road watching, SOG's pool of good agents continued to shrink. Tribal recruiters were willing to go along with

SOG's sabotage role, and some were even willing to work under the EWOT scheme, but they still demanded that they send back some members to eventually set up an autonomous area.[36] In the words of Colonel Singlaub:

> [The high-quality recruits] would not go back to the simple task of counting trucks or of running an intelligence net in North Vietnam unless there was some hope, some promise that they would be able to retrieve their former positions of power and responsibility among their own people. Since we could not promise them that they could ultimately lead their people in these areas, they not only refused to go as intelligence agents themselves but could not, in good conscience, recommend to any of their tribal members to go.[37]

With minority recruitment drying up, SOG increasingly leaned toward South Vietnamese army recruits. This was reflected in teams like ROMEO, which combined five soldiers from the 2nd Infantry Division with five ethnic Vietnamese civilians. Already in training for a year, the ten ROMEO agents were selected to be the first new team to be deployed under the EWOT program.[38] Their mission would be to watch Route 103, a short feeder spur that ran west along the edge of the Demilitarized Zone toward the main Ho Chi Minh Trail network.

As Team ROMEO underwent final preparation, SOG was giving consideration to new means of infiltration into North Vietnam. For over two years, Chinese-piloted C-123s had been the vehicle of choice. However, their accuracy had not been the best. Moreover, with the introduction of more sophisticated Soviet air defense weapons along the Ho Chi Minh Trail and the North Vietnamese panhandle—the primary focus of EWOT—fixed-wing aircraft were increasingly vulnerable.

SOG had few alternatives. The more sophisticated C-130 had been vetoed by the State Department earlier in the year. Air America helicopters, last used to insert Team ATLAS in 1962, were unavailable because SOG, a military outfit, did not want to borrow CIA assets. A more promising possibility was the use of U.S. Air Force–piloted helicopters staging from Thailand. In September 1965, the American ambassador in Bangkok had approved in principle heliborne SOG missions staging from Nakhon Phanom, at that time a small airstrip just inside the Thai border. However, the helicopters themselves had yet to arrive in Thailand.[39]

Another possibility was the use of South Vietnamese air force helicopters. This was not a new idea. Beginning in 1961, H-34s had for two years infiltrated South Vietnamese commando teams along the Ho Chi Minh Trail. By all accounts, their performance had been outstanding, even under the most trying weather and topographic conditions. But for some reason, this had been all but forgotten by the time SOG was formed in early 1964. Indeed, when SOG planners gave initial thought to methods of infiltration into North Vietnam, the use of South Vietnamese helicopters was rejected because of the mistaken notion that South Vietnamese aviators were not up to the task. It was not until the fall of 1964 that Colonel J. E. Johnson, the SOG chief of operations, checked the historical record and argued otherwise.[40]

More recently, South Vietnamese helicopter crews had again proved their mettle in covert operations. Supporting the initial SHINING BRASS forays into Laos, four unmarked H-34s had been dispatched to Nha Trang in October 1965. Some of the most experienced Vietnamese rotary-wing aviators went with them, including some with colorful call signs like "Spider" and "Cowboy."[41] Their performance had been superb, inserting and extracting the mixed American–South Vietnamese reconnaissance teams with professional precision.

Because of their SHINING BRASS record, these same Vietnamese air force H-34 crews were selected to insert Team ROMEO. On the morning of 19 November, the ten Op 34A agents were flown to Khe Sanh. Still three years before it would gain infamy as the scene of a pivotal battle between U.S. Marines and North Vietnamese regulars, at that early date Khe Sanh was a little border post just six kilometers from the Laos frontier and less than forty kilometers south of the Demilitarized Zone.

At 0300 hours, ROMEO boarded three H-34s and lifted off from Khe Sanh. In the lead aircraft were three of the agents, their SOG case officer, two American gunners, and an American copilot. In the pilot's seat was Captain Nguyen Phi Hung, alias "Moustachio."[42] The rest of the team was divided among the remaining two helicopters.

Heading north, Moustachio led the armada into cloudy skies. Crossing the Demilitarized Zone, he nosed into a sharp descent toward the selected landing zone. As the helicopters' wheels touched down, three ROMEO commandos sprinted for the tree line. The scene was repeated two more times as the remaining helicopters disgorged their passengers. With the sun fast fading, Moustachio throttled up and banked south.

EWOT was off to a good start.

15

PREMONITIONS

The EWOT honeymoon did not last long. To be sure, there was early promise. At the beginning of 1966, SOG believed that it had nine teams on the ground in North Vietnam, a total of seventy-eight agents. Its two most recent teams—ROMEO in November 1965 and KERN, a nine-man unit parachuted near the busy Mu Gia Pass in March 1966—managed to make radio contact after infiltration. They were acting on intelligence from CINCPAC suggesting that Hanoi was upgrading several roads for use as infiltration routes.[1] But euphoria was soon overtaken by the growing sentiment that SOG's long-term agent operations, intended as a critical strategic lever against Hanoi when first launched in 1964, were being reduced to a truck-counting sideshow.

SOG had mostly itself to blame for the decline. According to a 1966 internal review, SOG belatedly admitted its agent operations had been guided by "ambiguously worded mission statements" for the first year and a half.[2] Adding to the confusion was the organization's military structure, with most of its officers serving only twelve-month tours. With little overlap, and with minimal prior training in agent handling, these officers did not have the background or time to seriously revamp, much less cancel, bureaucratically entrenched programs.

Although SOG was prepared to admit its past shortcomings, it was doing little to correct them. When the Airborne Operations Section's newest mission statement was promulgated in June 1966, it was merely a rewording of the EWOT road-watching concept unveiled the previous year.[3]

On a more positive note, however, SOG spent the year looking for better technology to beef up its capabilities. Communications, in particular, were in dire need of updating. The mainstay of northern teams was still the RS-1 radio. This set was not only cumbersome to carry and noisy to operate but also vulnerable to new North Vietnamese direction-finding equipment and adverse weather effects on its operation.[4] Worse, during those times when the weather was sufficiently clear to allow transmission, BUGS—the CIA's radio relay site in the Philippines—could not handle all of the traffic from the northern teams at once. The resultant long delays in communications— each team averaged just one report per month—canceled out the rapid road-watch intelligence that was vital to the EWOT mission.

To correct this, SOG wanted a new radio. A leading contender was the Delco Model 5300. A high-frequency transmitter, the Delco 5300 could handle either voice or Morse communications. It was small and used a battery, a big advantage over the RS-1's bulky hand-cranked generator, and already was used by CIA road-watching teams in Laos. SOG ordered two sets in April 1966. Procurement delays ensued, however, leaving SOG with no new radios by year's end.[5]

Air support was another area in need of improvement. While North Vietnam's air defenses were being constantly updated, SOG's ability to penetrate those defenses was not keeping pace. Already, SOG's Nationalist Chinese C-123 crews were worried about upcoming missions to resupply ARES, the singleton infiltrated in 1961, and EAGLE, a six-man team infiltrated into western Quang Ninh in June 1964.[6] Both were near the deadly antiaircraft rings around Haiphong. Plans in February 1965 called for a C-123 to make a single drop to EAGLE, which, in turn, would cache some rations for ARES. Delays ensued, and by the time the idea was revisited later that year, Hanoi had already revolutionized its air defenses with the introduction of Soviet-made surface-to-air missile (SAM) batteries. Facing SAMs, the Chinese refused the mission outright.[7]

Empathizing with its pilots, SOG searched for a new means of resupplying its highest-risk teams. One solution was to use high-speed aircraft—even jets—although this concept had its limitations. For one thing, high speeds made it difficult for the pilots to see ground signals. Moreover, since the target would be near urban centers teeming with security forces, if a drop was off—even by a matter of seconds—it might alert North Vietnamese officials to the presence of a nearby team.[8]

Nevertheless, the concept of high-speed resupply flights went ahead. To test the idea, the South Vietnamese air force stepped forward. To that point, the air force's contribution to SOG missions in North Vietnam had been conspicuous by its almost total absence. Of the three Vietnamese C-123 aircrews that had completed advanced training in Florida in 1964, one had been killed during training, one quit, and the last was eventually dropped from the program in the spring of 1966 after repeatedly failing to complete any of its assigned resupply missions.[9]

Looking to improve on this dismal record, General Nguyen Cao Ky, who had pioneered the northern infiltration flights back in 1961 and had led the first bombing missions into North Vietnam in February 1965, offered the use of his elite 83rd Tactical Group. Flying unmarked A-1G propeller-driven fighter-bombers and going by the call sign Thanh Phong—Vietnamese for "kamikaze"—Ky's collection of aviators were the best in his air force. To prove it, one of the unit's A-1Gs raced across the Demilitarized Zone in April

South Vietnamese A-1G being loaded with a fake napalm canister for a covert re-supply mission in North Vietnam. (Conboy collection)

1966 and headed toward the hills near Route 103. Spotting ROMEO's ground signal, the pilot dropped twin napalm canisters from under his wings. The two steel tubs tumbled toward the triple canopy, but instead of explod-ing in a shower of jellied fuel, the canisters crashed harmlessly into the forest floor. Inside, they were stuffed with clothes, food, and ammunition for the Op 34A agents. The South Vietnamese air force completed four more high-speed resupply missions into the North Vietnamese panhandle that year.[10]

Then the U.S. Air Force gave it a try. Rather than prop-driven A-1s, it used F-4 Phantom jets from the 366th Tactical Fighter Wing at Danang. The target was EAGLE, the team in western Quang Ninh. While other American jets conducted nearby air strikes as a diversion, a pair of the squadron's F-4s headed toward the drop zone at 350 knots and just sixteen meters off the ground. Spotting EAGLE's ground signal, they ejected their disguised napalm canisters. Team members later claimed to have successfully recovered the supplies inside.

While high-performance aircraft solved the resupply problem, there re-mained the challenge of infiltrating new teams. The mainstay of the insertion effort, the C-123, was beginning to show its age. Its electronic counter-measures package and radar, in particular, were increasingly impotent in the face of Hanoi's air defenses. The Chinese crews also found the plane ill suited for nap-of-the-earth flying in marginal weather conditions.[11]

Knowing the C-123 would need an eventual replacement, in the spring of 1965 SOG had requested the C-130 as an alternative. It was turned down. That September, SOG again proposed the use of C-130s with U.S. Air Force crews. After additional justification was submitted to the Pentagon three months later, Defense Secretary McNamara ultimately relented: SOG would get its planes. In bowing to SOG's request, his decision was based not only on the C-130's heavier payload and faster speed but also on the fact that, since ROLLING THUNDER, American planes were routinely in North Vietnamese airspace, so there was no longer a need to sanitize the C-130 or use deniable aircrews.[12] Were a SOG C-130 to be downed, it would not spark the diplomatic outcry and embarrassment that might have resulted a year earlier.

The C-130s destined for SOG were not standard models. The crews, too, were specifically trained for the mission. Preparations had begun in the spring of 1966 when a select detachment of U.S. Air Force pilots and airmen began intensive low-level flight practice at Pope Air Force Base, North Carolina. By summer, they were joined by four new MC-130E Combat Spear aircraft painted in a velvet black finish. Each had a detachable yoke fixed to its nose for use with the Fulton Skyhook extraction system.

That October, the four aircraft and crews arrived at temporary quarters in Nha Trang. While they were officially listed as a detachment of the 314th Troop Carrier Wing, they answered solely to SOG. After some in-country practice, they graduated to conducting a handful of leaflet drops over North Vietnam.[13] Finally, on Christmas Eve they were ready for their first agent drop, a two-man reinforcement for Team TOURBILLON. Aircraft commander Leon Franklin was at the controls.

"We departed Nha Trang, overflew Danang, and then headed inland," he recalled. "We were flying with two pilots, a flight engineer, two navigators, and a third pilot who helped read the maps." As the C-130 neared the target, Franklin scanned the ground for a signal, but he saw nothing. Banking the plane around, he went back for another look. This time the correct signal was there: flame pots arranged in an inverted "L." The agents went out the back ramp, and Franklin headed for home. "We didn't encounter any hostile fire," he recalled.[14]

Although the first MC-130 infiltration was a success, SOG was having new doubts about the viability of parachute insertions. Not only did parachutes carry the possibility of serious injury, but past SOG experience had

Calling card printed by members of the 20th Helicopter Squadron's PONY EXPRESS Detachment. "Gommer" was the nickname given to indigenous agents and commandos. "T.P.R.S." stands for "This Place Really Sucks." (Conboy collection)

shown airborne methods, even with improved navigational equipment, could not guarantee a team would land in the intended drop zone. Only helicopters could deliver a team with precision. Moreover, a team inserted by chopper could be operational almost immediately.[15]

This point of view was bolstered by the November 1965 success of Team ROMEO in southern Quang Binh. While H-34s and South Vietnamese air force crews in that case had proved a winning combination, SOG felt that a better choice was the U.S. Air Force's CH-3. The CH-3 not only had 50 percent more speed but also had more than 50 percent greater payload-carrying capability than the H-34. This meant that just two CH-3s—one being used as an emergency "high bird"—could accomplish the same task as a three-ship H-34 formation.

The CH-3 was a relative newcomer to Southeast Asia. In October 1965, eight of these unarmed aircraft had arrived at Nha Trang and were assigned to the Air Force's 20th Helicopter Squadron. The following April, six of the squadron's helicopters, code-named PONY EXPRESS, were transferred to Nakhon Phanom air base in Thailand, ostensibly to help train Thai aviators in counterinsurgency techniques.[16] From this launch site, a wealth of targets within the North Vietnamese panhandle were within its range. Moreover, a refueling stop at one of the CIA's guerrilla outposts in northern Laos made landing zones elsewhere in North Vietnam readily accessible.

With secret agreement from the Royal Thai government, arrangements were concluded for SOG to use the helicopters at Nakhon Phanom during inserts into North Vietnam. This had a precedent of sorts: since the fall of 1965, SOG C-123s had been making brief refueling stops in Thailand while en route to North Vietnam. From Bangkok's perspective, however, the question of using Thai-based U.S. helicopters to insert South Vietnamese commando teams into North Vietnam was more diplomatically sensitive. As a result, the Thai government insisted that when the teams arrived at Nakhon Phanom, they would be taken in a blacked-out van to an isolation area until time to board their helicopters. Should a flight be aborted, the South Vietnamese commandos were not to remain overnight in Thailand.

The first team set for CH-3 infiltration was code-named HECTOR. HECTOR, in fact, was two subteams in one. According to this latest plan, the first HECTOR subteam—HECTOR A—would insert into North Vietnam and establish road-watching sites. It would later be joined by the second increment—HECTOR B—which would focus on making limited contact with local villagers. This binary arrangement, it was felt, would give the agents better odds of gradually assuming the full EWOT mission.[17]

On 22 June, the fifteen members of HECTOR A shuttled to Nakhon Phanom. Their target was directly east of the air base and just inside the North Vietnamese border near Route 137, a major traffic artery that fed through the rugged Ban Karai Pass toward the Ho Chi Minh Trail. As had increasingly been the case with SOG agents, HECTOR was entirely composed of ethnic lowland Vietnamese, many of them recruited directly from the South Vietnamese army.[18] Their commander, Captain Nguyen Huu Luyen, was the highest-ranking officer to ever head a long-term team.

Keeping in mind Thai sensitivities, HECTOR A spent little time at Nakhon Phanom. Bundled across the airfield to two waiting CH-3s, they took to the sky and headed across the narrow waist of the Lao panhandle. Gaining altitude to traverse the Annamite Mountains and avoid antiaircraft fire, the U.S. Air Force crews guided their helicopters over the border and into western Quang Binh. With twilight fast approaching, the aircraft ferrying the team settled into a clearing. Within minutes, the agents had unloaded their supplies off the rear ramp, and the helicopters were heading back toward Thailand.

HECTOR A quickly came up on the radio and reported its position to be secure. This cleared the way for the second increment of agents, HECTOR B, to go to Nakhon Phanom on 23 September. Boarding a CH-3, they

Eight members of Team SAMSON, along with other agent trainees, pose at Long Thanh prior to insertion in October 1966. (Courtesy Le Van Tinh)

infiltrated into the same drop zone without incident, then disappeared into the bush to link up with their sister unit.[19]

In Saigon, SOG waited for HECTOR B to make radio contact. Days passed with no word. HECTOR A, when quizzed, claimed that it could not locate any of the eleven reinforcements.

Undaunted by the mysterious loss, SOG pressed ahead with its next scheduled launch. The team, SAMSON, was an eight-man composite of five ethnic groups. Its mission was to land by CH-3 inside Laos and walk across the border to the Tay Trang Pass south of Dien Bien Phu. From that vantage point, the agents could observe Route 4, the major supply conduit to communist forces in northernmost Laos. In doing so, SOG was showing its lack of creativity: both the insertion inside Laos and the road-watching mission near Dien Bien Phu read like a copy of that given to REMUS four years earlier.

On 5 October, SAMSON departed Nakhon Phanom. Refueling at a CIA outpost inside Laos, the two CH-3s continued north to the border and off-loaded the team. SAMSON immediately came on the air, another apparent success.[20]

SOG waited three months for its next launch. The team, code-named HADLEY, consisted of eleven ethnic Vietnamese. Like SAMSON, it was to land just inside Laos and cross the North Vietnamese border by foot. The target was Route 8, a major thoroughfare feeding through the Nape Pass and down the Lao panhandle.

In addition to watching North Vietnamese traffic from the nearby hills, HADLEY was also supposed to make its way to the road and install a seismic intrusion device (SID).[21] Resembling a giant nail, the device had been field-tested by the CIA in Laos, where its motion detectors were able to differentiate between vibrations caused by passing pedestrians and vehicles. Traffic data from the device would be periodically collected by the team and relayed back to Saigon.

During the third week of January 1967, HADLEY's Vietnamese case officer, Captain Nguyen Van Vinh, flew to Nakhon Phanom for a briefing by the PONY EXPRESS detachment. Vinh, who went by the call sign Marc, already had four years of experience in the program. An engineer by training, he was the first chief of the Long Thanh demolitions course in 1963, and since 1965 had been promoted to full-fledged case officer.

At Nakhon Phanom, Marc was shown slides of potential landing zones in easternmost Khammouane Province. Agreeing on one, he traveled back to Saigon and together with his SOG counterpart, Captain Frederic Caristo, briefed the team. Caristo, a short, robust Green Beret with a flair for languages, had joined the Airborne Operations Section the previous fall. Together they explained to the agents that they would insert with only three days of food. Traveling light, they would be able to cover the thirty kilometers to their road-watching perch in about forty-eight hours. Once there, they could then call in a nighttime C-123 drop with more provisions.

On 26 January, HADLEY flew to Nakhon Phanom. Accompanied by Marc, the commandos loaded aboard one CH-3 and took to the skies. A second, empty CH-3 trailed behind as they traversed Khammouane Province and approached the border. With the sun rapidly setting, the lead pilot headed toward what he thought was the correct clearing. The CH-3 touched down, and the eleven agents, laden with minimal supplies, scurried off the rear ramp and into the bush. Nose forward, the aircraft lifted, made a slow turn, and headed west.

As the helicopter gained altitude, Marc peered from the side window. Immediately, his heart sank. One hill removed from the landing zone was a wide dirt road. When he had been shown the slides during the prelaunch briefing, no roads were in sight. They had landed at the wrong clearing. Marc was not alone in his fears. In the second helicopter, one of the crew members raised them over the radio. "Sir, wrong LZ?" he asked the aircraft commander.

"He's right," echoed Marc into his lip microphone.

The helicopter turned back. Landing once again, Marc and a Vietnamese cargo handler ran off the rear ramp and headed for the edge of the clearing.

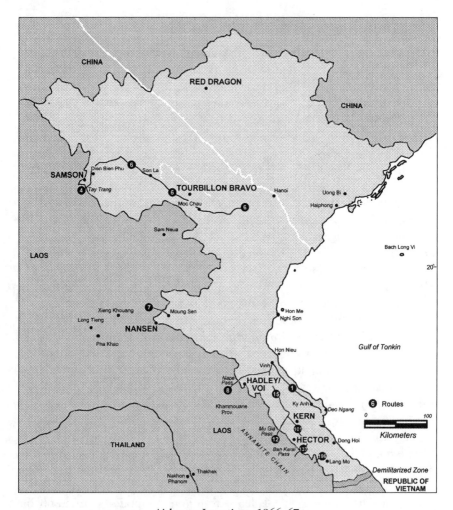

Airborne Insertions, 1966–67

Together they shouted the names of the team members. Nobody responded. For nearly five minutes they yelled, but still there were no answers.

On the other side of the landing zone, a water buffalo wandered out of the tree line. The presence of a domesticated animal could only mean a village was nearby. From the ramp, a U.S. Air Force flight engineer motioned for the two Vietnamese to return to the aircraft. Reluctantly, they boarded the helicopter and took to the darkening skies.

Back at Nakhon Phanom, Marc awaited radio contact from HADLEY. With him were HADLEY's food bundles, prepositioned there for an immediate drop to the team. After the proscribed forty-eight hours passed with no word, he went to Danang and boarded the backseat of a South Vietnamese A-1G. Three times over the next two days, he overflew HADLEY's intended rendezvous site in the hopes of seeing a panel or pen flare signal. He saw nothing.

Two days later, Caristo telephoned Marc from Saigon. The CIA, he was told, had just intercepted a communist radio transmission indicating a commando team had been found inside the North Vietnamese border near the Nape Pass. HADLEY, they reluctantly concluded, had been captured.

Or maybe not. Eighteen days later, BUGS picked up a surprise transmission. After giving the correct security code, the HADLEY radioman claimed that the team had been hit and was still trying to evade communist troops.

The message set off a debate in Saigon. Was the team responding under North Vietnamese control? After all, nearly three weeks had passed since its insert. In HADLEY's case, there were other reasons to suspect the worst. Every time SOG radioed a question, the team responded almost immediately. Past experience had shown Op 34A agents to be slow in answering; HADLEY, by contrast, was overly efficient.[22]

Strong evidence of duplicity came in early September. During a CIA debriefing of an escapee from a Pathet Lao detention camp in Khammouane Province, the ex-prisoner reported having overheard guards talk of eleven South Vietnamese commandos who had landed by chopper near the Nape Pass earlier that year. All were reportedly captured, along with twenty-two rifles, which they broke before surrendering.[23]

The CIA interrogation should have left little doubt regarding HADLEY's true fate. Still, SOG felt compelled to corroborate the escapee's tale. This led to planning for an unusual four-man operation. The team, code-named VOI (Vietnamese for "elephant"), was to parachute into the North Vietnamese panhandle ostensibly for an EWOT mission. In reality, the four agents were given high-powered binoculars and a telephoto camera and were to infiltrate near the alleged bivouac site used by HADLEY. There they were to lie and wait for a parachute resupply to HADLEY, then photograph whoever came to the drop zone to recover the supplies.

On 18 October, case officer Marc accompanied VOI into an MC-130. Cutting inland, the plane continued along the Lao border until reaching Ha Tinh Province. As the ramp lowered, Marc watched the team leap into the slipstream. He then turned his attention to the radio set in the rear of the plane. The VOI agents had been instructed to contact Marc the moment they landed. As the minutes passed, however, the radio remained static. As the aircraft cut a wide orbit, Marc transmitted a series of questions in hopes of eliciting a response. The static continued. VOI had disappeared.[24]

16

SUSPICIOUS MINDS

Team HADLEY's problems were only the tip of a very large iceberg. Although there were difficulties with the airborne insertions going back to the beginning, SOG seemed willing to ignore them. Then, in October 1966, SOG case officer Aaron "Greg" Dorough received an emergency call in the middle of the night ordering him to Long Thanh. A Green Beret captain, Dorough had arrived earlier in the spring to oversee all Op 34A teams in the North Vietnamese panhandle. Among them was ROMEO, the ten-man unit inserted just over the Demilitarized Zone that had been sending back infrequent data on trail traffic for the past eleven months. At Long Thanh, Dorough's South Vietnamese counterpart handed him a short translation of a message received via BUGS.[1] From the team's radioman, it stated simply: "ROMEO ALREADY CAPTURED."[2]

As if to erase that bombshell, ROMEO immediately sent a series of further messages claiming that the team was safe after all. SOG officers were mortified. Not only was this the first concrete evidence that one of its teams was transmitting under duress, but the North Vietnamese security service had the audacity to try to continue radio play despite being blatantly exposed.[3]

Keeping its true feelings in check, SOG went along with the charade and continued normal contact with ROMEO.[4] More bad news followed. In December, Hanoi announced the capture and trial of KERN, the nine-man team that had been operating near the Mu Gia Pass. Infiltrated in March, KERN had inexplicably gone off the air in September.[5]

In March 1967, another team, this time SAMSON, was exposed over Hanoi radio.[6] Like KERN, SAMSON had made its last radio contact exactly three months earlier.

During June, yet another team appeared in Hanoi. HECTOR A, which had made its last radio contact in March, was now facing spy charges.[7] The emerging pattern could not be mere coincidence: teams were going off the air for ninety days before being suddenly exposed. Clearly, SOG was being systematically humbled by Hanoi.

Even SOG's older established teams were being unmasked. Heading the list was TOURBILLON, the saboteurs infiltrated back in 1962. Landing at a drop zone secured by CASTOR—which had been captured within days and doubled—TOURBILLON, too, was arrested and turned from the beginning.

In hindsight, there had been numerous signs over the years about its true fate. During September 1963, for example, Saigon had radioed plans to exfiltrate TOURBILLON on account of its good performance. The agents should have been thrilled by the news, but instead they claimed that an injury suffered by the team's radioman prevented their overland movement into Laos.

Unwittingly, the CIA had stumbled across the weakness in North Vietnamese attempts to subvert its teams: Hanoi would always balk at any request to exfiltrate agents it had already doubled. The agency, however, failed to recognize this and took TOURBILLON's excuse at face value. Plans to extract the team were subsequently put on hold.

The following November, TOURBILLON was again involved when a C-123 received antiaircraft fire while attempting to resupply the team. The Chinese aircrews were convinced it was not a chance encounter and for a time refused to revisit the site. Still, TOURBILLON remained in SOG's good graces.

In September 1966, TOURBILLON was again told to prepare some of its members for exfiltration. By then, the team's original agents had been in the field for over four years. But once more, TOURBILLON was surprisingly cool to the idea. It was only after considerable prompting that Maurice and Captain George Lawton, the team's South Vietnamese and SOG case officers, secured their agreement to allow some members to be extracted by CH-3.

Lawton, a West Pointer, had been under pressure since arriving at SOG in November 1965. Word that no team going north had ever returned was spreading around Long Thanh. Morale and recruitment were falling fast.[8] Bringing part of TOURBILLON home would go far in reversing this situation, even if it meant the risky proposition of sending an unarmed CH-3 into a flak trap.

On 8 September, Lawton and Maurice went to Nakhon Phanom, boarded a CH-3, and headed north. The plan called for them to make radio contact en route to make sure the landing zone was secure. When they called TOURBILLON, however, the radio mysteriously fell silent. Unsuccessful in raising the team, Lawton signaled the pilot, and the mission was canceled.[9]

A few days later, TOURBILLON reestablished contact. SOG was finally becoming suspicious that not all was well, but it chose to go ahead with a scheduled reinforcement by two agents. Hedging its bets, SOG gave one of the agents a secret safety code to be innocently inserted in his tenth message back to Saigon.

On Christmas Eve 1966, the two agents jumped into a drop zone marked by TOURBILLON. The following month, during his tenth message to BUGS, the reinforcement radioman included the distress signal.[10] As with ROMEO, SOG opted to continue communication without exposing its hand.

Tainted along with TOURBILLON was its sister team, VERSE. Eight agents trained in road-watching techniques, VERSE had parachuted during November 1965 into a drop zone secured by TOURBILLON. The teams split, with VERSE moving to a neighboring district in Son La Province to observe truck traffic.[11]

For over a year, VERSE remained above doubt. With TOURBILLON showing duplicity, however, VERSE came under suspicion. In June 1967, SOG notified the team to prepare for a helicopter exfiltration. In a routine that was becoming as painful as it was predictable, VERSE concocted an excuse and went off the air.[12] Three months later, Hanoi announced its latest spy trial.[13]

Another long-running team exposed during this period was BELL. Seven saboteurs parachuted into Yen Bai Province in June 1963; the team had been captured within three days and its radioman coerced into making radio contact with Saigon.[14] Because no distress signal was ever transmitted, SOG believed BELL was secure when it took over the team from CIA control in 1964.

By that time, the North Vietnamese were growing tired of SOG's continued penetrations of their airspace and were contemplating ways of shooting down a C-123. The easiest method to do this—setting up a flak trap near a drop zone—was used sparingly because Saigon would certainly conclude that the team was doubled. Another method—using antiaircraft fire to down a plane on its way to a drop zone—was also discounted because most of North Vietnam's antiaircraft batteries were clustered around populated areas rather than the mountainous rural routes favored by the SOG planes.

Hanoi settled on a third method: send another plane to shoot down the intruding aircraft. The only problem was that in the spring of 1964, North Vietnam's fledgling air force had no fighters. It did, however, have a single American-made T-28B that had been kept in storage outside Hanoi. How it acquired the T-28 was a tale in itself. In September 1963, a disgruntled pilot in the Royal Lao Air Force—himself a Thai national who had once before defected from the Thai air force to Laos—defected once again, this time to North Vietnam. Not sure what to do with the pilot or his plane, the North Vietnamese quietly placed him in custody and covered the T-28 with oil to prevent rust.

For six months the plane was all but forgotten. Then, in April 1964, the North Vietnamese general staff ordered that it be made ready for action. This was more difficult than it sounded. The plane, after all, came with no maintenance records. Nor did any of North Vietnam's pilots have experience flying the T-28. Still, technicians did what they could to inspect the plane and make repairs. When they started it up, it worked. Excited by their success, they gave the newest member of their air force tail number 963, representing the ninth month of 1963, the date the plane landed in their country.

But who would fly it? The search settled on two instructors at the aviation school, Nguyen Van Ba and Le Tien Phuoc, both of whom had been among the first contingent of pilots trained in China in 1960. Over the following weeks, the pair spent hours flying from Hanoi's Gia Lam airfield.

Learning to fly the T-28 was only half the battle. A greater difficulty was how to locate and intercept a C-123 once it crossed the border. Because some of the Op 34A teams had already been doubled, Hanoi knew the general time frame and flight path for resupply or reinforcement missions. For teams dropping to new locations, however, North Vietnam's primitive radar network could not provide any specific intercept coordinates. Figuring they would have to rely on their own eyesight, pilots Ba and Phuoc took a low-tech approach by playing Ping-Pong and volleyball at night to develop what they called "supernatural" vision.[15]

Training continued over the next three months. Then, one night in mid-summer, a command staff car pulled onto the runway. From the backseat stepped General Van Tien Dung, chief of the General Staff. He shook hands with the stunned pilots, then asked for a progress report. Ba and Phuoc briefed the general on aerial tactics and noted that they had only tested the plane's 12.7mm machine guns on ground targets.

"We're sorry that we have not yet had enough means to fire live rounds in flight," said Ba.

The general pointed to the sky. "We'll use an enemy aircraft as the target."

On 29 July, they had their first crack. That night a SOG C-123 parachuted Team BOONE into Nghe An Province, then headed back south along the North Vietnamese panhandle. Thirty minutes before they reached the safety of the Demilitarized Zone, the Chinese pilot, Captain Tien-tsung Chen, got a tap on the shoulder from his electronic countermeasures operator. A signal was on their tail, he was told, and closing.

Banking slightly, Chen looked back and saw a red pulsing light at the same altitude as their own. Diving, he headed into a layer of clouds. A few minutes later, the C-123 was back in the clear night sky. The unidentified plane, however, was still keeping pace to their left. Chen again dove into the clouds. The Demilitarized Zone was just ahead, but their pursuer clung fast. Not until they crossed the seventeenth parallel did the mystery plane turn around and head north. SOG officials in Saigon, unaware that Hanoi had refurbished the ex-Lao T-28, listed the July incident as unresolved.

The North Vietnamese, meanwhile, were having trouble keeping their makeshift fighter aloft. Its tires and engine were wearing out, and without spare parts it faced imminent grounding. Pure luck provided the solution. On 18 August, an antiaircraft unit in western Quang Binh Province downed a Royal Lao Air Force T-28 that had strayed across the border. Its pilot, a Thai volunteer named Chem Bumrungon, provided detailed information on the T-28 during his interrogation. Better still, his plane, though badly damaged, was a gold mine of spare parts.

Their T-28 again flight-worthy, Ba and Phuoc spent the remainder of the year trying to catch a C-123. However, even when Hanoi was forewarned that a transport would be resupplying one of its doubled teams, the T-28 could not locate the plane in the vast moonlit sky.

Finally, after eight months and twenty failed attempts, Hanoi received a break. On the night of 14 February 1965, SOG relayed a message to its Yen Bai team, BELL, that reinforcement agents were on the way and a drop zone should be prepared that night.[16] The North Vietnamese quickly passed word to every radar outpost in the panhandle to be on their highest alert. Reports soon filtered in: an aircraft had passed over Thanh Hoa and was heading northwest.[17]

Given a final update, Ba and Phuoc boarded their T-28 and were airborne. Heading on an interception course for Yen Bai, they studied the cloud banks below. "Occasionally we would come up on a layer of clouds, see a reflection of moonlight and think it was the enemy aircraft," recalled Ba. "We could close on the target, but would be mistaken."

With little to go on, they guessed that the C-123 would use the highest mountain in the area, a fifteen-hundred-meter peak, as a landmark on their final run to the drop zone. They were right. After a few circles around the peak, Phuoc, in the rear seat, spotted the transport. "That's it!" he cried. "Very long wings!"

Ba also saw the C-123 bobbing in the turbulence, its interior lights visible through the open rear ramp. Maneuvering the T-28 underneath, he slowly climbed to within one hundred meters of his target. Then, zeroing the machine guns on the glowing exhaust from one of the engine cowlings, he squeezed the trigger. Tracers spit toward the C-123, hitting its left engine and stitching its belly. In Ba's words, "The enemy aircraft rolled and disappeared into the blackness of the night."[18]

Believing the C-123 had crashed, Hanoi was elated.[19] But the SOG plane was not downed. A few minutes before the attack, the Chinese crew had aborted the mission because it could not spot the flame pots prepared by BELL. The pilot, Captain Lee-chin Yei, was just banking the plane to the west when it was hit. As the bullets ripped into the fuselage, he wrestled for control of the aircraft, then careened downward toward the jungle canopy.

Leaking hydraulic fluid forced the landing gear down and made it difficult for Yei to control the flaps. Knowing the plane could not make it back to South Vietnam, he instead headed south for the Thai border.

In the rear of the plane, Team GECKO—the code name given to the seven agents preparing to reinforce BELL—hung on for dear life. Nguyen Van Ru, the team leader, yelled for calm. Two of his agents were wounded, one with shrapnel in his shoulder, a second with a bullet fragment in his ankle. Crumpled in a pool of blood on the floor of the plane was one of the Chinese parachute delivery officers. A quick check showed he was dead.

The stricken plane called ahead to Nakhon Phanom air base for emergency landing clearance. Nothing like the sprawling military base of later years, Nakhon Phanom at that early date was a quiet aviation backwater. Only a handful of Thai and U.S. Air Force personnel were there when the damaged plane coasted to the far end of the runway. By sunup, a slightly larger crowd had gathered around. What they saw was an unmarked plane with a Chinese crew and a commando team armed to the teeth. The aircraft was riddled with thirty-one bullet holes, mostly in the tail. Thai officials, who had yet to give permission for SOG landing rights, were not amused.

After a few hours of quiet negotiations, American officials hustled the crew and commandos back to Saigon. The Chinese crew returned to Taipei and was awarded its country's highest medal for bravery.[20] Team GECKO was disbanded, its men merged into a new team destined to reinforce EASY in Son La.[21]

Back on the ground, Team BELL claimed not to have heard the aerial engagement—odd considering that it took place nearly over its head. Although BELL's denials raised questions, SOG again made plans to reinforce the team with fresh agents. On 12 May, the reinforcement team, code-named DOG, headed north. Bad weather, however, forced an abort.[22]

For the next year, BELL—if its radio transmissions were to be believed—was almost constantly on the move. Hanoi manipulated its radio play with precision, if not a flair for the dramatic. In late 1966, for example, it claimed that the team had encountered North Vietnamese troops and engaged in a full-blown firefight, losing two members but managing to evade the dragnet.

Still believing the team was secure, in mid-January 1967 SOG devised a plan to exfiltrate BELL by CH-3 helicopter.[23] CINCPAC approved the concept, which was passed to SOG case officer Austin Wilgus for implementation. Wilgus, a U.S. Army Special Forces captain coming off a tour in West Germany, had joined SOG the previous October and inherited the files for BELL. He immediately informed his agents of the proposed extraction. Just like earlier teams, however, BELL had plenty of excuses for why it could not leave North Vietnam. "In our radio code, the North Vietnamese troops were called 'monkeys,'" remembered Wilgus. "BELL kept telling me that they could hear 'monkeys chattering in the trees,' which meant that North Vietnamese troops were near their team location and that it was not a good time to try an exfiltration."

In message after message, BELL said that it could still hear monkeys in the trees. Finally, during the first week of February, BELL signaled that an extraction was possible. Wilgus rushed to Nakhon Phanom to brief the PONY EXPRESS crews. Wilgus himself would be flying in an MC-130 command ship, while three CH-3s made the recovery.

On the afternoon of 8 February, one day before Vietnam's Tet lunar New Year, the aerial armada lifted off from Thailand. From the MC-130, Wilgus made radio contact with BELL and confirmed that the landing zone was still secure. There was a brief scare when his aircraft entered North Vietnamese airspace. "We had a radar lock-on from an approaching plane," said Wilgus. "Over the headset I heard the electronics countermeasures operator tell the pilot, 'We'll know who it is when they go by.' I remember thinking to myself, 'If it is a MiG, then it'll be too late when they go by.' It turned out to be an F-105 heading for Hanoi."[24]

Below the MC-130, Major Alton Deviney was the aircraft commander in the lead CH-3. Flying low over the North Vietnamese landscape, he guided his helicopter into Yen Bai Province. Reading the terrain, he spotted the landing zone and headed earthward. As he hovered over the clearing, however, nobody appeared. Overhead, Wilgus tried to raise BELL, but there was only silence.

Fearing a trap, Deviney powered up and climbed back into the sky. As he cleared the first set of mountains, tracers bracketed his chopper. One bullet ripped through the cockpit, breaking the windshield and smashing the navigation and communications equipment. Unable to speak with the rest of his flight, Deviney trailed the two other CH-3s back toward Laos, where he managed to land his crippled aircraft at a CIA forward base.[25]

North Vietnam's security services, having milked BELL for all it was worth, abruptly ceased radio transmissions in March. Three months later, like clockwork, Hanoi announced its latest spy trial.[26]

The cracks in SOG's agent operations were growing wider.

17

STRATA

Although long-term agent operations were no longer a priority, SOG grew larger as it was handed new responsibilities. By January 1967, SOG numbered 207 Americans, up from a mere handful three years earlier. On the Vietnamese side, the increase was even greater, climbing from 470 in 1964 to over 1,700 by early 1966.[1] Most of these new men were assigned to SHINING BRASS, which that June entered its second phase when it began using platoon-sized Hornet Forces to attack targets in Laos identified by its cross-border reconnaissance teams.

Another new SOG mandate involved the search for the growing number of American servicemen missing in action. Studies showed that almost half of all failed rescues resulted from slow reaction time. If the helicopters did not reach the scene in thirty minutes or less, the odds of a successful rescue plummeted. CINCPAC had determined that MACV should have an organization that could continue recovery operations after normal search-and-rescue procedures were exhausted. MACV gave the assignment to SOG.

Colonel John K. Singlaub, who replaced Blackburn as chief of SOG in May 1966, handpicked U.S. Air Force Colonel Harry "Heinie" Aderholt to design the new program. Aderholt was one of the few senior officers in the Air Force with an appreciation for special operations. For several years in the early 1960s, he commanded the Far East detachment of the 1045th OE&T Group, the same joint U.S. Air Force–CIA unconventional warfare outfit that earlier had helped train the crews parachuting agents into North Vietnam. More recently, he had overseen the deployment of U.S. Air Force special warfare teams to Southeast Asia from their base at Eglin Air Force Base in Florida.

Aderholt's idea was to forge an intelligence clearinghouse and action arm for resolving missing-in-action cases under one roof. The Joint Chiefs of Staff approved the concept and on 17 September MACV formally created the Joint Personnel Recovery Center (JPRC) as a separate staff function within SOG. Aderholt was named the center's first chief.

In scanning the list of missing American servicemen, the JPRC staff quickly determined that the bulk of the missing were downed pilots—and most of those were in North Vietnam. So as its first order of business it decided to create its own commando teams that could insert into the north to search remote crash sites, neutralize ground opposition, and administer first aid when necessary. Formalized in October as the Safe Area Activation Team (SAAT) program, the plan called for a cadre of airborne-qualified indigenous commandos to be cross-trained as medics and radio operators. Heading the high-priority program from the Vietnamese side would be Captain Do Van Tien—alias François—the same case officer who had recruited the first singleton back in 1960.

That same month, the JPRC visited Long Thanh looking for recruits. Two dozen were chosen from the camp's pool of agent trainees, primarily Vietnamese along with a few ethnic minorities. A program of instruction emphasizing first aid and communications was worked up by SOG's Airborne Operations Section, while François and three top recruits traveled to Clark Air Force Base in the Philippines for six weeks at the U.S. Air Force's Jungle Survival School.[2]

In the midst of this training, the JPRC got a call for help. On 12 October, Canasta 572, a U.S. Navy A-1 piloted by Lieutenant Robert Woods, was shot down over southern Thanh Hoa Province. Ejecting from his plane, Woods managed to land safely in an expanse of jungle fifty-eight kilometers from the coast. His wingmen promptly relayed the coordinates offshore to the aircraft carrier *Intrepid*.

Launching from the *Intrepid*, an HH-3 Sea King helicopter was soon over Thanh Hoa. Spotting Woods, the crew attempted to lower a line through the thick canopy. On the end of the cable, however, was a doughnut-shaped flotation collar, which, though suitable for sea rescues, became hopelessly stuck in the treetops. Worse, North Vietnamese troops appeared on the scene, and their sporadic small-arms fire kept rescue helicopters at bay for the next day.

After repeated failures, the JPRC was brought in on 14 October. The U.S. Navy, it was told, wanted a commando team to accompany the helicopters and secure Woods's position on the ground. While this was exactly the type of mission that the JPRC was designed for, its SAAT teams were not yet available. Looking for an alternative, the center asked SHINING BRASS for the loan of its best reconnaissance team.

In October 1966 that distinction belonged to Spike Team OHIO, a combined unit numbering three Green Berets, eight Nung commandos, and a Vietnamese interpreter.[3] The team leader, Sergeant Richard Meadows, was well known for bravery and coolness under fire. Earlier in the year, he had earned accolades from General Westmoreland when he returned from a Laos mission with a load of new artillery sighting devices—proof positive that the North Vietnamese were smuggling big guns down the Ho Chi Minh Trail.

Meadows was in Laos with OHIO when a voice on the radio ordered them to find a landing zone and wait for immediate extraction. By midnight on 14 October, the entire team was aboard the *Intrepid* for a hasty briefing on the status of Lieutenant Woods.

At sunup, OHIO was on deck waiting to board two Sea Kings. This time, in place of the flotation collars, the team would use jungle penetrator devices specifically designed for breaking through thick forest canopy. But storm clouds closed in over Thanh Hoa, and the mission was scrubbed for the remainder of the afternoon. Woods was now into his third day on the ground in North Vietnam.[4]

The morning of 16 October dawned clear, and at first light the team members divided among two helicopters and lifted off *Intrepid*'s deck. As they reached Thanh Hoa, the lead helicopter dipped down over the aviator's last known position near a tall tree with distinctive white bark. As Meadows recalled, "When I was young, I remember a blight had hit the Appalachian chestnut trees and turned them blonde. This tree looked the same way, so I nicknamed it the 'chestnut tree.' I used this as a reference point and told the pilot to land us 800 meters away."[5]

Going down in pairs aboard jungle penetrators, OHIO quickly assembled on the ground. As the sound of helicopter blades receded, the team waited for the normal background chorus of bird and insect noises to return. Meadows then motioned his teammates to slowly patrol out of the forest in skirmish formation toward the "chestnut tree."

Moving up a low rise, the recon team picked its way through the thick vegetation. Less than one hundred meters from their target, the Nung pointman motioned them to an abrupt halt. Meadows edged forward and saw a well-worn trail hidden under the canopy.[6]

For fifteen minutes, they sat in silence watching the jungle trail. Then, faintly in the distance, came the sound of Vietnamese voices. Meadows sank to the ground, trying to hide his frame in the foliage. Four North Vietnamese soldiers appeared on the trail and immediately spotted Meadows. Bursting from the brush, he fired a burst from his Swedish K submachine gun. Within seconds, bullets were flying through the trees. The assistant team leader, Sergeant Charles Kerns, looked around at the Nung commandos. "During an earlier operation, the Nung had peeled away from a hilltop," recalled Kerns, "and Meadows had been forced to lead them back up. It had been a big loss of face for them. When we came under fire this time, they turned toward me with big grins on their faces as if to say, 'We're not running this time.'"[7]

As one, OHIO raced forward. By the time the team reached the trail, the four North Vietnamese lay dead. With the element of surprise now gone, the Americans began to yell for Woods. But once they did, the surrounding forest came alive with bugle calls. The dead patrol, they realized, was part of a much larger force sweeping through the area.

Vastly outnumbered, the rescuers were now in need of rescue. Meadows called the *Intrepid* for an emergency extraction. With the helicopters incoming, OHIO retraced its steps to the original insertion point. By the time the HH-3s materialized overhead, the commandos had been on North Vietnamese soil for almost four hours. But they were not yet out of danger; the sound of bugles was closing in.

Dividing the team in two, Meadows called for Kerns and half the Nung to ride the jungle penetrator into the first chopper. After that, Meadows, Sergeant William Anthony (the third American on OHIO), and the remaining commandos boarded the second helicopter.

As the two Sea Kings turned toward the Tonkin Gulf, the jungle erupted into a maelstrom of lead from the converging North Vietnamese. The second aircraft with Meadows and Anthony managed to escape the bullets, but the first was not so lucky. A round slammed into the armor plating on its side door, knocking the door gunner to the floor in an unconscious heap. Shrapnel slashed through the cabin, ripping the crew chief's nose and gashing the copilot in the arm and one of the Nung in the leg. Kerns took a shard in the head, which started bleeding profusely.

The stricken helicopter began to vibrate and lose altitude. The pilot, who alone had managed to escape serious injury, shouted for everyone to don life vests. With the carrier task force almost within reach, the Sea King sputtered, then lurched into the sea. Pitching on its side on impact, it took on water and began to sink. Passengers and crew leaped free just as the HH-3 was swallowed by the waves. A motorboat from the destroyer *Henley* soon arrived and whisked them to safety.

SOG's attempted rescue inside North Vietnam showed the pitfalls of such missions. Not only had its best reconnaissance team failed at finding Woods (SOG later learned that he was captured on 14 October), but the commandos had nearly become prisoners themselves. Still, when the JPRC got a second call on 4 December, it again turned to SHINING BRASS.

This time, eight planes with thirteen crewmen were downed over North Vietnam during a single twenty-four-hour period. Emergency radio signals were beeping across North Vietnam, including one near Dien Bien Phu. Intending to focus its efforts in that valley, the JPRC relayed a request to Kontum, the SHINING BRASS launch site in South Vietnam's Central Highlands. Captain Frank Jaks, the launch site's operations officer, took two of his best reconnaissance teams and rushed to Nakhon Phanom. Like OHIO's mission from the *Intrepid*, they drew up plans to take helicopters into Dien Bien Phu and eliminate any opposition on the ground. The mission was code-named Operation ROWBOAT.[8]

Before implementing ROWBOAT, an RF-101 reconnaissance plane flew

Sergeants Richard Meadows (third from left) and Charles Kerns (right) with Team OHIO aboard the USS *Intrepid* following their rescue mission in Thanh Hoa Province, October 1966. (Courtesy Charles Kerns)

over the area for a visual check of the crash site. The pilot saw nothing, and there was no longer any signal from the emergency beepers. Without anything to go on, ROWBOAT was canceled on 8 December.[9]

As the two SOG teams returned to Kontum, the SAAT commandos were nearly ready for their baptism of fire. Four teams already were operational, and an additional four awaited training.[10] But before any of them had a chance to taste combat, Saigon had a change of heart. Probably because it belatedly realized the slim chances of success, MACV dissolved the SAAT program in the spring of 1967.

Almost immediately, the teams found new jobs. Since early in the year, SOG's Airborne Operations Section had been toying with a new concept called Short-Term Roadwatch and Target Acquisition, abbreviated as STRATA. The plan called for Vietnamese commando teams to infiltrate the North Vietnamese panhandle, transmit real-time intelligence, and exfiltrate after about four weeks. In many respects, this sounded like the SHINING

BRASS forays in Laos, which had been renamed PRAIRIE FIRE in early 1967. The Joint Chiefs of Staff, in fact, had proposed in May that PRAIRIE FIRE teams be extended into the North Vietnam panhandle.[11] But while this concept had its advantages—no language barriers when communicating with overhead aircraft, for example—it also carried the possibility of Americans being captured or killed on North Vietnamese soil. This risk alone was too much for Washington, and the idea died on the vine.

Instead, the Joint Chiefs approved STRATA as an all-indigenous alternative. Conveniently, the four operational SAAT teams had recently become available. Changing the acronym at the top of the ledger, the rescuers were now road watchers; François, the former SAAT chief, assumed command of STRATA.

On the American side, the first STRATA chief was Major Austin Wilgus, the same case officer who had tried to extract Team BELL earlier in February. With STRATA now his priority project, Wilgus was given control over the four ex-SAAT teams, each of which numbered between ten and thirteen commandos. While they already had seven months of Long Thanh training, most of it covered topics that had nothing to do with road watching. Beginning instruction anew, they learned the reconnaissance ropes through midsummer. As a graduation exercise, they conducted a series of training forays into Laos.

The first team into Laos, called STRATA 111, began its mission from Khe Sanh, the SOG forward launch site used earlier during the ROMEO infiltration. Boarding a South Vietnamese air force H-34, the team headed west toward the border. Dipping toward an isolated clearing, the chopper dropped off the commandos and circled east.

While nobody intended for the team to see heavy action on its first outing, things did not go according to plan. A few hours into the mission, the team members began to detect movement on all sides. Communications intercepts later indicated they had landed in the middle of the North Vietnamese 325th Division.

In the midst of a hornet's nest, the fact that the STRATA members were disguised as North Vietnamese regulars—complete with pith helmets, khaki fatigues, and AK-47 assault rifles—provided little comfort. Quickly spotted, they ran for five kilometers, all the while radioing frantically for an extraction. Breaking contact, they found a clearing and waited for the H-34s. When the choppers finally arrived, a dozen men jumped in; one remaining member—known as the "Big Cambode" because of his size and ethnicity—was missing. Hearing this, an H-34 circled back to the clearing for a final look. There they found the Big Cambode, sitting on the ground and nursing a bullet wound on his buttocks.[12]

A second training mission had better luck. In August, STRATA 112 was inserted into Laos from SOG's launch site at Dak To in the Central Highlands. Its job was to recon a segment of the Ho Chi Minh Trail, and once again the commandos anticipated little action. Boarding two H-34s, they inserted without incident. Working their way toward the trail, they found a few huts on the first day. The following morning, they were spotted and called for a helicopter extraction. Despite heavy cloud cover, the H-34s landed and delivered them safely back to Dak To.[13]

With only this limited experience, STRATA prepared to shift toward North Vietnam. Just as in their training missions, the commandos would be dressed like North Vietnamese troops.[14] The teams would carry PRC-74 tactical radios, which would allow them to make instantaneous voice communication with spotter aircraft overhead. Nearly all of their approved target areas were in the North Vietnamese panhandle astride routes leading across the Annamites to the Ho Chi Minh Trail.

The first to head north was STRATA 111. Its mission: to watch traffic along Route 101 in Quang Binh, a feeder road that plugged into Route 12 before channeling through the Mu Gia Pass on its way to the Ho Chi Minh Trail.[15] Equipped with heavy binoculars on a tripod, the team would conduct its spying from nearby Khe Sai Mountain.

At sunup on 24 September, the STRATA commandos climbed into a CH-3 at Nakhon Phanom. To minimize their profile on the ground, only seven of the team's thirteen members would be going. Nearby, Major Wilgus boarded a C-130 command-and-control ship that would monitor the insert from overhead.

"We infiltrated them at first light," recalled Major Alton Deviney, the same CH-3 flight commander on the abortive mission to extract Team BELL. "The mountains where we put them in were steep and sharp, and the jungle was extremely thick."[16]

While the harsh topography meant there was little chance of hostile troops in the area, it also hindered movement of the team. As the commandos soon learned, covering the six kilometers to their intended observation point would be all but impossible. Worse, they ran out of water, then two members became sick. On 28 September, STRATA 111 called for an extraction.[17]

Because he was familiar with the terrain, Major Deviney got the job of pulling the commandos out. If he succeeded, it would mark the first time a SOG agent team had successfully been pulled out of North Vietnam. Wilgus gave Deviney a call before departing. "He told me that he would be in

STRATA 111 in North Vietnamese fatigues and headgear prior to the team's insertion into North Vietnam, September 1967. (Conboy collection)

the C-130 command ship not too far away, and that I would have all the cover for the mission that was needed."

True to his word, Wilgus arranged for a flight of U.S. Air Force T-28 fighter-bombers to scramble from Nakhon Phanom once the two CH-3s departed. Heading east, both sets of aircraft rendezvoused over the landing zone, only to find it socked in by bad weather. "I told my high bird to stay on top of the clouds," said Deviney. "I would try to get under them." He dropped his CH-3 through a tight hole, popping into the clear a mere thirty meters above the pointed karst pinnacles.

Behind him, the second CH-3 edged downward. The aircraft commander, Major James Villotti, was only two months into his tour and was carrying an 8mm movie camera to record the event. As the mountains came into view, he stared in awe. "I don't know how anyone could travel over such extreme terrain," he later commented. "It reminded me of the Badlands covered with rainforest."[18]

Spotting the place where he had originally dropped STRATA 111, Deviney moved closer. Waving from the mountaintop was the entire team, apparently having barely moved over the previous four days. "You could not land because of the brush and trees," said Deviney, "though I could get close

Major Alton Deviney, CH-3 commander during the first STRATA insertion, September 1967. (Courtesy Alton Deviney)

enough to bring them up on a hoist." But as the chopper settled in above the karst, gunfire popped from a ridgeline 450 meters away.

Unarmed and vulnerable, Deviney yelled for T-28 support. Despite the cloud bank, the fighter pilots managed to squeeze through the hole. Racing toward the ridgeline, they peppered it with white phosphorus rockets. The gunfire immediately ceased, and the chopper continued winching up the commandos from the ground. Three were safely aboard when a fire warning light flashed in the cockpit. Out of time, Deviney hovered even lower until the chopper's belly scraped the bushes. The crew chief, Sergeant Ralph Hohl, then tossed down a rope and pulled the remaining four Vietnamese aboard hand over hand. As soon as the last man's feet cleared the ground, Deviney added power and climbed steeply back through the clouds.

Although STRATA 111 had gathered almost no data of interest, MACV was delighted that the jinx was broken. A SOG team had finally been recovered from North Vietnam. Major Deviney earned a Silver Star; Villotti, the Distinguished Flying Cross. Cover letters from General Westmoreland personally thanked the crews for their "efficient and professional manner" during a "deep penetration into hostile territory."[19]

Less than a month later, STRATA tried again. By this time, Major Wilgus had rotated out of Vietnam and was replaced as chief STRATA case officer by Major Victor Calderon. A Green Beret on his second tour in Vietnam, Calderon assembled the second team, STRATA 112, and briefed the members on their target. For this outing, they would infiltrate northern Quang Binh Province and watch the key intersection where Route 15 merges with Route 12 and plunges south toward the Mu Gia Pass. Their insertion point would be a wide expanse of mountainous jungle eight kilometers to the northwest. This time, they would forgo helicopters and use SOG's more traditional parachute entry.

On the evening of 23 October, the ten members of STRATA 112 donned padded tree-jumping suits and filed into an MC-130 at Tan Son Nhut air base. Circling over the Tonkin Gulf, they arrived over the drop zone at low altitude. At the jumpmaster's command, two "sticks" of five men stepped off the rear ramp.

Like most of the agent teams before them, STRATA 112 was dispersed during the drop. Ngo Phong Hai, one of the radiomen, had lost sight of all his teammates by the time he reached ground. As he crashed through the forest canopy, his body was jarred to a stop well off the jungle floor.

Frightened by the noise made during his landing, Hai stayed still until sunup. As the first shafts of morning light filtered through the canopy, he

Architects of the STRATA program: François, Major Austin Wilgus, and Major Victor Calderon. (Courtesy Victor Calderon)

cautiously climbed down from the tree and soon linked up with Mai Van Hop, the team's demolitions man, who had also spent the predawn hours hanging in a tree. Walking back to where Hai had landed, they located his radio bundle stuck high in the branches. Unable to climb up, they took a small piece of C-4 explosive from Hop's demolitions kit, fixed it to a long bamboo pole, and set it aflame. Hai eased the pole next to the radio and burned through the parachute cord holding it fast. The radio fell into the waiting arms of the men below.[20]

Five hours later, all ten members of STRATA 112 managed to reassemble. As he gathered his men, Lieutenant Nguyen Van Hung, the team leader, was visibly concerned. None of the surrounding terrain corresponded to anything on the map sheets they carried. Moreover, some of the men had seen a village nearby—and the drop zone was supposed to be unpopulated.

As it turned out, STRATA 112 was dropped clear across the district near the Ha Tinh provincial boundary. To get their bearings, the team members began to meander through the forest. Local villagers soon found signs of their movement and notified the authorities. On the morning of 31 October, they were ambushed near the banks of a wide stream. Sergeant Pham Ngoc Linh, the team's second in command, charged through the cordon, spraying bullets as he ran. Three commandos died in the firefight, and another was killed the following day.

Shaking their pursuers, the commandos fled south to the Quang Binh border. While they managed to make radio contact with U.S. Air Force aircraft, the team could not pinpoint their own location. Spotters tried in vain to locate the team, but the thick jungle made that all but impossible. The North Vietnamese search parties were careful not to give themselves away, watching quietly from under cover as the aerial search unfolded. They knew the helicopters would soon fly away and the hunt could resume.[21]

Out of food, the commandos were forced to roast some cassava roots in an open pit. Villagers saw the smoke and notified the militia. The hunt was on again. For the next week the North Vietnamese chased the commandos down like animals. One small group was surrounded on the afternoon of 4 November and captured, the rest within the next few days. One commando, Ngo Phong Hai, the team's backup radioman, ran for ten more days, evading North Vietnamese patrols as he waited vainly for rescue. On 17 November, exhausted and completely out of ammunition, he surrendered.[22]

Down in Saigon, meanwhile, Major Calderon was given emergency orders to report to Bolivia to help train that nation's elite rangers in the wake of the capture and execution of the guerrilla Che Guevara.[23] Deprived of a case officer, STRATA was placed on indefinite hold.

18

RED DRAGON

Among the most sensitive SOG missions were those conducted in concert with the Republic of China. This marriage followed indirectly from Chiang Kai-shek's dream of retaking the mainland, which he had lost in 1949, and vanquishing Mao Tse-tung's People's Republic. From almost the beginning, the U.S. government had actively fanned the generalissimo's hopes. Washington, for example, initially lent support to a pro-Nationalist guerrilla army taking shape in the hills of Burma. Beginning in 1951 and over the next two years, this front made no less than seven forays against China's southern underbelly, all without success.[1]

After this failed Burmese campaign, Chiang had spent the mid-1950s building his army. Behind the scenes, the CIA supported low-level shipping interdiction by Nationalist maritime commandos. By 1957, this had escalated into occasional probes against the mainland by ranger teams. The largest of these, on 2 October, involved a twenty-eight-man party that raided the Pehling Peninsula; they withdrew after being hit by artillery and machine-gun fire.[2]

With these coastal strikes causing China just minor discomfort, Chiang Kai-shek was determined to strike farther inland. For these operations, he envisioned deep penetrations by airborne commando teams. To support this, Chiang in September 1957 personally gave the U.S. ambassador to Taipei plans for the creation of a special forces corps that would jump inside China and rally the population. While leery of such provocations, the following February Washington authorized its military assistance mission in Taiwan to help raise a three-thousand-man special forces group.[3]

Not satisfied with just a single group, Chiang ordered the creation of two more special forces formations over the next two years. He also began to drop them inside China. During one mission in late April 1960, the CIA assisted with the insertion of a five-man team into Anhui Province. According to Taiwanese intelligence, this team was to be met by five hundred pro-Chiang sympathizers. Instead, it landed amid a dam construction project and was immediately on the run. Making radio contact with Taiwan, they pleaded for a resupply. But international politics made that impossible. A CIA U-2 spy plane had just been shot down over the Soviet Union, prompting the Eisenhower administration to temporarily halt further aerial missions over the communist bloc. Frantic, the team leader relayed a series of expletives to his CIA case officer before being captured.[4]

Taipei's poor track record did not deter Chiang. By the summer of 1961, he had four special forces groups totaling 12,000 airborne commandos, the largest concentration in any Asian nation. In addition, he had created a 5,500-man Anti-Communist National Salvation Corps composed of former mainlanders; this formation, too, was intended to play a direct, if ambiguous, role in overthrowing the communist Chinese.

Despite boosted numbers, the Republic of China's unconventional warfare campaign remained thin on success through the early 1960s. Typically, most airborne teams were captured soon after landing.[5] In many cases, China's formidable air defense system did not even let the infiltration aircraft reach their drop zones: at least five RB-69 aircraft, the mainstay of the infiltration effort, were shot down through 1964.[6]

With the skies growing too dangerous, Chiang's commandos turned toward the sea. Their biggest operation came in the summer of 1963, when two ships loaded with twenty-six members of the Anti-Communist National Salvation Corps headed toward Vietnamese waters. By 23 July, the boats had reached Bach Long Vi, a small, uninhabited atoll midway between Haiphong and the Chinese island of Hainan. Five days later, they sailed directly north, stopping off the coast of Quang Ninh Province. From there, the commandos transferred to motorized launches and made for shore. Their intention was to infiltrate along the border between North Vietnam and China, then head inland and establish a pocket of anticommunist resistance.

The commandos had barely beached their craft before North Vietnamese border units closed in. In the ensuing chase, seventeen commandos were captured, seven were killed, and two committed suicide.[7]

Unbeknownst to Taipei, two weeks earlier the South Vietnamese had tried to infiltrate a maritime commando team, code-named DRAGON, into the same corner of Quang Ninh Province. With this first incident no doubt fresh in their memories, the North Vietnamese had been able to mobilize instantly against the Nationalist Chinese.

While this operation might suggest a complete lack of coordination between Taipei and Saigon, such was not the case. In fact, military links between the two nations date back to May 1960, when Chiang sent three officers to Saigon for an assessment mission. Three months later, a contingent of South Vietnamese frogmen headed to Taiwan for scuba training. The following February, Ngo Dinh Can, Diem's influential brother, visited the Republic of China and suggested that Taipei station scuba instructors in South Vietnam.[8] While these instructors never materialized, a team of Chinese special forces was dispatched later that year for service in the Mekong Delta.

Landing boats used during the ill-fated infiltration by twenty-six commandos from the Republic of China's Anti-Communist National Salvation Corps, Quang Ninh Province, July 1963. (Vietnam News Agency)

While in the delta, the Chinese commandos worked with Father Nguyen Lac Hoa. A unique blend of anticommunist reactionary and Catholic clergyman, Father Hoa had been a lieutenant colonel in the Chinese army when Chiang Kai-chek held the mainland. After Chiang fled to Taiwan, Hoa headed south toward French Indochina. He eventually found safe haven in Diem's Catholic-friendly South Vietnam. Moving to An Xuyen Province in the southernmost Mekong Delta, Hoa began to organize his followers into a home guard. Assisted by the Chinese special forces team, they soon swept the Viet Cong out of their locale.

While Hoa's main focus was in An Xuyen, part of his paramilitary interest was directed north. Toward these ends, he maintained close contact with the Presidential Liaison Office's Lieutenant Colonel Tung and Captain Linh, directing them toward potential agent recruits among the Catholic refugee community. He also brought to their attention an elderly South Vietnamese army captain named Luong Hang. An ethnic Nung, Luong was soon hired as the Presidential Liaison Office's case officer for its Nung commando trainees.[9]

With the fall of Diem in November 1963, Father Hoa's star also dimmed.[10] Contacts between Saigon and Taipei, however, continued to grow. Already, Chinese C-123 aircrews were handling the bulk of infiltration missions into North Vietnam. Building on this foundation, South Vietnamese army General Nguyen Van Thieu traveled to Taipei in June 1964 to discuss other forms of military assistance.[11] Two months later, MACV and the South Vietnamese army agreed to the establishment of a Republic of China Military Mission. This was formally established in October, with its fifteen members primarily devoted to advising the South Vietnamese in psychological and political warfare techniques.

Saigon was hungry for more than just a small military mission. In August 1965, Prime Minister Nguyen Cao Ky went to Taipei to sound out possibilities and returned with assurances of more technical and material assistance. In addition, the Republic of China ambiguously hinted that it was prepared to respond to other requests.[12] This vague pledge became clear later that month when Lieutenant Colonel Ngo The Linh, then head of covert maritime operations, traveled to Taipei to discuss staging agents from South Vietnam into North Vietnam and China. All of the agent candidates were to be furnished by South Vietnam and trained in Taiwan. Taipei also promised to provide false documentation and speedboats to infiltrate some of the agents directly from South Vietnam. Others would infiltrate from Cambodia and Laos, presumably aboard commercial air flights.[13]

As quickly as these promises were made, the proposed collaboration turned into a unilateral Nationalist Chinese effort. By September, with no input from the South Vietnamese, four agents had sneaked into mainland China as legal travelers via Phnom Penh and Vientiane.[14] It was not until early the following year that covert cooperation with Taiwan was again proposed. This time, SOG was to have a primary role.

SOG's flirtation with the Republic of China is best understood in the context of relations between North Vietnam and China. During the 1960s, ties between the two communist countries had degenerated into an odd mix of anti-Western camaraderie and historical animosity. At the bottom of all the comradely rhetoric was the historical fact that the Vietnamese viewed China with deep suspicion.[15] Old antagonisms were exacerbated when the Soviet Union significantly increased its military aid to Hanoi in 1965, a move that left Beijing quietly fuming. While China maintained a facade of communist solidarity with North Vietnam, many foreign observers suspected bilateral relations were stretched taut below the surface.

These strained ties provided both Washington and Taipei with some unique unconventional warfare opportunities. In May 1965, Taipei's defense minister Chiang Ching-kuo, the son of Generalissimo Chiang, proposed air-dropping commandos into southwest China to harass Hanoi's supply lines.[16] Four months later, Washington sounded out Taipei on the possibility of parachuting Nationalist Chinese agents near the North Vietnamese border region to monitor Beijing's lines of communications.[17] In encouraging such a move, U.S. policy had turned on its head: since 1956, Washington had repeatedly lectured self-restraint with regard to mainland operations, but nine years later it was actively encouraging the Nationalists to conduct these very same activities. Chiang knew better than to waste such an opportunity.[18]

Each side had different motives for its actions: the United States wanted intelligence, while Taiwan saw an opening for the introduction of agents into China's Yunnan Province. This ambition was of some concern to Washington, which realized Taipei would be prone to turn what was basically a reconnaissance foray into a more provocative operation. The solution: introduce SOG into the equation.

In switching from a primarily Nationalist Chinese operation to a joint venture with SOG, the parameters for the operation quickly changed. Instead of sending Chinese agents directly into Yunnan Province, SOG lobbied to place a long-term team along the Chinese border in Lao Cai Province. This team would perform an EWOT mission of watching road, rail, and river traffic flowing southeast from China toward Hanoi.[19]

Not surprisingly, SOG's Lao Cai concept was too tepid to excite the Nationalists. But in a compromise move, Taipei agreed to shift the drop zone northeast into Ha Giang Province. Rugged and thin of population, Ha Giang had little of the logistical network found in Lao Cai. Ha Giang, however, had a long, remote border that jutted into China. According to reworked plans, a Vietnamese team would first jump into Ha Giang and secure the drop zone for a month, after which a Chinese team would be dropped to join them. From there, they would eventually head north into China.

The plan was overly optimistic. SOG's own record with long-range teams was spotty; Taiwan's was even worse. Despite the disheartening precedent, however, plans proceeded. Taipei was especially eager to infiltrate commandos into the mainland, especially when it could do so under the protective umbrella of the United States. While the benefits for SOG were not as apparent, the secretary of defense was notified of the plan in October 1966, and CINCPAC offered approval the following May.[20]

At Long Thanh, formation of the Vietnamese half of the Ha Giang team had begun in August 1966. Acting as case officer was Major Luong Hang, the Nung discovered earlier by Father Hoa. Going by the call sign Mathieu, Hang was considered the perfect choice for such a collaborative effort with Taipei on account of his ethnic background and fluent Chinese.

Under Mathieu's direction, twelve commandos were chosen from the thirty-man class of agents then undergoing training at Long Thanh. Code-named RED DRAGON, all were ethnic Vietnamese natives of northern North Vietnam. Chosen as its leader was Nguyen Thai Kien, a veteran of several battles against the Viet Minh along the Chinese frontier during the First Indochina War. Coming south after 1954, he had joined the South Vietnamese army's airborne group, then was among the original group of army lieutenants seconded to SOG in late 1965 to act as indigenous leaders for the SHINING BRASS reconnaissance teams running missions into Laos.

Through the beginning of 1967, RED DRAGON received instruction at Long Thanh. All members were cross-trained in demolitions and various weapons systems to include 3.5-inch rocket launchers. They also received intensive instruction in the Chinese language.

On 24 February, RED DRAGON was paired with its Chinese counterparts. Totaling thirteen men, they were drawn from the Republic of China special forces. Given the sensitivity of their presence, they were given a variety of cover designations. On financial records, for example, they were listed as either "Nung RED DRAGON" or "RED.DRAGON," the period between words used to distinguish them from their Vietnamese counterparts. Each Chinese member was also given a Vietnamese alias.[21]

For six months, the two RED DRAGON contingents went through the paces at Long Thanh. For graduation, they were loaded aboard a plane in August and parachuted near Dalat for a live-fire field exercise against roving Viet Cong bands. Making contact, they killed two communist guerrillas, captured two others, and recovered five carbines.[22]

By the second week of September, the Vietnamese half of RED DRAGON, now down to eight members, underwent final preparation. The commander, Kien, was promoted to captain, while his deputy, Pham Xuan Ky, moved up one rank to master sergeant. Mathieu, joined by his SOG counterpart, Captain Frederic Caristo, gave the men their final briefing. Caristo told them they needed to establish contact within three days or they would be presumed captured. Their mission, the case officers stressed, was to sit and wait for the Nationalist Chinese special forces before heading north into China. Behind them was a map of North Vietnam, with a white circled area extending from Ha Giang into China. One of the RED DRAGON communications specialists, Le Trung Tin, assumed this area indicated a liberated zone.[23]

On 21 September, the eight commandos donned tree-jumping suits and boarded an MC-130. Nearly all of their supplies were packed into a single large bundle. The bundle had a beacon inside, and each of the agents carried a special SOG homing device disguised as a transistor radio. By following

Captain David Kriskovitch trains with Team RED DRAGON near Dalat for its mission into North Vietnam, summer 1967. (Courtesy David Kriskovitch)

the beacon to the bundle, all of the agents would be able to quickly converge after their jump.

Lifting into the darkening sky, the plane made a short hop to Nha Trang. From there, it flew over the Tonkin Gulf in a wide counterclockwise arc. Taking full advantage of the aircraft's advanced avionics, the pilot dropped low and skimmed west along the rugged Chinese border.

At 0200 hours over Ha Giang Province, the rear ramp lowered. The team was divided into two even sticks. According to plan, the bundle and the team leader would go out first, followed in rapid succession by the radiomen and the rest of the team. What had not been in the plan was the fact that nearly every member of RED DRAGON became airsick. Whether from nerves or the bumpy flight, the commandos—not to mention the one Vietnamese and two American jumpmasters—took turns vomiting on the floor of the plane.[24]

When the green light came on, RED DRAGON stood on weakened legs. Looking to set a strong example, Kien and the bundle disappeared into the void. It was to no avail. Claiming sickness, one of the demolitions experts, Trinh Quoc Anh, fell to his knees and refused to jump.[25] Seeing this, a second member balked, followed by a third. A full minute passed as the jumpmasters tried to encourage, cajole, and otherwise force RED DRAGON out the rear. Kien and the bundle, meanwhile, drifted into the distance. Eventually, six more team members jumped. No amount of pleading could get Anh off the plane; he ultimately rode the MC-130E back to South Vietnam.

Last off the ramp was Nguyen Huu Tan, a Catholic from Thai Binh. The team's medic, Tan could see other parachutes spread below him in the bright moonlight. He could also hear the sound of trucks and saw lights from a military border camp; he was certain they were seen on descent.

Crashing through a bamboo grove midway up a slope, Tan released his harness. The commandos had been told to retrieve their parachutes and dissolve them with a special acid compound. But Tan's chute was stuck high in the bamboo, so he left it and fled the drop zone. Because of the delay aboard the plane, he had landed southwest of the intended target some fifty kilometers from the Chinese border. Although the area was sparsely populated, a road ran through the area, guarded by a large North Vietnamese military garrison and a Chinese antiaircraft battery.[26]

Reckoning that the supply bundle was located in the valley below, Tan tried to activate his homer. As a result of the wide dispersion of the drop, however, the beacon was out of range. Swedish K submachine gun in hand, he headed down the slope where he suspected the other commandos had landed. Within a day, he managed to stumble across Le Trung Tin, one of the team's two radiomen. Tin's homer was not working either, making their chances of finding the bundle containing food, uniforms, and GRC-109 long-distance radio exceedingly remote. His handheld HT-1 radio was also not functioning in the mountains, meaning they could not contact the rest of the team.[27]

For two days, the two commandos picked their way through the forest in a futile search for their teammates. Alone and hungry, they finally decided to escape toward Laos. Just one day later, North Vietnamese patrols closed in, and Tin and Tan were captured without a struggle.

Three other members of RED DRAGON had only slightly better luck. Landing in the valley, they managed to link up the day after the jump. Closer to the bundle, their homers had registered, leading them in a northern direction. They walked for nearly a week but still failed to find the supplies. By that time, the North Vietnamese had fully mobilized and were sweeping the lowlands; all three commandos were soon surrounded and captured.[28]

A few days later, the final two members of RED DRAGON were in custody. Isolating the radiomen, contact was soon made via BUGS. At their final briefing, the commandos had been given just three days to come on the air. Now, nearly two weeks after their jump, they were asking Saigon to overlook the lag. For SOG, this was too much to swallow. Mathieu, however, took their story at face value and demanded that a resupply be flown. Accordingly, on 17 October an F-4C jet raced over Ha Giang and dropped a set of disguised napalm canisters.[29]

As it turned out, SOG was not alone in smelling duplicity. Taiwan, too, began to have second thoughts and kept its commandos in the isolation area at Long Thanh. Before they went north, it was decided to send some Vietnamese reinforcements to verify the status of the original team. The new team, RED DRAGON ALPHA, would have only two members. One of them was Trinh Quoc Anh, the original RED DRAGON member who had balked in September.

More than just a standard reinforcement mission, RED DRAGON ALPHA would be played with a twist. The team would jump in, stay two weeks to verify RED DRAGON was secure, then be pulled out using the Fulton Skyhook System. The Fulton Skyhook had been featured in the 1965 James Bond movie *Thunderball,* and it indeed looked like a gadget worthy of 007. Invented by Robert Fulton, from the family of steamboat fame, the system was intended as a means of quickly extracting agents from deep inside the communist bloc without the need to land a plane. The person to be exfiltrated put on a harnessed oversuit with a 250-meter cord attached to a helium balloon. As the balloon rose in the sky, it would be snagged by a transport aircraft fitted with a specially configured yoke on the nose. With the cord secured in the yoke, the agent would be yanked off the ground and pulled up into the slipstream behind the plane. He would then be winched into the open ramp at the rear of the aircraft.

While the Fulton Skyhook looked very dangerous, a U.S. Marine had successfully tested it back in August 1958. Four years later, the CIA formulated plans to use the system to free Allen Pope, its imprisoned B-26 pilot in Indonesia.[30] Although that mission was eventually scrubbed, dozens of live tests followed, with the first dual pickup in March 1964, and the first side-by-side dual pickup in May 1966.[31]

By that time, the Skyhook had found its way to Vietnam. In the fall of 1966, the first MC-130E aircraft delivered for SOG use had detachable

Fulton yokes on the nose. Also delivered were a limited number of Skyhooks packed in aerodynamic metal canisters and designed to be dropped to downed airmen deep inside North Vietnam. This plan was put to the test on 12 March 1967, when a Fulton canister was dropped by jet to Edwin Goodrich, a U.S. Air Force aviator whose RF-4C was shot down in Son La Province. Goodrich, seriously injured, was killed during capture before he could reach the canister.[32]

Besides rescuing downed airmen, SOG recognized further possibilities for the Skyhook. In June 1967, plans were drawn for a reinforcement team to drop to REMUS near Dien Bien Phu. Its mission was twofold. First, the two-man team would be able to verify the status of SOG's most successful team. Second, it would carry and be trained in the use of wiretaps. The technology at that time called for agents to physically activate a tape machine when they heard a conversation come through the lines. Once they had exhausted their supply of tapes—estimated at about thirty-three days—the two agents would have them in hand when they exfiltrated by Skyhook.[33]

In preparation for this first Skyhook mission, a Fulton system was delivered to Long Thanh. A side-by-side configuration was to be used to yank out the two agents on a single pass. Stepping up to the challenge, the two REMUS reinforcements performed a single test snatch without incident. Then, on 22 August, they jumped into the REMUS drop zone with their wiretaps and a Skyhook canister. Before the Skyhook could be used, however, REMUS radioed a message saying that a North Vietnamese patrol had uncovered the cached equipment.[34]

Despite this failure, SOG assembled RED DRAGON ALPHA and readied it for a test snatch. Understandably, the commandos were leery of the technology. To allay their fears, two Americans decided to prove its safety. The first was Lieutenant Colonel Jonathan Carney. A slim military intelligence officer, Carney was head of SOG's Airborne Operations Section. The second, Roland Dutton, was a muscled U.S. Special Forces major who commanded the advisory contingent at Long Thanh.

Putting on harnessed oversuits with straps leading to a single helium balloon, Carney and Dutton sat next to each other on the dirt in front of a throng of commando trainees. As planned, the MC-130E flew low over the Long Thanh airfield and snagged the balloon in its yoke. Initially, the two Americans lifted without incident and drew in behind the airplane. Once they were in the slipstream, however, the difference in their weights made them oscillate wildly. The smaller Carney slammed repeatedly into Dutton, breaking all the bones around his eye sockets and nose.[35]

When the plane landed, the bloodied pair stepped onto the tarmac. Despite their injuries, they had convinced the jittery Vietnamese that the sys-

Lieutenant Colonel Jonathan Carney and Major Roland Dutton brace for a twin Skyhook test at Long Thanh, December 1967. (Courtesy Roland Dutton)

tem worked. RED DRAGON ALPHA was scheduled to jump the following month, January 1968.

All the while, RED DRAGON's case officer, Captain Fred Caristo, remained convinced his agents were compromised. For once erring on the side of caution, SOG put RED DRAGON ALPHA on permanent hold, and Taipei called its special forces team home.

But Mathieu was just as certain that his agents were good. By the spring of 1968, however, he lost any say in the matter when he was reassigned as the Strategic Technical Directorate's first covert operative in Hong Kong.[36] There his mission included collecting intelligence on Beijing's support for North Vietnam and recruiting Chinese agents.[37] Given his ethnic background and linguistic ability, hopes were high that he could foster some good contacts. To Saigon's utter disappointment, however, Mathieu spent a year without showing any results for his efforts. Then, without a trace, he and his entire family disappeared. While desertion was suspected, defection was never ruled out.

19

SHORT-TERM TARGETS

Nguyen Nhu Anh, one of the two commandos on RED DRAGON AL-PHA, was homesick. A Catholic, he had spent Christmas 1967 locked in the isolation area of Long Thanh. Six days later, Anh was still there to usher in 1968. He was not alone. On New Year's Day, thirty-three fresh faces filed into the adjoining row of Quonset huts. By the end of March, nearly eighty new arrivals had packed Long Thanh tight. One-quarter were ethnic Cambodians recruited from around the Mekong Delta.[1]

All were destined for STRATA, the road-watching effort initiated the previous September. While the program had seen only limited success—one team had been recovered, the other was missing in its entirety—MACV felt it offered enough promise to warrant major expansion. This was underscored in a 17 March 1968 memo, which called for the program to be built up to ten teams.[2]

Overseeing the program was a new STRATA case officer, Major George "Speedy" Gaspard. A marine during World War II, Gaspard was later commissioned as a U.S. Army infantry officer and became part of the original contingent of Special Forces formed in 1952. This was his second Vietnam tour, having earlier worked with CIA-sponsored paramilitary border forces during 1963.

When Gaspard first arrived at Long Thanh, STRATA missions had been on hold for a full five months. The delay was partly due to the communist Tet Offensive, launched at the close of January 1968, which had thrown South Vietnam into chaos. Forced to turn its assets inward to deal with the offensive, SOG found little time to pursue operations in the north.

By March, the communist blitz had lost steam, and pressure was mounting to restart STRATA. None of the new recruits had finished training, so Gaspard made do with the project's three original teams. To start, he moved them to a new forward operations base at Monkey Mountain, a karst pinnacle located near Danang. Isolated at the end of the Son Tra peninsula, Monkey Mountain was long a favorite SOG locale. Already, several small camps housing Biet Hai commandos had been erected along its rocky base. Next to these, STRATA built its own secure compound.

Monkey Mountain was ideal for STRATA on two counts. First, it gave the commandos more room than the cramped Long Thanh facilities. More important, it put them closer to the Demilitarized Zone: just north of the boundary was Quang Binh Province, STRATA's main target. From the field, deployed STRATA teams could now directly communicate with the forward operating base via PRC-74 tactical radios.[3] In doing so, they bypassed the earlier inefficient arrangement of relaying messages through BUGS in the Philippines, speeding communications and making STRATA's intelligence more timely.

Before launching his first operation, Gaspard reviewed the lessons learned on the previous two outings. STRATA 112's disastrous parachute insertion was foremost in his mind, so the decision was made to launch all future missions from Nakhon Phanom in Thailand using U.S. Air Force CH-3 helicopters. Strict guidelines from the Thai government remained in force, meaning that STRATA commandos could stay at Nakhon Phanom for only short layovers; in the event of a weather delay, they had to fly back to Danang.

Another lesson concerned team size. STRATA teams were originally configured as large as ten men apiece. Too unwieldy, STRATA teams were now to run with no more than eight and as few as four.[4]

Early STRATA commandos also carried too much equipment. "[There were commandos who] weighed 124 pounds soaking wet carrying as much as 80 pounds or a little better," quipped one U.S. adviser. To solve the problem, SOG eliminated unnecessary extras. Bulky telescopes with tripod mounts, which several members had already abandoned in the field, were removed from their load. Food and ammunition were kept to a minimum; should more be needed, resupply flights from Nakhon Phanom were planned. And with the teams running with fewer men, there was no longer a need to carry walkie-talkies for intrateam communication.[5]

Gaspard was satisfied with this lighter configuration, and during the third week of March he finalized plans for the first mission of 1968: a foray by the veterans of STRATA 111 into the karst maze west of Lang Mo, a key village in Le Ninh District of Quang Binh Province. A well-traveled road, labeled Route 196, ran southwest from Lang Mo toward the Laos border and fed into the Ho Chi Minh Trail. There was evidence that the nearby Giang River was also being used by the North Vietnamese to move supplies south. "Surveillance of this area will provide information on the status and use of these two routes of movement," read MACV's analysis. "In addition, valuable targeting data can be developed for 7th [Air Force]."[6]

On the afternoon of 17 March, STRATA 111 flew into North Vietnam. The insertion went off without a hitch, and as the sound of the helicopter blades faded into silence, the team moved off the landing zone toward its road-watch site. Early the next morning, it ran into two squads from a local militia unit. For twenty minutes they exchanged fire, with the North Vietnamese getting the worst of it. At least three militiamen were killed or wounded, and, in the confusion, the team withdrew. That night, it contacted Danang and reported the fight.

On the third day, 19 March, the team was more careful. Three times the commandos spotted militia patrols looking for them in the distance. Avoiding contact, they moved on, planting antipersonnel mines as they left. They continued for the entire day, hearing at least three explosions in their wake.

Early the next morning, the team tried making contact with an orbiting forward air control plane. In a special arrangement, one U.S. Air Force O-2 spotter aircraft from Nakhon Phanom was dedicated to the STRATA program. With a STRATA adviser aboard, the plane crossed the Annamite chain and homed in on the signal from the team's PRC-25 tactical set.[7] Unfortunately, the commandos could offer no clear coordinates from under the thick jungle canopy, and it was another two days before the forward air controller could actually pinpoint the team on the ground.

By that time, the mission had run its course and it was time for extraction. Back at Nakhon Phanom, Major Kyron Hall of the 20th Helicopter Squadron got the call to fetch the STRATA commandos. As he neared the pickup point, he was struck by the ruggedness of the karst. The team was atop one particularly steep outcropping appropriately nicknamed the Candlestick. Hall eased his helicopter toward the top of the long, thin ridge, which he recalled was "about the size of my living room," but found the rocky spine too narrow to touch down. Hovering in space, he dropped a ladder. The agents scrambled up one by one to safety.[8]

This was the second extraction for STRATA 111, and for that reason alone SOG considered the mission a success even though little useful intelligence was gathered. "Team found no evidence to determine whether or not significant infiltration traffic is passing through," read a SOG report.[9] Not surprising considering the rugged terrain. Men and supplies heading to the southern battlefield would most likely stick to the lowlands, not the mountaintops.

Gaspard decided to send his two untested teams into North Vietnam. The first was STRATA 113, which on the morning of 31 March launched from Nakhon Phanom into the same general target area. Seeing no activity of note, the team was extracted a week later.

Although short on results, the mission marked another milestone in the STRATA program: the same helicopter that picked up STRATA 113 dropped off the next team, STRATA 114. In addition to road watching, the new team was charged with spreading SSPL propaganda and sowing M-14 antipersonnel mines along trails in the vicinity. Very quickly, it ran into trouble. Two days into the scheduled ten-day mission, the team encountered a

North Vietnamese patrol. Bullets flew, but STRATA 114 withdrew before anyone was hit.

Moving south along Route 196, the team radioed Danang on the afternoon of 11 April to say it was positioned overlooking the road. For the next twenty-four hours the team members watched, then on 12 April SOG ordered them to cross the route, take pictures of what they saw, plant the mines, and leave a batch of SSPL leaflets.

The commandos moved slowly, checking for signs of North Vietnamese activity. Reaching a small crossroads believed to be a checkpoint, they scattered leaflets and planted an SSPL flag, then placed a few mines as a rude surprise for anyone stopping to look. An hour later, with the team safely out of the area, a few muffled explosions confirmed that the road was indeed in use.

STRATA 114 still had two days to go before extraction. But by then the commandos had already run out of water and wanted to go home. As it turned out, water was shaping up to be the biggest limiting factor in the program. It was the dry season in the North Vietnamese panhandle, which was good for helicopters looking for landing zones but left most water holes empty. To compensate, SOG had considered outfitting the commandos with extra canteens but rejected the idea because of weight considerations. Similarly, a proposal to lift a large water bladder into the target area was vetoed as too cumbersome.[10]

The thirsty team waited until 15 April before a chopper picked them up. Once again, little of note was learned from the mission. Still, SOG got the satisfaction of showing the North Vietnamese that STRATA could come and go in their own backyard.[11]

For future missions, SOG added four new targets to the STRATA area of operations, bringing the total to thirteen. Three areas were outlined in Quang Binh Province, two of them farther north than any previous STRATA targets. The fourth, added in May, was just north of the Demilitarized Zone at Lac Xa, known as Bat Lake to the Americans. Hanoi was extending a road through the area, which Saigon feared would facilitate the movement of troops and supplies to battlefields in the south.

By the time the next STRATA mission was launched in May, Monkey Mountain was teeming with new agents just graduated from Long Thanh. First to see combat was STRATA 120. This team consisted of six men: two were fresh Vietnamese recruits, two were former members of the aborted RED DRAGON ALPHA mission, and two were Nung who had seen action the previous year in a CIA-sponsored guerrilla unit in southern Laos.

Assembling at Nakhon Phanom, the team filed into a CH-3. Like the long-term agent teams of earlier years, the men were outfitted with an odd mix of North Vietnamese fatigues, sterile weaponry, and American radios. If

STRATA target areas were located near roads and choke points used by the North Vietnamese to move men and matériel to the Ho Chi Minh Trail and into South Vietnam.
(Courtesy George Gaspard)

captured, they were to repeat weak cover stories that their advisers were Cau-
casians of unspecified nationality.[12] Just who they were trying to fool was
unclear.

Flying high over the Annamites, the team landed near Lang Mo. A few
hours later, the commandos spied a North Vietnamese patrol heading down
a small jungle path. Spooked, they raised Danang and asked for an extract.
SOG said no; they had not been spotted and would continue the mission.

Maneuvering forward, they reached a vantage point above Lang Mo.
Then they vanished. Over the next nine days, SOG tried to find the team,
flying extra spotter planes and making emergency radio broadcasts every
hour, including blind messages over the Voice of the SSPL. On 26 May, the
team was officially declared missing.[13]

Although SOG would never learn what happened, STRATA 120 had met
its fate on 18 May, four days after insertion. While taking an afternoon break,
the team leader, Nguyen Dinh Lanh, moved off to check out a stream they
would soon have to cross. Moments later, the rest of the team heard shouts—
"Surrender! Surrender!"—followed by gunfire. Lanh died in a hail of bullets.

Hearing this, the two Nung commandos began a wild volley of return fire while the remaining three agents fled into the thick brush. "I was twenty years old and very afraid," recalled Nguyen Nhu Anh, one of two ex–RED DRAGON ALPHA members on the team. "Most of my training was not practical, and we had never seen real combat before."[14]

Dashing through the jungle, all five survivors eventually managed to reunite. In their flight, they had shed most of their equipment, keeping only their weapons and some food. Still, they had managed to shake their pursuers. Climbing a hilltop that evening, they spread a fluorescent signal panel in the event a plane came overhead. Without a radio, it was their only chance for a rescue.

Waiting in the baking sun, the men soon ran out of water, and the two Nungs decided to search for a stream. Joining them was Trinh Quoc Anh, the same commando who had refused to parachute into Ha Giang Province as part of RED DRAGON, and then missed out on a second chance when the RED DRAGON ALPHA mission was canceled. Now on his third team, he had at long last made it to North Vietnam—and was no doubt regretting it.

As the three departed, the remaining two commandos stayed on the hilltop. Within an hour, they heard rifle shots in the valley below. Fleeing in the opposite direction, they were spotted on 24 May and captured. In prison, they learned that the earlier rifle shots had come after the members of the water party got into an argument. Tempers flared, and Trinh Quoc Anh was shot dead. The rifle reports had quickly attracted the North Vietnamese, who arrested the two Nung.

On 14 May, the same day that STRATA 120 inserted into North Vietnam, STRATA 111 also went in. Picking up where they left off two months earlier, the commandos were deposited on the Candlestick karst spire near Route 196. Major Kyron Hall was again at the controls of the CH-3.

For two days the team reported no contact; then, on 17 May, it heard rifle shots and barking dogs. The men stayed put until the danger passed, then moved off the karst toward their road-watching spot. Eight days later they were still moving toward the road through rough terrain. They were extracted without incident on 30 May.

The day after STRATA 111 inserted, one of the new teams—STRATA 122—headed north. It consisted of just four men, three of them brothers. All were veterans of a long-term agent mission along the North Vietnamese frontier the previous year. To the disappointment of SOG, that mission had been aborted in its opening stages after the team called for a premature exfiltration from inside Laos. Frustrated by such poor results, all of the members had been fired except for the three brothers and one other Vietnamese agent. Unwilling to waste these assets, SOG repackaged them as Team VANG and made tentative plans in the spring of 1968 to insert the four on a long-term mission. Thinking better of it, SOG canceled VANG and instead incorporated the team into the STRATA program.[15]

Once inside North Vietnam, STRATA 122 had little chance to prove its mettle. After just two days on the ground, it reported one of its members to be gravely ill. A forward air controller managed to spot the commandos—they had barely moved from their insertion point—and an exfiltration was launched five days later. Once back at Monkey Mountain, the team resigned.[16]

Despite such meager returns, SOG continued with its rapid-fire insertion of STRATA commandos. In late May, STRATA 113 conducted a second mission and was safely extracted. Then, on 6 June, STRATA 114 went on its second outing into the Lang Mo area, this time to survey a narrow road winding southwest into Laos. The men quickly found themselves in the middle of a North Vietnamese truck convoy heading toward the Ho Chi Minh Trail. But the air force was already aware of the activity. On 10 June, the team frantically reported that bombs were falling nearby, with some exploding as near as three hundred meters. SOG established a "no bomb" zone around the team, an order that must have surprised air force pilots who thought they were bombing North Vietnamese supply lines with no chance of hitting friendly troops.

But the bombs had little impact. STRATA 114 reported that none of the air strikes hit the road, and for the next two days the team watched as convoys of heavily loaded trucks passed by. Later the group crept up to a truck park and motor pool containing some sixty vehicles hidden from view under the thick jungle canopy.

The team's good luck did not last. On 12 June, the team leader and his executive officer and a radioman failed to return from a short reconnaissance patrol. Hearing rifle fire and grenade explosions in the distance, the remaining four team members moved away. They were extracted on 18 June.[17]

STRATA 115, a new team, was inserted the following day. The mission was noteworthy for two reasons. First, it was conducted in a new target area in southern Ha Tinh Province, farther north than any previous insert. Second, the team was the first of four consisting entirely of ethnic Cambodians. The use of Cambodians in STRATA was interesting considering that they were ostensibly posing as North Vietnamese natives and were often assigned with spreading SSPL propaganda. It was a case of deniability gone awry.

Over the next week, the team moved toward its road-watch site. Running short of rations, it called for resupply. Responding, SOG arranged for a

South Vietnamese air force A-1 to drop a set of modified napalm canisters. The supplies were recovered, and the team continued on. On 27 July, it ran into a North Vietnamese patrol and lost one commando in a brief firefight. Two days later, it was pulled out safely, although the helicopter was hit as it climbed off the landing zone.

At almost the same time, STRATA 111 returned for its fourth outing. On 20 June, the commandos landed in karst about sixteen kilometers north of the Demilitarized Zone. For four days the commandos were on the move, with no sign of North Vietnamese activity. Then, on 24 June, they were spotted. They radioed Danang to report the situation; then, unwilling to stand toe to toe with a superior force, the commandos withdrew, planting mines to slow any pursuit. It worked. Explosions ripped through the jungle as STRATA 111 ran for safety.

Three days later they again ran into trouble, and this time they were forced to stand and fight. The team reported that three North Vietnamese soldiers went down in the first fusillade, but a bullet also struck one commando in the leg. They called frantically for extraction.

Major Gaspard happened to be in Nakhon Phanom when the call for help came in. To his dismay, STRATA's standard mounts from the 20th Helicopter Squadron were all off doing something else. Scrambling around the air base for an alternative, Gaspard spied some idle CH-3s from the 21st Helicopter Squadron and asked to use them. As it turned out, the two squadrons were worlds apart. By prior agreement with MACV, only the 20th had permission to conduct team infiltrations. The 21st, by contrast, was tasked solely with dropping sensors along the Ho Chi Minh Trail. The squadrons' choppers might have been the same and their respective crews equally talented, but the two missions could not be mixed.

Gaspard was livid. His team was on the verge of being overrun, and the only thing standing between it and a rescue chopper was red tape. Raising Saigon on the radio, he argued his case. Word soon came back: he had special permission for onetime use of assets from the 21st. But precious hours had gone by, and the clock was still ticking.

Armed with this approval, he quickly got the squadron commander to release two of his CH-3s. Gaspard boarded the lead aircraft. Reaching the landing zone, the crew spotted the beleaguered team. As A-1E prop-fighters put down suppressing fire, one of the helicopters approached to make the rescue. As usual, the terrain was too rugged to allow them to set down, so a hoist was lowered. The wounded team leader was winched to safety, then the second chopper moved in to pick up the rest of the commandos.

But the rescue was only half the battle. Although the team was near the Demilitarized Zone and less than nineteen kilometers from SOG's forward operations base in Quang Tri Province, restrictions prohibited Thai-based choppers from landing in South Vietnam. They would have to fly back across Laos to Nakhon Phanom. Gaspard did manage to get permission to refuel at Quang Tri before flying on to Thailand, a move that made the regulation seem even more ridiculous.[18]

The story might have ended on this heroic note, but during the team's debriefing some inconsistencies came to light. Pressured for clarification, one of the members finally admitted that the team leader shot himself in the foot to force an extraction. The desperate claim about being surrounded by an enemy battalion turned out to be a total fabrication. STRATA 111 was immediately disbanded for this major breach of trust. Still, the eleven Americans on the "rescue" force received the Distinguished Flying Cross for their efforts.[19]

Over the summer of 1968, STRATA continued to grow. Now going by the name Op 34B—as opposed to long-term agent missions, still known as Op 34A—the program churned out a string of new teams from Long Thanh, taking in larger numbers of junior officers and sergeants from the South Vietnamese army. Although most recruits were still civilians, the infusion of military veterans began to noticeably improve the overall quality of STRATA teams.[20]

While the teams might be becoming more competent, their intelligence haul remained insignificant. Of the six STRATA missions launched between late June and the end of July, not one uncovered information of any great value. "The teams would always report the same messages," lamented Major François, the Vietnamese STRATA commander. "Some forests, some streams."[21]

Worse, the program was starting to take heavy casualties. On one of the missions, STRATA 115, a Cambodian team on its second insert, ran into a North Vietnamese patrol after eighteen days on the ground. Following a fierce firefight, the Cambodians scattered. Three managed to stay together, distribute some SSPL leaflets, then call for an extract. The other four went missing.[22]

The loss of the STRATA 115 commandos was hard-felt. When they were first recruited, SOG had hoped the historical animosity Cambodians felt toward ethnic Vietnamese could be harnessed as a strong motivating factor. This proved to be the case: Cambodian STRATA members soon earned a reputation as the best the project had to offer. They remained on the ground inside North Vietnam longer than most other teams, but their presence in the program also stripped the last shreds of credibility from the SSPL. If some North Vietnamese officials were still worried about this "indigenous resistance movement" supposedly gaining strength in their backyard, they learned the truth when they caught Cambodians with SSPL leaflets in hand.

The final mission of July went to STRATA 119. This team had a unique lineage. In its ever-expanding search for prospective agents, SOG had arranged for a Vietnamese recruiter to visit Laos in July 1967. He went no farther than the capital, Vientiane, where he scoured shanties on the outskirts for ethnic Tai minorities who had fled from the North Vietnamese border region. Thirteen volunteers were quickly selected and shipped down to Long Thanh.

Trained for the remainder of 1967, the Tai were then divided into two teams, QUA and AXE. QUA fared poorly in training and was ultimately sent packing back to Vientiane. AXE did better and was set for a long-term mission in the Tai tribal stomping ground of northwestern North Vietnam.

The commander of AXE, Lo Van Thong, was no stranger to combat. Born in Lai Chau Province, he had first joined the French GCMA and fought in the hills of his home province. After North Vietnam went communist in 1954, he crossed the border and melted into the substantial pocket of Tai tribesmen in northeastern Laos. There he eventually signed up with the Royal Lao Army and served a two-year stint. After that, he made his way down to Vientiane and found work as a driver with the U.S. embassy.

After several months of training, AXE was whittled down to five members. One of them was Lo Van Thong's own son, Lo Van On, who had joined his father at Long Thanh during November. In April 1968, the team got word that its long-term mission was canceled. Instead, the team members were handed over to Op 34B and, augmented by two Vietnamese radiomen, became STRATA 119.[23]

On 29 July, the team inserted by helicopter south of Lang Mo. For a week, it moved without seeing anything of note. After that, things changed considerably; the commandos could barely move without seeing constant signs of the North Vietnamese.

On 10 August, just two days before its planned extraction, STRATA 119 spotted a North Vietnamese patrol conducting a sweep. Fearing they were detected, Thong ordered his men to lay low.

The North Vietnamese soldiers approached, then cut off at a right angle and disappeared into the jungle. When the danger passed, one of the radiomen contacted an orbiting O-2 and asked for instructions. Given the amount of activity in the area, the forward air controller asked for target coordinates.

Consulting a map, the STRATA members were stumped. The heavy canopy prevented them from spotting local terrain features. Taking one other commando with him, Thong went to look for the tallest tree in the area. As he left, his eyes met those of his son. Earlier they had made a vow: if things got bad, they would run west and not stop until they got back to Vientiane.[24]

After scaling a small hill, the pair came upon a towering hardwood with enough branches to allow for an easy climb. The two commandos ascended it with ease. Near the top, they looked out in all directions. All they saw was a green carpet.

While they were still high above the jungle floor, shots rang out in the valley below. Their hearts pounding, the two STRATA members stayed in the tree for another hour. Cautiously patrolling back toward their deserted base camp, they heard the sound of helicopters in the distance. The rest of the team had been rescued and was on its way back to Nakhon Phanom.

Remembering the pact with his son, Thong headed west. For ten days, he pushed toward the Lao frontier. Just short of the border, he and the other commando ran headlong into a North Vietnamese patrol. In shackles, they were sent north to a Hanoi prison.[25]

20

DENOUEMENT

While the STRATA program was disappointing, compared with the agent program it was a success. By the close of 1967, Hanoi's repeated public unveiling of captured teams left SOG's long-term operation a tattered shell. In March 1968, Colonel Singlaub belatedly moved to see what was worth salvaging. Disguising his order as a research project, he called on his case officers to prepare historical studies of their respective teams. Appended to each would be a security review, which was the true reason behind the exercise.[1]

As the case officers set about doing this, they learned a terrible secret: SOG's most successful team, REMUS, was under hostile control. Hanoi, in fact, had captured the team two months after its insertion way back in April 1962. The charade was easily pulled off because three REMUS agents, including its team leader, proved highly cooperative in captivity.[2]

Hanoi had gone through unprecedented pains to keep REMUS above suspicion. For example, after the team was tasked in the fall of 1963 to mine a road leading into Dien Bien Phu, the North Vietnamese had actually orchestrated a bogus mine attack that jammed up traffic for a time.[3] And in August 1964, when SOG ordered REMUS to plant explosives along a bridge, Hanoi obliged by creating visible cracks in the structure—damage that was duly noted by American aerial reconnaissance.[4]

The REMUS deception scheme intensified in early 1965. That January, the team was reinforced by four saboteurs carrying 4.5-inch rockets to attack the Dien Bien Phu airfield. Intercepting the team as it landed, the North Vietnamese took the rockets to a hill overlooking the Dien Bien Phu valley and fired them into a nearby cattle farm.[5] Bogus aircraft wreckage was then strewn along the airfield, which American aerial reconnaissance again managed to photograph.[6]

Not until mid-1965 did Hanoi have any problems with its counterespionage scheme. In May, SOG ordered REMUS to detach five of its original members for exfiltration via Laos. But as had been the earlier experience with TOURBILLON, the team reported a series of unfortunate events complicating extraction, claiming that one man was ill and a second needed to stay and care for him. Then the remaining three reported slow overland progress. Two months later, the trio mysteriously ceased radio transmissions.

Questions about REMUS deepened later that month when it received a resupply drop. Marc, the South Vietnamese case officer who had recently inherited responsibility for REMUS, went to Nha Trang to pack the supplies for his agents. Returning to the airfield the next morning, he quizzed one of the Vietnamese cargo handlers who had flown on the C-123: "I asked him how the drop went, and he said that he was very surprised. Usually, it was very hard for them to spot the ground signals from the teams because they were very small. But this time, the signal had been very big and bright, almost like an electric light. He said that REMUS was very careless and did not seem to be concerned about being spotted."[7]

But the intelligence kept flowing in, and SOG chose to overlook the growing suspicions. In November, REMUS reported that it had ambushed some vehicles near the border. It also began to relay useful information on road-building activities into Laos and gave poststrike results after the Dien Bien Phu airfield was hit by American aircraft.[8]

By 1967, SOG considered REMUS its most productive agent team. That summer the agents again bolstered that reputation by claiming to have found a telephone line leading into the Dien Bien Phu valley. SOG selected two radiomen from its pool of students at Long Thanh and cross-trained them in the use of wiretapping equipment. But before deploying the new agents, SOG hedged its bets with two further steps. Remembering the distress signal the TOURBILLON radioman sent earlier in the year, case officers separately took each of the reinforcements aside and gave secret challenge questions and safe answers to be inserted in a preselected message back to Saigon. They also trained the two agents in the use of the Fulton Skyhook. According to plan, once they exhausted their supply of wiretap tapes—estimated at thirty-three days—they would exfiltrate via the Skyhook. Just as with the later RED DRAGON ALPHA plan, a Skyhook extract would enable SOG to positively verify the status of REMUS.[9]

On 22 August, the two agents, Do Van Tam and Truong Tuan Hoang, boarded an MC-130 with their wiretapping equipment. As they approached the drop zone, the pilot sighted the correct ground signal at the proper alignment.[10] Three bundles went out the rear, followed by the two agents.

They would soon learn the truth. Landing precisely on the drop zone, they gathered up their parachutes while members of Team REMUS came out of the trees. "We had an identification code," recalled Do Van Tam, "they were supposed to say a one-digit number, and I would answer with a number that equaled ten." One of the shadowy forms said "seven," to which Tam replied "three." Then everybody smiled and shook hands. Moments later the smiles were replaced by guns and the two new agents found themselves prisoners. "I had trained for two years," said Tam, "and my mission had lasted less than twenty seconds."[11]

Perhaps suspecting that the reinforcement radiomen planned to alert SOG, Hanoi came up with some creative radio play. First it told Saigon that the cache holding the Skyhook equipment had been uncovered by a North Vietnamese patrol.[12] Then, before either radioman had a chance to transmit his safety signal, it reported Truong Tuan Hoang had died in an accident and Do Van Tam had perished from a snakebite.[13]

SOG was suspicious about the string of coincidences and ordered an immediate internal study to determine if past cases where reinforcement radiomen were killed or missing indicated a team was doubled.[14] Their findings were inconclusive, and SOG's confidence in REMUS, though guarded, was restored.

Then came the 1968 Tet Offensive. As reverberations from the communist attacks continued through the first few months of the year, the South Vietnamese military captured hundreds of North Vietnamese soldiers. It was during the interrogation of one of these prisoners in April that SOG received its biggest shock to date. A North Vietnamese lieutenant named Vo Cong, captured near Hue, claimed knowledge of a South Vietnamese commando team captured at Dien Bien Phu in 1962.[15]

To get firsthand details from the captive, Marc, the REMUS case officer, went to the prison camp to conduct his own interrogation. What he found was unnerving. If the prisoner's story was true, REMUS had been undone by a small act of carelessness. It seemed that in the summer of 1962 some children had found a makeshift stove and unburied garbage in the forest near Dien Bien Phu.[16] When border guards went to investigate, they found the REMUS agents were in the midst of receiving their first aerial resupply. Hearing the aircraft and seeing flame pots on a nearby mountaintop, the guards called for reinforcements and surrounded the team. All the agents were eventually captured, and they resumed radio contact with Saigon the following month.

Marc knew the story was true. The location and time matched with REMUS, and the month-long gap in radio communications after the first airdrop in 1962 also fit. To confirm his fears, he visited the prison a second time with a ream of photos. One showed the REMUS radioman; the others were a random selection of agents from different teams. Without hesitation, Vo Cong correctly pointed to the file photo of the REMUS radio operator.[17]

Angered and embarrassed, Marc reported his findings to Long Thanh. At the meeting were five SOG officers; a representative from the CIA; Colonel Tran Van Ho, the Strategic Technical Directorate commander; and Major Ha Ngoc Oanh, the same South Vietnamese case officer for the 1962 VULCAN raid who was now being groomed to assume command of all long-term agent operations.[18] All were shocked by the REMUS deception.

Seeking revenge, they made plans for a resupply mission with a deadly twist. Instead of supplies, the North Vietnamese officials awaiting the bundles would be hit by an airstrike.

The bombing mission was planned for 15 May. But just two days before that date, Hanoi radio announced REMUS had been captured.[19] In some ways, this news was even more devastating than knowing REMUS had gone bad. North Vietnam was clearly one step ahead of SOG, and the fact that Hanoi had forgone its normal three-month interval between last radio communication and spy trial strongly hinted at an intelligence leak.

That possibility should have come as no surprise. Problems with SOG's operational security, in fact, were legion. To be fair, some of these shortfalls predated the actual formation of SOG. For example, for several years the CIA had repeatedly used the same safe houses in Saigon for waves of agent trainees. Not only did this draw undue attention to the sites, but neither American nor South Vietnamese case officers lived at the houses; as a result, students went unsupervised at night, and it was not a stretch to imagine them roaming around the city to overcome boredom.[20]

Once SOG took over the operation, operational security, if anything, worsened. At Long Thanh, for example, long-term agents from different teams mingled with each other and, after late 1965, came into regular contact with dozens of commandos from the SHINING BRASS reconnaissance teams.[21] SOG officers also belatedly discovered that Long Thanh's South Vietnamese training cadre occasionally let students go to Saigon for rest and recreation.[22] And at Nha Trang, the packing sheds full of supply bundles for the agent teams were located in an area with minimal security. Names and other data for each northern team were clearly marked on individual supply bins.[23]

But these atrocious security procedures were not the main reason for Op 34A's dismal showing. The problems went back much farther in time. The CIA's very first team, CASTOR, had been quickly captured and doubled, giving Hanoi a revealing window into the program from its inception. Second, timely advice from China, which had been the target of similar operations, was no doubt critical in helping Hanoi keep abreast of the covert campaign's graduated increase in pace and scope. Third, the airborne insertion methods were inaccurate and predictable. It did not take much counterintelligence acumen to listen for the sound of aircraft in the night sky and then watch for parachutes. Fourth, for those teams that were able to survive the insertion, North Vietnam's omnipresent security apparatus and a society riddled with informants made it almost impossible for them to remain undetected for long. Finally, by late 1965, improved direction-finding equipment made it easier for Hanoi to find incoming teams.[24] Against these factors, the long-term agents barely stood a chance. Colonel Singlaub's internal security review, completed in April 1968, finally revealed the fatal flaws in SOG's agent operations. All of its teams, it concluded, with the exception of EASY in Son La, were now thought to be under hostile control.

In retrospect, this conclusion was not surprising. Besides EASY, SOG had just five teams and one singleton in radio contact. Three of these teams—HADLEY, ROMEO, and TOURBILLON—were already known to be doubled. And it was no leap of logic to figure that EAGLE, which clung unconvincingly to the claim it was undetected in a heavily populated province for four years, and RED DRAGON, which had been strung across an entire district upon insertion, were also under North Vietnamese control.

That left only ARES, the program's lone—and longest-running—singleton. ARES had been captured within a month of his insertion in April 1961, and, looking back, there was plenty of reason to suspect he was bad. One junk had been lost while resupplying him in January 1962, and a shore party from a second disappeared on a similar mission in August 1963. While these incidents were discounted at the time as bad luck, SOG began to suspect something was amiss when, year after year, the intelligence content of his radio messages remained consistently low. "He mostly told us about the weather," recalled Marc, who had taken over as the singleton's case officer by 1966. And on the rare occasions when he did provide more substantive information, like bomb damage assessment for airstrikes around Haiphong, he often reported schools and hospitals were being hit—claims that sounded suspiciously like Hanoi's own propaganda.[25]

By early 1967, Saigon began to express frustration with ARES. The agent, however, had a ready excuse. His RS-1 radio was too unwieldy, he said, and he had to depend on his brother to operate the hand-cranked generator. To correct this, Marc scheduled a high-speed resupply with an F-4C Phantom using disguised napalm canisters. This mission was timed to coincide with a major airstrike against Haiphong, which would camouflage the presence of an additional fighter near the port.[26]

On the late afternoon of 1 May, the airstrike and resupply began as scheduled. Racing across Quang Ninh Province, the Phantom pilot spotted the proper signal—smoke from two adjacent fires—and dropped the canisters. ARES later reported that he recovered the bundles. Inside were ten solid gold rings—to barter for medicine—and a Delco 5300 radio set and battery pack that he could use without help from his brother.

The bundles also contained something else—three innocuous letters to be delivered by the agent to addresses in Thailand. SOG had its suspicions about ARES, but in the past it had found no way to check up on his excuses.

ARES had never been augmented with other agents—the high level of military and commercial activity around Haiphong made this all but impossible—which meant there was no reinforcement radioman who could send back a secret safety signal. And given his proximity to urban areas, SOG could hardly attempt a CH-3 exfiltration.

So SOG turned to the CIA, which came up with the idea of sending the letters. Each was in a sealed envelope with instructions that they all be postmarked from Hanoi. ARES was not told that one of the letters had bogus classified information written inside the envelope in invisible ink, the presumption being that curiosity would get the best of the North Vietnamese security service, who would damage that envelope in an attempt to develop the invisible message.

Three weeks later, two of the envelopes arrived in Bangkok. The third—containing the secret message—failed to arrive. Quizzed about this, ARES claimed that, on his way to the post office, an airstrike forced him to jump into a bomb shelter at roadside. The third letter, he said, had gotten soiled, preventing him from posting it.[27] SOG found the coincidence too much to swallow.

But still Saigon refused to fully sever contact with its agent. In December, ARES was told to again prepare a drop zone for a high-speed resupply. Upon hearing this, ARES protested, urging his case officers to find a different means of delivering bundles. For SOG, this straw broke the camel's back. Quite obviously, the North Vietnamese, speaking through the singleton, were using him to expose newer forms of delivery technology that SOG might be developing. Refusing to take the bait, Saigon canceled the mission.[28]

By the time of the April 1968 security review, then, SOG already felt most of its teams were damaged goods. Still, the scope of its findings was an embarrassment. To be certain, Singlaub asked the CIA and MACV intelligence to launch their own independent study. Their results, released in June, were even more distressing: all of the teams, including EASY, were probably bad.[29]

As it turned out, the suspicions about EASY were justified. Inserted in August 1963, the team had quickly established radio contact. What Saigon did not know was that the two REMUS reinforcement agents on the same plane had been immediately captured in Lai Chau and informed the North Vietnamese that another team had jumped in Son La. With this information, Hanoi launched a manhunt. Three weeks later, it had seven of EASY's eight members in custody; the last was shot dead six days later.[30]

Using the EASY radiomen, the North Vietnamese were able to resume communication with Saigon without drawing undue attention. Inheriting the bad team, SOG reinforced it in July 1964 with five more agents. Radio play continued over the next year, with reinforcements dropped on another three occasions. Thirty-five commandos were eventually dispatched to help EASY, the largest number for any single Op 34A team.

In the end, it was sheer size that focused suspicion on EASY. SOG was expected to believe not only that the equivalent of a platoon was hiding in the forests of Son La but also that they had been able to spread a modest resistance net without attracting Hanoi's attention. In January 1964, for example, EASY claimed to have made contact with the relatives of some of its Hmong members. Later in June, the team reportedly recruited some of these assets and distributed rifles.[31] Even for SOG, which had shown its gullibility on frequent occasions, the ability of EASY to perform these feats without detection stretched the bounds of credibility.[32]

To confirm its suspicions, in March 1968 Saigon told the team to prepare four members for exfiltration. Realizing the game was up, EASY broke radio contact. By the time the June security review was completed, there had been no word from the team for two months. Then, on 7 August, Hanoi unveiled its latest set of prisoners, and SOG's long-term agent operations effectively ended.[33]

If SOG's shortcomings were becoming obvious to those on the ground in South Vietnam, it often seemed as if the policy makers in Washington were not seeing the same picture. A mere month after Singlaub's security review revealed the extent of Hanoi's success in thwarting the agent operations, Clark M. Clifford, President Johnson's new secretary of defense, asked the Joint Chiefs "what should be done in the event that the discussions with the North Vietnamese in Paris fail to proceed satisfactorily toward a peaceful settlement." On 4 June, General Earle Wheeler, chairman of the Joint Chiefs, responded by suggesting that, if the Paris talks broke down, the military could respond by renewing many old Op 34A missions. Suggestions included expanding STRATA operations, resuming maritime sabotage along the coast, and infiltrating "new long-term agent teams into NVN for intelligence collection as approved on a case-by-case basis at the Washington level." Finally, SOG could take steps to "expand the credibility of the SSPL" by developing new assets inside North Vietnam. Skeptics could be forgiven for wondering how a plan that had not worked for the past eight years was to suddenly result, as the Joint Chiefs wrote, in "exploit[ing] fully North Vietnamese vulnerabilities" if they failed to cooperate at the peace table in Paris.[34]

Only one year earlier, when Clifford was President Johnson's chairman of the Foreign Intelligence Advisory Board, he had been asked to review the operations against North Vietnam. "I can't for the life of me see why this great country can't get a few spies into this pipsqueek little country," he concluded in frustration.[35] Now Clifford was being told to try again.

21

GUERRILLAS IN THEIR MIDST

SOG found a way to capitalize on the failure of its long-term agents. In the fall of 1967, plans were drawn up to insert eighteen new teams over the next year. But there was a twist: all of these teams would be phantoms, part of a concerted psychological campaign designed to make Hanoi think dozens of commandos were on the loose when none actually existed. The new program was code-named FORAE, but this "notional"—or imaginary—concept harkened back to the original wording of Oplan 34A, which had called for "phantom resistance movements, and psychological development of actual resistance."[1]

Psychological warfare against North Vietnam dated back to early 1961 with the advent of leaflet drops and plans for gray radio broadcasts. These stations combined real and bogus information, leaving listeners in doubt about their origins.[2] Two years later, Herbert Weisshart's team of experts had inaugurated the notional SSPL resistance movement. That year also saw the beginning of deception supply drops, which involved bundles parachuted over remote corners of North Vietnam where no long-term teams were located. These deception bundles were carried on the same aircraft as real agent teams and dropped en route, thereby drawing attention away from actual drop zones. Ten fake drops were conducted through December 1963, the last of which included a special firecracker package meant to simulate a small-arms firefight.

Another program implemented in 1963 was a "black letter" campaign. Dozens of letters were sent to North Vietnam from third countries, primarily Hong Kong. Some were intended for harassment, others harped on benign propaganda themes, while some were meant to smear specific North Vietnamese officials by including incriminating messages that would likely be intercepted by Hanoi's censors. One letter-writing campaign was aimed at a group of North Vietnamese officers allegedly sympathetic to South Vietnam.[3]

After the creation of SOG in January 1964, the Pentagon was supposed to shoulder psychological operations. However, while a U.S. Army major was named nominal chief of SOG's Psychological Operations Group, true expertise remained with the CIA. For that reason, the agency's Weisshart was given the title of SOG special assistant and allowed to retain de facto control over the mental bullets fired at Hanoi.

Continuing as before, leaflet missions were flown near Hanoi by SOG C-123s on the nights of 18 and 31 May—to coincide with Ho Chi Minh's and Buddha's birthdays, respectively.[4] Deception drops resumed on 27 June when a fake team was supplied during the same flight on which a real team, EAGLE, was inserted.[5] The black letter campaign increased, with up to one hundred letters per week being sent via Hong Kong by November.[6] Black radio broadcasts, too, were on the rise, reaching ten hours per week during the same month, while the Voice of Freedom (VOF), a new gray Vietnamese-language station run by SOG, could be heard for more than eight hours a day.[7]

Over the next two years, SOG's Psychological Operations Group—with strong input from the CIA—continued to expand in pace and scope.[8] The letter-writing campaign was expanded in 1966, with a special emphasis on exploiting the growing number of North Vietnamese military prisoners of war. One operation, code-named CANDY, used cooperative prisoners to write letters home praising the good life in South Vietnam. Other campaigns emphasized the self-destructiveness of Hanoi's war. MARS was a series of "semicontrived" letters, supposedly written by captured North Vietnamese soldiers, notifying the next of kin in North Vietnam about the death of their loved ones and giving "details" of how they died. Also included were stories about the hardships suffered by communist soldiers in the south and the rising casualties on the battlefield. By the end of 1966, MARS was sending north about five such letters per week.[9]

Radio programming was also boosted. The Voice of Freedom, for example, was able to add Cantonese shows during 1966. Prepared with the assistance of psychological warfare experts from Taiwan, the Cantonese program sandwiched music between news segments that hinted at the historical animosity between Vietnam and China, and even touched on contemporary contentious issues like conflicting claims to islands in the South China Sea.[10] The intended result was an exacerbation of strains between Hanoi and Beijing.

During the same year, the Voice of Freedom also began a segment entitled "Letters from the North." This started after some pieces of mail, many of them highly sentimental and addressed to family members, were collected off the bodies of dead North Vietnamese soldiers. After these were read over the air, SOG got reports that mothers were seen crying at the communist party headquarters in Hanoi. Realizing it had an effective tool, it expanded the segment with a diversionary twist: for every five real letters read per week, there were two fake ones that contained coded messages for notional SOG agent teams. In a variation on this theme, the Voice of Freedom also began "Bridge to the North," which listed the names of dead North Vietnamese identified on the battlefronts. Also read were captured documents that named the locations of jungle cemeteries.[11]

Besides radio warfare, leaflets—some of them in special shapes to increase wind drift—were being dropped in record numbers by SOG planes and scattered along the shore by special 81mm mortars mounted on Nasty boats. SOG also began parachuting gift kits over the north that included medicine, toys, food, defector passes, and unmarked radios designed to pick up SOG's black stations. Similar kits, dubbed "baskets of cheer," were handed out to fishermen detained by the Biet Hai.[12]

While psychological operations appeared to be gaining momentum, there were voices of dissent. One of these was SOG's own chief, Colonel John Singlaub. As an unconventional expert, Singlaub was beyond reproach. A World War II veteran of Jedburgh operations in France and OSS missions in the Asian theater, he had been seconded to the CIA in the early 1950s and was instrumental in organizing agent networks in northern China and Korea. In May 1966, he was handpicked by the SACSA, General William R. Peers, to be the new commander of SOG.

Under Singlaub's watch, certain aspects of SOG's psychological warfare campaign were soon brought into question. In particular, he was critical of leaflet drops over North Vietnam. These drops had started when no American aircraft were officially over North Vietnam, Singlaub noted. At that time, the themes presented in the leaflets were black or gray. By 1966, however, U.S. planes were swarming the skies of North Vietnam, and the source of the leaflets was clear. Their themes, as a result, had shifted toward white, or factually based, propaganda.[13] Such overt messages, Singlaub argued, had little to do with covert warfare and were a waste of SOG assets. He lobbied to have the missions stopped, but entrenched bureaucracies kept them going.[14]

Misguided leaflet missions were only one of Singlaub's worries. Increasingly, SOG's monopoly over long-term agent operations in North Vietnam was under fire. Within MACV itself, the intelligence section wanted a share of the pie. Some of its intentions were outlined in July 1966 when Brigadier General Joseph A. McChristian, MACV's assistant chief of staff for intelligence, held a closed briefing for Pentagon brass. Among McChristian's plans was a program for using some of the Vietnamese refugees in northeast Thailand to collect information on North Vietnam. Already, representatives from MACV intelligence and their senior counterpart, the South Vietnamese chief of collection, had visited Bangkok to explore the concept.[15] McChristian also intended to build an isolated training base on the uninhabited island of Hon Cua, 240 kilometers south of Saigon. There MACV intelligence would train action agents and special reconnaissance teams for theaterwide use. Finally, the general revealed an ambitious scheme for training and employing North

Vietnamese defectors (called *hoi chanh,* meaning "ralliers") as agents and reconnaissance teams inside North Vietnam. These ralliers would not only collect intelligence, organize stay-behind nets, and recruit agents in place but also be inserted into North Vietnamese prisoner groups prior to any exchanges or repatriations.[16]

There were questions about whether SOG was the right organization to run such a mission. After all, its long-term agent operations were a disaster. Although security compartmentalization meant that SOG's failures were not widely known, enough details had leaked by 1967 to make its uninspired performance a tempting target for challenge by other organizations. What's more, SOG was sometimes its own worst enemy. When CINCPAC promulgated the group's latest mission statement that April, for example, the objectives read like a throwback to its original mandate of 1964.

Washington was no help at all. The White House had steadfastly refused to condemn Op 34A despite obvious signs of decay. In fact, President Johnson had claimed early in March that the program provided "virtually the only human intelligence we are able to obtain from rural North Vietnam."[17] These sentiments were echoed in early October, when a Defense Intelligence Agency report claimed SOG's agents "have frequently provided unique information of considerable intelligence value," particularly on things such as road and bridge construction "which were not otherwise available." Of seventy-nine reports it evaluated from the first half of the year, 45 percent were rated as containing either great or moderate intelligence. Another 52 percent were of at least "slight" value.[18]

General Westmoreland, the MACV commander, knew better. Involved in SOG planning almost from the start, he had seen firsthand the shortcomings of Op 34A. The general was particularly concerned that CINCPAC's latest mission statement for SOG differed little from its first. The simmering Vietnam conflict of early 1964 bore little resemblance to the full-blown Vietnam War of 1967, yet SOG's orders seemed to take no account of these changes. The lack of insight and imagination was disturbing.[19]

Voicing his concerns, on 16 October Westmoreland asked for Washington to send a joint survey team to evaluate SOG's efforts, particularly its North Vietnam program. On 1 November, the requested team—comprising fifteen members from the CIA, DIA, SACSA, CINCPAC, and the various services—landed in Saigon. Briefed by the SOG hierarchy for six days, the officials came away with two strong impressions. First, it seemed SOG was well aware it faced serious problems. Second, SOG already was contemplating a boost in psychological operations as part of a reorientation in northern operations.

Not by coincidence, these changes in SOG came shortly after the arrival of two key officers. In August, Lieutenant Colonel Thomas Bowen took over as head of the Psychological Operations Group. He was no stranger to the task, having served one of his two prior years in MACV as the psychological warfare officer in its Special Warfare Branch. The following month, the Airborne Operations Section was turned over to Lieutenant Colonel Jonathon Carney. A veteran of two wars, Carney was unique. Unlike the Green Berets who had monopolized that slot to date, he was a military intelligence officer. Immediately, he had his staff augmented by more intelligence officers conversant in agent handling.[20]

Together, Carney and Bowen reviewed operations to date. Their findings were not encouraging. The SSPL, theoretically the centerpiece of the psychological campaign in the north, was doing little beyond running a radio station and kidnapping fishermen. It had been warning the communist rulers that it would urge the population to "take more direct action against the government and reassert people's power" if Hanoi's "subordination of national interests to party interests did not change," but four years had passed since the SSPL's formation, and there was no action to back up the words.[21]

Airborne operations, meanwhile, could find no formula for success after more than three years running. "We were all amateurs," Carney recalled. "And we had no business sending brave young men on missions which had almost no chance of success."[22]

With Bowen and Carney at the helm, old themes like deception drops and notional agents would no longer simply be a sideshow. Instead of trying to divert Hanoi's attention away from the real long-term agent teams, deception missions would now take center stage, with a total of eighteen phony teams operational by the following September.

Approved by the chief of SOG on 29 November, Op 34A began a full-scale reconfiguration. In its first step, a series of three notional teams were to be established in a line along the eastern edge of Lai Chau Province. Each team would be located by a bundle drop but no agents.

On the night of 29 December, an MC-130 with the phantom supplies departed Nha Trang. Arriving over Lai Chau at low altitude, the crew flew up to the northern provincial border, then made a clockwise arc to begin its run down the Song Da River valley. In the rear, loadmasters eased the pallets near the edge of the ramp as the first drop zone approached. At 0430 hours, the crew reported its mission was complete.

In Saigon, SOG waited for further word from their plane. None came. Assuming the worst, a photo reconnaissance sortie was launched over the mountains of Lai Chau. The search focused on the karst twenty kilometers northeast of the provincial capital, where the MC-130 had last made radio contact. In addition, the U.S. Special Forces training team at Long Thanh was put on alert, ready to drop into North Vietnam to remove classified radio gear.[23] After three photo missions and one electronic search, however, no wreckage was found.[24]

Despite the loss of the MC-130, psychological operations still appeared to be the best option available. For a second opinion, Westmoreland organized an Ad Hoc Evaluation Group to evaluate SOG's performance and future course. Heading the group was Brigadier General Albert Brownfield. A World War II veteran with a background in armor, Brownfield had seen his share of special operations. During the 1950s, he served with the airborne doctrine section at Fort Bragg, and in 1960 with the U.S. military advisory group in Laos. Then, in 1964, he had been intimately involved with SOG as General Krulak's deputy in SACSA.

As Brownfield set about critiquing SOG, the Pentagon took notice. None was more interested than the new SACSA, General William E. DePuy. Ever since assuming office in March, DePuy had been perplexed by the inverse relationship between SOG operations and results. In terms of intelligence gathered and sabotage conducted, Op 34A's record was getting worse—yet Hanoi's reaction was growing more shrill. While perhaps not achieving its intended results, clearly the program was still having an effect. Puzzled by this, in the summer of 1967 DePuy ordered his men to look for ways of achieving these same ends without such a high cost in agent lives. SACSA's conclusions, reached just before the joint survey team was dispatched to Saigon in November, pointed toward deception operations.[25]

Continuing with this theme, at year's end DePuy ordered his Special Operations Division to conduct an expanded study of the North Vietnamese media to look for specific weaknesses that could be exploited through deception. Published in March 1968, the report noted Hanoi's population control system was its key vulnerability. "Hanoi interprets allied special operations in North Vietnam as a major facet in the US strategy," it concluded. "As such, it views these operations with considerable alarm." Indeed, North Vietnam was paranoid of threats to its total control, and any perceived threat would elicit repressive measures that would ultimately be counterproductive. This explained why Hanoi's reaction was so shrill despite Op 34A's dismal record. For the North Vietnamese, it did not matter if an agent team succeeded or failed; it represented a breach of control either way. By extension, deception operations could simulate breaches without losing agents.[26]

At the same time, others were jumping on the deception bandwagon. On 14 February, General Brownfield's Ad Hoc Evaluation Group published its final report, which advocated focusing SOG almost exclusively on two objectives: "Creation of psychological impact and development of an intelligence capability." In addition to concentrating on mainstays like the SSPL and notional agent teams, the report also suggested innovative steps such as drone and balloon delivery of leaflets from Nasty boats and ground locations in Laos, and the use of floating radio transmitters in the Tonkin Gulf. The following month, MACV released its comments to the findings of the November survey team. Agreeing that northern operations should be reoriented toward deception operations, it also argued that at least four real teams be inserted during 1968 to give substance to the notional campaign. The report also suggested that SOG seek to covertly insert articles in Third World newspapers and magazines known to be distributed inside North Vietnam, and, on a more sinister note, place the SSPL "in a more powerful position" by exploring the possibility of "selective assassination of hated NVN officers."[27]

Westmoreland agreed wholeheartedly. In a message to DePuy on 16 February, the MACV commander emphasized that SOG had not convinced North Vietnam to "cease all support of subversion/aggression in SVN"—the original intent of Op 34A. Since the SSPL was not enough to force Hanoi to "re-evaluate" its actions, and since the long-term agent teams were accomplishing nothing, Westmoreland pointed out that "this re-evaluation is . . . not likely to occur unless those in command in Hanoi believe (fear) that their political leadership is in some real danger." This "fear," he continued, would only come if the entire covert effort in North Vietnam was focused on convincing the communist leaders that they were up against something large and powerful.[28]

While SOG was being hit by advice from several directions, all of it was pointing in the same direction. Codifying these views, on 14 March 1968, MACV verbally approved a psychological reorientation to SOG's campaign against North Vietnam. At long last, Op 34A was on the road to developing a well-integrated mission statement predicated on North Vietnamese vulnerabilities and SOG's true capabilities.[29]

In pursuing its diversionary mission, SOG could build on the long-standing SSPL foundation. In the early days, the SSPL had been surprisingly effective. With its Voice of the SSPL mixing diatribes against Saigon, Hanoi, Washington, and Beijing (Hanoi's most important ally prior to 1965), North Vietnamese authorities were thoroughly confused about the real source behind the front. For a time, there were indications Hanoi thought Moscow—then competing with Beijing for dominance in the communist world—was the sponsor. One communications intercept even hinted that the North Vietnamese attributed management to a pair of its lieutenant colonels who had defected to the Soviet Union in 1964.[30]

By the fall of 1967, however, Hanoi had no doubt about the SSPL's true sponsor. American aircraft, after all, were the obvious source of leaflet drops, and triangulation of the SSPL's radio waves prior to 1967 would have shown its origins south of the Demilitarized Zone. (To frustrate direction-finding equipment, beginning in June 1967, Voice of the SSPL was relayed by a U.S. Navy NC-121 orbiting the Tonkin Gulf.) In an article published in the government journal *Hoc Tap* in September, readers were told that the SSPL "exists only in the minds of the American imperialists and their lackeys," and that its radio stations were merely tools "advertising America's deceitful 'peaceful intentions.'"[31]

Still, there were good reasons for SOG to maintain the charade. For one thing, there was ample evidence that midlevel village cadre and cooperative managers—those who had access to radios—listened to the Voice of the SSPL. Also, it did not matter whether Hanoi believed a real resistance movement was lurking in the countryside. What did matter was that the communist leaders knew some of its population was listening to SSPL radio and reading SSPL leaflets, a breach of control it could not tolerate.[32] In fact, Hanoi was concerned enough about SOG's psychological operations that during the initial stages of the Paris peace talks North Vietnamese negotiators included demands that the United States stop dropping leaflets and withdraw "psychological war commandos," as well as end the kidnapping of North Vietnamese during maritime operations.[33]

In the spring of 1968, SOG launched its coordinated psychological assault on North Vietnam. As before, black radio operations centered around the Voice of the SSPL.[34] Leaflet drops, too, went unabated, as did the flow of black letters from third countries. The latter, in particular, was expanded. Since it began the campaign in 1964, SOG had used North Vietnamese nationals living abroad as the alleged authors. In early 1968, SOG was using an unwitting leftist Japanese fishing organization as the originators of the letters, and it had plans to continue the letter-writing program with notional overseas leftist organizations.[35]

Both SOG and its South Vietnamese counterpart also began attempts to discredit specific North Vietnamese military officers as dissident elements in secret contact with Saigon, under a project code-named POLLACK. Various methods were used, including letters and messages using "easily discovered secret writing" dropped in deception bundles. While there was never any confirmation on whether or not the operation was successful, in early 1969 communications intercepts revealed that one North Vietnamese general—a target of the campaign—was inexplicably relieved of his divisional command and recalled to Hanoi.[36]

But the main focus was on notional teams, with two new airborne diversionary operations organized under the heading of Op 34C. The first, code-named OODLES, was an expansion of the notional team concept started during the ill-fated MC-130 mission in late December. As before, SOG would drop phantom supply bundles to locate the fake teams. In addition, special remote-activated radio packages were developed that would automatically begin sending messages to BUGS. In return, Saigon would periodically have its black radio stations beam back instructions and family messages. One project encompassing diversionary supply drops—including some fitted with nonfunctional gadgets designed only to confuse technical analysts—was code-named URANOLITE.[37]

Other methods were devised to support OODLES. For example, SOG instructed TOURBILLON—one of its earlier teams known to have been turned—to link up with one of the fake units.[38] In addition, SOG case officers visited Saigon hospitals and gathered expired blood supplies. This blood was then mixed in large blocks of ice and fitted to a parachute harness. When a C-130 arrived over a notional team location, ice blocks, a few of which contained the blood, were parachuted from the rear. The ice would soon melt, leaving behind an empty parachute and a patch of human blood on the jungle floor. The North Vietnamese, it was hoped, would conclude an agent had been injured during a team insertion.[39]

SOG's second airborne diversionary operation was the brainchild of Major Bert Spivy, a West Pointer and Special Forces officer who had arrived that spring to head Op 34C. Spivy's idea was to make use of some of the North Vietnamese military prisoners who were swelling southern prisons in the aftermath of the Tet Offensive. These detainees, he reasoned, were a perfect—albeit unwitting—source for diversionary troops. "The original name for the project was MOCHA, because you can't distinguish the coffee from the cream. We then went through a number of names with dairy themes, such as MILK and MILKRUN, before settling on BORDEN."[40]

In April, Spivy and a small staff from Op 34C began to look for their first volunteers. To allow speedy collection and avoid compromise, they were allowed to canvass American division-level detention facilities. Each SOG man was armed with a letter signed by Brigadier General Phillip Davidson, MACV's top intelligence officer, which read, "Selected prisoners of war are to be released to his custody for transportation to such locations as he may designate for special processing."[41]

Reviewing personnel records, Op 34C sought out North Vietnamese prisoners who were healthy, literate, and cooperative.[42] "The BORDEN agent had to be smart," added Captain John Mullins, a Long Thanh adviser, "so he could convincingly pass a cover story and not turn himself in the minute he was inserted."[43]

A couple dozen prospective volunteers were taken to the isolation compound at Long Thanh. Known in Vietnamese as Khu Cam (Forbidden City), a section of the isolation area had been specially modified for BOR-

DEN. "Everything was bugged," said Major Stanley Olchovik, the Long Thanh detachment commander. "Where they slept, where they ate, where they took showers. We listened and watched them at all hours to see who was dependable."[44]

For three weeks, the recruits were assessed and oriented. After SOG gained their cooperation, they were taken on tours of Saigon. This had a profound effect on many. "When they saw all the prosperity, you could see the lights go off in their heads," recalled Mullins. "Some of them got really gung-ho."[45]

At the end of this first phase, about half of the volunteers were found to be unsuitable. Before being returned to the prison camps, these rejects were fed disinformation about hundreds of ex-prisoners being trained for covert missions back north. SOG was certain these magnified stories would eventually make their way to the ears of Hanoi's spy network, which was believed to have penetrated the prison system.

For those BORDEN volunteers still at Long Thanh, two weeks of agent training began. It was intentionally conducted in groups so the ralliers might compromise themselves. Their mission, they were told, was twofold. First, they were to return to their old unit in the field and pose as an escapee or present some other rehearsed cover story. If successfully reintegrated, they were to collect intelligence on their way to the battlefield, then redefect. Each agent was marked with ultraviolet paste on the forehead and fingernails; this would be their means of identifying themselves once they rallied to allied forces. Second, they were to induce defections among their peers. To mark potential defectors, they were all given a tube of ultraviolet paste.

SOG, of course, did not expect all of the BORDEN agents to carry out their assignments. Some, if not most, would probably reveal their mission soon after insertion. Even so, their clumsy attempt at encouraging defections—and their tales of fellow ralliers at Long Thanh—would serve the purpose of sowing suspicion within the North Vietnamese army. Should the agents actually be able to merge back into their original units and then make their way south, that would be an added bonus.

In early September, the first wave of BORDEN agents was ready. Before leaving, they all sat down to a lavish meal in Saigon. To maximize their impact, plans called for the bulk of them to be individually parachuted or helicoptered near their old units in South Vietnam, Laos, or Cambodia. Four more were scheduled to go to North Vietnam, two of whom were to jump from the same plane at different locations.

In short order, the insertions began, and by month's end a new batch of recruits was rushed to Long Thanh. Meanwhile, BORDEN case officers began experimenting with variations on their deception theme. Major Spivy's assistant, Captain David Faughnan, recalls:

In theory, the BORDEN agents would rally and wait in prison camps once they got south. To further this idea, we selected plants and put the ultraviolet mark on their foreheads and inserted them into camp. BORDEN control people, including myself, visited the sites and, with great show, put the ultraviolet light on the foreheads of many prisoners. When the plants were discovered, big welcome home ceremonies were held in the compound in the view of the true prisoners. We knew that North Vietnamese intelligence would latch on to these happenings and would reinforce what we were doing.[46]

Another innovation combined BORDEN with the OODLES notional teams. For one of the North Vietnam drops, a BORDEN agent was told he would be the guide for an entire long-term commando team. Shortly before his scheduled jump, this agent was introduced to his fellow teammates, who happened to be disguised members of the South Vietnamese training staff at Long Thanh. Donning parachutes, they filed into an MC-130 and overflew the drop zone in Nghe An Province. The BORDEN volunteer jumped first into the night sky, but the rest of the team remained aboard the plane. Once captured, it was expected that he would convincingly swear more commandos were at large.[47]

In late September, the BORDEN case officers got a pleasant surprise. A handful of agents did manage to find their way back to allied hands and were calling Long Thanh to fetch them. One of them, code-named KILO, had jumped into Laos, rejoined his unit, and defected to U.S. Marines near Hue. Eager for more, KILO was readied for a second mission. This time, the officers explained, he would be going to North Vietnam as a single reinforcement for an existing long-term team. Left unsaid was the fact that the team was a notional OODLES unit.

Putting on a parachute for the second time, KILO boarded a SOG plane and headed north. He had ultraviolet paste on his nails, which he would supposedly use to identify himself to the other agents on the ground. After leaving the aircraft over Nghe An Province, he was never seen again.[48]

While it is difficult to fully calculate success, diversionary operations by November 1968 had made considerable headway. Of the eighteen OODLES teams planned for the calendar year, fourteen had been raised over the radio, eight had been supplied by phantom bundles, and two were reinforced by BORDEN agents. In some cases, American intelligence intercepted word that North Vietnamese troops were alerted to look for notional teams, including the unit KILO was supposed to augment.[49] At long last, SOG appeared to be hitting its stride.

22

URGENCY

It had taken four years of trial and error for the Airborne Operations Section to arrive at a winning formula. No less painful was the evolution of SOG's maritime operations. Topping their list of problems was the fact that each new mission plan was outdated almost before the ink was dry. Frustrated in the search for new mandates, the Naval Advisory Detachment consistently pursued stale formulas.

Nowhere was this more true than with MINT operations. While still listed as their primary mission, SOG maritime operators increasingly found little to interdict. The U.S. Navy's SEA DRAGON patrols had seen to this, denuding the Quang Binh and Ha Tinh coastlines—SOG's former hunting ground—of most sea traffic.[1] Forced to look farther north in Nghe An and Thanh Hoa Provinces, in 1967 the Nastys were sinking about nine small boats a month.

Like MINT, the Naval Advisory Detachment's ongoing LOKI campaign was also generating yawns. While Danang was still snaring some thirty prisoners a month—and had even drawn up ambitious plans for coordinating the capture of a North Vietnamese MiG pilot downed at sea—the detainees were giving up little in the way of exploitable intelligence.[2] The fishing industry in North Vietnam occupied just a thin slice of the population, and it had been milked of all it was worth.

Behind the stagnating program was a chorus of complaints from the underemployed Biet Hai commandos. Reduced to three action teams by the close of 1967, they were used on just a dozen CADO raids during the year, ten of which produced no results.[3] Efforts to augment their combat pay by using them as gunners on MINT missions had fallen short, so an additional assignment was invented in September 1966. Known as SOTROPS, for Southern Training Operations, this scheme had the action teams and their American advisers making beach assaults against Viet Cong sanctuaries along the coast near Danang.

In theory, SOTROPS were designed as dress rehearsals for northern raids. In reality, CADO missions were not materializing, so the southern operations proved to be the only serious combat many of the Biet Hai ever saw. In this, they gave a good account of themselves through the winter monsoon season ending in early 1967. Later that year, with the onset of another monsoon cycle, the Naval Advisory Detachment looked to expand the concept to the Mekong Delta in southern South Vietnam. There it promised to give the U.S. Navy's riverine force a SEAL-type capability for reconnaissance, raids, and prisoner snatches.

The Mekong assignment, it quickly became apparent, was nothing like North Vietnam. The base of operations was the *Benewah*, a converted barge on the My Tho River acting as command center for the riverine force. This, in turn, was anchored off Dong Tam, a man-made peninsula of dredged mud that was home to a brigade from the U.S. Army's 9th Infantry Division. Clusters of floating platforms—some festooned with artillery pieces, others acting as helipads—ringed both Dong Tam and the *Benewah*, giving it the odd air of an urban militarized oasis in the middle of a desolate swamp.

So it was here that two Biet Hai teams, NIMBUS and ROMULUS, found themselves looking past the perimeter of Dong Tam toward endless tracts of snake-infested mangroves. Almost immediately, things got off to a bad start. More adept with the trigger of a submachine gun than the steering wheel of a truck, one of the ROMULUS commandos accidentally backed his vehicle over his Naval Advisory Detachment adviser. Hearing screams, he reversed direction—and ran over the adviser a second time.[4]

Short one American, NIMBUS and ROMULUS began a month of Mekong operations. On alternate nights, one team, accompanied by two advisers, would board a patrol boat at Dong Tam and head up the My Tho. A second, empty patrol boat followed. Once the boats got near an insertion point, the first would cut its engine and drift toward the bank. The second would continue up the river, the sound of its motor camouflaging the insert. After continuing for a couple of kilometers, the empty boat would circle back, allowing the first boat to restart its engine and ease back into the middle of the river.

Swampy terrain and dense vegetation made for slow progress toward the target. Once there, the commandos could be confident that the hamlet was hostile; most had an armed Viet Cong presence. Worse, the entire region was a free-fire zone at night, and, because the team was operating in secret, allied artillery did not know it was there.

In October, NIMBUS got orders to reconnoiter one particular village deep in the swamps. Unlike their previous nocturnal forays, which usually were aimed at snatching a prisoner for interrogation, the commandos were to remain in place throughout the daylight hours to gauge traffic around the village.

Choosing three of his best commandos, the senior NIMBUS adviser, U.S. Marine Gunnery Sergeant Charles Duncan, accompanied by one U.S. Navy SEAL, departed Dong Tam at 2200 hours and raced up the My Tho River.

Infiltrating without incident, their luck turned bad as soon as they started patrolling. About one hundred meters to their left, a single rifle shot cracked. As the patrol moved through the night, the shots continued—always just off to their left. The commandos knew what was happening: Viet Cong guerrillas were signaling the progress of their team.

Shortly before sunup, Duncan arrived near the targeted village. To his left was the NIMBUS team leader, a Catholic warrant officer who had been fighting communism for the past two decades. Another Biet Hai was to his right; the SEAL and the last commando were off to the rear.

As the sky lightened to gray, the village came into focus. Immediately the commandos knew something was wrong. All of the children and women were mobilized and probing the nearby jungle. It was apparent they knew government commandos were in the area.

Hearing movement to his rear, Duncan twisted in the grass. A head popped up, and for a second he thought it was one of his NIMBUS commandos. "He was wearing black pajamas, and we were wearing black pajamas," said Duncan. "But he had a carbine, and we had AK-47s."[5]

The Viet Cong reacted first. Squeezing the trigger, he pumped a shot into Duncan's hip; a second bullet hit his buttocks. Rolling to bring his rifle free, the wounded Marine emptied half a magazine into the guerrilla's stomach.

Drawn to the fire, the entire village erupted. Duncan rose to flee but was bleeding heavily and could barely walk on his wounded leg. The NIMBUS team leader grabbed him, and they began leapfrogging toward the river. By the time they reached water, their radio had been destroyed, leaving them no way of contacting Dong Tam. Out of ideas, they lowered themselves into the river and tried to hide among the water lilies lining the shore.

As the Viet Cong worked their way up to the bank, they instantly spotted the Biet Hai and opened fire. A fierce firefight erupted, with each of the commandos wounded in the crossfire. Desperate, Duncan ordered the SEAL—the best swimmer—to go for help; he was eventually rescued by a tugboat steaming upriver.

Alone with his commandos, the wounded marine adviser fired off his last shots, then tried to swim out to deeper water. Shedding his clothes and inflating his life vest, Duncan kicked with his single good leg, only to be pushed back by the incoming tide. From shore, the Viet Cong withheld fire as they watched the hapless commandos exhaust themselves in the current.

Floundering in the My Tho with Viet Cong strung along the riverbank, NIMBUS again got lucky. Oblivious to the firefight that had just taken place, a sampan wandered into range. Training an AK-47 on the boat captain, the NIMBUS team leader forced him to pull alongside. Seeing their quarry about to escape, the Viet Cong opened fire. With bullets flying, the three Vietnamese clambered aboard, pulling a naked but grateful Duncan over the side.

Although the mission had gone awry, it was only the nearly fatal results that separated it from many others. Coincidence rather than sound intelligence dictated whether or not the teams managed to snatch an important prisoner. "Most of what we did was pure luck," Duncan later recounted. "When we went into a village, it was just luck if there was somebody to grab."[6]

With NIMBUS temporarily out of action, ROMULUS was left to pick up the slack. Once more, chance played the key role. Approaching a village in the dead of night, U.S. Marine Gunnery Sergeant Robert "Tony" McMillan and his Biet Hai kidnapped a middle-aged male and spirited him back to a waiting patrol boat. Under interrogation, he was revealed to be the senior Viet Cong intelligence chief for the sector. Better yet, in his bag was a diagram of Dong Tam, apparently the target of an upcoming attack. "The details on the sketch were amazing," said Major W. H. "Duff" Rice, the Naval Advisory Detachment officer leading the Mekong contingent. "The teams really proved their worth that time."[7]

Although the Biet Hai fared well during SOTROPS, the exercises did little to offset mounting troubles for SOG's maritime section. The crunch came at the close of 1967, when the Joint Survey Team and General Brownfield's Ad Hoc Evaluation Group were reviewing SOG's performance. Restating the obvious, both commissions concluded the Naval Advisory Detachment was sorely in need of new direction.

Frustrated, Danang considered shifting toward a psychological focus. This was a logical tack considering that the SSPL had ostensibly been the sponsor of maritime operations almost since inception. But by 1968 the SSPL's supposed base in North Vietnam—in reality Paradise Island off the South Vietnamese coast—was a farce. It was inconceivable that fishermen, men intimately familiar with the sea, could be fooled into thinking that they were on the mainland. As one SOG report pointed out, "The smell of salt water, the amount of sand tracked throughout the detainee area, and the sound of the surf combined with the sun setting in the west where the ocean was located must have indicated to some of them that they were on an island."[8] Said one South Vietnamese radioman associated with the notional front: "Paradise Island was supposed to be a secret location in the north. However, the fishermen we kidnapped were smart and good at navigation. During one interrogation, a fisherman came to us and said, 'Twenty years ago, I was on this island.' He even knew its name, Cu Lao Cham. He had been blindfolded when he arrived, so we asked how he knew. He said that as soon as he landed, he felt the sand and knew exactly where he was."[9]

There were other holes in the SSPL myth. For one thing, the Nasty boats, which, as part of a national liberation front were supposed to be independent of the United States and South Vietnam, were openly supported by American naval vessels and carrier-based aircraft. Also, their primary mission—sinking northern boats—flew in the face of a liberation movement. The interdiction mission was "cutting our own throats insofar as trying to establish a rapport with the coastal population was concerned," concluded one SACSA official. "It gradually got through our thick skulls that this did not make too much sense."[10]

Although the SSPL was a transparent sham, there was no denying it was having a pronounced effect, though not exactly the one SOG had hoped for. Increasingly, fishermen were trying their best to get kidnapped—just so they could partake in the amenities of Paradise Island. "[We] cured them of all diseases while they were being held, but we also had to force feed them in order to increase their weight and the size of their stomachs," said SOG commander Singlaub. "Each individual who was brought south and returned to the north would have gained an average of over 20 pounds and, obviously, would be in better condition than he was when he left NVN [North Vietnam]."[11]

Besides medical benefits and better cuisine, the detainees got the popular "basket of cheer" when leaving. These gift kits were also coveted by the local authorities, who were confiscating half the contents. To compensate, SOG began to give each fisherman two baskets: one to hide and one to surrender to communist cadre. By the second half of 1967, some fishermen were showing up at Paradise Island as many as three times. Upon return, their extended stomachs demanded more food than the northern regime could provide, causing further dissatisfaction.[12]

SOG kept track of this as best it could, poring over interrogation transcripts for signs of how well the program was working. Fishermen who had been captured on more than one occasion reported that, upon their return to North Vietnam, local communist officials gathered up the gift boxes—all of which were marked "To NVN compatriots and pupils, a humble gift"—redistributing them to their own families. At the same time, they told the fishermen that the radios were meant to explode, and the food and clothes were laced with poison. But everyone knew this was untrue, and at least one fisherman readily told his interrogators that these government officials were "good for nothing" because they confiscated these small tokens from ordinary people.[13]

Naturally, Hanoi reacted harshly, issuing a shrill decree on counterrevolutionary crimes in October 1967 that promised death to those guilty of "fifth-column" activities, such as helping others to defect.[14] Nineteen of the twenty-one crimes outlined in the document could be linked to SOG, particularly maritime operations. "Hanoi's screams were getting louder and louder," said one SACSA official, "and they seemed to be giving us credit for doing a lot more than we actually were doing. They were seeing a lot of ghosts in their backyard. . . . We had several cases come up where apparently innocent North Vietnamese were tossed in the hoosegow for dealing with 'spy-commandos' who actually were never even there."[15]

By the time knowledge of this decree made its way to MACV in March 1968, SOG was also reorienting the airborne half of Op 34A toward diversionary operations. Following suit, the Naval Advisory Detachment decided on a diversionary realignment of its own. As with its airborne counterparts, OODLES and BORDEN, the maritime version—code-named URGENCY—was designed to make Hanoi think a lot was going on in its backyard.

Actually, the Naval Advisory Detachment had set the stage for diversionary maritime operations in the summer of 1967 when it planned to train fishermen detained at Paradise Island as low-level agents. Inserted back north, the fishermen would collect intelligence for two to three months, then sail out to sea for a prearranged rendezvous with a Nasty boat. Just as with the later BORDEN operation, SOG entertained little hope that the agents would actually complete their mission. Rather, SOG's interest was in stoking Hanoi's paranoia and diverting resources as the authorities detained, interrogated, and investigated all other returned detainees. After receiving approval from the Joint Chiefs of Staff in August, SOG inserted two maritime agents on 13 September, code-named PERGOLA and GOLDFISH, off the coast of Thanh Hoa Province. As expected, they were never seen again.[16]

During the first quarter of 1968, SOG began its full-blown diversionary campaign at sea. With an additional two patrol boats added to the inventory, by midsummer the Naval Advisory Detachment was able to conduct operations on almost a daily basis.[17] They trolled the coast looking for fishing fleets (to improve the SSPL's image, junks were no longer being sunk), and the blindfolded fishermen were hustled down to Cu Lao Cham, which had been expanded to handle two hundred detainees at a time. There the fishermen were subjected to two months of interrogation and SSPL indoctrination. Beginning in September 1967, some of the captives were enticed into writing letters to their families in South Vietnam before leaving Paradise Island. Beginning the following month, a select handful of fisherman were allowed to defect to South Vietnam. Their defections were carried on television and in the newspapers, which described their good treatment by the SSPL.[18]

Most fishermen were simply released back into North Vietnamese waters aboard rattan basket boats filled with gifts. Some were given SSPL "redemp-

Commander Ho Van Ky Thoai (second from left), chief of the Coastal Security Service, inspects a Nasty boat in Danang, 1968. (Courtesy Ho Van Ky Thoai)

tion coupon leaflets" and instructed to secretly hide them near their villages. Other fishermen were told to look for hidden SSPL members near their homes by using common hand signals—such as scratching one's shoulder. "If such information is relayed to the security police, which is relatively certain," read one SOG report, "the security police will be busy arresting innocent people with itchy shoulders."[19]

A few detainees were segregated from the rest of the group. Like BORDEN, these candidates were given an evaluation course to determine their potential as low-level agents. Among this group, two were weeded out as unsuitable. For this pair, the Naval Advisory Detachment conjured up plans to use them as unwitting pseudo-agents. After money and other incriminating material was secretly planted in their clothes, both were released far north of their homes near the city of Vinh. According to a senior SOG official:

One of them, an ethnic Chinese, was fed disinformation that the Chinese government was looking to encroach on the North Vietnamese fishing industry. When he was released in the north with other Vietnamese, there were documents to this effect hidden in the lining of his shirt. The Nastys were shelling the coast with leaflet mortars repeating this same line. The idea was to make Hanoi suspicious of Chinese maritime intentions.[20]

The remaining URGENCY candidates were given a quick agent primer. Like the previous year's PERGOLA and GOLDFISH experiment, they were to remain in place for up to three months, collect low-level intelligence, then make their way to sea and try to flag a passing Nasty. Of the 328 fishermen sent to Cu Lao Cham in the first ten months of 1968, eleven were reinserted as URGENCY agents. None returned.

Beginning in July 1968, SOG decided to "more fully utilize Paradise detainees in special operations designed to enhance the credibility of the SSPL." One proposal, code-named HATTORI/PARFAIT, called for some detained fishermen to be organized into three-man cells that would form a pseudo-organization in select coastal communities. Once released, these cells were "oriented toward passive support of SSPL psychological and agent operations." Another plan, code-named YELLOW JACKET, proposed "insertion" of a North Vietnamese fishermen, "under controlled narcosis," into the mountains near the border with Laos. The object was to convince Hanoi that the SSPL extended beyond the coast. YELLOW JACKET was never approved.[21]

For the North Vietnamese authorities, the increased tempo of SOG's maritime campaign begged a response. But Hanoi had few options. Its shore batteries, while a nuisance, had yet to hit a Nasty. Coastal militia garrisons were also useless for anything other than defending against the rare CADO raid. Moreover, their collection of Soviet and Chinese patrol boats did not dare wander far from port for fear of being sunk by a U.S. Navy SEA DRAGON patrol.

Improvising, Hanoi conjured up a primitive countermeasure long on stealth and short on technology. Two naval detachments were formed, each equipped with unmotorized bamboo rafts. From a distance, they looked like innocent fishing junks. Up close, each packed an array of recoilless rifles, handcrafted mortars, rocket-propelled grenades, and machine guns. The idea was for these rafts to wander out to sea amid a flotilla of civilian fishing vessels for cover. Should some Nastys try to make a snatch, the rafts would spring their ambush.

At 0200 hours, 17 August 1968, three rafts departed their base in Nghe An Province. Their target was an area of open sea about thirteen kilometers from shore favored by the fishing fleets. The winds were moderate and visibility good. A little over three hours later, they were in position.

For the remainder of the morning, the three boats remained in place. Around them, the sea was alive with fishermen casting nets and setting tackle. While plans called for them to maintain their vigil through the following day, they did not have to wait that long. At 1340 hours, shore radar reported three Nastys heading south along the coast, apparently in search of fishermen.

A second detachment of four armed rafts was ordered to reinforce the vicinity. Before that could happen, however, the ambush began to fall apart. The skies darkened, the wind picked up, and the seas turned choppy. As the rest of the fishing fleet headed for shore, the original three rafts were now conspicuous and vulnerable. Making matters worse, the radar operators at the closest station finished their shift and went home before replacements arrived. The shore-based command post was suddenly blind.

At 1534 hours, the three Nastys spotted the rafts alone at sea. Ten days earlier, a Nasty patrol had encountered a similar pack of six armed boats. All had been sunk at that time, although six South Vietnamese sailors were killed in the encounter. Recognizing this second ambush for what it was, the Nasty skippers cautiously approached to within five hundred meters and shouted surrender appeals over their loudspeakers. The rafts responded with rocket fire.

The fight was one-sided, but at first the rafts gave as good as they got. While the Nastys stood their distance and fired their 40mm guns, the rafts struck back with grenades and homemade mortars. One shell hit a Nasty on its superstructure, killing four sailors. As this boat limped away, the other two kept up their 40mm barrage. By 1630 hours, the rafts were reduced to flotsam. Seven North Vietnamese crewmen went down with their craft, nine were captured, and two managed to swim to safety.[22]

The Nastys won this battle, but it was one of the last. Politics again intervened. In Washington, fallout from the Tet Offensive still colored policy, and by the fall of 1968, public opinion had turned against the war. President Johnson reacted by imposing more restrictions on the military, including the covert war. Paradise Island was one of the casualties: the last detainee was sent back to North Vietnam on 22 October, and the facility was closed.[23] SOG's war at sea was all but over.

23

CLOSING THE GATE

The call came to MACV headquarters on the morning of 29 October 1968: President Johnson wanted to see General Creighton Abrams in the White House immediately. Abrams had just become MACV commander in July, but, as Westmoreland's deputy since early 1967, he knew the situation in Vietnam as well as anyone.

Abrams secretly flew out of Tan Son Nhut airport and arrived in Washington on 31 October, just in time for an early morning meeting with Johnson.[1] The general knew from highly classified discussions going on since early summer that the president was leaning toward a cessation of all bombing north of the Demilitarized Zone in exchange for Hanoi's promise to negotiate an end to the war.

Not surprisingly, the military opposed a bombing halt. The Joint Chiefs had advised the president that if the halt went into effect without "substantive reciprocal agreement" by Hanoi, the result would "carry substantial and heavy risks, both military and political." General Abrams pointed out that "we could not assume the enemy would act in good faith."[2]

The president wrestled with these arguments, but the war was a crushing weight on his shoulders, and he wanted a quick solution. The previous March, Johnson had announced that he would not seek reelection, a decision precipitated by the worsening situation in Vietnam. Now, alone in the Oval Office with his Vietnam commander, the president wondered aloud if the bombing halt was the right decision. "If you were president, would you do it?" he asked Abrams.

Like other military men before him, Abrams was unable to be candid with the president. He also probably knew that Johnson had already made his decision. "I do think it is the right thing to do," Abrams said, apparently unwilling to vent his previous objections. "It is the proper thing to do."[3]

That night, Johnson announced the bombing halt to the American public. Negotiations in Paris were bearing fruit, he said, and "as a result of these developments, I have now ordered that all air, naval, and artillery bombardment of North Vietnam cease."[4]

Abrams returned to Vietnam knowing that the war had changed. He was now commanding an army in retreat. In Saigon, he stoically passed on the news that the bombing halt was a reality. In an irony-tinged message to his subordinate commanders, he said that "this comes at a time when U.S. and allied forces have achieved a dominant position of strength in relation to the [North Vietnamese] forces." He also noted sarcastically that "it is anticipated that the North Vietnamese forces will immediately cease their violation of the DMZ and will refrain from attacks on [South Vietnamese] cities."[5]

As far as the public knew, the bombing halt was just what it implied—an end to air attacks against North Vietnam. But the halt was actually being broadly interpreted to include all operations in North Vietnam, including covert activities north of the seventeenth parallel. When SOG was told three weeks before the bombing halt that its activities were also likely to be suspended, the reaction was one of disbelief. Halting further covert operations in the north, argued former SOG chief Blackburn, would once and for all reveal the American hand behind SSPL operations. And there was no going back. "It can't be reconstituted," he pointed out. Halting operations in North Vietnam also gave Hanoi a propaganda victory, observed Blackburn. Although the communists knew the SSPL to be nothing more than a shell, they could now turn around and claim that resistance "activities had been destroyed."[6]

Colonel Singlaub, who had been replaced as chief of SOG in August by Colonel Stephen Cavanaugh, agreed:

[A cessation would cause] a complete compromise of the covert operations because it [is] just unrealistic to expect that the mythical resistance movement that we used as the cover for the conduct of these operations would standdown their operations because of the U.S. standdown. . . . The fact that the [SSPL] was forced to standdown at the same time expose[s] the very direct connection between the two, and this is what we worked so hard to avoid.[7]

There were other objections as well. The United States had started covert operations in North Vietnam when overflight restrictions were in place, noted SOG Deputy Chief Robert Gleason, so why cancel covert operations because overflight restrictions were reimposed? In doing so, Washington risked being painted as an unreliable ally. After all, it had recruited, trained, and deployed the agents that went north—and now was withdrawing support for nontactical reasons.[8]

While such arguments were persuasive in SOG's mind, the White House was undeterred. In mid-October MACV moved to rein in covert operations ahead of the anticipated halt. On 22 October, the last fisherman was sent home from Paradise Island. The next day, helicopters from Nakhon Phanom scrambled to pull the last two STRATA teams out of North Vietnam.[9] Five days later, one final BORDEN agent was sent north. By the time dawn broke on 1 November, SOG was abiding by the restrictions in both letter and spirit.

Not all of SOG's operations were affected by the bombing halt. By late 1968, the overwhelming majority of the group's assets were occupied by cross-border forays into Laos and Cambodia, neither of which was touched by the president's ruling.[10] But for those sections focused on North Vietnam, there was no longer a mission. In fact, it seemed that suddenly the Pentagon, which had been so supportive of the northern operations in the past, was now criticizing their legacy. STRATA operations were an "unproductive failure," lamented the CINCPAC, Admiral John McCain, shortly after the halt.[11] Maritime forays, he said, had done little more than gather some anecdotal data from the fishing community.[12] Diversionary operations, whose success was hard to quantify, were all but ignored.

Despite the harsh reviews, the Pentagon did not scrap SOG's North Vietnam sections entirely. Rather, SOG was told to retain its northern capabilities at maximum readiness should the call to use them ever come again. In some cases, this took almost no adjustment. The Naval Advisory Detachment, for example, expanded on its SOTROPS experience by focusing all of its boats and action teams on CADO-type operations against Viet Cong targets along the South Vietnamese coast.

Psychological operations also kept to a heavy schedule with little change. Further leaflet drops were halted, as was the development of an aircraft-launched balloon leaflet delivery system,[13] but the section was able to continue its assault on the airwaves with regular broadcasts of Voice of Freedom and Voice of the SSPL.[14]

But for the heart of Op 34—airborne operations—major changes were in store. Prior to 1 November, this section had expanded into three related campaigns: 34A for long-term agents, 34B for STRATA, and 34C for OODLES and BORDEN. Because these were all but shut down by the bombing halt, SOG felt compelled to change its organizational chart. On 8 December, Op 34 was renamed Op 36, the Airborne Studies Group. Two subsections were recognized: 36A, handling agents and diversionary activities, and 36B, for STRATA.

Op 36A inherited no fewer than five operations from the pre-halt days. The first, OODLES, consisted of fourteen notional teams located in the hills of North Vietnam. While these teams could no longer be resupplied with ice-block parachute rigs and phantom bundles, they were able to continue beaming family morale messages over the Voice of the SSPL.

The second inherited operation was BORDEN. Just as during its first year of operation, groups of ralliers were taken to Long Thanh and trained en masse. Most were then returned to the prison camps with inflated tales of the program. The remainder were then inserted into Laos, Cambodia, and communist-controlled areas of South Vietnam. At its peak during the first half of 1969, there were a dozen BORDEN infiltrations per month, some of them grouped as two- and three-man teams. A total of forty-three volunteers were inserted by year's end.[15]

Op 36A also inherited the long-term teams still in North Vietnam. A total of five teams—EAGLE, HADLEY, RED DRAGON, TOURBILLON, and the singleton ARES—were still in radio contact with Saigon. For the past year, SOG had been painfully aware that all of these were under North Vietnamese control. In some cases, Hanoi had not even tried to hide this fact. For example, ARES began to ask probing questions in February about the negotiating positions taken by Washington and Saigon at the just-opened Paris peace talks.[16]

Hoping to close this embarrassing chapter, SOG decided in early 1969 to use the five remaining teams in a diversionary capacity. Four of them were told to make their way toward exfiltration sites. The last, ARES, was ordered to prepare a cache for a notional agent in the Haiphong area. Unable to comply, both RED DRAGON and TOURBILLON went off the air. A third team, HADLEY, reported in March that it had crossed the border into Laos and was awaiting pickup.[17] SOG was sure the claim was a ruse but decided to go through the motions of a search. Major Stanley Olchovik, who had served a prior tour in Op 34A, was pulled from a desk job in Saigon and dispatched to Nakhon Phanom. "I took a spotter plane along the border," recalled Olchovik, "but I couldn't see a thing."[18] Shortly thereafter, HADLEY's radio fell silent.

This left two teams still on the books. SOG told them to finalize exfiltration plans and inform Saigon. Pushed for a decision, EAGLE finally went silent in November. By year's end, only ARES—who had been the first long-term agent back in 1961—clung to his transparent radio play.

The final two programs under Op 36A's control had yet to be tested. The first was as a so-called Strategic Intelligence Team (SIT), conceived in the spring of 1968 as a kind of urban STRATA. Whereas STRATA haunted the remote karst along the border, SIT agents were supposed to infiltrate close to populated areas along the North Vietnamese panhandle. A pilot team of nine agents, all of them born in North Vietnam, had been recruited over the summer and began training in October. When the bombing halt went into effect the following month, however, the SIT concept withered on the vine. All nine agents were turned over to the STRATA program in early 1969.[19]

The second program yet to be implemented was the gray singleton concept. Under this plan, North Vietnamese ralliers would be documented as soldiers and infiltrated by boat to the coast near Vinh. Collecting low-level intelligence, they would eventually make their way south any way they could. This concept, of course, had ample precedent. Prior to 1964, the CIA had repeatedly attempted to infiltrate long-term singletons by boat, always without success. This time, however, the ralliers-cum-agents were only supposed to go for short missions. In this sense, they more resembled BORDEN minus the diversionary dimension.[20]

Following CINCPAC approval in September, two *hoi chanh*—both former residents of Vinh—were selected as the first gray singletons. Sent to Danang, they practiced infiltrating by rubber boat. But like the SIT team, the bombing halt came before they could head north. Rather than waste the two assets, their South Vietnamese case officer, Marc, brought them south for use in Cambodia.

On 1 December, the first singleton, code-named ROMA, walked across the border. While Prince Norodom Sihanouk's government in Phnom Penh professed to be diplomatically neutral, Sihanouk had years ago ceded de facto control over the kingdom's eastern extreme to the combined forces of North Vietnam and the Viet Cong. From this swath of territory, the communists had established a string of heavily defended base areas from which they could stage into South Vietnam, then withdraw to the safety of Cambodian soil. Outgunned on their own territory, Cambodia's military turned a blind eye to such blatant violations of their sovereignty.[21]

One of the largest communist strongholds, known as Base Area 350, was in Kratie opposite South Vietnam's Phuoc Long Province. Into this hornet's nest went ROMA. Back in Saigon, SOG waited for its singleton to return. He was never seen again.

Smarting from this loss, Marc and his Op 36A counterparts turned toward their second singleton, a Vinh native by the name of Dinh Cong Ba. Code-named AURORA, he was also to be documented as a North Vietnamese soldier and would try to penetrate a Cambodian base area. Instead of Kratie, he was targeted against Mimot, opposite Tay Ninh Province. To track his progress, SOG this time equipped their agent with a special homing device disguised as a canteen.

After boarding a chopper alongside Marc and Major John Carter, the commander of Op 36A, AURORA was dropped on the South Vietnamese frontier. He ran from the landing zone, pausing to hide a PRC-25 tactical radio before starting his seven-kilometer hike toward the town of Mimot. Once there, he was to gather low-level intelligence as an overflying aircraft plotted his movement with the homing device. He would then return to the landing zone and use the PRC-25 to call for extraction.

Initially, all went well. While Marc and Major Carter camped for the week at a border outpost, AURORA arrived at Mimot. Five days later, he began his return journey and reached the landing zone. Then his homer suddenly fell silent. Overflying the area in an O-2 spotter plane, Marc used a loud-speaker in an unsuccessful bid to contact the agent. Communications intercepts later revealed he was captured.[22]

With two failures in two attempts, Op 36A's record with singletons was showing no improvement over the earlier CIA effort. Still, with SOG's mandate calling for proficiency in the technique, it tried once more. This time SOG turned toward members of the Cao Dai, an indigenous Vietnamese religious sect centered in Tay Ninh that blended the diverse influences of Jesus, Buddha, author Victor Hugo, and other philosophies. During the earlier Diem regime, the Cao Dai had been persecuted, leading many adherents to flee across the border to the safety of Cambodia. Nearly all had returned after the assassination of Diem, but not before they had established business ties and friendships in the same border areas now being used as communist sanctuaries.

After recruiting the first Cao Dai agent, SOG sent him toward Mimot in April 1969. Going by the code name DIEHARD, he was promptly arrested by border officials as he crossed the frontier. The resourceful agent was able to convincingly portray himself as a local trader and bribe his way to freedom. Once back in South Vietnam, however, he promptly quit. Undeterred, SOG recruited another Cao Dai and sent him into Cambodia under the same code name. In all, three different DIEHARD agents were successfully sent on cross-border forays during a one-year period.[23]

These small successes prompted Op 36A to recruit a fourth sect member in mid-1969. Going by the code name FASTAGE, this agent, living near an open market on the Tay Ninh border, had developed good connections during his Cambodian exile with military authorities in Svay Rieng and Kompong Cham Provinces. These contacts proved useful that September, when FASTAGE was able to obtain revealing photographs of the audience at Ho Chi Minh's funeral taken by a member of the Cambodian government delegation attending the service. Later that year, FASTAGE scored another coup when he acted as middleman between SOG and a Cambodian military officer who had information on the remains of an American chopper crew that had crashed just inside the Cambodian border. Following from this contact, the bodies of two servicemen were exhumed from a Svay Rieng grave site in February 1970.[24]

While Op 36A could now point to concrete results from its singleton effort, little of the experience was applicable to northern operations. The operating

Photograph delivered to SOG via its Cao Dai singleton agent FASTAGE, showing Prince Sihanouk (white jacket, second from left), his wife, Monique, and Pathet Lao leader Soupannouvang (fifth from right) at the funeral for Ho Chi Minh, September 1969. (Courtesy Allan Tureson)

environment in Cambodia, after all, was a far cry from North Vietnam. And the Cao Dai, while fertile for Cambodian contacts, had no inroads north of the Demilitarized Zone.

The same was true for Op 36B, the new coordinating body for the STRATA program. Once the SOG darling that had captured Westmoreland's imagination when it was first launched in September 1967, STRATA had come under much criticism in the immediate aftermath of the bombing halt. Some of the harshest words came from its own SOG advisers, many of whom faulted their commandos for a pronounced lack of aggression. "I got the feeling that every time we inserted them, they found a hole to hide," summed up Captain Roy Meeks, their assistant chief of operations.[25]

A few, however, found redeeming features in the program. STRATA teams, for example, had averaged thirteen days on the ground in North Vietnam; by comparison, American-led reconnaissance teams staging into Laos usually counted their missions in hours. This was because the Americans tried to capture prisoners or stage flashy ambushes, reflected SOG's Lieutenant Colonel Ernest T. Hayes. STRATA agents, more interested in staying alive than gaining glory, were content with simply observing.[26]

Electing to keep STRATA intact, SOG did with these road watchers what it had done with BORDEN and the singletons—redirected them south of the Demilitarized Zone. Thus, the STRATA commandos were now little different from the joint U.S.–South Vietnamese reconnaissance teams long operating in Laos and Cambodia. The only distinction was that STRATA, in keeping with its deniable status, was outfitted in sterile gear (except for radios) and kept its all-indigenous roster.

On 5 January 1969, STRATA conducted its first mission since the bombing halt. Boarding CH-3s from Thailand, it landed in the Lao panhandle. Two days later, another team headed out from Nakhon Phanom. Both groups were recovered without incident.

At that point, SOG did the unexpected. Ditching the last vestiges of STRATA's claim to deniability, it began outfitting the teams with American-made M16 rifles and permitted U.S. Special Forces advisers to accompany the commandos into combat.[27] With these changes, STRATA was now no different than the standard PRAIRIE FIRE reconnaissance teams. On 12 January, the first group of American-led STRATA agents ventured into Laos on a U.S. Army UH-1 chopper. Perhaps predictably, the emboldened team got into a firefight, killing seven North Vietnamese. Three days later, it withdrew without casualties.[28]

More American-led missions followed. The peak came in early March, when Monkey Mountain received reports of a Lao jungle camp holding U.S. prisoners. "We had two sources of information on the camp," said Captain Richard Meadows, the same Green Beret who had led the abortive carrier-based rescue into North Vietnam during 1966. After receiving a battlefield commission for his heroics in Laos, Meadows was on his second SOG tour, this time as STRATA operations officer. "I had a STRATA team on standby at the launch site, but at the last minute I was told that there were three [PRAIRIE FIRE] platoons getting hit in Laos, and they wanted STRATA to take off the pressure."[29]

The stricken SOG platoons were part of two large military operations being conducted along the Lao frontier. The first of these, code-named DEWEY CANYON, was targeted against the hills north of Route 548, a strategic path used by the North Vietnamese to shuttle men and arms from the Ho Chi Minh Trail across the border and into the A Shau Valley, an important North Vietnamese pipeline into northern South Vietnam. The second operation, MASSACHUSETTS STRIKER, moved against the A Shau from the south.

Both thrusts initially caught the North Vietnamese by surprise. It was the middle of the monsoon, and Hanoi figured MACV would not risk a major push while logistics and air support were hindered by rains. It had figured wrong. On 22 January, three battalions from the U.S. Marine 9th Regiment helicoptered into the hills north of the A Shau, then moved south in three prongs.

Recovering from their initial shock, the North Vietnamese increased resistance as the marines uncovered several enormous weapons caches. On 18 February, they rushed the forward lines, only to be pushed back over the course of the next four days. By then the marines had reached the border and crossed it, uncovering more caches, including one with a dozen 122mm guns.

At that point, the U.S. Army's 101st Airborne Division moved into the valley and established a pair of fire support bases. On 1 March, the paratroopers surged forward under MASSACHUSETTS STRIKER, reinforcing the gains already made by the marines. As part of this second operation, elements of a PRAIRIE FIRE exploitation company based in Danang were lifted to the Lao border.

As the SOG company touched ground, the North Vietnamese zeroed in and took them under heavy fire. But the 101st Airborne Division had plenty of fighting on its hands, so SOG had to reinforce itself. They scrounged up a company from the southern part of the country to help take off some of the pressure. With an American-led STRATA team at point, the commandos were ordered to insert farther north on the border to relieve some of the pressure.[30]

On 7 March, the fresh SOG troops landed in Laos. They were unofficially dubbed Task Force Meadows, because the indefatigable Captain Meadows had landed with his STRATA pathfinders. But as soon as they arrived, the task force got word that the Danang company had been rescued. Their diversion no longer necessary, they made their way toward the South Vietnamese border. "The mission was only supposed to last five days," remembered Meadows. "But when we weren't going to get picked up in time, we decided to head toward the marines because we thought they had food."[31]

The marines, it turned out, were in worse shape than the SOG commandos. In the field for nearly a month, the 1st Battalion, 9th Marines, had seen some of the heaviest fighting in DEWEY CANYON. One onslaught had been so intense that Lieutenant Westley Fox, a company commander, earned the Medal of Honor for his spirited defense. The constant skirmishes and poor weather combined to make resupply difficult, leaving them with little food to spare.

Calling for an extract, Task Force Meadows was lifted out on 15 March. Four days later, the marines followed. A total of 1,617 North Vietnamese were confirmed dead and 1,461 weapons captured. The North Vietnamese A Shau stronghold had been breached, but the operations were not enough to sweep the valley clean.

Once more Op 36 assets had done well, and once more they had focused their energies on operations that had little bearing on their underlying mandate. Using STRATA as light infantry offered few lessons applicable in North Vietnam.

In Washington, meanwhile, the highest levels of government were emphasizing the need to maintain contingency forces for unconventional warfare in the north. In January, SACSA had quizzed MACV on its preparedness for such operations.[32] The White House also weighed in, asking the Joint Chiefs of Staff on 1 February if it had "a capability in-country or elsewhere to counteract [Hanoi's increasing aggression] with guerrilla attacks against North Vietnam?" President Richard M. Nixon, in his new job for less than a month, could be forgiven for his ignorance of SOG's past history. General Earle Wheeler, the chairman of the Joint Chiefs, pointed out that there was not much that could be done along those lines because "we have no assets in NVN." If the United States wanted to open new clandestine attacks against the north, the president "should consider the use of sea-launched, air dropped, or helo-inserted groups." In other words, go back to what SOG had been doing before 1968.[33]

In Saigon, MACV responded with a mixed bag of proposals. Of the dozen possible scenarios, most were fast attacks by CADO teams or heliborne PRAIRIE FIRE assets. "Our feeling was that these would be largely harassment operations, a repetition of 1964 all over again," lamented SACSA's Captain Bruce Dunning. "This type of hit-and-run raid and harassing operation would not have any long-range or significant impact on the Hanoi regime," he concluded.[34]

One MACV contingency, however, showed potential. The success of BORDEN led some Op 36 case officers to contemplate forming an entire reconnaissance team composed of ralliers.[35] As it turned out, the idea was not original. In early 1968, SOG's PRAIRIE FIRE section had pioneered plans for a *hoi chanh* squad that could do everything from reconnaissance to kidnapping. Under the code name THUNDERCLOUD, three teams of three ralliers each were formed. With them dressed and equipped like their former comrades, it was hoped the disguise would give the agents greater longevity on the Ho Chi Minh Trail.[36]

The plan worked—up to a point. Indistinguishable from a real North Vietnamese patrol, the teams managed to conduct several forays without incident. On one mission, said a SOG officer, "they were able to walk up to another North Vietnamese Army soldier, convince the soldier that the members of the team were his comrades in arms, and to capture him."[37] But in other cases the teams were short on discipline. During one attempted kidnapping of a North Vietnamese officer, they shot their prisoner and fled.[38]

For their part, the Americans were short on patience. Disappointed by a lack of solid results after just a few months, THUNDERCLOUD was canceled by mid-1968 and its commandos incorporated into a regular PRAIRIE FIRE team.[39]

THUNDERCLOUD was dead, but Op 36 resurrected its spirit in early 1969 as the EARTH ANGEL program. Approved by CINCPAC in February, the initial scheme repeated the THUNDERCLOUD formula of three teams of three ralliers apiece. Unlike THUNDERCLOUD, however, they would be used strictly for road watch and reconnaissance. Significantly, the South Vietnamese code name for the program was DE THAM, the name of a guerrilla leader in northern Vietnam who had led a thirty-year resistance campaign against the French early in the twentieth century.

On 8 April, the first EARTH ANGEL team was lifted into the field. Its target was a ferry and dock landing inside Cambodia. Because South Vietnamese and American helicopter pilots were understandably leery of picking up an all-indigenous team dressed like North Vietnamese soldiers, the agents were instructed to walk home. As the case officers waited along the border, however, two ralliers failed to appear.[40]

Things only got worse. On 30 April, an EARTH ANGEL team was set to insert near Khe Sanh to confirm the presence of the North Vietnamese 3rd Division. But as it approached the landing zone, antiaircraft fire brought down the helicopter.[41] Two other teams were able to insert into Laos during May, but both were disbanded after they were caught fabricating reports.[42]

Sensing that the program was rapidly becoming a fiasco, Op 36 restructured it over the summer. By July, ten new agents—picked according to a new psychological profile—were training at Long Thanh. The changes worked: seven of the next eight EARTH ANGEL missions were considered a success.

With this improved record, the ralliers were handed a critical assignment in November. For the previous three months, a pair of U.S. Special Forces border camps in the Central Highlands, Bu Prang and Duc Lap, had been under communist pressure. A full-blown siege began on 28 October, with heavy artillery fire coming from inside Cambodia. It was the EARTH ANGEL's task to find the big guns.

At the end of the first week of November, a two-man team headed for the border. One of the members, Le Thanh Nam, was a Catholic from Nghe An. He had left the north in February 1968, walking down the Ho Chi Minh Trail for 105 days. As a combatant in the 304th Division, Nam did not have a taste of heavy combat until 23 December. He defected later that same day and ended up in the central Chieu Hoi center near Saigon. In June 1969, he was among the ten volunteers sent to Long Thanh. Since then, he had been

A U.S. officer poses with members of EARTH ANGEL at Camp Long Thanh, 1971. (Conboy collection)

on two successful reconnaissance forays into Cambodia, both of them against his old unit.[43]

The other team member, Nguyen Dang Vieng, had come south in late 1967 and was assigned to the 2nd Division in South Vietnam's Central Highlands. He rallied in late May 1969 and spent just three days in the Chieu Hoi center before being diverted to Long Thanh. This was his second mission.[44]

For twenty-four hours, the pair worked their way slowly through the brush. On the second day their luck ran out. Running headlong into a North Vietnamese patrol, they were disarmed, taken to a jungle campsite, and thrown into a pit covered by bamboo grating. An adjacent pit housed six South Vietnamese soldiers, and a third contained two American helicopter crewmen. A pair of North Vietnamese platoons guarded the enclosures.

For the next three weeks, the agents languished in their earthen cell. Through interrogation, their captors discovered they were ralliers, which prompted a round of severe beatings. The guards openly discussed plans to execute the two as traitors.

On the twenty-sixth day of their confinement, the bamboo grating came off. Their leg irons were unlocked, and a single armed guard motioned them toward the jungle's edge to relieve their bowels. As they reached the foliage,

Nam continued forward. Training his weapon on the commando, the guard followed a few paces behind. As he came abreast of Vieng, the rallier lunged. Nam then spun around and wrestled away the rifle. Leaving the guard in an unconscious heap, they bolted into the jungle.

Twenty-four hours later, on 9 December, the two arrived at a government-controlled outpost. After word was passed to SOG, Major Carter, the Op 36A commander, arrived by chopper early the following morning to conduct a debriefing. He was particularly interested in the two American prisoners seen at the jungle site. Nam volunteered to act as pathfinder for a rescue team; Vieng, suffering from malaria, was forced to stay behind.

Later that same afternoon, a heliborne task force, with Nam in the lead helicopter, assembled in Phuoc Long Province. At the same time, SOG inserted an American-led reconnaissance team to independently locate the prison.[45] Before anything was found, however, the two American servicemen, Sergeant Vernon Shepard and Warrant Officer Michael Peterson, materialized from the jungle.[46] The North Vietnamese, perhaps anticipating the imminent raid, had elected to spring their captives. While his services were not used, Nam was presented a brick of cash as a bonus.[47]

The escape of the two agents ended the year on a high note, but it also underscored the fact that Op 36 was excelling in areas only tangentially related to its core mission. Despite advances with the singletons, STRATA, and EARTH ANGEL, SOG was no closer to reaching proficiency in North Vietnam contingencies than it had been the previous January.

24

BACKDOOR

SOG operations in North Vietnam were all but ended by the bombing halt, but the CIA was playing by a different set of rules. Suddenly the agency had the upper hand in an undeclared turf war with the Pentagon that had been raging for years.

The infighting had come to a boil back in 1965, when SOG began operating in Laos, and continued unabated for the next four years. The first battle erupted when EWOT, the early road-watching effort, became the focus for Op 34A. Hearing of this, the CIA station in Vientiane offered swift protest, claiming SOG's reconnaissance agents might compromise in-place teams the agency already had on the Lao side of the border. More likely, the case officers wanted to stave off any road-watching competition from MACV.[1]

Adding to the widening rift was the U.S. ambassador to Laos, William Sullivan, who steadfastly opposed any kind of SOG operations in Laos. In a scathing letter to MACV commander General Westmoreland on 23 April 1965, he called SOG's plan to run reconnaissance operations in Laos "wistful" and said it was it was "farfetched to think of storming the Ho Chi Minh Trail with a bare-bottomed bunch of [hill tribesmen]. If there is any serious intent to break up the real marrow of the Ho Chi Minh Trail in the areas where the Vietnamese truly protect it by organic battalions, we had better start thinking in terms of regiments and divisions, and not tribal assets."[2]

SOG was not swayed, however, and the turf war continued. When MACV did not back off from its commitment to such operations, Sullivan fired back by approving CIA plans to use Laos as a springboard for unilateral intelligence forays into North Vietnam. The pilot team, consisting of Hmong guerrillas, walked from Sam Neua Province for a brief stay inside Son La.[3]

Soon after the Son La mission, strained relations improved somewhat. This came after the inauguration of Southeast Asia Coordination (SEA-CORD) meetings at Udorn Royal Thai Air Force Base during 1966. Attended by Sullivan, SOG chief Singlaub, Vientiane station chief Ted Shackley, and a handful of other CIA representatives, these monthly trysts were effective in eliminating some conflicts. "Sullivan imposed artificial lines," said Singlaub. "But the CIA occasionally agreed for SOG to cross those lines."[4]

One result of the SEACORD meetings was an agreement for SOG to launch limited recruiting drives in Laos. Heading the effort was Major Lo Ngan Dung, the ethnic Tho officer who was the first Office 45 airborne adviser back in 1961. Now stationed at the South Vietnamese embassy in Vientiane, Dung in August 1966 selected fourteen Hmong for training at Long Thanh.[5] Plans called for this Hmong team—code-named NANSEN—to establish a rear base along the Lao border opposite Nghe An, then make forays into North Vietnam over a three-year period.[6]

In preparation, NANSEN was put through seven months of instruction. American advisers at Long Thanh were impressed by the quality of the Hmong compared with the standard Vietnamese recruit.[7] Sometimes, however, the training produced comical results. "When they did practice parachute jumps," remembers one fellow student, "they always deployed their reserve chute open after their main chute was open, and their helmets were always falling off in the air because they forgot to secure the chin straps."[8]

In March 1967, the team was declared mission-ready. Before leaving, it was joined by three ethnic Vietnamese radio operators—all brothers—and one Vietnamese translator. On 22 April, the ensemble went to Nakhon Phanom, transferred to a CH-3, then headed north. A second CH-3 followed, this one piled with three months' worth of supplies—the theory being that NANSEN would stash the food at a secure Lao campsite to minimize the need for a quick resupply.[9]

Landing in a border clearing, the helicopters disgorged their cargo and left. Alone, NANSEN gathered the supplies and waited. And waited. Only after constant prompting over the radio from Saigon did the agents cautiously venture toward the border. Just as quickly, they hurried back to their bivouac. The next month, they again tiptoed into North Vietnam, then sprinted west to Laos until reaching a friendly Hmong outpost. Frustrated with NANSEN's nonresults, SOG recalled the four Vietnamese and disbanded the team.[10]

Following the NANSEN episode, SOG recruitment efforts in Laos sputtered. Major Dung made one last attempt, identifying thirteen Black Tai refugees in July and packing them off to Long Thanh. When half had to be repatriated because of ill health and poor motivation, the program ground to a halt.[11]

The failure fed Ambassador Sullivan's ire. In May he had complained about expanding SOG reconnaissance operations inside Laos, noting that "opportunities for SOG . . . considerably exceed their abilities."[12] Sullivan's tone turned more sarcastic five months later when Pentagon plans included expanding PRAIRIE FIRE operations. He believed that these missions "were totally disproportionate to the amount of paper which [they] consume; and it would not become more effective even if it were more liberally permissive." The root of the problem, Sullivan argued, was the fact that operations were carried out "by a gung-ho group who, by their very nature, are always attempting to exceed the political limitations of more reasonable men everywhere." When Sullivan turned down what he considered overzealous missions, he was fully aware that he was acquiring a reputation for micromanagement. He waved aside the criticism, noting that "this is largely a problem of morale for overgrown adolescents and I certainly don't wish to disappoint their inevitable image of parental rigidity."[13]

In contrast to SOG's frustrations, the CIA station in Laos continued to make headway with unilateral operations into North Vietnam. In this, 1967 proved a pivotal year. Across Laos, CIA-sponsored paramilitary forces were making strong territorial gains, prompting speculation that the tide of war was about to swing decisively in favor of the government. Behind this momentum, guerrilla teams began venturing up to the North Vietnamese border—and occasionally across it.

The first instance took place in early June, when Air America H-34s staging from Luang Prabang twice inserted a twelve-man road-watching team along the provincial boundary between Son La and Lai Chau. Showing little imagination, the team was inserted for a third time into the same vicinity near month's end. Not surprisingly, North Vietnamese troops were waiting. Nine of the Lao team members were killed in a fierce firefight.[14]

Seven months later, the CIA was back in North Vietnam, this time closer to the infamous Dien Bien Phu valley in Lai Chau. Site of a key North Vietnamese military base camp controlling activities into northern Laos, the valley was also home to the Black Tai ethnic minority. Recruiting a team of these hill tribesmen from refugees around Luang Prabang, the agency gave them three months of reconnaissance training. At 1000 hours on 5 January 1968, they were lifted by U.S. Air Force CH-3 helicopters to a grassy plateau south of the valley. Faring slightly better than the previous team, this new group lasted one day before it was hit. Scattering, three members headed for the border and were lifted out under fire; the remaining eight were killed or captured.[15]

Still fixated on Dien Bien Phu, the CIA readied a third team during the spring. This one consisted of North Vietnamese ralliers—the agency's precursor to SOG's EARTH ANGELs. Outfitted with a sophisticated wiretap, the team was inserted by Air America on 19 May along the Lao side of the border. Walking to their target, the agents managed to operate for over two weeks without compromise.[16] Then they got sloppy and decided to supplement their rations by throwing a grenade into a pond to catch fish. Alerted by the blast, North Vietnamese border guards closed in for the kill. Only one team member managed to reach Lao government lines.[17]

Some forays were directed against the North Vietnamese panhandle, where the CIA was trying its hand at STRATA-type reconnaissance missions. On 26 April, for example, a CIA road-watching team, led by a Thai civilian code-named SUN, was inserted by U.S. Air Force CH-3s directly west of Nakhon Phanom just inside the Quang Binh provincial boundary.[18] From their perch high in the mountains, the commandos quickly established contact with their CIA adviser in Savannakhet. Showing far greater longevity than their STRATA counterparts—probably because they stayed in the hills and refrained from venturing into the lowlands to lay mines or plant leaflets—SUN and his teammates were able to remain undetected through midsummer. "They were cordial at first," remembers their case officer. "But as the weeks dragged on, they started getting nasty. By the time they were extracted, they were asking, 'Are you trying to kill us?'"[19]

Other teams followed during the second half of 1968.[20] All of them followed a similar script: local hill tribesmen dispatched back to their ethnic stomping grounds to conduct shallow, passive reconnaissance forays. Offensive, action-type missions were, as yet, not condoned.

This changed dramatically in the summer of 1969 with the arrival of a new U.S. ambassador in Vientiane. In manner and style, McMurtrie "Mac" Godley was a far cry from his predecessor. Where Sullivan was comfortable wearing bow ties and attending cocktail parties, Godley preferred rolling up his sleeves and touring outlying provinces. And where Sullivan micromanaged American military efforts and was at constant loggerheads with MACV, Godley, handpicked by the new Nixon administration, was a team player. Significantly, he had just completed a tour as ambassador in the Congo, where the CIA had recently finished a major paramilitary operation against communist Simba insurgents. Given his proven ability to work with the agency in that case, many in Washington were hoping Godley could "pull another Congo" in Laos.

Very quickly, the war in Laos mushroomed into a semiconventional slugfest pitting government forces against entire North Vietnamese infantry divisions. Along with this increase in scope and intensity, CIA officials suddenly found that earlier restrictions on action operations into North Vietnam had evaporated. In the words of a senior CIA official, "We were now encouraged to bring the war to the enemy."[21]

The tool by which they would do this was the Commando Raiders. Conceived in late 1968 as a kind of "super guerrilla," the Commando Raiders were to be given months of intensive unconventional warfare instruction under the auspices of U.S. Special Forces advisers at Phitsanulok, Thailand.

The first eighty candidates, chosen for their physical condition, completed training during the second half of 1969 and returned to Laos in ten teams of eight apiece. Half went to the southern half of the country and were posted to a CIA base near Savannkhet; the others, consisting of ethnic Hmong tribesmen, were sent to the northeastern guerrilla outpost at Pha Khao.

Given their intensive instruction, hopes were high that the Commando Raiders would be able to perform a wealth of sensitive strategic missions. Chief among these were cross-border raids into North Vietnam. In early 1970, the concept was put to the test. Loading into Air America Bell choppers, a team of Savannakhet commandos armed with five 60mm mortars was ferried east. Given the prohibition on overflights into North Vietnam, the Air America crews stopped at the border and unloaded the passengers. From there, the commandos hiked fourteen kilometers into Ha Tinh Province, stopping outside a North Vietnamese military camp. Fifty mortar rounds later, the base was in flames and the commandos were sprinting back toward Laos.

Following this successful baptism of fire, fifty more southern recruits were sent to Phitsanulok. Upon their return, they were stationed in southernmost Laos on the Bolovens Plateau. Together with the Savannakhet contingent, they initiated a string of cross-border strikes into the North Vietnamese panhandle during the second half of the year. Some of the missions were a repeat of the first, with the commandos making shallow stabs using mortars or recoilless rifles against military rest stations or vehicle parks.[22] Other missions, sometimes lasting no more than a few minutes, had the raiders landed high in the Annamites with makeshift rocket pods CIA technicians had outfitted with fat bicycle tires. While the helicopter idled, the commandos would wheel a pod to the edge of the mountain and fire toward targets in the North Vietnamese lowlands below.

In the northeast, meanwhile, the Commando Raider contingent at Pha Khao found similar cross-border employment. For this group's first mission, the CIA was eager to revisit Dien Bien Phu. Looking to get Hanoi's attention, the mission was to involve seven Air America Bell helicopters and thirty-two commandos armed with two-shot rocket pods. On 22 February, the armada carried the raiders to a landing zone just inside the Lao border. As planned, they carried the rockets to a perch overlooking the target valley and fired. Communications intercepts later revealed they hit a North Vietnamese military base camp while a senior officers' meeting was in session.[23]

During May, the Pha Khao raiders prepared for a second foray. This time their target was the village of Muong Sen, six kilometers inside Nghe An Province. Immune from American aerial interdiction since the 1968 bombing halt, Muong Sen had grown into a major depot for military supplies headed toward battlefields in northeastern Laos. Recent intelligence indicated a shipment of tanks had arrived at the village, which the commandos intended to destroy with mortars and shoulder-fired M72 light antitank rockets.

On 23 May, twenty-one raiders boarded Bell helicopters and headed for the border. Crossing into Nghe An, they took a circuitous route toward the tank park. Despite their precautions, within thirty-six hours North Vietnamese border guards stumbled across one of their bivouac sites. During a week-long manhunt, seven commandos were killed and ten captured. Only four Hmong managed to make it back to government lines.[24]

The southern raiders, too, were encountering problems. In October, the Savannakhet contingent walked into Quang Binh and happened across a heavily defended antiaircraft site. Spotted by guards, the raiders were forced to flee—minus their team leader—back to Laos.

In April 1971, the Savannakhet unit geared up for another raid. This time, two dozen commandos were to carry three 81mm mortars across the border for an attack near the Mu Gia Pass. By then, however, Hanoi had become wise to the repeated use of a handful of border landing zones. As the raiders moved away from the mountain clearing, North Vietnamese soldiers pounced. Not until five weeks later did the first of five survivors evade back to government lines. It was the last time Savannakhet commandos would venture across the border looking for targets.

25

EXCEPTIONS TO THE RULE

Bright and early on 1 January 1970, ARES radioed Saigon with New Year's greetings. Then his radio fell silent.[1] SOG waited until June before formally writing off its final North Vietnam agent, followed by the final shutdown of the daily JENNY NC-121 aircraft orbiting over the Tonkin Gulf—used to transmit SSPL broadcasts and family messages to notional teams. Finally, links were cut with the CIA's radio relay site in the Philippines.[2]

Although SOG appeared to be washing its hands of the long-term agent business, the Pentagon still expected the organization to remain prepared to go back into North Vietnam—just in case. In May, Admiral McCain fired off a strongly worded message to the chairman of the Joint Chiefs of Staff suggesting that SOG resume maritime strikes north of the Demilitarized Zone. He also advocated using U.S. Navy SEALs operating from a modified special warfare submarine, the *Grayback,* to attack North Vietnamese radar facilities, lighthouses, and shipping.[3]

Before any of this could take place, however, the Vietnam War took a giant step west. In an effort to eliminate communist sanctuaries in eastern Cambodia, American and South Vietnamese forces that month spilled across the Khmer frontier. As was so often the case during the war, military victory turned to political defeat at home when protests erupted across the United States, prompting President Richard Nixon to repeat promises of a phased withdrawal of American combat troops from Southeast Asia. He called his plan "Vietnamization," a policy of encouraging the South Vietnamese to assume responsibility for their own defense.

SOG felt the changes immediately. In July, Colonel John F. Sadler took over as SOG commander and quickly discovered that he was presiding over a much different program than that of his predecessor. Sadler found that his job "was marked by increased requirements, tighter controls, added restrictions on some programs, some minor reorganization and increased emphasis on improvements and modernization of the STD."[4]

For the moment, manpower was not a big problem. While the U.S. Army in Vietnam was drawing down quickly, SOG strength remained constant—about sixteen hundred Americans and eight thousand Vietnamese during 1970.[5] However, as Colonel Sadler pointed out, one of his main tasks was to help the Strategic Technical Directorate expand in both size and capability.

In some cases, months of stagnation had taken a toll. Within the STRATA program, for example, the number of teams had dropped from ten in early 1969 to just four a year later.[6] Most of the remaining members were of poor quality; many were deserters from the regular army. And with American advisers no longer allowed to accompany agents into the field, morale was low.[7]

Despite such problems, SOG felt STRATA was worth salvaging. Unlike SOG's other reconnaissance efforts, STRATA already had an all-indigenous roster that meshed perfectly with the goals of Vietnamization. To build on this, American Special Forces advisers began to pour into Monkey Mountain near Danang.[8] By midyear, Op 36B had brought the total back to nine teams, each numbering a dozen commandos. In order to prepare them for a wider variety of North Vietnam contingencies, agents were now cross-trained in such diverse skills as demolitions, ambushes, prisoner snatches, and tapping phone lines.[9]

The focus soon paid off. On 2 October, a STRATA team was lifted into northeasternmost Cambodia on the program's maiden raiding mission. Locating a bridge, the commandos set charges underneath, hoping to drop it as traffic passed overhead. But before they finished rigging the explosives, a Cambodian man peddling by on a bicycle spotted them. One commando ran over and stopped the Cambodian at gunpoint, then, assuming the mission was compromised, called for a helicopter extraction. As they bundled their prisoner aboard and took to the sky, the bridge went up in a plume of fire and smoke.[10]

Other elements of SOG felt the effects of Vietnamization. Within Op 36A, new projects were being added and old ones rapidly expanded.[11] Among the latter was the EARTH ANGEL program. From three teams in late 1969, a total of ten were planned by the close of 1970. These ralliers continued to impress SOG with their singular dedication to mission. According to one adviser, "The EARTH ANGEL agent was a product of northern society. They would hold self-criticism sessions at night, just like they had done in the North Vietnamese Army. The never balked at a mission, never gave any disciplinary problems. They were extremely motivated, almost without parallel."[12]

Such high motivation often led the *hoi chanh* to take high risks. On one mission, for instance, a team was ambushed and the radio operator taken prisoner. When forced to send a message to base, he included the duress code. Then, in a final act of defiance, he radioed his own coordinates and called for an airstrike. "We launched the strike," remembers Major G. H. "Wick" Zimmer, the Op 36A commander. "And the radioman was able to escape in the confusion and eventually make it back to Long Thanh."[13]

Despite the team's bravado, EARTH ANGEL derring-do did little to rebuild its potential for North Vietnam operations. SOG admitted as much in

October 1970 when a senior CINCPAC representative visited Long Thanh. Taking aside Major Zimmer, the officer asked how long it would take SOG to mount renewed operations north of the Demilitarized Zone. "I have no problem with recruits," replied Zimmer. "But it will take nine months to get ready, and then you can count on ninety-percent casualties."[14]

The reason behind the question soon became apparent. On 21 November a small team of heliborne raiders flew deep into North Vietnam on a mission to free American prisoners held in the Son Tay prison camp thirty-seven kilometers west of Hanoi. When the team landed, it found the camp empty—the prisoners had been moved only weeks earlier. The raiders flew away with no serious casualties. In the flurry of accusations following the "failure" of the mission, several points were ignored. Because of the Son Tay raid, North Vietnam moved all American POWs together in Hanoi, revamped its early warning and air defense system, and shifted some of its conventional units back north to guard Hanoi. The communists were severely shaken by this single operation, something that years of CIA and SOG missions had failed to accomplish. In a single swift stroke, the raid managed to alter North Vietnamese tactics and made them fear retaliation for the poor treatment of American prisoners. Most important, the raid illustrated that special operations forces were capable of penetrating North Vietnam almost at will and, in the words of one study, "demonstrated that it was possible to bring the war home to the people of North Vietnam through direct, highly visible actions. Such raids, carefully chosen for psychological impact and high assurance of success, could have been important factors in influencing the attitudes of the average North Vietnamese." Taking that thinking to the next level, the study concluded that future missions of this type could "neutralize key individuals or destroy key targets, as well as to capture or examine new items of enemy equipment."[15]

Significantly, no SOG assets were used at Son Tay; all of the raiders were drawn from Stateside elements of the U.S. Army Special Forces. Op 36, theoretically in charge of MACV's covert contingencies in North Vietnam, had not even been consulted, an especially telling omission considering that one of the key planners was Donald Blackburn, the former SOG chief. Part of the reason, no doubt, stemmed from the need to keep total secrecy in the run-up to the raid.[16] Unlike a Vietnam-based team, an all-American strike force could rehearse the mission in the United States with less fear of exposure. Perhaps, too, there was concern whether SOG had the ability to conduct such a precision raid.[17]

SOG was, however, given a chance to capitalize on the Son Tay raid. In December, the psychological operations staff began exploiting Hanoi's fear of further raids by adding bogus correspondence about the effects of the rescue mission to the "black letter" campaign. One letter, ostensibly sent by a North Vietnamese citizen residing outside the country, pointed out that:

> The situation of our North has become tenser and tenser especially since the American landing on Son Tay Province last November to liberate captured American pilots. . . . The Americans and Southern traitors have paid great attention to their soldiers' fate. . . . They cried out fiercely to denounce our evil actions and searched for all means to ask our State to exchange war prisoners with them. Many movements were organized to support their claims. But our State rejected squarely such demands of theirs. . . . Not only the US but many other world countries raised their voices to criticize our maltreatments toward captured American soldiers and considered such actions inhuman. . . . [They question Hanoi, asking:] "Why didn't your DRVN Government respect the Geneva Convention about war prisoners though having signed it?" We could not answer them correctly.[18]

Presumably the letter—just one of many such black letters sent to North Vietnam—would be opened by communist authorities, who might be led to believe there was a groundswell of discontent over how the Hanoi government was handling the issue of American prisoners.[19]

Although Washington gave SOG only a psychological operations role in the mission to rescue American prisoners, policy makers did not have any problem with at least rekindling some of SOG's northern operations. In early December 1970, General Abrams and Admiral McCain discussed a range of SOG strikes against North Vietnam in order to put pressure on Hanoi during stalled Paris peace talks. Proposed operations included shipping interdiction, shore bombardment by Nasty boats, cross-beach missions, kidnapping of fishermen, and even an airborne STRATA raid against a petroleum complex in southern Quang Binh.[20]

Even those with minimal institutional memory should have recognized the unrealistic optimism contained in the CINCPAC scheme. In resurrecting themes from SOG's past—MINT, LOKI, CADO, airborne sabotage—McCain showed little appreciation for the lessons learned prior to 1968. Back then, such pinprick attacks had virtually no effect on the North Vietnamese economy or, more important, Hanoi's desire to pursue its war effort in South Vietnam. That they would fare any better in late 1970 was doubtful.

MACV should have known better. But in a case of shared amnesia, Abrams signed off on the optimistic covert plan on 14 December. Over the next week, MACV fine-tuned the plan. One contingency received the most attention: a STRATA raid code-named PERRY RUN. Jumping at low level from an MC-

130, the STRATA commandos were to land in the hills twenty kilometers south of Dong Hoi, cross a river, and demolish their target. The biggest stumbling point, according to the planners, was in getting an unescorted MC-130 across the Demilitarized Zone undetected. But little concern was given to the proposed length of the mission—nine days—even though past experience showed sabotage teams were lucky to survive just twenty-four hours.[21]

PERRY RUN may have been far-fetched, but it looked positively coherent next to other plans in the works. One SOG contingency plan written in September, for instance, speculated on unconventional options in the event of internal uprisings in North Vietnam. SOG had not even come close to capitalizing on potential northern unrest at its zenith, so how it would accomplish such a mission now that operations north of the Demilitarized Zone had been shut down for almost two years was a mystery.[22]

In another airy departure, Saigon in October ordered the disbandment of the entire Luc Luong Duc Biet (LLDB), the South Vietnamese Special Forces organization that for the past seven years had operated out of paramilitary border camps alongside their American counterparts, then ordered the best LLDB veterans to be retrained as core for a new Strategic Technical Directorate subsection called the Special Mission Service (SMS). Headed by Lieutenant Colonel Ngo The Linh, the same officer who earlier commanded Office 45 and the Coastal Security Service in Danang, the 1,450-strong Special Mission Service was assigned a full range of unconventional contingencies in the north.[23] On paper, at least. Given the problems inherent in coordinating even small raids, the inflated mandate of the Special Mission Service was wishful thinking at its most fanciful.

Still, MACV was determined to get back into North Vietnam, and in early 1971 it looked like there might be an opening. With Vietnamization in full swing, the South Vietnamese army prepared for its first solo conventional cross-border campaign. Code-named LAM SON 719, it was to be a multidivision swipe into the Lao panhandle against the heart of the Ho Chi Minh Trail. Significantly, no American ground troops would be taking part, though they would fly most of the helicopters.[24]

On 8 February, LAM SON 719 officially kicked off as thousands of South Vietnamese infantrymen, rangers, paratroopers, and tankers spilled into Laos. Anticipating heavy North Vietnamese resistance, Saigon had tasked SOG with conducting a series of diversionary parachute drops both north and south of the main thrust. As a further diversion, the November 1968 restrictions were temporarily waived, and MACV was given permission to stage limited strikes along the North Vietnamese coast.

In planning the strikes, MACV dusted off the covert maritime options proposed by CINCPAC the previous December. In January, these had been further refined into five separate operational plans, one each for CADO raids, shore bombardment, attacks on fishing junks, attacks on shipping, and interdiction of military infiltration trawlers.[25] Of these, the Joint Chiefs in early February approved the plan covering attacks on shipping.

On the evening of 10 February, three Nastys departed Danang. Like a throwback to the old MINT patrols, the trio raced to the northern Quang Binh coast and began prowling for targets. Approaching a motorized junk, they opened fire. In its attempt to evade, the North Vietnamese vessel turned toward shore and ran aground. Encountering a second junk, the Nastys pulled alongside, captured the crew, and set demolition charges. A one-hundred-ton cargo vessel was also hit, with two wounded crewmen plucked from the flaming wreck. A fourth ship managed to escape.[26]

One week later, the Naval Advisory Detachment readied a second interdiction patrol. Two Nastys left Danang early that evening and headed back for northern Quang Binh. This time the North Vietnamese were ready. Over the previous week, they had ordered a pair of fishing junks be outfitted for a maritime ambush. Just as had been done in the summer of 1968, both vessels were festooned with machine guns, rocket-propelled grenades, and recoilless rifles.

After picking up the Nastys on radar, the armed junks were hurried to sea. For the next two hours, they saw nothing. Radio reports, however, told them the South Vietnamese boats had circled north of their position and sunk a gunboat and a tanker.[27] Hearing this, the two junks pushed farther out to sea in the hope of intercepting the Nastys on their return run.

They soon got their wish. At 2240 hours, the two South Vietnamese boats approached in line formation from the northeast. When they got within two hundred meters, the junks opened fire. Firing illumination rounds, the Nastys responded in kind. Both sides traded shells for an hour, with the North Vietnamese receiving seven casualties. At midnight, the Nastys broke contact and sped south. SOG rated the mission a "great success."[28]

If the Quang Binh raids had been intended as a diversion for LAM SON 719, Hanoi barely noticed. Although the South Vietnamese troop columns managed to briefly seize their targets in Laos, stiff North Vietnamese resistance soon had them reeling back over the border. Rather than an example of how far Vietnamization had progressed, LAM SON 719 instead became a symbol of failure. Television cameras recorded soldiers retreating in a panic, many of them clinging to helicopter skids.

With the ill-fated operation over, SOG scrambled to bolster its maritime capabilities in case it was again called upon to venture north of the Demilitarized Zone. Plans to insert commando teams all along the North Vietnamese coast, code-named CLAY DRAGON, remained on the books, as did the ongoing mission to intercept and destroy North Vietnamese trawlers ferrying supplies to the south (Operation BOSTON ANTIQUE). Most ambitious was GLYNN REEF, SOG's blueprint for "destroying or disrupting" Hanoi's fishing industry. It never launched any of the missions.[29]

Hoping for one more try, SOG added a new weapon to its inventory. By March, technicians at Danang had outfitted captured Soviet-made 122mm rockets to the sides of four Nastys. With an eleven-kilometer range, the rockets were intended to give the boats an enhanced capacity for striking North Vietnamese shore targets. SOG would never get the chance to use them.[30]

26

THE QUIET ONE

The Nevada night was clear, lit by a full moon. Beneath the star-studded sky, the desert air was crisp and quiet. The only sound was a fire crackling on the white sand of a dried lake bed. Anyone watching the peaceful scene would not have noticed anything unusual, but from the sky, the fire was part of a pattern of flame pots signaling a position on the ground.

An airplane engine hummed in the distance, growing louder as it approached the lake bed. Soon a dark silhouette loomed directly over the first flame pot, coasting sharply toward the ground. The little DHC-6 hit the salt flats with a bounce, engines whining as the props reversed directions, then came to an abrupt halt well short of the second flame pot.

Pausing momentarily, the pilot vectored the plane to the side and added power. Pulling back the wheel, he climbed back into the sky, banked into a wide orbit, then came in line for another landing. This was repeated all night, every night, for a week.

It was all very secretive. No one was supposed to know that the pilots training in the Nevada desert were from Taiwan, members of the same elite 34th Squadron that had been supplying SOG with C-123 crews since 1964.

Besides its SOG duties, the bulk of the squadron's activities centered on the insertion of agent teams into mainland China. By 1964, improved air defenses along the mainland led the unit to shift its focus toward ROBIN missions, the code name for RB-69 patrols along the Chinese coast to collect electronic data on Beijing's radar and antiaircraft coverage. It was this background, plus their deniable status, that made the Chinese crews the logical choice for a new CIA project in early 1971 involving a different aircraft, the De Havilland DHC-6 Twin Otter.

At first glance, the DHC-6 seemed an unlikely candidate for clandestine operations. Readily available on the commercial market, it was used by small airlines for short hauls of up to twenty passengers. But the CIA especially liked its impressive short takeoff and landing capability, enabling the Twin Otter to squeeze into crude jungle airstrips. So the agency outfitted one airframe with a Teledyne LORAN C prototype, giving it long-range navigational ability accurate to within eight meters.

With covert operations in mind, nine members of the 34th Squadron ventured to Nellis Air Force Base in Nevada for three months of DHC-6 conversion training. While the crew members were never told, they assumed they were being prepared for missions into China.

In May, the contingent returned to Taiwan. Arriving, too, was the LORAN-equipped Twin Otter along with a single instructor from Air America. After a perfunctory checkout, the crew flew the plane to southern Laos and landed at a guerrilla base code-named PS 44.[1] Located just twenty-six kilometers north of the town of Pakse, PS 44 was isolated in a world all its own. "The terrain around PS 44 was like a truncated ice cream cone with a single goat trail to the top," recalled one CIA official. "The ground consisted of shale with a thin layer of soil. When the rains came, the whole place came into blossom like Arizona."[2]

With the limited security afforded by PS 44's geography, the CIA turned it into perhaps its most sensitive base in Laos. Already home to a contingent of Commando Raiders, simple living quarters—dubbed "The Hotel"—were built for the Chinese aircrew. The Twin Otter was housed in a special hanger.

The Chinese immediately went to work. To acclimatize them to their new surroundings, they were initially tasked with flying supply drops during daylight hours. "We did missions all across Laos," said Chuang-wen Yu, head of the Chinese contingent. "Some were up near the North Vietnamese border, where the mountains were beautiful. They reminded me of my home in Guangxi Province. None of the missions were too difficult. Compared to mainland penetrations and the ROBIN flights, Laos was easy."[3]

Greater challenges were on the immediate horizon. With the pinpoint accuracy afforded by the LORAN C, the CIA wanted to use the Twin Otter in conjunction with Commando Raider missions. Initially, these missions were conducted inside Laos by Air America crews. On 25 July, for instance, an American-piloted DHC-6 was used as an airborne relay link during a raider insert along the border opposite Dien Bien Phu.

Shortly thereafter, the CIA drew up plans for a more ambitious strike into the North Vietnamese panhandle. This time, the commandos would parachute from a Twin Otter with 81mm mortars and improved white phosphorus rounds. Unlike previous raider missions, this insertion would be well inside the North Vietnamese border, placing the commandos close to their target, a surface-to-air missile site. Given the need for deniability in the event of a shootdown, the aircrew would be Chinese.

After several weeks of training, the raiders were ready. "We did night jumps at Phitsanulok, and more when we got back to Laos," remembers case officer Tom Poole. "There was lots of money spent in preparation, but the mission never happened. It was aborted at the last minute. No reason was given."[4]

Cancellation of the missile site attack did not spell the end of Taipei's connection with North Vietnamese operations. By early 1972, Vietnamization was well under way, and attention in Washington was turned toward a possible cease-fire with Hanoi. But policy makers were not betting on it, and one of the CIA's tasks became the installation of wiretaps to maintain a steady intelligence feed following the departure of American forces from the Indochinese battlefield.

Listening in on phone conversations was not new to the Vietnam War. Since 1966, taps into North Vietnamese phone lines along the Ho Chi Minh Trail by both SOG and CIA guerrilla teams had regularly yielded useful tactical information. By 1971, these taps were reaching new levels of sophistication. Using voice-activated devices, part of a technology code-named THRESHOLD, conversations were now directly relayed to orbiting planes or helicopters.[5]

The North Vietnamese no doubt realized their conversations were vulnerable. Sensitive information, therefore, was often passed via other means, such as couriers, and North Vietnamese patrols frequently examined telephone lines for signs of tampering.

Deep inside North Vietnam, however, Hanoi's precautions slackened. So when overhead imagery in 1971 pinpointed an elevated line twenty-four kilometers southwest of Vinh, it was an intelligence coup too good to miss.

Installing a tap that far inside North Vietnam was easier said than done; nothing like it had been attempted before. The target itself was relatively isolated from villages and roads. But any CIA infiltration to the line from Laos would have to bypass ground and air defenses covering the Ho Chi Minh Trail. In addition, all the choppers in the current Air America inventory were too slow and loud, making them vulnerable to interception by the four MiG-21 jet fighters stationed at the Vinh air base. Something more silent and less visible was needed.

The job went to the "Quiet One," the name given to a top secret helicopter being developed by Hughes Aircraft, which was building it as part of a Pentagon-funded program under the U.S. Army's Air Mobility Research and Development Laboratories. "The most effective way to silence a large piece of rotating machinery is to turn it off," said scientists from Hughes in 1970. "Obviously we can't go that far and still have a flying machine, so we did the next best thing and slowed everything down."

To slow its experimental chopper, Hughes began with the base frame from their OH-6A light observation helicopter. By adding one extra main rotor and two extra tail blades, the necessary lift and thrust were maintained at substantially lower revolutions per minute. A muffler was added to stifle the roar of jet engine exhaust, and the entire power plant was wrapped in a cocoon of sound-blanketing material to absorb stray engine noises. The engine air intake was similarly treated with soundproofing materials, and the airflow was redirected to prevent transmission of the jet engine's characteristic compressor whine. Even the tips of the main rotor blades were reshaped to reduce the severity of tip vortex phenomenon, a kind of whirlwind generated by the blades that is a major contributor to chopper noise output.[6]

On 8 April 1971, Hughes officially unveiled the Quiet One to the public. It truly lived up to its name. During a demonstration to the press, a standard OH-6A passed overhead at thirty-one meters. Almost everyone could hear its rotors when it was still almost two and a half kilometers away, and one and a half kilometers after it had passed by. When the Quiet One flew over, its noise could not be detected until it was within 278 meters, and the sound receded just as quickly. At 155 meters overhead, it could not be heard in a quiet residential neighborhood. And even though the pilot was able to reduce engine and rotor levels to as little as 67 percent of normal in-flight levels, the extra blades allowed for an additional six-hundred-pound increase in payload lift and twenty-knot higher airspeed.[7]

The Department of Defense dropped funding for the modified OH-6A after the first prototype was built. But with the helicopter's obvious potential for clandestine infiltrations, the CIA quietly picked up the project. Beginning with the modifications already incorporated on the Quiet One, further state-of-the-art changes were made. To add strength, the five main rotor blades were fed into a special titanium hub. Then the power plant was improved with a better transmission and a special water-alcohol injection system that lowered engine temperature, allowing the chopper to pull more power for takeoff. Because of anticipated higher payloads, a reinforced skid was added. Four different optional fiberglass gas tanks were fitted for the backseat to increase range. On either side of the helicopter, short struts supported two aerodynamic pods. One housed an inertial navigation system (INS), a navigation device using gyros, accelerometers, and a computer to track both desired and actual path. A LORAN C, more accurate than the INS, went in the other pod. Wrapped under the cockpit chin was an AN/AAQ-5 forward-looking infrared (FLIR) system. Hooked to a pair of liquid nitrogen tanks fixed to the belly, supercooled FLIR sensors measured minute differences in temperature by reading electromagnetic radiation emanating off the landscape; this was translated onto two television screens—one for the pilot, the other for the copilot—as a clear thermal image. Infrared spotlights were affixed to the skids and frame to enhance the performance of night-vision goggles to be worn by the crew.

On 28 April 1971, only three weeks after Hughes unveiled the Quiet One, two pilots were hired by Air America to begin an intensive familiarization program with the CIA's new rotary-wing acquisition; a third pilot was later added to the program. All three had extensive U.S. Army experience either as instructors or in low-level night flying. For the next two months, they became proficient with SU-50 night goggles and the FLIR system while flying nap-of-the-earth practice flights around Area 51 in Nevada.

In July, the three pilots flew to Tainan, Air America's main base of operations on Taiwan. There they met up with a contingent of fixed-wing pilots from the 34th Squadron that had been undergoing rotary-wing training since April. The three Americans were designated as instructors for six of the Chinese; the other students would be coached by two more Air America instructors on the S-58T, a new and enhanced version of the H-34 that sported a pair of turbo-shaft power plants.[8]

High in seniority yet short on experience, the six OH-6A students initially trained with the Hughes 500, the helicopter's civilian counterpart. Three months later, two modified versions (the CIA had built a second prototype) were secretly flown to Tainan. Unofficially dubbed the Hughes 500P, both airframes were used for training through the spring of 1972.[9] By that time, however, the American instructors were voicing serious reservations about the ability of the Chinese to operate the sophisticated aircraft. Of additional concern was the fact that the senior liaison officer, Lieutenant Colonel Henry Lu, insisted on flying the Hughes even though he was supposed to handle only administrative duties.

In April 1972, in an attempt to provide cover for the modified helicopters that would soon be arriving, two unmodified Hughes 500s were sent to Udorn and assigned to Air America. Within days they were flying supply and medical evacuation missions in Laos.

Two months later, the two Hughes 500Ps had their main rotors removed and were loaded into a single Air America C-130 transport. Flown directly to the isolation area at Takhli Royal Thai Air Force Base, they were reassembled and shuttled to PS 44. Already at the site were the Chinese crews for the S-58T and the Twin Otter.

Soon after, the Chinese Hughes 500P cadre arrived with orders to prepare for a single mission: infiltrating a Commando Raider team near Vinh to plant a tap on the phone lines identified a year earlier. In support, a Twin Otter would act as an airborne relay post, while a pair of S-58T choppers would orbit along the mountain foothills as a rescue contingency force in case the Hughes was downed inside North Vietnam. All of the aircraft would be piloted by Taiwanese to afford Washington deniability.

To increase proficiency in night flying, the Hughes 500P pilots began nightly mission profiles along streambeds near PS 44. "We were under pressure," said Lieutenant Colonel Lu, the Chinese liaison officer, "to get ready so the tap could get information while Kissinger was in Paris for the peace talks."[10] Within a month, however, pilot error claimed one of the two modified choppers as it landed hard in front of the hanger. While problems with the night-vision goggles were blamed, the accident compounded lingering reservations about the ability of the Chinese to handle the aircraft. Given the heavy investment in the program, the need for success now overrode concerns for deniability. As a result, the six Chinese were sent back to Taiwan in early September, along with the S-58T and Twin Otter crews.[11]

With the Chinese contingent gone, two of the original three Air America instructors were told they would together fly the modified Hughes to Vinh. On 28 September, the two pilots moved back to PS 44. Also arriving was James Glerum. Since 1968, Glerum had been deputy chief at the CIA's Udorn headquarters that oversaw paramilitary operations in Laos. Scheduled to rotate home, he instead had his tour extended and was sent to PS 44. There, he was named overall manager for the unfolding Vinh operation. As Glerum remembers:

> The group at PS 44 was an entertaining mix of air crews, technicians, air operations officers, and paramilitary specialists. Except for the latter, most had never lived and worked under such primitive conditions and had to make some significant adjustments. Although the site's terrain gave us fair security, there was nothing to the north or east between us and the North Vietnamese Army. After trying for a week to organize a workable defense and evasion plan, I gave up hope and kept an S-58T nightly on the landing zone near our quarters, hoping we could get everyone on board if something unpleasant happened.[12]

With an all-American aviation crew, the Hughes 500P pilots began nightly profiles. A handful of practice flights later, they were pronounced ready to launch the operation.

The only other factor was weather. For such a mission, optimal lunar and weather conditions were a quarter-moon with slight overcast. This would permit enough moonlight and starlight for the night goggles without back-lighting the chopper's silhouette from the ground. Moon phases could be predicted; the weather, however, could not be forecast with the same degree of accuracy.

As the pilots waited for the right conditions, a pair of Lao commandos were practicing wiretapping. Their training initially centered on how they would exit the hovering chopper. First, they practiced parachuting from the back of the Hughes, only to find there was insufficient clearance from the tail rotor. Then they tested a mini–Sky Genie (a onetime friction device developed by American smoke jumpers). Both these methods were dropped in favor of a rolled ladder fixed out the back door.

Once the method of exit was selected, the commandos practiced descending the ladder, then scaling a mock telephone pole erected along a lotus-choked streambed northeast of PS 44. Because the Vinh line was in the midst of a forest, the CIA assumed the pole was constructed of local wood. Using a tap hidden inside a glass insulator stolen from downtown Vientiane, the commandos used an industrial stapler to attach it to the top of the pole.[13]

By mid-October, the monsoons in the North Vietnamese panhandle were drawing to a close. There would be a quarter-moon the third week of the month, providing a narrow window of opportunity. Before the mission could be launched, however, one last preparation was necessary. Unlike the early taps used on the Ho Chi Minh Trail, it would be too dangerous for teams to go back to retrieve tapes. And unlike the THRESHOLD taps introduced in 1971, an orbiting aircraft could not be expected to overfly Vinh to record transmissions.

For the North Vietnam tap, therefore, the transmissions in Vinh had to go all the way back to collection facilities at Nakhon Phanom. This necessitated placing a pair of relays to boost the tap's signal. One of them, a "spider relay" that resembled a two-meter, solar-powered, olive flower petal, would be slung under the Hughes 500P during infiltration and deployed on a hill overlooking the tap. A second, larger relay had been carried by an S-58T during the second week of October and deployed during daylight hours atop a peak seventy-two kilometers northeast of Thakhek.

Just when all looked ready, Murphy's Law intervened. On the night before the scheduled launch, the lead pole climber was bitten by a scorpion and had an allergic reaction. "Although disappointed," recounted Glerum, "I did enjoy writing the cable to headquarters on that event."[14]

After a quick recovery, the commandos were again ready. On the night of 21 October, the weather was cooperating to the fullest: quarter-moon, a sprinkling of stars, a pale wash of clouds. Final clearance came from Vientiane, and the Hughes flew from PS 44 to Thakhek. There it landed in a remote corner of the town's airstrip and waited as a Twin Otter acting as airborne command post took up an orbit to the east. At midnight, the chopper lifted off and headed toward the Annamite Mountains. Five minutes later, the crew returned to Thakhek. The FLIR had malfunctioned, and the mission was scrubbed.

Five days later, the moon and weather allowed for another attempt. Again, the FLIR broke down after takeoff from Thakhek. Three weeks later, the temperamental FLIR forced a third abort. Technicians were then called in to give the infrared system a thorough overhaul; they pronounced it in good working order.

With frustration mounting, the Hughes flew in darkness to Thakhek during the last week of November. The weather was cooperating, and so was the FLIR. Lifting silently from Thakhek, the chopper flew the one-hour trek deep into North Vietnam without incident. But after the LORAN guided it into the target valley, the helicopter met a solid sheet of fog. With its night-vision goggles useless, the crew had no choice but to abort the mission for a fourth time.

In Paris, meanwhile, U.S. National Security Adviser Henry Kissinger arrived on 4 December to attend a critical phase in the peace talks with North Vietnamese leader Le Duc Tho. Negotiations bogged down, and pressure was mounting for the CIA to get the Vinh tap in place so that it might yield advantages during Kissinger's deliberations.

While headquarters felt the pressure, those at PS 44 stayed calm. After poring over high-resolution aerial photography for weeks, the Hughes crew was certain it could get to the target and back. Said one of the pilots, "I knew every hill, every stream, every rock on the way to the target."[15]

Project manager Glerum, too, held few doubts. "I have never been more confident of a mission," he remembers. "I sat in back during a few of the training runs, and I was in awe over their proficiency. It was a good plan, and I thought it would succeed as soon as the weather cooperated."[16]

Another opening came unexpectedly on 6 December. American jets pounded the area both north and south of Vinh, one of the few bombings north of the Demilitarized Zone since the November 1968 halt. Nixon had ordered the attacks to prod North Vietnamese negotiators, who were stalling at the Paris peace talks. With the next Hughes infiltration attempt scheduled for later that day, the Pentagon discreetly rerouted some of the strikes to divert attention away from Vinh. A total of ninety sorties were flown by the U.S. Navy, as well as multiple B-52 bombing runs across Quang Binh.[17]

That night, the weather was good. The Commando Raiders, AK-47s strapped across their backs and each carrying a sack with the taps, boarded the rear of the chopper. For the fifth time, the crew flew to Thakhek and refueled. After typing the mission coordinates into the LORAN keyboard, the Hughes took off at midnight. Heading northeast, it flew at an altitude of sixty-two meters.

Forty-eight kilometers outside Thakhek, the terrain leveled out. The crew increased speed and lowered to thirty-one meters as the helicopter flew over known North Vietnamese antiaircraft positions along the Ho Chi Minh Trail. No shots were fired. Sixteen kilometers farther along, the valley gave way to the foothills of the Annamite Mountains. The crew members stayed close to the hilltop but were forced to lower their speed as they climbed the 2,167-meter-tall range. Out to the right, the pilot peered down on the occasional rice paddy layered up the narrow mountain valleys. The landscape was a pale green glimmer in his night goggles. Peasants worked the fields under the safety of darkness, but none noticed the Hughes 500P's muffled rotor as it passed overhead.[18]

Following behind the Hughes, two American-piloted S-58Ts filed through Thakhek and headed for the Annamites. At the crest, they entered long racetrack orbits, preparing to act as rescue aircraft in the event the infiltration helicopter was downed.

The Hughes 500P, meanwhile, picked up speed going down the east side of the Annamites. Weaving into North Vietnam, the copilot studied the LORAN readout and called directions until about two kilometers from the target. Then the pilot banked slightly, studying the terrain through his goggles until he made a visual identification of landmarks memorized from the reconnaissance photographs. At that point the copilot donned a second pair of goggles as the helicopter approached a clearing. The clearing was actually a fresh bomb crater that, given its proximity to a nearby bridge, appeared to be the result of poor aiming. In reality, the bomb had been intentionally diverted for the express purpose of creating a landing zone for this mission.

As the helicopter gingerly lowered into the crater, the pilot realized he could get close enough to the ground so the commandos could jump. They had planned to use a ladder if necessary. Adjusting their assault rifles across their backs, the commandos jumped from the hovering aircraft (all doors had been removed to improve visibility and lower weight). In seconds, the helicopter was gone, and the landing zone was silent.

Climbing above a 340-meter mountain to the west, the crew members searched for a suitable spot atop the triple canopy to place their underslung spider relay. Hovering above the foliage, the pilot hit a switch with his left hand. One of three retraining cables holding the relay was cut by a squib charge, unfolding the device like an ironing board. As the pilot threw a second switch, the device opened its solar pedals. Orienting the relay toward Nakhon Phanom, the pilot threw the last switch, dropping the relay onto the jungle. It hung from the treetops, perfectly camouflaged.

That accomplished, the crew moved off the hill and found a dry streambed nearby. Ordered to wait twenty minutes before returning for the commandos, the pilot settled the aircraft onto the rocks. He misjudged the landing, and a sharp boulder lanced the chopper's underbelly, piercing a liquid nitrogen tank and disabling the vital FLIR for the return journey. Then a radar detector fixed on the top of the cockpit (set to scan for radar-controlled guns or marauding MiGs) began beeping. It sounded like a scream in the silent jungle. Deciding that MiGs were less of a threat than the noise, the nervous pilot turned it off.

At the landing site, the commandos quickly located the telephone pole. But it was made of cement, not of wood as expected, rendering their stapler useless. Flustered, the commandos made another mistake. When the two taps were affixed with tape, they were accidentally both placed on the same line, an error that would later cause some static as the phone conversations were relayed west. Once the taps were in place, the commandos retraced their steps to the landing zone. Exactly twenty minutes later, the Hughes returned, picked them up without incident, and flew for one hour directly back to Nakhon Phanom.

On 7 December, the day after the taps were on the line, the North Vietnamese delegation to the Paris talks grew intransigent. A week passed with both sides still hopelessly deadlocked, so on 18 December, President Nixon launched LINEBACKER II, a massive increase in the bombing campaign against North Vietnam. After twelve days, the LINEBACKER onslaught forced Hanoi back to the negotiating table with an apparent change of heart.

By that time, Kissinger had a secret ace: the Vinh tap was providing a stream of information from inside the north. Kissinger, for example, knew when his North Vietnamese counterparts were lying about their troop movements into South Vietnam. He also knew of their candid discussions about the damage caused by LINEBACKER II. Functioning through the peace negotiations—signed on 25 January 1973—and Kissinger's subsequent February visit to Hanoi, the tap offered invaluable insights into Hanoi's mind-set during the final days of the Vietnam War.

27

LAST MISSIONS

While the CIA was patiently preparing its mission to Vinh, SOG plotted its own return to North Vietnam. Its capacity for northern contingencies had peaked in mid-1971 at the height of Vietnamization. Within Op 36A, for example, the EARTH ANGELs showed sufficient promise to put a sixteen-man group through airborne training that summer at Long Thanh.[1] On their first parachute insertion, the *hoi chanh* managed to mine roads in northeastern Cambodia for twenty days before exfiltration.[2]

STRATA also continued to expand its capabilities. Over the summer, teams practiced firing M72 rockets at oil drums floating off Monkey Mountain. Once proficient, they were used on a series of successful sampan-killing missions along rivers in eastern Cambodia. STRATA agents were also used on several low-level parachute infiltrations into Cambodia, including one ten-man insert.[3]

Perhaps the greatest gains were seen in the Strategic Technical Directorate's new northern strike force, the Special Mission Service, officially formed on 1 January 1971; unconventional warfare instruction commenced at Nha Trang the following month. With authorized strength set at five groups of nine twelve-man teams, the first Special Mission Service class, consisting of experienced South Vietnamese special forces veterans, finished orientation by May. A second class started training in late March, and a third in early June. By November, the service's first complete group, officially titled Group 71, was mission-ready.[4]

On the psychological operations front, SOG continued to think up ways to demoralize Hanoi, although by 1971 most of its efforts were aimed at North Vietnamese and Viet Cong soldiers along the Ho Chi Minh Trail or inside South Vietnam. One of the few new programs directed north of the Demilitarized Zone began in November 1971 at the behest of the National Security Council. One month earlier, massive flooding in Hanoi and three surrounding provinces prompted a leaflet drop and broadcasts over black radio stations authorizing soldiers from the worst-hit areas to leave the ranks and return to their devastated homes to assist in the reconstruction process. The "leave orders" were signed by the North Vietnamese minister of defense, General Vo Nguyen Giap. Although SOG never learned if the plan worked, packets of leaflets were later found on several dead North Vietnamese soldiers.[5]

260

These were encouraging moves, but they were too little, too late. In accordance with Nixon's Vietnamization pledge, thousands of American troops and advisers were coming home from Vietnam. On 1 October, Op 36 was deactivated as a separate unit and merged with SOG's Ground Studies Group, which focused on missions in Laos and Cambodia. In accordance with this downsizing, Op 36A was reduced and renamed the Special Operations Detachment (SOD); Op 36B, also at reduced size, became Detachment B.[6]

That same month, the Special Mission Service was also revamped. Even before it had a chance to test any of its unconventional warfare skills in North Vietnam, the service was informed that its new mission was strategic reconnaissance in Laos. Starting instruction anew on 18 October, Group 71 was sent to Long Thanh for a reconnaissance course.[7] Two newly formed sister elements, Groups 72 and 75, joined it the following spring.[8]

The change in the Special Mission Service's mandate was fortuitous. On 30 March 1972, Hanoi launched the so-called Easter Offensive with a three-pronged attack across the Demilitarized Zone and over the border from Laos. North Vietnamese divisions also hit Binh Long Province along the Cambodian border, placing the provincial capital of An Loc under siege for more than two months. In the Central Highlands, Hanoi's troops threatened to cut South Vietnam in two. By the end of April, three South Vietnamese divisions were all but out of action, and Quang Tri, Saigon's northernmost provincial capital, had fallen. Facing their greatest challenge to date, the generals in Saigon needed all the troops they could spare for in-country tactical missions. Commando penetrations into North Vietnam were very far from their minds.

While South Vietnam struggled to cope with the onslaught, Vietnamization continued. On 30 April, SOG was deactivated and replaced by a smaller outfit known as Strategic Technical Directorate Advisory Team 158.[9] Within Team 158, the Special Operations Detachment was only seven men, with another seven assigned to Detachment B. Both were ordered to refocus their efforts toward internal missions against the advancing North Vietnamese forces. On 23 May, Detachment B placed its STRATA assets under the operational control of the Special Mission Service, which had shifted its staff to Hue. Two days later, several members of the Special Operations Detachment, along with twelve South Vietnamese counterparts and a dozen EARTH ANGELs, also departed for Hue to link up with the Special Mission Service. Together with STRATA, the *hoi chanh* began intelligence-gathering forays north into communist-held Quang Tri.[10]

Not all of the Special Operations Detachment's attention was focused on reconnaissance. During the final days of May, MACV approved plans for a

Vietnamese singers attend a party at Long Thanh to boost morale for the fledgling Thanh Long commando group, June 1972. (Conboy collection)

diversionary operation in Quang Tri. Major Nguyen Phan Tuu, the senior BORDEN case officer since that program's inception, was chosen to lead the new project. "We had not run any BORDEN missions for almost a year," recalled Tuu. "I made my headquarters at the Thanh Hoa Hotel in Hue, and got two volunteers from among some recent North Vietnamese prisoners. We only had enough time to give them about a week of training."[11]

The Special Operations Detachment got the idea for the diversionary operations from a successful World War II ruse that fooled the Germans into thinking the Allies were going to land in Greece rather than Sicily. One of the American advisers had read a book about the operation and decided a similar plan would work against the North Vietnamese.[12]

To carry out this scheme, the Special Operations Detachment found a fresh North Vietnamese body, dressed it in South Vietnamese fatigues, and strapped on a malfunctioning parachute. Into the pockets went documentation showing him to be leader of a South Vietnamese commando team, as well as a codebook with radio frequencies and passwords. At the beginning of the second week of June, a Vietnamese air force C-47 dropped the body into the A Shau Valley.[13]

A few days later, the two BORDEN agents were helicoptered into the same area with orders to link up with a team allegedly on the ground. Resurrecting an old OODLES ploy, parachute-fitted ice blocks and resupply bundles were also dropped over the area.

On 11 June, a North Vietnamese patrol stumbled across the bloated corpse. Eight days later, the two BORDEN agents were discovered along with some of the resupply bundles. Using the codebook, the North Vietnamese also intercepted what they believed was radio traffic to two more commando teams closer to the Demilitarized Zone. On 25 June, messages told these two teams to support an alleged airborne and amphibious landing starting in two days' time. North Vietnamese forces scrambled to react to their intelligence coup, sending a few units back north to deal with a possible attack to their rear. Planners in Saigon considered the diversionary effort a success.[14]

By then, South Vietnamese forces were getting their second wind. While Saigon prepared to roll back North Vietnam's advances, Washington planned reprisal strikes north of the Demilitarized Zone. In May, the Nixon administration temporarily lifted the November 1968 bombing halt and allowed American aircraft to mine harbors and bomb targets inside North Vietnam. On the clandestine side, the Joint Chiefs and CINCPAC the following month began piecing together a diverse special operations blitz named Contingency Plan (Conplan) 5108.[15]

Word of Conplan 5108 reached Team 158 on 25 May. While stretched thin with deployments to Hue, the Special Operations Detachment and Detachment B were immediately brought into the planning process.[16] The operation, they were told, was to include such varied elements as notional teams, EARTH ANGELs, BORDEN, and airdrops of counterfeit currency. The centerpiece was a company-sized airborne raider force specializing in demolitions. By that time, however, no such raiders existed. STRATA, while previously trained in sabotage for North Vietnam contingencies, was now fully occupied with reconnaissance around Quang Tri. The Special Mission Service, originally intended as an unconventional strike force for North Vietnam, was also busy with in-country reconnaissance.

Starting from scratch, Saigon decided to build a new group of commandos code-named THANG LONG, the ancient name for Hanoi. Recruitment posters were immediately placed at select military bases around the country. One who answered the call was a STRATA team leader in Hue, Lieutenant Tran Viet Hue. "I saw a notice calling for people to 'invade the north,'" he recalled. "This sounded good, so I reported to Long Thanh along with another lieutenant from STRATA and three noncommissioned officers. There were also some men from [SMS] Groups 71 and 72, including three Cambodians."[17]

By 4 June, THANG LONG counted sixty-nine volunteers. They were placed in a small secure corner of Long Thanh normally reserved for Khmer intelligence agents. Lieutenant Colonel Nguyen Van Hy, previously the Long Thanh camp commander, was placed in charge. The Special Operations Detachment senior adviser, acting as counterpart to Hy, had serious reservations from the start. He wrote them down: "They assembled on a Sunday and immediately went absent to Saigon. They gathered enough by Tuesday the 6th to start training as a 'raid-commando' force. The quality is not uniform, to say the least. They are concentrating on demolitions and communications. About fifteen are not airborne-qualified, which doesn't seem to bother anyone in the STD. The compound is so crowded that sanitation is almost non-existent."[18]

From this shaky foundation, things continued to deteriorate. On 29 June, the Special Operations Detachment reported:

> We drew a lot of equipment to support THANG LONG. I hope we never have to issue it to them. They are ninety percent a sorry lot. [STD commander] Colonel Nu gave them a pep talk and a party to improve their morale and discipline on 17 June—immediately afterward they began fighting with their officers and among themselves. They ditch classes in droves, going down to the village and highway rest stops. To top it all off, Lt. Colonel Hy yesterday confiscated four vials of heroin and a quantity of opium. Their living and mess area is bad. I'm going to recommend that they be cut down to no more than three teams. . . . They should—the remainder—be sent to jail. Lt. Colonel Hy is trying hard, but he can't be everywhere at once.[19]

Other aspects of Conplan 5108 were scarcely any better. Several EARTH ANGEL teams, slated to have a sabotage role in the operation, were still running missions into Quang Tri. Because they needed to begin immediate training in demolitions, the Special Operations Detachment recommended that they be brought back to Long Thanh and replaced by Khmer intelligence teams sitting idle at the camp. By month's end, however, the Strategic Technical Directorate staff had yet to make a decision, and the EARTH ANGELs were still languishing in Hue.

Slow progress was also seen in Thailand, where a Special Operations Detachment delegation had gone on 20 June to coordinate support. Pending CIA approval, diversionary operations, consisting mostly of radio traffic to notional teams, were to center around a dummy launch site at Nam Phong, an agency-sponsored training base south of Udorn. In addition, U.S. Air Force helicopter assets at Nakhon Phanom were to be used for heliborne insertions. The senior air force commander at the air base, however, was anything but cooperative; only after intercession by an air force general at

Udorn did he reluctantly agree to release his aircraft within seventy-two hours of the operation's commencement.[20]

While the Special Operations Detachment struggled to scrounge together some airborne teeth for Conplan 5108, the remnants of the Naval Advisory Detachment were working to forge a maritime component. By this time, however, few assets remained on hand. Back in April, all of Danang's Nasty boats had been returned to the U.S. Navy. In the same month, half of the four remaining action teams were turned over to the Coastal Rescue Force, a new outfit intended to help with the recovery of downed airmen along the North Vietnamese coast.

By May 1972, then, the Coastal Security Service counted just two Swift boats and a pair of action teams, none of whom had been used on North Vietnam raids since 1968. The Naval Advisory Detachment, meanwhile, was reduced to only four U.S. Navy SEAL advisers.[21] When CINCPAC that month recommended supplementing Conplan 5108 with a seaborne raiding force capable of insertion by boat, helicopter, or submarine, it was clearly beyond South Vietnamese means. Recognizing this, thirty-one action team members were sent to Subic Bay on 10 June for special warfare instruction under the auspices of the U.S. Navy's Underwater Demolitions Team 11/Western Pacific Detachment. Over the next nine weeks, the students were trained in diving, demolitions, and raids. They also practiced submerged exits from the submarine *Grayback*.[22]

By mid-August, the new maritime strike force was back at Danang awaiting further orders. Meanwhile, down at Long Thanh, progress remained slow. Drug problems plagued THANG LONG, leading the Special Operations Detachment to focus its attention on the EARTH ANGELs. Three different targets inside North Vietnam had been selected in late September for the *hoi chanh*, including a petroleum pipeline northeast of Hanoi near the border between Ha Bac and Lang Son Provinces.

Getting the EARTH ANGELs to and from the pipeline was not going to be easy. For insert, they were going to take an MC-130. While the plane's sophisticated avionics enabled it to fly a nap-of-the-earth profile, the MC-130 crew would be nudging some of the thickest air defenses in North Vietnam, spearheaded by an array of heat-seeking surface-to-air missiles. The planes were not exactly equipped to deal with the threat. "I was aboard when an MC-130 inserted two teams into Cambodia," recalled the Special Operations Detachment's chief adviser. "That time, the back ramp opened a crack and an airman with a flare gun stood guard for any approaching rockets. It was not too reassuring." Besides rockets, North Vietnam had perhaps the most experienced collection of MiG pilots in the communist bloc. When asked about the MiG problem, the MC-130 squadron commander said curtly, "We will run the MiGs into the ground."[23]

If all that sounded like bombast and oversimplification, the exfiltration plans were even worse. "We envisioned them riding a train to near Laos," said one Special Operations Detachment officer. "Basically, they were on their own."[24]

Despite the suicidal nature of the mission, the EARTH ANGELs were motivated to go. "They would have succeeded getting in and doing the job," said the senior Special Operations Detachment adviser. "No doubt about it."[25]

In the end, Conplan 5108 went the way of all the other post-1968 unconventional warfare schemes targeted against North Vietnam—nowhere. On 31 October, all American support for the Coastal Security Service came to a halt.[26] That same month, THANG LONG was disbanded. Thirty of the best members were retained as agent teams with an undetermined mission. Detachment B was also dissolved, while the Special Operations Detachment was reduced to only two men on 25 November.[27]

As Saigon dismembered its final means of conducting unconventional warfare in North Vietnam, peace talks in Paris deadlocked. When the Nixon administration finally decided to apply decisive military pressure against Hanoi in December, it was not with commandos but rather with B-52 bombers.[28]

Eventually, the strong-arming worked. By mid-January 1973, Hanoi was on the verge of signing a peace treaty. To show good faith, the Joint Chiefs on 18 January ordered Saigon to terminate planning for Conplan 5108. A similar message came from CINCPAC on 27 January.[29] By then, the signatures of the North Vietnamese negotiators were on the agreement. On paper at least, the Vietnam War was over.

28

DEFEAT

On 9 February 1973, a senior American military delegation arrived at Saigon's Joint General Staff headquarters for a meeting with South Vietnam's top brass. But instead of battle plans, they discussed budgets. American aid was about to end, and the 1.1-million-man South Vietnamese army was going to have to fight alone.

They would have a head start, however. Just one year earlier, Washington had lavished Saigon with additional material assistance, part of a plan called Operation ENHANCE. This goodwill gesture was designed to rebuild the South Vietnamese military, still reeling from the 1972 Easter Offensive, and at the same time prepare Saigon for a fight that was sure to get worse after the last American soldiers left. Tanks, ships, and aircraft came by the hundreds—some 685 planes and helicopters were delivered during the last three months of 1972 alone.[1]

Tactical support had been equally generous. For over a decade, American advisers had extended down to the division, regiment, and even battalion levels, while American aircraft had been instrumental for both airlift and airstrikes.

The Paris Peace Accord, however, marked the beginning of a new era. Further U.S. defense funding was now to be sharply curtailed. The agreement, signed on 27 January 1973, dismantled MACV, the centerpiece of American military assistance, and allowed only a small Defense Attaché Office (DAO) in its place. Only fifty U.S. military personnel and a handful of civilians were permitted within the Defense Attaché Office, which was expressly forbidden from offering advice on tactics and operations. The war now belonged completely to the South Vietnamese.[2]

This was the new reality Saigon's generals faced during their meeting. In somber tones they sorted through what to keep and what to cut in the coming days of a leaner war machine. Considering that Hanoi's military threat had been increasingly conventional over the past few years, airplanes and tanks were high on the list of military priorities. Down near the very bottom was clandestine operations. Vietnamization had already taken a heavy toll on the Strategic Technical Directorate, but now it was difficult to make a case for keeping it around at all. According to one Special Mission Service reconnaissance team leader:

When the Americans were supporting us, we could count on fighter support and plenty of helicopters on standby. By 1972, we had to depend on Vietnamese helicopters, and sometimes we could not count on more than one at a time. In the SMS, we had to cut our teams from twelve men down to six, because six was the maximum number we could get out on ropes from one helicopter in an emergency. By early 1973, we could not even count on one helicopter; we ended up going in and out mostly by foot.[3]

With the Strategic Technical Directorate having trouble conducting even in-country missions, continued covert operations into North Vietnam were merely a fantasy. Further American funding for South Vietnam's unconventional warfare units, agreed the generals, would come to an end. Group 68, the Strategic Technical Directorate's residual force for northern contingency operations, was earmarked for deactivation.[4]

In February and March, the United States and North and South Vietnam held a series of prisoner exchanges. As stipulated in the Paris Peace Accord, all captured American and allied military and civilian personnel were to be returned within ninety days. Complying in part, North Vietnam set free 591 Americans and several hundred South Vietnamese by the close of March. Significantly, not a single Biet Kich was among them. Hanoi, it turned out, had charged all agents caught in the north with espionage, which it did not consider a military crime. While no such distinctions were made in the Paris Accord, North Vietnam decided the Biet Kich were not eligible for release. Yet neither Saigon nor Washington pressed Hanoi: both consistently maintained weak denials that such covert operations ever took place.

The Biet Kich captured in North Vietnam were not the only commandos kept in prison. Nearly all other Strategic Technical Directorate personnel captured in Cambodia or Laos—estimated at several dozen—remained behind bars.[5] There were a handful of exceptions. Lieutenant Hong Tran, a STRATA team leader captured in southern Laos in early 1971, was one of only two STRATA members to come home in 1973.[6] Debriefed upon his return, Tran revealed that Hanoi knew quite a bit about the secret missions.

"When Tran was interrogated in North Vietnam, he was shown clear photos of STRATA officers taken from on top of the water tower inside the main STRATA compound at Monkey Mountain," said one of his debriefers. "They obviously had a spy at the base who was pretending to service the water tower."[7]

With hindsight, the fact that the North Vietnamese had a source inside Monkey Mountain should have come as no surprise. According to a Strategic Technical Directorate major, "There were dozens, if not hundreds, of local personnel working as cooks and maids and drivers at each STD compound. Few of them had any serious background checks. These people had tremendous access around each base—they cleaned everything from bedrooms to briefing rooms. Many assumed that they were illiterate villagers, but I wonder how many were communist plants?"[8]

While knowledge of an agent inside Monkey Mountain gave Saigon's counterintelligence crowd something to contemplate, it was too late to make any difference. By early 1974, South Vietnam's grip on the countryside was eroding in the face of steady communist encroachment. In December, North Vietnamese troops besieged Phuoc Long, a provincial capital about 120 kilometers north of Saigon. One month later, they overran the city, their biggest victory since the cease-fire.

Half a world away, Washington responded to the violations with weak protests about Hanoi's "aggressive behavior." Encouraged by the limp American response, the North Vietnamese military felt sufficiently confident to move up its timetable for an all-out invasion of the south. On 8 March 1975, they kicked off the so-called Ho Chi Minh Campaign with a series of well-coordinated attacks down the length of South Vietnam.

Whipsawed by the multiple North Vietnamese thrusts, South Vietnam's war machine withered. First to fall was the Central Highlands. Saigon's continued tactical blundering then resulted in a chaotic retreat toward the coast by several South Vietnamese army units during the second week in March. With North Vietnamese tanks and infantry in pursuit, the country was effectively cut in half.

To the north, the South Vietnamese army had instructions to defend enclaves around Hue and Danang at all costs. Four divisions were available, including two—the 1st Infantry and the marines—that were rated among the best in the South Vietnamese order of battle. But with the Central Highlands falling apart, morale, even among elite troops, was at rock bottom. By the third week of March, soldiers and refugees were streaming south from Hue.

As the noose tightened around Danang, two Strategic Technical Directorate units, a group from the Special Mission Service and STRATA, continued to operate in the field. Three Special Mission Service teams had been conducting shallow forays beyond the receding government front line in the forlorn hope that they might find a weak spot in the North Vietnamese juggernaut. It was little more than a suicide mission.

"On March 23, we were told to walk with a marine platoon northwest of Danang and mine the highway approaching the city," recalls Lieutenant

Nguyen Cong The, a team leader. "When we got there, we were told over the radio that no evacuation choppers could get us. We were cut off and surrounded, and finally surrendered three days later."[9]

Back in Danang, marines and soldiers were swimming through the surf to commandeer boats back to Saigon. Minus its three teams lost in the field, the Special Mission Service headquarters joined the exodus.

On nearby Monkey Mountain, Major Le Huu Minh, the STRATA commander, watched the chaos. A former commander of the EARTH ANGEL program, Minh had taken over STRATA in late 1974. "The marines were coming out to Monkey Mountain and leaving in boats," he said. "All of my teams were in the field, so I got on the radio and gave them the 'Red Order,' which meant that they were supposed to make their own way down to Saigon."[10]

By nightfall on 30 March, Danang was in communist hands. The next day, the Joint General Staff slapped together a new plan to reconstitute the remnants of the South Vietnamese army and defend the southern half of the country. Unimpressed by the last-ditch maneuver, the Defense Attaché Office estimated that Saigon would fall in as little as three months. A Defense Intelligence Agency assessment on 3 April gave South Vietnam just thirty days.[11]

Such pessimism was fully warranted. By the third week of April, sixteen North Vietnamese divisions were positioned for a three-pronged attack on the capital. Out of ideas, the Joint General Staff simply tossed all available units into a last line of defense. Everything was thrown onto the battlements, including some residual elements of the Strategic Technical Directorate. East of Saigon stood what remained of the Special Mission Service. Ten kilometers to the north was Major Minh and his handful of STRATA stragglers. On the west at Long Thanh was Group 68, which had steadfastly resisted disbandment and remained in the order of battle despite the lack of any possibility of renewed missions into North Vietnam. The last Group 68 commander, Lieutenant Colonel Truong Duy Tai, had years earlier commanded Biet Hai forces at Danang.

"Group 68 had about 150 men in mixed reconnaissance teams," recalled Tai. "We were supposed to be used for cross-border operations, including North Vietnam, but nobody talked about this anymore. Many of my best men were Cambodians; they were sticking around to the very end."[12]

But not everyone stayed around for the final fight. On 21 April, President Nguyen Van Thieu resigned and flew off to exile. With him went the chairman of the Joint General Staff, General Cao Van Vien. Spying General Vien's personal aircraft abandoned at Tan Son Nhut, the Strategic Technical Directorate commander, Colonel Doan Van Nu, boarded the plane with his family and fled the country on 28 April.

The next morning, Major Minh, the STRATA commander, radioed head-quarters for orders. Nobody answered. He gathered his remaining men, and they marched back to Saigon. "When we got there," said Minh, "we saw the STD leadership had fled and the SMS was boarding about five barges to es-cape to the U.S. Seventh Fleet in the South China Sea. I told my men to join them."[13]

On the morning of 1 May it was all over. A tense silence hung over Saigon as North Vietnamese troops poured into the city. The interim South Viet-namese prime minister, Duong Van Minh, had offered unconditional sur-render the day before, enabling North Vietnamese tanks to symbolically crash through the gates of the presidential palace unopposed.

Taking over the central radio station, a communist spokesman ordered South Vietnamese military officers to report to their normal units. As in-structed, several key Strategic Technical Directorate officers arrived at their headquarters near the main gate to Tan Son Nhut. Among them was Fran-çois, the former STRATA commander who had recruited the original sin-gleton to North Vietnam, ARES.

"I had planned to leave the country," he said. "The STD headquarters, which was in contact with the U.S. embassy, had been assured that we could get out with our families. But then the top officers in the STD were gone, and the U.S. embassy was busy getting their own people out. I got stuck behind."[14]

Alongside François was Marc, sporting the rosettes of a lieutenant colonel for his last assignment as chief of logistics. They were joined by Jacques, now a major acting as last head of the Strategic Technical Directorate security sec-tion; STRATA commander Minh; and the Group 68 chief, Lieutenant Colonel Tai.

North Vietnamese soldiers surrounded the five men with fixed bayonets and marched them off to "reeducation," a communist euphemism for incar-ceration mixed with indoctrination. François was released in 1978, appar-ently for cooperative behavior while in prison.[15] Marc remained for over a dozen years.[16] Minh and Tai did not see freedom for sixteen years. Jacques died from the harsh treatment.

Like the war itself, covert operations against North Vietnam were a failure. Designed to convince Hanoi that conflict in the south would be an expen-sive undertaking, in the end SOG as a whole did not have much impact on Hanoi's conduct of the war. Three basic reasons lie behind this failure, all of them embedded in the complex political definitions of the conflict. First, during the early 1960s the United States publicly announced that it had no intention of overthrowing the government of North Vietnam. Whether right or wrong, this policy severely constrained the options open to special operations planners. Second, the structure built to oversee special operations in Southeast Asia was removed from the battlefield and placed in the hands of political decision makers. MACV had no authority over non–Defense Department organizations, leaving all major operational decisions to Washington. Finally, the U.S. government consistently tied the conduct of special operations to conventional political and military events. Although Op 34A missions inside North Vietnam were ostensibly conducted by non–U.S. nationals and therefore "deniable," they were in reality inextricably linked to American war aims. When Washington declared a unilateral bombing halt north of the seventeenth parallel in November 1968, covert action was also stopped. Considering that the United States denied any connection to these secret missions, the simultaneous halts were clear evidence that the opposite was true.

With hindsight, it is clear that all the agent operations were doomed from the start. Precedent, after all, foretold disaster. By the time the first agent crossed the Demilitarized Zone in 1960, the CIA already had plenty of evidence that blind missions into closed communist societies did not work. Whether these lessons remained unlearned because of the agency's penchant for compartmentalization, or because there were simply no better ideas, the Saigon station ended up using the same failed ideas from previous cold war endeavors.

The miscue stemmed from larger policy misunderstandings, something that plagued all aspects of the war. The first miscalculation was the decision to allow North Vietnam to use the surrounding countries—as well as its own backyard—as inviolate sanctuaries. Since the 1954 Geneva Accords divided Vietnam, Hanoi ignored the sovereignty of its neighbors in Laos and Cambodia, not to mention South Vietnam. American policy was confined to bolstering the regime in South Vietnam, and policy makers viewed Laos and Cambodia as sovereign nations to be dealt with separately. Hanoi, on the other hand, regarded the region as three parts of a single whole—Vietnam, Laos, and Cambodia were all one Indochina. Communist strategy knew no borders. Rather than use conventional forces to thwart these sanctuaries, Washington declared them off-limits—and then allowed covert operations to get around the rules.

Reliance on covert operations also stemmed from a desire to keep the war "small." President Kennedy had envisioned a bold new counterinsurgency force—which included a covert component—while his successor, President Johnson, emphasized the secret side designed to fight the war quietly, away from public view. Johnson attempted to escalate the war unnoticed, afraid to be labeled "soft on communism" if he failed to confront Hanoi, yet unwilling to alter the course of his Great Society reforms at home. Instead of choosing between mobilizing the nation for war or concentrating on domestic policy, Johnson tried to have it both ways, and he failed badly. But part of the president's decision to choose a nonexistent middle ground was the delusion that covert operations could accomplish what he felt a conventional commitment to war could not: destroy the enemy's will to continue to support the revolution in South Vietnam, and do it cheaply and quietly.

Johnson's misunderstanding was very likely based partly on the success of earlier covert operations around the world. He certainly understood the many differences between earlier operations and those in South Vietnam, and as former vice president during the Bay of Pigs fiasco, Johnson was well aware of the consequences of failure. Unlike in the Bay of Pigs incident, Johnson was not relying purely on special operations; in Vietnam, they were to be an extension of a burgeoning military presence. But any covert operation—no matter how large—would always be inferior to the conventional North Vietnamese military presence. Despite the obvious mismatch, in the earliest days of the war the United States was willing to try and meet Hanoi's open escalation with a covert one in the hopes that somehow this would be regarded as a credible threat.

Johnson also favored Op 34A because it carried little likelihood of reciprocal escalation—either from Hanoi or from an outside power such as China. In this, Johnson probably calculated correctly. North Vietnam never openly indicated that it would risk escalation over the covert raids because it did not regard Washington's secret war as anything more than a nuisance.

Still, for more than three years the CIA followed a flawed formula that had proved unsuccessful throughout the Far East since the early 1950s. Only on the eve of losing the program to the Defense Department in late 1963 did the agency admit its failure. By the time the military took over, there was ample evidence—as well as an opportunity—to break with the past. Agency misgivings, however, fell on deaf ears. Submerged in bureaucratic rivalry, the Pentagon misinterpreted CIA warnings as sour grapes over losing its mission.

Once the American troop buildup began in 1965, and conventional war became the mainstay of Washington's strategy, covert action continued, though by that time its purpose was no longer clearly defined. Given that America was now meeting the threat to South Vietnam head-on, Op 34A became little more than a frill. Since destabilizing the Hanoi regime was never seriously considered, and given the rigidity of North Vietnamese control of its population, the operations had little effect.

If anything, SOG's military mind-set—tackling the operation with more men and bigger budgets—compounded the problem it inherited. Annual rotation of American advisers and staff robbed the group of institutional memory and helped perpetuate the fiasco for another three years. Between 1961 and 1967, fifty-four teams totaling almost five hundred men ventured north, only to be captured or killed almost immediately upon arrival.[17] Only in late 1967, with the growing list of setbacks too long to ignore, were the long-term agent operations halted. In their place were short-term teams— STRATA—and while they were the first to infiltrate into North Vietnam and then come out safely, their intelligence-gathering capabilities were limited.

In 1970, almost two years after the North Vietnam bombing halt brought an end to Op 34A, the Defense Department conducted an exhaustive top secret study of SOG operations. Without exception, key SOG figures from the 1964–68 era expounded on the shortcomings of the program. Covert agent operations in North Vietnam, they agreed, had not worked for the CIA, did not work for SOG, and almost certainly would not work in the future. Many concluded that notional operations made up of phony teams to convince Hanoi that agents were penetrating their backyard had a better chance of success without such a high cost in human lives.

The Pentagon did not fully take these lessons to heart. On several occasions between 1969 and 1972, plans surfaced to restart the covert operations in North Vietnam. Most of the contingencies read like a pre-1968 script, underscoring what one Pentagon official called "the frustration syndrome": it was better to conduct some sort of unconventional warfare in North Vietnam, no matter how ill-conceived, than to do nothing at all.

The irony of all this was that CIA and SOG operations, especially during the crucial period leading up to the Tonkin Gulf incident in August 1964, probably had the opposite of the intended effect. True, any penetration of North Vietnam triggered paranoia in Hanoi. But this was not maximized until the advent of the notional campaign in late 1967. In the meantime, the amateurish nature of agent operations in the north enabled Hanoi to rally public opinion against the United States, gave the communists the moral high ground for claims of patriotism, and provided an excuse for further crackdowns.

So it should come as no surprise that the covert program failed. Yet some believe that there were more nefarious reasons. "The enemy had to have known the teams were coming," wrote one SOG veteran. "To have played the game so effectively and so long, the North Vietnamese had to have moles in Saigon, right in the bowels of SOG."[18]

But there is no real evidence of any such thing. While the communists had high-level agents in the Saigon government and in all likelihood had penetrated the South Vietnamese army command as well, they have never claimed to have had any high-level moles within the covert operations machinery, and there is no reason to believe they would be hiding such infor-

mation. Their most dramatic coup—the "turning" of the singleton ARES—
is well documented. A plant high up in the Strategic Technical Directorate
would certainly have been cause for even more bragging.

Besides, the North Vietnamese did not need an agent inside SOG to defeat the covert operation into their homeland. Lack of imagination in planning, faulty execution of missions, and poor operational security were more
than enough to account for the failures. What some see as an uncanny knack
for capturing agent teams almost immediately upon insertion was in reality
just plain old common sense and effective security on Hanoi's part. Commandos routinely point out that their missions were often planned using old
maps, which accounted for the many mistaken drop zones. Especially in the
early days, parachute insertions were at best inexact because of a lack of sophisticated navigation equipment. Unpredictable winds often separated
teams during their drop, and they frequently landed near populated areas.
Given the presence of militia in almost every village and Hanoi's iron grip
on the North Vietnamese people, it was unthinkable that the appearance of
strange faces would go unreported for long.

In the final analysis, covert operations against North Vietnam became an
end rather than a means. Throughout the long war, they became a crutch
that allowed Washington to put off making any hard decisions about expanding the war, thereby diluting the effect that Op 34A might have had on
North Vietnam if there had been a clear and pointed purpose. Political constraints and a lack of understanding of the enemy doomed it from the start,
but policy makers consistently believed that covert operations—no matter
how poorly conceived—were better than nothing. General Westmoreland
summed it up best when he observed that "in a war that as much as any in
history pitted will against will, it was worth a try."[19]

EPILOGUE

"Victory has a hundred fathers and defeat is an orphan," lamented President Kennedy after the failure of the CIA's Bay of Pigs operation in 1961. The Vietnam War was only a brushfire at the time, and although it grew into a conflagration that did not burn out for more than a decade, the orphan of defeat was still there, waiting in the ashes. No one has claimed it to this day.

Of course, there are many orphans of the Vietnam War—most of them real rather than rhetorical. The commandos of Op 34A are certainly among these, although their plight is no more compelling than that of the millions of other South Vietnamese soldiers and civilians displaced by the war. If there is a difference, however, it is that they alone ventured into the enemy's home ground, and for this they often took the brunt of the new regime's vengeance. The term *biet kich* became synonymous with "traitor," and much of Vietnamese society has been loath to forgive and forget. The result has been discrimination, unemployment, and poverty.

The United States provided little succor for the commandos who once served so faithfully. During the 1980s, Hanoi made it clear that it was willing to let them go, but Washington threw up roadblocks. In the years immediately after Saigon's fall, cold war sentiments paved the way for easy entry into the United States for almost anyone fleeing communist tyranny. But by 1982 anticommunist fervor was offset by mounting concern over the number of immigrants swelling America's borders. This sentimental shift suddenly made it difficult for even former allies to come to the United States. Despite the fact that there were only a handful of former commandos, they were not welcomed.

The culprit was the U.S. Immigration and Naturalization Service (INS), which administered the Vietnamese refugee program with a capricious and seemingly uncaring hand. From the American embassy in Bangkok, Thailand, a single INS representative held sway over the former commandos' appeals for entry into America. Applications for emigration were sent from Vietnam by the commandos—along with documentation of their SOG affiliation and a prison release form—to the Bangkok office where they were processed. After up to a year, or even more, a decision was made. For the commandos waiting resignedly in Saigon, the answer almost always came back negative.

The INS decided that, to qualify for the immigration program, the commandos (and other former members of the South Vietnamese military) must have spent at least three years in a reeducation camp after the fall of Saigon in 1975. Although many of the Op 34A commandos had spent more than ten years in prison during the war, the INS ruled that their political persecution did not begin until after the war was over—before then they were simply prisoners of war.

To make matters worse, no one at the INS had any real knowledge of the Op 34A program. When a commando applied for refugee status claiming that he parachuted into North Vietnam on a secret mission, he was usually greeted with disbelief—not an unreasonable response considering how unbelievable the covert operation must have seemed to outsiders. But a little checking with knowledgeable sources would have shown that the stories were true. Documents and personal accounts abounded; all it took was simple research.

Stories of INS inflexibility piled up. Nguyen Van Ngo, a member of Team TELLUS, was captured on 7 June 1963 and released from a reeducation camp on 15 April 1978—just fifteen short days short of the three-year cutoff. Despite the fact that some of his teammates were already in the United States, Ngo was denied a visa.

Duong Long Sang, a maritime commando with Team CANCER, was captured on 7 June 1963 and held in a communist prison until 12 May 1982. Two of his teammates had immigrated to the United States, but Sang was refused entry by the INS because he "failed to establish pre-association" with SOG. The decision was made despite the fact that Sang produced a photo of himself and two teammates, as well as an official prison release form stating that he was a commando.

Ngo Quoc Chung, the leader of Team PACKER, was captured during a mission on 4 July 1963. Chung, a veteran of Dien Bien Phu, was known as a particularly recalcitrant commando throughout his prison and reeducation time. He was finally released in October 1987, but as punishment for his failure to toe the communist line, he was given no release papers by Vietnamese officials. The INS refused to hear his case, despite ample documentation of his history with the CIA.

The list went on and on, but only a few people outside of Vietnam followed the commandos' saga. Then, in April 1995, the U.S. ambassador to Thailand, David F. Lambertson, sent a cable to Washington suggesting that the INS reconsider its rejection of so many commandos. "We believe they [the commandos] qualify," read the cable, "based on their associations with U.S. policies and programs and serving long incarcerations." Lambertson also acknowledged the obvious by noting that the commandos were captured "while engaging in U.S.-directed missions to collect intelligence, conduct military and psychological operations, or to render assistance to downed American air crews."[1]

Lambertson's cable, which was quickly made public, prompted the INS to review its selection process for the Op 34A commandos, especially those previously rejected. The result was that most of those formerly rejected were finally allowed to enter the United States. Only public scrutiny of the process made this possible.

At about the same time, the Op 34A drama entered the courts. On 20 April 1995, Miami-based attorney John C. Mattes filed suit in the U.S. Court of Federal Claims in Washington, D.C., on behalf of 281 former commandos (most of them already residing in the United States) asking for $11,240,000 in back pay. Mattes arrived at the figure by taking the commandos' yearly salary—about $2,000—and multiplying it by their prison time.

The U.S. government, Mattes argued in the suit, failed "to continue the commandos' salaries until the return of all the commandos from captivity." He claimed this was done deliberately by Washington, which declared all the commandos dead in 1969 rather than continue to pay benefits to the families, despite ample evidence that many were alive and in prison.

In a startling interview contained in the MACSOG Documentation Study, Colonel John J. Windsor, U.S. Marine Corps, the SOG operations officer in 1965 and 1966, said that his commanders felt that the "agents' monthly pay to their relatives back in Saigon should be discontinued." Windsor admitted that this was done by "gradually declaring so many of them dead each month until we had written them all off (paid them) and removed them from the monthly payrolls."[2]

Financial records recently uncovered in the National Archives support this claim. They show death gratuity payments for commandos that SOG knew were in prison, not dead. Some of the teams were declared dead despite the fact that the North Vietnamese had publicly tried and sentenced the captured commandos to prison. The stories were covered by the press.

Still, in order to prevail in court, Mattes had to overcome a past ruling on a similar case. In 1981, a Chicago-based attorney, Anthony Charles Murray, sued the U.S. government on behalf of Vu Duc Guong, a maritime commando captured in March 1964 during a mission north of the Demilitarized Zone. Guong was asking for $449,201 in back pay plus $21 million in damages. The case was dismissed because of an old precedent known as the *Totten* Doctrine. In 1875, the estate of a former Civil War spy claimed the U.S. government owed him money for his espionage work on behalf on the Union. The Supreme Court was unsympathetic and ruled that any action was barred because the secrecy of *Totten's* work "precludes any action" taken to enforce the contract. "This condition . . . is implied in all secret employs of the government in time of war, or upon matters affecting our foreign relations, where a disclosure of the service might compromise or embarrass our government in its public duties." In other words, any secret contract with the U.S. government is ultimately unenforceable. This precedent still applies.[3]

The courts never heard the new case, however. Growing awareness of the covert program pushed the commandos back into the public spotlight, and it was only a matter of time before Congress noticed. On 19 June 1996, more than a dozen former commandos filed into a hearing room to listen as senators expressed outrage and promised to make amends.

"The truth is we sent heroic Vietnamese commandos into North Vietnam to do America's bidding," said Senator John Kerry, a Massachusetts Democrat. "We can't make up for the extraordinary suffering, for the years of having turned away. But we can honor their service and make it clear to those we wish to join us in the struggle for freedom and democracy that we are big enough to admit mistakes and to move to rectify them." Immediately after his testimony, Senator Kerry left the room to introduce an amendment to the 1997 Defense Authorization Bill for over $20 million, about $40,000 for each commando. Not a single senator voted against the measure.[4]

Senator Bob Kerry, a Nebraska Democrat and former Navy SEAL who won the Medal of Honor in Vietnam, cosponsored the bill. "In my view," he said, "the United States simply owes them the money. I did not require a hearing for me to reach that conclusion."[5]

But the harshest words came from Pennsylvania Republican Arlen Specter, chairman of the Senate Select Committee on Intelligence. "The United States wrote them off," he said. Specter called American actions "callous, inhumane. . . . This conduct is criminal. Leaving them behind—that's homicide, that's premeditated." Specter was so incensed by the Defense Department's reliance on the "ridiculous" *Totten* case that he hinted he might sponsor a bill to strike it down as a legal precedent.

Today the commandos are receiving their due. Congressional action forced the Defense Department to establish a commission to oversee compensation. As of May 1999, it had received almost 1,200 claims (of which about 332 were approved) and paid out about $13.5 million.

The process continues. As Senator John Kerry said, the United States has admitted its mistakes and is rectifying them.

NOTES

Chapter 1. Trojan Horses

1. *The Pentagon Papers,* as published by the *New York Times* (New York, 1971), p. 27. Hereafter referred to as *NYT Pentagon Papers.*

2. The first wave of Vietnamese immigrants—primarily persecuted Catholics and followers of a deposed Vietnamese prince—arrived in Thailand 150 years before World War II. The second wave fled to Thailand in 1946 when the French reimposed their rule over Indochina. See Peter Poole, *The Vietnamese in Thailand* (Ithaca, N.Y.: Cornell University Press, 1970), p. 23.

3. Correspondence with Donald Gregg, 7 February 1997.

4. NSC memorandum, subj: Discussion of NSC meeting on 21 January 1954, Declassified Documents Reference System (hereafter DDRS) 1996-2764.

5. Cecil B. Currey, *Edward Lansdale: The Unquiet American* (Boston: Houghton Mifflin, 1988), p. 136.

6. White House Memorandum, 18 May 1954, DDRS 1996-1066.

7. *NYT Pentagon Papers,* p. 55.

8. CIA Memorandum, subj: Biographic Register for Dang Van Sung, 1963 [no day or month given], DDRS 1976-24F.

9. Interview with Dang Van Sung, 11 March 1996.

10. MAAG-Indochina was formed in June 1950 to assist "the forces of France and the Associated States of Indochina." On 1 November 1955, it was replaced by MAAG-Vietnam, which would advise the newly created Republic of Vietnam.

11. *The Pentagon Papers,* Gravel edition, vol. 2 (Boston: Beacon Press, 1975), p. 649.

12. Interview with Jack Shirley, CIA case officer, 7 August 1995.

13. *Nhung Hoat Dong Pha Hoai va Lat Do cua CIA o Viet Nam* [CIA Subversion and Sabotage in Vietnam] (Hanoi: People's Public Security Publishing House, 1990), pp. 67–76.

14. Morrison interview with David Zogbaum, 9 June 1997.

15. *The Pentagon Papers,* Gravel edition, 1:580.

16. With still more Vietnamese volunteering for American instruction,

Lansdale drew up contingency plans for creating a second training site within the Clark Air Force Base reservation in the Philippines. According to the proposal, advisers would be provided by Freedom Company, a CIA-backed venture established by Lansdale during his previous Asian tour as a means of channeling Filipino unconventional warfare assistance to other Far East nations. See *NYT Pentagon Papers,* p. 62. While Clark was used as a holding site, Conein claims that all primary training remained at Saipan. Interview with Lucien Conein, 16 July 1995.

17. Howard R. Simpson, *Tiger in the Barbed Wire: An American in Vietnam, 1952–1991* (Washington, D.C.: Brassey's, 1992), p. 127.

18. *Pentagon Papers,* Gravel edition, 1:578–579.

19. Interview with Lucien Conein.

20. Interview with Gilbert Layton, commander, Combined Studies Division (Saigon), 2 March 1993.

21. *NYT Pentagon Papers,* p. 65.

22. Interview with Bui Van Ninh, 29 March 1996. The law professor, Dr. Vu Van Mao, would briefly serve as head of the South Vietnamese government in April 1975.

23. *Nhung Hoat Dong Pha Hoai va Lat Do cua CIA o Viet Nam,* pp. 77–79; correspondence with Nguyen Nhu Anh, 26 May 1996. Anh was imprisoned for two years along with five of the VNQDD spies.

24. Interview with Dang Van Sung.

25. Currey, *Edward Lansdale,* p. 164.

26. *Cong An Nhan Dan Viet Nam, 1954–1964* [Vietnam People's Public Security Force, 1954–1964] (Hanoi: Institute of Public Security Science, Ministry of Interior, 1994), p. 44.

27. This was not the first spy ring to be made public. Eight months earlier, North Vietnamese authorities announced the capture of an alleged stay-behind network, which they claimed took orders from both Saigon and a French national living in Hanoi. The Frenchman was immediately thrown out of the country. Eleven of the fourteen accused spies were given prison sentences, and the ringleader, Nguyen Quang Hai, was executed. No evidence was ever presented at the trial showing that the Saigon government or the CIA was involved with this group of agents. Later that same month, a North Vietnamese paper ran an editorial entitled "Alertness Against Spy Rings." Given that the authorities were already aware of the Dai Viet agents, the editorial was probably aimed as much at them as at the group just placed on trial. See Foreign Broadcast Information Service (hereafter FBIS), East Asia edition, 21 March 1958, p. EEE1; 24 March 1958, p. EEE7; 26 March 1958, p. EEE5.

28. FBIS, East Asia edition, 7 April 1959, p. 18.

29. Interview with Nguyen Nhu Anh. Given the length of time it took to uncover the VNQDD spies, an embarrassed Hanoi chose to conduct the 1965 trial without publicity. However, dated photos of the event are on record at the Vietnam News Agency photograph department in Hanoi.

30. "Bai Noi Chuyen cua Dong Chi Bo Truong Tai Hoi Nghi Suu Tra Doi Tuong Chinh Tri Lan Thu 3" ["Speech by the Comrade Minister of Interior at the Third Conference on Investigation of Political Subjects"], p. 8. The meeting was held between 23 September and 1 October 1977.

Chapter 2. Singletons

1. Correspondence with Tran Khac Kinh, Deputy Commander, Presidential Liaison Office, 1 December 1995.

2. Morrison interview with David Zogbaum; Morrison correspondence with David Zogbaum, 4 November 1998 To ensure that Dr. Tuyen shared information, the CIA station provided a secret ink but retained control of the developing solution.

3. The CIA was inconsistent regarding stay-behind networks in Southeast Asia. In Thailand, the police stay-behind cadre had been formed with CIA assistance in 1952. By 1957, with a Chinese invasion seen as increasingly remote, this program was quietly dropped. During this same year, however, Washington felt neighboring South Vietnam sufficiently threatened by a Chinese invasion to warrant the creation of a specialized stay-behind force in that country.

4. Tung was also in charge of the military network inside the Can Lao, Diem's elite secret party created to provide leadership for mass front organizations. Correspondence with Edward Regan, 23 April 1997.

5. Interview with Tran Gia Loc, 7 January 1997.

6. Morrison interview with David Zogbaum. Besides the scant—and, with hindsight, fictitious—reporting from Tuyen's organization, the CIA was able to glean some details about conditions inside North Vietnam circa 1958 by interviewing a Senegalese deserter and a French academic, Dr. Gerard Tongas, both of whom had grown disenchanted with North Vietnamese communism after living for several years in Hanoi.

7. Correspondence with Edward Regan.

8. Interview with Ngo The Linh, 20 June 1996.

9. For a brief period, Office 45 was also known as Bureau E.

10. Interview with Lu Trieu Khanh, Presidential Liaison Office officer, 21 June 1996.

11. Interview with Thomas Fosmire, 14 March 1995.

12. Interview with Do Van Tien, 26 April 1996.

13. Hanoi has given several reasons for Pham Chuyen's defection. According to one, Chuyen sought revenge after his family was the victim of injustice during the harsh land reforms of the late 1950s and his father committed suicide: *Cong An Nhan Dan Viet Nam,* p. 150. In a slightly fictionalized account written with the cooperation of police involved in the case, Chuyen is portrayed as searching for a former girlfriend who went south: Vo Khac Nghiem, *Cuoc Dau Tri Muoi Hai Nam* [A Twelve-Year Battle of Wits] (Quang Ninh: People's Public Security Publishing House, 1995). According to Do Van Tien, however, Chuyen never mentioned the alleged suicide of his father or a lost girlfriend in South Vietnam. Rather, he said only that he had defected because his wife jilted him.

14. Interview with Do Van Tien.

15. Interview with Nguyen Van Nghe, 24 June 1996. As the PLO's finance officer, Nghe was in charge of procuring the junk at Vung Tau.

16. *Chong Biet Kich* [Resist the Commandos] (Hanoi: People's Public Security Publishing House, 1961), pp. 6–17, 25.

17. *Lich Su Quan Chung Phong Khong* [History of the Air Defense Branch], vol. 1 (Hanoi: People's Army Publishing House, 1991), p. 151. Hanoi claims there was a string of aerial provocations and bombing runs throughout that year. However, Hanoi was able to offer no evidence that any bombings or airborne infiltrations occurred during 1959 or 1960.

18. Ibid., p. 152.

19. *Chien Si Bien Phong* [The Border Defense Soldier], vol. 1 (Hanoi: People's Public Security Publishing House, 1984), p. 220.

20. *Lich Su Bo Doi Bien Phong* [History of the Border Defense Troops], vol. 1 (Hanoi: People's Public Security Publishing House, 1990), p. 59.

21. Ibid., p 54; *Cuoc Dau Tri Muoi Hai Nam,* p. 174.

22. Correspondence with Tran Khac Kinh.

23. There is some question as to ARES's insertion date. MACSOG documents give the date as February 1961, but North Vietnamese accounts are quite clear that it was in April. Since Hanoi's accounts are more detailed, we have used the April date. See MACSOG Documentation Study (hereafter MDS), "Airborne Operations," 10 July 1970, p. C-b-63; *Cong An Nhan Dan Viet Nam,* pp. 149–152.

24. *Cong An Nhan Dan Viet Nam,* p. 150. An erroneous account claims that fishermen found the skiff on 23 February buried in the sand: *Chien Si Bien Phong,* vol. 2 (Hanoi: People's Public Security Publishing House, 1990), p. 123.

25. Interview with Do Van Tien.

26. *Cong An Nhan Dan Viet Nam,* p. 150.

27. Ibid., p. 151. According to another account, the arrest took place on 23 March: *Chien Si Bien Phong,* 2:123.

28. *Cuoc Dau Tri Muoi Hai Nam,* p. 240; *Cong An Nhan Dan Viet Nam,* p. 151.

29. After arriving at Ha Long, a smaller skiff headed toward shore with the supplies for ARES. Both the skiff and the junk were captured and the entire crew imprisoned. *Cong An Nhan Dan Viet Nam,* p. 151.

30. Interview with Hoang Cung, 27 July 1995.

31. Interview with Do Van Tien.

32. *Cuoc Dau Tri Muoi Hai Nam,* p. 275.

33. Between December 1960 and September 1961, HIRONDELLE made five brief forays across the Demilitarized Zone. On his sixth mission, he was captured on 17 September after infiltrating Nghe An Province. Interview with Ngo The Linh.

34. TRITON, whose real name was Nguyen Chau Thanh, was a Catholic recruited to operate within that community. Spotted while sleeping near the Vinh bus station, he drew immediate suspicion and was quickly put under surveillance. Two days later, he was captured close to the Demilitarized Zone, apparently while trying to escape back to the south. For a full account, see *Cong An Nhan Dan Viet Nam,* pp. 203–205.

35. Dang Chi Binh, *Thep Den* [Black Steel], vol. 2 (Glendale, Calif.: Dainamco Publishers, 1989), pp. 206–207.

36. Correspondence with Edward Regan.

37. Interview with Bui Van Ninh.

38. *Cong An Nhan Dan Viet Nam,* pp. 211–212.

39. Unknown to the CIA, after its Dai Viet stay-behind network was exposed in 1959, there still remained two pockets of Dai Viet sympathizers within the heavily Catholic cities of Thai Binh and Nam Dinh. Both of these groups, however, were penetrated by North Vietnamese authorities and were quietly arrested en masse during mid-1960. Ibid., pp. 121–122.

40. Correspondence with Edward Regan.

41. Interview with Do Van Tien; correspondence with Edward Regan. Claiming that the two murdered agents, Vu Van Mung and Pham Quang Truc, were missing in action, the U.S. government paid death benefits to the two families. See MACSOG Financial Records, FY 65, Entry 69-228, Box 1, Folder 8.

42. WOLF, whose real name was Hoang Khung, was quickly captured and died in prison. See Hoang Khung's death gratuity in MACSOG Financial Records, Entry 69-228, Box 8, Folder "SOG Vouchers, July–December 1964."

43. On 28 January 1964, a military court in Haiphong sentenced the six sailors to lengthy prison sentences. See FBIS, East Asia edition, 28 January 1964, p. JJJ2. The date of their capture is given as 20 August in *Cong An Nhan Dan Viet Nam*, p. 151.

44. Interview with Nguyen Van Vinh, 13 January 1995. Vinh, a South Vietnamese intelligence officer, extensively reviewed the ARES case file when he assumed responsibility for running that agent in 1965.

45. *Chien Si Bien Phong*, 2:123.

Chapter 3. Airborne Agents

1. *Chong Biet Kich*, pp. 18-19, 28.

2. Interview with Ngo The Linh.

3. Correspondence with Tran Khac Kinh.

4. MDS, "MACSOG and the Strategic Technical Directorate: Inception, Organization, Evolution," p. B-66.

5. The Tai and Muong, recruited from the South Vietnamese 22nd Division at Kontum, were to form one airborne ranger company within the 1st Observation Group; the Nung, chosen from the South Vietnamese 5th Division, would form a second. These two minority companies, joined by two more recruited from among ethnic Vietnamese, were to be used during cross-border missions into the Lao panhandle as part of a CIA-sponsored operation code-named TYPHOON. Correspondence with Tran Khac Kinh.

6. Interview with William Colby, 19 June 1992; interview with Lawrence Ropka, U.S. Air Force, 20 June 1995. In 1959, Air America became the new corporate name for Civil Air Transport.

7. Interview with Jim Keck, 3 November 1995.

8. Anthony Cave Brown, ed., *The Secret War Report of the OSS* (New York: Berkeley Books, 1976), p. 314. Colby, in retrospect, claimed he had doubts his sabotage missions severely hampered the Nazis, who were able to quickly repair the railroad. Interview with William Colby, 2 June 1992.

9. Nguyen Cao Ky, *How We Lost the Vietnam War* (New York: Stein and Day, 1984), p. 27.

10. *Foreign Relations of the United States*, Vietnam, 1961–1963, vol. 1 (Washington, D.C.: U.S. Government Printing Office, 1991), p. 16 (hereafter *FRUS*).

11. National Security Memorandum No. 28, subj: Guerrilla Operations in Viet Minh Territory, 9 March 1961. See also Memorandum for the President from Dep. Secretary of Defense Roswell Gilpatric, subj: Operations Against North Vietnam, 29 March 1961.

12. *FRUS,* Vietnam, 1961–1963, 1:17.

13. In 1961, Office 45 began opening subbranches in Vientiane (code-named Comete, Savannakhet (Hercule), Bangkok (Alto), and Paris (Venus) The purpose of these subbranches was to gather information and recruit North Vietnamese expatriates. See MDS, "Strategic Technical Directorate," p. B-t-2. Opened over the next two years, most consisted of little more than a single South Vietnamese intelligence officer attached to the local embassy or consulate. Interview with Ngo The Linh.

14. *United States–Vietnam Relations, 1945–1967,* book 2 (Washington, D.C.: U.S. Government Printing Office, 1972), p. 18.

15. William Colby and Peter Forbath, *Honorable Men* (New York: Simon and Schuster, 1978), p. 172.

16. *NYT Pentagon Papers,* p. 124.

17. For a detailed examination of the changing missions see MDS, "MACSOG and the Strategic Technical Directorate: Inception, Organization, Evolution," pp. B-60–B-65.

18. *Van Kien Dang* [Party Documents], vol. 4 (Hanoi: Public Security Scientific Research Institute, 1977), p. 137.

19. "Facts and Figures Concerning U.S. and U.S. Agents' Sabotage Activities in North Vietnam" (Hanoi: Ministry of Foreign Affairs, 1963), p. 59.

20. *Chien Si Bien Phong,* 1:229; *Tay Bac, Lich Su Khang Chien Chong My, Cuu Nuoc* [The Northwest Military Region, History of the War of National Salvation Against America] (Hanoi: People's Army Publishing House, 1994), pp. 128–129.

21. *Chong Biet Kich,* p. 3.

22. Interview with Ngo The Linh. In 1977, Hanoi claimed—with considerable exaggeration—that Khai "commanded all of the commandos who were inserted into the north": *Ba Noi Chuyen cua Dong Chi Bo Truong Tai Hoi Nghi Suu Tra Doi Tuong Chinh Tri Lan Thu 3,* p. 75.

23. *Chien Si Bien Phong,* 1:236.

24. An Austroasiatic minority, the Tai are especially numerous in Vietnam's Lai Chau and Son La Provinces. Depending on the predominant color of the women's clothing in any particular Tai settlement, tribes are subdivided into Black, Red, or White Tai.

25. *Lich Su Bo Doi Bien Phong,* 1:66; interview with Lo Van Sinh, DIDO team member, 26 July 1995. According to one account, members of DIDO passed out berets and local money to villagers prior to their arrest: *Tay Bac, Lich Su Khang Chien Chong My, Cuu Nuoc,* pp. 129–130.

26. *Van Kien Dang,* 4:147.

27. *Chong Biet Kich,* pp. 74–75.

28. Interview with Ha Van Chap (via Nguyen Van Vinh), 20 October 1996.

29. "Mat danh CASTOR bi giai ma," [Code name CASTOR is decoded], article from *Su Kien & Nhan Chung* [Events and Witnesses], December 1994, p. 32.

30. *Lich Su Quan Chung Phong Khong*, 1:176; *Chien Si Bien Phong*, 1:241.

31. Interview with Jim Keck.

Chapter 4. Second Wind

1. "Mat danh CASTOR bi giai ma," p. 32.

2. *Xu An Vu May Bay Gian Diep Biet Kich C-47 cua My-Diem* [Trial Related to the Affair of the American-Diem C-47 Spy-commando Aircraft] (Hanoi: People's Army Publishing House, 1961), p. 19.

3. During this same time frame, Hanoi doubled ECHO—the team that parachuted into Quang Binh Province—and had it reestablish radio contact with Saigon. As ECHO had earlier radioed that the team members were under pressure and attempting to escape to the Demilitarized Zone, Saigon was immediately suspicious when ECHO came back on the air and claimed they had eluded capture. Concluding ECHO was under communist control, Saigon maintained the charade until terminating contact in August 1962.

4. U.S. officials occasionally translated the PSO's title as the "Topographical Exploitation Office."

5. Interview with Lawrence Ropka.

6. The group's 2 Detachment, based in Okinawa, handled the 1045's Far Eastern assignments.

7. Interview with David Clarke, 9 July 1995.

8. Interview with Jim Keck.

9. Interview with Lawrence Ropka.

10. Interview with Bui Van Tu, EUROPA team member, 17 March 1995; *Lich Su Co Yeu Bo Doi Bien Phong* [History of the Cryptology Branch of the Border Defense Troops (Draft)] (Hanoi: General Staff of the Border Defense Troops Headquarters, 1989), p. 41.

11. Nguyen Cao Ky notes that there was poor weather over North Vietnam during the night of the crash. To date, the wreckage of the C-54 has not been found. Interview with Nguyen Cao Ky, 5 May 1995; interview with David Clarke; interview with Lawrence Ropka.

12. The Laos mission, code-named NORTHERN STAR, began in January 1961 but was abruptly canceled the following month after a Chinese-piloted C-47 was shot down over northeastern Laos.

13. Interview with Ken Rockwell, Air America navigator, 22 September 1995.

14. Interview with Ngo The Linh.

15. Interview with Tran Viet Nghia, ATLAS team member, 20 November 1992.

16. Interview with Wayne Knight, one of the H-34 pilots, 25 October 1995.

17. Interview with Nguyen Huu Hong, ATLAS team member, 26 April 1996.

18. Just as the PLO was renamed the PSO, the 1st Observation Group was redesignated Group 77 because the former title was publicly exposed during the trial of the three VIAT aviators shot down in July. Group 77 took its number from the day and month—7 July—when President Diem took the reins of government in 1954.

19. Interview with Vong A Giong, radio operator, Team TOURBILLON (via Nguyen Van Vinh), 29 December 1995.

20. "Mat danh CASTOR bi giai ma," p. 32.

21. *Chien Si Bien Phong*, 2:124; *Chien Si Bien Phong*, 1:66.

22. Interview with Vuong Van Tang, team member, TOURBILLON, 18 February 1995.

23. Interview with Vong A Giong.

24. *Lich Su Bo Doi Bien Phong Thanh Hoa* [History of the Border Defense Soldiers in Thanh Hoa] (Hanoi: People's Public Security Publishing House, 1994), p. 57.

25. Interview with Pham Cong Thuong, team member, EROS, 18 February 1995.

26. According to North Vietnamese accounts, the three EROS agents in Laos were captured on 8 October 1962: *Lich Su Boi Doi Bien Phong Thanh Hoa*, p. 58. However, two of the commandos—Ha Cong Quan and Pham Cong Thuong—claim that they were not arrested until 12 June 1963. Prison release documents issued to these commandos corroborate the 1963 date. Interview with Pham Cong Thuong; interview with Ha Cong Quan (via Ha Van Son), 22 March 1995.

27. *Cong An Nhan Dan Viet Nam*, p. 202.

Chapter 5. VULCAN

1. *Dictionary of American Fighting Ships*, vol. 2 (Washington, D.C.: Office of the Chief of Naval Operations, 1963), pp. 54–55.

2. Twelve Swatows arrived in 1958, and another dozen came in 1959.

Because of frayed relations between Hanoi and Beijing at the time of the book's publication, the official Vietnamese naval history does not mention the nomenclature or origin of these vessels. See *Lich Su Hai Quan Nhan Dan Viet Nam* [History of the Vietnam People's Navy] (Hanoi: People's Army Publishing House, 1985), p. 56.

3. It is possible that a Swatow was used to intercept one of the CIA's motorized junks in January 1962 while resupplying ARES near Ha Long Bay. At that time, the North Vietnamese counted the Swatows and some forty small patrol boats in their naval order of battle. Because their official naval history is unclear on the matter, it is unknown which of these intercepted the junk.

4. Edward J. Marolda and Oscar P. Fitzgerald, *The United States Navy and the Vietnam Conflict: From Military Assistance to Combat, 1959–1965* (Washington, D.C.: U.S. Government Printing Office, 1986), pp. 202–203.

5. Ibid., p. 202.

6. Interview with Jack Mathews, 11 March 1996.

7. Interview with Tom Fosmire.

8. The contingent returned from Taiwan in December 1960. Those members hailing from the navy—totaling one officer and seven men—were used as cadre for the Lien Doi Ngoui Nhia (Frogman Unit), formally established in July 1961.

9. Interview with Hoang Cung, *Nautilus 2* crewman.

10. Robert Destatte interview with Le Van Kinh, 30 December 1996.

11. Ibid.

12. *Chien Si Bo Doi Bien Phong,* 1:381–382.

13. *Lich Su Hai Quan Nhan Dan Viet Nam,* p. 78.

14. Ibid.; also see *Chien Si Bo Doi Bien Phong,* 1:386–387; Destatte interview with Le Van Kinh.

15. Destatte interview with Le Van Kinh.

16. *Lich Su Hai Quan Nhan Dan Viet Nam,* p. 78.

17. "Facts and Figures Concerning U.S. and U.S. Agents' Sabotage Activities in North Vietnam," p. 47.

18. One year later, on 28 June 1963, communist agents set off two bombs hidden in bicycles placed outside the window of the CIA compound in Saigon. Two CIA officials were wounded, including Lou Conein, who was cut on his neck and back by flying shrapnel. Ten South Vietnamese passersby were killed—including five children playing soccer in the street—and another forty-six wounded. See *Le Journal d'Être Orient,* 1 July 1963.

Chapter 6. Bang and Burn

1. CIA report, "North Vietnamese Violations of Laos," 19 May 1964, DDRS 1976, no. 145D.

2. "Mat danh CASTOR bi giai ma," p. 32.

3. *Chien Si Bien Phong,* 1:395.

4. Ibid., p. 390.

5. Despite the radio messages, TARZAN had actually been captured the day after it was inserted. Correspondence with Nguyen Minh Hung, TARZAN team member, 23 November 1997.

6. Evan Thomas, *The Very Best Men* (New York: Simon and Schuster, 1995), p. 293.

7. Interview with Than Van Kinh, team member, PEGASUS, 6 September 1994.

8. The May team, code-named JASON, was composed of five ethnic Vietnamese. Prior to launch, they had been given the names and addresses of Lieutenant Colonel Linh's relatives living in Ha Tinh and Quang Binh Provinces. The team was captured before it could make any contact. Six years later, a reconnaissance team operating near Mimot, Cambodia, found a North Vietnamese film of JASON's mock trial. Interview with Ngo The Linh; interview with Nguyen Van Vinh; FBIS, Far East edition, 28 October 1963, p. JJJ2.

9. *Tay Bac, Lich Su Khang Chien Chong My, Cuu Nuoc,* p. 134; interview with Tien-tsung Chen, Chinese air force pilot, 27 February 1996.

10. Interview with Hoang Van Thai, team member, NIKE, 26 July 1995; interview with Pham Cong Hoan, team member, MIDAS, 27 July 1995; interview with Lang Van Duc, team member, MIDAS, 26 February 1995; interview with Nguyen Van Ngo, team member, TELLUS, 26 July 1995; interview with Bui Van An, team member, BART, 26 April 1996.

11. In April 1962, President Kennedy promised the Republic of China two C-123 transports for covert drops in mainland China. In September the number was increased to five, with the proviso that two be made available for operations in Vietnam. State Department background paper, "Visit of Chinese Minister of Defense Chiang Ching-kuo," September 1965, DDRS no. 2166-1998.

12. Flight log entries for Tien-tsung Chen. One C-123 crashed on Taiwan during training. Of the remaining four, only two were in Vietnam at any one time.

13. Interview with Tien-tsung Chen.

14. GIANT was captured soon after landing. For an account of the team's trial, see FBIS, Far East edition, 28 October 1963, p. JJJ1.

15. Interview with Ngo Quoc Chung, team member, PACKER, 27 February 1995.

16. Flight log entry of Tien-tsung Chen.

17. Interview with Tran Gia Loc.

18. There was a fresh spring in the area, and the team leader recalled that civilians frequently came to fill their pots there. The team was spotted and quickly captured. Interview with Moc A Tai, team leader, DRAGON (via Ha Van Son), 7 October 1995; *Chien Si Bien Phong,* 1:396–397.

19. Prior to June, two teams—BELL and TARZAN—were in radio contact. In mid-June, however, the North Vietnamese security service abruptly terminated radio play with TARZAN after Saigon unsuccessfully tried to re-supply the team. The TARZAN agents were not brought to trial until November 1964. Correspondence with Nguyen Minh Hung.

20. FBIS, Far East edition, 9 July 1963, p. JJJ16.

21. Interview with Nguyen Van Ngo, team member, TELLUS, 26 February 1995; FBIS, Far East edition, 19 September 1963, p. JJJ6.

22. Interview with Pham Quang Canh, team member, PACKER, 26 July 1995.

23. The team with the greatest longevity was PEGASUS, which managed to evade capture for eleven days. See *Viet Bac, 30 Nam Chien Tranh Cach Mang* [Viet Bac Military Region, 30 Years of Revolutionary War], vol. 2 (Hanoi: People's Army Publishing House, 1992), p. 71; interview with Than Van Kinh.

24. Members from eight different teams were executed during 1963. For mention of some of the death sentences, see FBIS, Far East edition, 5 December 1963, p. JJJ1, and 24 January 1964, p. JJJ7.

25. For anti-Catholic rhetoric, see *Van Kien Dang,* 4:212; "To Develop Revolutionary Vigor of the Masses and to Strengthen the Struggle Against Counter-Revolutionaries," Hanoi Domestic Service, as reported in FBIS, Far East edition, 9 December 1963, p. JJJ7.

26. *Lich Su Quan Chung Phong Khong,* 1:176.

27. Ibid., p. 177; interview with Tien-tsung Chen.

Chapter 7. Nasty Boats

1. "Facts and Figures Concerning U.S. and U.S. Agents' Sabotage Activities in North Vietnam," pp. 36–37.

2. Interview with Tom Fosmire.

3. The four action teams were code-named CANCER, CHARON, NEPTUNE, and ZEUS.

4. MDS, "MACSOG and the Strategic Technical Directorate: Inception, Organization, Evolution," p. B-86.

5. Marolda and Fitzgerald, *The United States Navy and the Vietnam Conflict*, pp. 91–93.

6. Ibid., p. 203.

7. Ibid.

8. Interview with William Hamilton, CIA maritime officer, 4 August 1994; MDS, "Maritime Operations," p. C-d-3.

9. Department of Defense News Release no. 671-63, 13 May 1963; *Washington Post*, 16 May 1963.

10. Marolda and Fitzgerald, *The United States Navy and the Vietnam Conflict*, p. 206.

11. Interview with William Colby.

12. Interview with William Hamilton.

13. For three years, these would be the only Swifts in South Vietnam. Not until 1965 did the U.S. Navy select the Swift as one of its coastal interdiction craft for use against communist seaborne resupply efforts. See Thomas J. Cutler, *Brown Water, Black Berets* (Annapolis: Naval Institute Press, 1988), pp. 85–86.

14. Interview with Truong Duy Tai, 9 October 1995.

15. Ibid.; interview with Ngo The Linh.

Chapter 8. Sacred Sword Patriot's League

1. Thomas, *The Very Best Men*, p. 356.

2. MDS, "Comments on MACSOG's Operations and Intelligence," interview with Lt. Col. Ernest T. Hayes Jr., SOG Plans Officer, p. B-n-48.

3. Ibid., interview with Col. John T. Moore Jr., p. B-n-30–B-n-32.

4. *NYT Pentagon Papers*, p 124.

5. A complete account of Vang Pao's military career is found in Kenneth Conboy and James Morrison, *Shadow War: The CIA's Secret War in Laos* (Boulder, Colo: Paladin Press, 1995).

6. A second South Vietnamese recruiting team, code-named BION, approached the North Vietnamese frontier on 23 October. Despite its claims, the CIA did not believe that BION actually crossed the border, and the team was subsequently disbanded.

7. *Cong An Nhan Dan Viet Nam*, p. 255; interview with Nguyen Huu Tan, 27 February 1995. Tan, a commando captured in 1967, was imprisoned with Vang Cha.

8. Brown, *The Secret War Report of the OSS*, p. 542.

9. Thomas, *The Very Best Men,* p. 72.

10. *Cong An Nhan Dan Viet Nam,* p. 256; MACSOG 1968 Command History, p. F-III-4-C-2.

11. MDS, "MACSOG and the Strategic Technical Directorate: Inception, Organization, Evolution," p. B-103.

12. MDS, "Comments on MACSOG's Operations and Intelligence," interview with Col. William R. Becker, Chief, SOG Air Operations, pp. B-n-10–B-n-11. Selective plausible deniability was not unique to the North Vietnam operation. For its Tibetan guerrilla operation, the CIA used British weapons and stateless Polish aircrews—as well as radios and aircraft of obvious U.S. origin.

13. Ibid., Moore interview, p. B-n-25.

14. MDS, "Operations Against North Vietnam," p. C-3.

15. Delmar Sefton, *Black Boomerang* (New York: Viking Press, 1962), p. 39; Brown, *The Secret War Report of the OSS,* pp. 537–538.

16. Interview with Herbert Weisshart, 15 May 1997.

17. Correspondence with Herbert Weisshart, 23 March 1997.

18. Ibid.

19. In 1963, the CIA already had one black radio station—Radio Red Flag—beaming into North Vietnam. Red Flag purported to be a dissident communist organization inside North Vietnam that was anti-Beijing and pro-Moscow. MDS, "Psychological Operations," p. C-a-36.

20. MACSOG ultimately wrote a detailed "history" of the SSPL, claiming it was composed of ex–Viet Minh, VNQDD, and Dai Viet members. The bogus history claimed that the SSPL was founded in April 1953, had staged an anti–land reform revolt in Nghe An Province, and promulgated its manifesto at a secret jungle base in December 1961. Ibid., pp. C-a-14–C-a-15.

21. Interview with Herbert Weisshart.

22. SWAN was captured during its third day on the ground. See *Cong An Nhan Dan,* p. 257, and *Viet Bac, 30 Nam Chien Tranh Cach Manh,* p. 71.

Chapter 9. Switchback

1. Colby, *Honorable Men,* p. 220.

2. Thomas, *The Very Best Men,* p. 187.

3. Interview with Ngo The Linh; Morrison interview with Robert Myers, 25 October 1996.

4. Interview with Robert Myers.

5. MDS, "MACSOG and the Strategic Technical Directorate: Inception, Organization, Evolution," p. B-108.

6. Interview with William Colby, 21 October 1995.

7. William Colby, *Lost Victory* (Chicago: Contemporary Books, 1989), p. 165.

8. John Newman, *JFK and Vietnam* (New York: Warner Books, 1992), p. 434.

9. MSD, "MACSOG and the Strategic Technical Directorate: Inception, Organization, Evolution," p. B-9.

10. Ibid., pp. B-10–B-11.

11. *Pentagon Papers,* Gravel edition, 3:150.

12. Interview with William Colby.

13. MDS, "Operations Against North Vietnam," p. C-2; *Pentagon Papers,* Gravel edition, 3:150.

14. In hindsight, it was learned that the benefits to operational security offered by the safe house arrangement were offset by the fact that trainees were not supervised at night, making the temptation to roam the streets of Saigon undoubtedly too great to bear. Moreover, repeated use of the same safe houses made it probable that communist agents had identified at least some of the sites.

15. Interview with Charles Gutensohn, 7 November 1995.

16. MDS, "Operations Against North Vietnam," p. C-3.

17. Marolda and Fitzgerald, *The United States Navy and the Vietnam Conflict,* pp. 336–337.

18. *FRUS,* Vietnam, 1961–1963, 4:734; *Pentagon Papers,* Gravel edition, 3:151; *NYT Pentagon Papers,* p. 273. Today McNamara denies his enthusiasm for the covert program. "Many of us who knew about the 34A operations had concluded they were essentially worthless," he wrote thirty years after the fact. While his statement is true in hindsight, McNamara is being less than candid about his views at the time. See Robert S. McNamara, *In Retrospect: The Tragedy and Lessons of Vietnam* (New York: Times Books, 1995), p. 130.

Chapter 10. New Management

1. *FRUS,* Vietnam, 1961–1963, 4:724.

2. *Pentagon Papers,* Gravel edition, 3:151, 153.

3. Ibid.

4. Ibid., p. 152.

5. MDS, "MACSOG and the Strategic Technical Directorate: Inception, Organization, Evolution," p. B-172.

6. Ibid., p. B-173.

7. Saigon message no. 3943, Ambassador Lodge to SecState and JCS, 21 January 1964, DDRS 1990.

8. MDS, "MACSOG and the Strategic Technical Directorate: Inception, Organization, Evolution," pp. B-173–B-174.

9. MACSOG 1964 Command History, p. A-1. Keeping the same initials, the Special Operations Group changed its name to the more ambiguous Studies and Observations Group during the second half of 1964.

10. MDS, "Operations Against North Vietnam," pp. C-5–C-9; "Military Pressures Against North Vietnam: Action and Debate—Jun 1964," *U.S.–Vietnam Relations, 1945–1967*, book 3 (Washington, D.C.: Government Printing Office, 1971), sec. IV.C.2a, p. ix.

11. The six agent teams included the singleton ARES from 1961, EUROPA, REMUS, and TOURBILLON from 1962, and BELL and EASY from 1963. CASTOR, the original airborne team, had inexplicably gone off the air in July 1963, supposedly while withdrawing overland toward Laos. EUROPA ended radio contact in January 1964 but was not stricken from the active rolls until year's end.

12. Morrison interview with Larry Jackson, one of the two CIA training officers at Long Thanh, 20 August 1996; Morrison interview with Ron Radda, the CIA case officer at Long Thanh, 5 October 1996.

13. *NYT Pentagon Papers*, p. 239.

14. MDS, "Operations Against North Vietnam," p. C-59.

15. MDS, "Comments on Command and Control," interview with Col. Clyde R. Russell, Commander, SOG, p. B-m-3.

16. William A. Buckingham Jr., *Operation Ranchhand* (Washington, D.C.: Office of Air Force History, 1982), p. 105.

17. MDS, "Comments on MACSOG's Operations and Intelligence," interview with Cmdr. Kenneth N. Bebb, Chief, Psyops Office, Special Operations, J-3, HQ PACOM, p. B-n-19. SOG was never given final clearance to launch these carrier-based mining operations.

18. Correspondence with Nguyen Van Cuong, member of the REMUS reinforcement team, 15 January 1995.

19. Interview with Nguyen Nhu Chuc, ATTILA team member, 28 April 1995.

20. *FRUS*, Vietnam, 1961–1964, 4:699–700; *NYT Pentagon Papers*, p. 276.

21. MDS, "Comments on MACSOG's Operations and Intelligence," interview with Col. Russell, pp. B-n-7–B-n-8.

22. Ibid., interview with Col. William R. Becker, Chief, MACSOG Air Operations, p. B-n-12. SOG's Air Operations Section was divided between Saigon and Nha Trang. The former was a staff function concerned with

formulating policy, while the latter was charged with conducting the actual operations.

23. MDS, "Airborne Operations," p. C-b-97.

24. MDS, "Comments on Command and Control," interview with Col. Russell, pp. B-m-3–B-m-4.

25. Tran Van Ho came from a military family: his older brother had commanded the Vietnamese air force, and a younger brother had been one of Lieutenant Colonel Tung's assistants in the Special Forces.

26. *Conduct of the War: A Study of Strategic Lessons Learned in Vietnam,* vol. 6, book 1 (Arlington, Va.: BDM Corporation, 1980), p. 8-37, n. 75.

27. MDS, "MACSOG and the Strategic Technical Directorate: Inception, Organization, Evolution," pp. B-237–B-238.

28. Ibid., pp. B-239–B-241.

29. MDS, "Summary of MACSOG Documentation Study," p. A-26.

30. MDS, "Comments on Personnel and Training," interview with Col. Becker, pp. B-q-10–B-q-11.

31. Interview with Tien-tsung Chen.

32. MDS, "MACSOG and the Strategic Technical Directorate: Inception, Organization, Evolution," p. B-174.

33. Interview with Tien-tsung Chen.

34. During that same month, the Chinese unknowingly escaped another antiaircraft trap near EAGLE, a team that had parachuted into Quang Ninh Province during June 1964. Twenty-six minutes from the drop zone, the C-123, filled with resupply pallets and a reinforcement team, aborted because of electronic countermeasures trouble. The team was lucky: the North Vietnamese had assigned three antiaircraft regiments to form a flak trap around the site. Entry in flight log of Tien-tsung Chen; *Quan Chung Phong Khong,* p. 17.

35. MDS, "Operations Against North Vietnam," p. C-12. SOG officers would later claim that they were forced to use drop zones previously selected by the CIA. See MDS, "Comments on MACSOG's Operations and Intelligence," interview with Colonel Becker, p. B-n-12. This excuse, however, rings hollow: CIA targeting could have easily been overridden, especially for sabotage teams whose mission was not necessarily wedded to a specific locale.

36. FBIS, Far East edition, 21 July 1964, p. JJJ18, and 3 August 1964, p. JJJ12; log entry by Tien-tsung Chen.

37. Details of the BUFFALO insertion can be found at the Vietnam News Agency, Hanoi, in the captions for photos of the Biet Kich team that parachuted on 19 June 1964. At ten men, BUFFALO was the largest airborne team to be inserted into North Vietnam.

38. Of the sixteen teams in training, only five were actually sent. Eleven teams—AURELIO, BEAR, *Renfort* BOUVIER, CATO, DAVID, *Renfort* EAGLE, ELM, LANCE, MARIUS, PHOQUE, and TWIN— were ultimately disbanded. See SOG financial records, "Avances aux agents partant en mission," entry 69-228, box 9, folder "SES Payroll— August."

39. For a breakdown of military and civilian members in the northern teams, see MACSOG Financial Records, July 1964, *Etat de Solde du Mois de Julliet [1964] Base de Long-Thanh*. Besides being given greater access to South Vietnamese army recruits, the SES had also been given control over BEAR, a team recruited by South Vietnam's Central Intelligence Organization (CIO). It had been the CIO's intention in 1963 to run a unilateral agent operation into North Vietnam outside the jurisdiction of the Special Branch. Following the creation of SOG, however, the CIO was ordered to halt any unilateral efforts and to remand the BEAR trainees to the SES. In the end, the BEAR agents experienced disciplinary problems in Long Thanh and were dropped from the program. Interview with Nguyen Van Vinh; SOG financial records, Memo from Capt. Nick to Lt. Col. Scharfen, 19 May 1965, subj: Corporal 1st Class Do Van Luc, agent from BOONE team, owed money to STS, box 9, folder STS.

40. Log entry by Tien-tsung Chen; MDS, "Comments on Personnel and Training," interview with Col. Edward V. Grossheusch, Chief, MACSOG Air Section, p. B-q-14.

41. Interview with James Hawes, a U.S. Navy SEAL adviser, 11 October 1996. On paper, SOG airborne operations were divided between the Saigon-based Airborne Operations Section, which was a staff function tasked with formulating policy and plans, and the Airborne Operations Group, which conducted the actual operations from Long Thanh. Because of the close physical proximity of Saigon and Long Thanh, the same officer held command of both the section and the group.

42. MDS, "Comments on MACSOG's Mission," interview with Capt. Bruce B. Dunning, U.S. Navy Special Operations Division, SACSA, p. B-i-9.

43. During recovery efforts on Monkey Mountain, a Vietnamese air force team took custody of the first seven bodies, listed them as the deceased aircrew, and buried the remains. Later investigation showed that one of these bodies was actually that of Sergeant Sansone, but Vietnamese officials refused to exhume it for positive identification. Not until the mid-1980s was the grave opened and Sansone's bones returned to the United States.

44. MDS, "Operations Against North Vietnam," p. C-60.

Chapter 11. Sea Commandos

1. On paper, SOG maritime operations were coordinated by the NAD at Danang, which was charged with the actual conduct of operations, and a Maritime Operations Section in Saigon, which was formed as a staff function within the SOG headquarters.

2. Steve Edwards, "Stalking the Enemy's Coast," *US. Naval Institute Proceedings*, February 1992, p. 58.

3. For a detailed account see Anthony J. Murray, "Our Covert Commandos: Why Are They Still in Vietnam?" *Chicago Reader*, 25 May 1984, pp. 17–28.

4. On 18 July, three of the NEPTUNE frogmen were sentenced. The fourth, Gioi, had been shot dead during capture. Guong and Ly, who were captured after one week on the run, received seven and eighteen years, respectively. Nhu, the team leader, was to spend life in prison; his brazen tattoo probably did not help his case. See FBIS, East Asia edition, 22 July 1964, p. JJJ2.

5. "Cancer Team Briefing and Operation," written by Lieutenant L. V. Bearce, Naval Advisory Detachment (courtesy of Ray Stubbe).

6. Xuong and Cau were captured four days later. Interview with Chau Henh Xuong, 21 April 1995.

7. One of the swimmers was killed, and the other, Truong Van Le, was captured. Details and photos of the mission are found in the Vietnam News Agency, Photograph Division, "Photos of Biet Kich attack, 0010 hours, 17 March 1964."

8. Marolda and Fitzgerald, *The United States Navy and the Vietnam Conflict*, p. 341.

9. Ibid., p. 397.

10. Ibid., p. 341.

11. *NYT Pentagon Papers*, p. 276; *FRUS*, 1964, Vietnam, 1:152, 154.

12. Besides the four new action teams raised by SOG, there were the four teams inherited from the CIA: CANCER, CHARON, NEPTUNE, and ZEUS. During the first half of 1964, SOG rearranged some of these ex-CIA agents in a confusing round of redesignations. By late summer CHARON and ZEUS were amalgamated into a single team code-named CUMULUS; Team CANCER was retained intact in the SOG order of battle; and the scuba-qualified Team NEPTUNE, which lost four swimmers in March, remained inactive through the spring of 1965 before being officially dissolved.

13. Interview with Truong Duy Tai.

14. MDS, "Comments on Personnel and Training," interview with Cmdr. Kenneth N. Bebb, p. B-q-26.

15. MACSOG 1964 Command History, p. IV-13.

16. Edwards, "Stalking the Enemy's Coast," p. 57.

17. Marolda and Fitzgerald, *The United States Navy and the Vietnam Conflict,* pp. 335–337.

18. MDS, "Maritime Operations," p. C-d-24.

19. On 26 April, the two gassers returned to Danang with improved fuel tanks. Because their sailors had not been trained by the U.S. Navy's MTT at Subic and the German skippers had already departed, neither boat was destined to see much action. That same month, the first two all-Vietnamese Nasty crews graduated from Subic and arrived in Danang. They initially used the first two Nastys, PTFs 3 and 4, which were on hand by late April for sea trials. On 14 May, two more boats, PTFs 5 and 6, arrived, enabling the original two Nastys to return to Subic the next day for fuel tank improvements. See MACSOG 1964 Command History, pp. IV-11, IV-14.

20. Interview with David Elliott, 21 March 1997.

21. Msg, COMUSMACV to CINCPAC, subj: PTF Lease, 29 May 1964; MDS, "Maritime Operations," pp. C-d-3, C-d-81, C-d-82. The Nastys were not officially transferred to the South Vietnamese until October 1964, partly because MACV felt that "in the event of a coup the PTFs [are] more likely to remain in a relatively neutral status" if they remained under U.S. ownership.

22. MDS, "MACSOG and the Strategic Technical Directorate: Inception, Organization, Evolution," p. B-405.

23. Msg, COMUSMACV to White House, 4 June 1964, p. 5.

24. MDS, "Operations Against North Vietnam," p. C-38.

25. Ibid., p. C-43. According to North Vietnamese accounts, the bridge was destroyed. *Lich Su Hai Quan Nhan Dan Viet Nam,* p. 89.

26. *Lich Su Bo Doi Bien Phong,* 1:80; *Chien Si Bien Phong,* 1:418.

27. One of the abandoned commandos, Vu Van Sac, was captured alive; the other, Nguyen Van Hoc, was killed in action. See Vietnam News Agency, Photograph Division, "Photos of Biet Kich attack at 0030 hours, 1 July 1964"; correspondence with Tran Thi Trung (widow of Nguyen Van Hoc), dated 20 July 1996.

28. The two missing commandos, Phan Trac Cuong and Do Minh Huy, were killed in action. See MACSOG Financial Records, "Listing of Personnel KIA or MIA for 1 April 1964 through 31 April 1965," folder Pacific, May 1965.

Chapter 12. Tonkin Gulf

1. Marolda and Fitzgerald, *The United States Navy and the Vietnam Conflict*, p. 407; MACSOG Financial Records, FY 65, TS 858, NND 964961, Entry 69-228, Box 1, Folder 11, "Payments for LOKI 3, 25 July 1964."
2. MDS, "Comments on SOG Mission," interview with Col. Russell, p. B-i-2.
3. Marolda and Fitzgerlad, *The United States Navy and the Vietnam Conflict*, p. 407.
4. MDS, "Comments on SOG Mission," interview with Col. Russell, p. B-i-2. Marolda and Fitzgerald, *The United States Navy and the Vietnam Conflict*, pp. 408–409.
5. MACSOG 1964 Command History, pp. IV-2–IV-4.
6. Hanoi's official account of the incident fails to mention any Swatow near Hon Me. See *Lich Su Hai Quan Nhan Dan Viet Nam*, p. 92.
7. Interview with James Hawes, 31 March 1996.
8. Marolda and Fitzgerald, *The United States Navy and the Vietnam Conflict*, p. 402.
9. Ibid., pp. 400, 404.
10. Edwards, "Stalking the Enemy's Coast," p. 60.
11. Marolda and Fitzgerald, *The United States Navy and the Vietnam Conflict*, p. 415.
12. Nearly all historians now believe that the second Tonkin Gulf attack never took place, and was probably just a case of nervous jitters by radar and sonar operators. For complete accounts of the two incidents, see Marolda and Fitzgerald, *The United States Navy and the Vietnam Conflict;* and Edwin Moise, *Tonkin Gulf and the Escalation of the Vietnam War* (Chapel Hill: University of North Carolina Press, 1996).
13. Interview with James Hawes; MACSOG 1964 Command History, p. IV-4.
14. George C. Herring, ed., *The Secret Diplomacy of the Vietnam War: The Negotiating Volumes of the Pentagon Papers* (Austin: University of Texas Press, 1983), p. 18.
15. *FRUS*, 1964, Vietnam, 1:598.
16. Ibid., p. 611; *The U.S. Government and the Vietnam War: Executive and Legislative Roles and Relationships*, pt. 2, 1961–1964 (Washington, D.C.: U.S. Government Printing Office, 1984), p. 287; Marolda and Fitzgerald, *The United States Navy and the Vietnam Conflict*, p. 425.
17. Marolda and Fitzgerald, *The United States Navy and the Vietnam Conflict*, p. 646.
18. McNamara, *In Retrospect*, pp. 136–137.

19. Ibid.
20. *NYT Pentagon Papers,* p. 267.

Chapter 13. Maritime Operations

1. *FRUS,* 1964, Vietnam, 1:646.
2. Ibid., p. 603.
3. Ibid., p. 646.
4. In the end, the last two were dropped, the T-14 (nicknamed *cochon*—French for "pig"—by CSS officers) because of spare part shortages, and the 106mm recoilless rifle because its fierce backblast could damage the Nastys. Interview with Ngo The Linh; MACSOG 1964 Command History, pp. IV-4, IV-19.
5. Dept. of Defense report, subj: Summary of Rolling Thunder operations through 31 March 1965, undated, DDRS 1988–1548.
6. MDS, "Maritime Operations," p. C-d-11.
7. The sole scuba-qualified team, NEPTUNE, was officially disbanded in the spring of 1965.
8. *NYT Pentagon Papers,* p. 301.
9. Initially, it was planned for the Nationalist Chinese to transfer from the Swifts to the Nastys. But after the South Vietnamese Navy crews proved sufficiently competent on the Nastys—and the Chinese showed less seafaring skill than originally thought—they remained on the Swifts for the duration of their tour. Interview with Truong Duy Tai.
10. MDS, "Maritime Operations," p. C-d-11.
11. Ibid., pp. C-d-38, C-d-42.
12. MDS, "Psychological Operations," p. C-a-160.
13. Vietnam News Agency, Photograph Department, photos and captions for "Biet Kich captured on night of 24 February 1966, Vinh Linh"; interview with Nguyen Van Vu, one of the two captured ATHENA swimmers, 26 February 1995. After this incident, ATHENA was disbanded and its members divided among the other Biet Hai teams.
14. *Chien Si Bien Phong,* 2:111–112.
15. Caught in swift currents and shifting tides, the four CANCER swimmers were carried far off target. Two were quickly spotted at sea and captured. The other pair made it to the mainland and were apprehended several days later. Interview with Duong Long Sang, one of the four CANCER combat swimmers, 7 September 1994; *Chien Si Bien Phong,* 2:111–112.
16. Interview with Bernard Trainor.
17. In their zeal to counter the Nastys, the North Vietnamese sometimes

hit the wrong target. On 17 March 1966, their navy attacked a commercial vessel off Quang Binh Province belonging to the Singaporean-based Hottuat Trading Company. The boat was sunk, and thirteen Chinese, Indonesian, and Singaporean crewmen were thrown in prison.

18. *Phao Binh Nhan Dan Viet Nam: Nhung Chang Duong Chien Dau* [People's Army of Vietnam Artillery Command: The Periods of Combat], vol. 2 (Hanoi: People's Army Publishing House, 1986), p. 184.

19. MDS, "Maritime Operations," p. C-d-67.

20. Later in 1966, the U.S. Navy sank a Swatow in the Tonkin Gulf and captured its commanding officer. During the prisoner's subsequent interrogation, the NAD forwarded a series of questions, among them why the North Vietnamese had decided to use a biplane to attack the Nastys. According to the officer, Hanoi had studied the U.S. reaction to the August 1964 Tonkin Gulf episode, especially the attempt by U.S. jets to sink North Vietnamese gunboats at sea. That attempt had been less than successful, leading Hanoi to conclude that jets were not an effective means of attacking boats. By contrast, it felt that a slow-moving An-2 could match the speed of a Nasty and successfully bomb it. Interview with Bernard Trainor.

21. Ibid.; MDS, "Maritime Operations," p. C-d-47.

22. Interview with Hiep Hoa Trinh, 9 July 1996.

23. Interview with Bach Van Dong, a Biet Hai commando who was on the operation, 7 June 1996.

24. Interview with Truong Duy Tai.

25. In the official account of the incident (which incorrectly gives the date as April 1966 rather than May), Hanoi erroneously claims its artillery destroyed all three boats. See *Phao Binh Nhan Dan Viet Nam,* 2:190–191. Reconnaissance photos taken after the bombing showed North Vietnamese soldiers crawling on the wreckage. Interview with Bernard Trainor.

26. Interview with Ho Van Ky Thoai, 22 February 1995; interview with Truong Duy Tai. Again, Hanoi erroneously claims that its shore-based guns sank the ship. See *Phao Binh Nhan Dan Viet Nam,* 2:189.

27. MSD, "Maritime Operations," chart CD-4, p. C-d-41; MACSOG 1966 Command History, p. 32.

Chapter 14. Frustration Syndrome

1. Beginning in 1962, the CIA had overflown Lao territory during the insertion of some of its long-term agent teams. Officially, however, it was not until 24 May 1964 that all restrictions on overflights of Laos were lifted. See MDS, "Airborne Operations," p. C-b-91.

2. Correspondence with Nguyen Van Luc, one of the commandos trained on the rockets, 31 January 1997.

3. Nguyen Van Vinh, who took over as the South Vietnamese case officer for REMUS in May 1965, clearly remembers the reconnaissance photos of the Dien Bien Phu airfield in the team's file history. Interview with Nguyen Van Vinh.

4. MDS, "Operations Against North Vietnam," p. C-15.

5. Besides the four commandos for REMUS, the other three teams included four agents (Team ALTAR) reinforcing REMUS on 22 October; seven men (Team GRECO) parachuted to BELL on 14 November; and six reinforcements for TOURBILLON on 19 December. All four insertions at the time appeared to be successful.

6. MDS, "Operations Against North Vietnam," p. C-15.

7. MDS, "Comments on Command and Control," interview with Capt. Dunning, p. B-m-23; MDS, "Comments on MACSOG's Mission," interview with Capt. Dunning, p. B-i-7.

8. MDS, "Operations Against North Vietnam," p. C-19; "Analysis of Military Effort in South Vietnam," Annex E—Special Operations, undated, p. 2.

9. MDS, "Airborne Operations," p. C-b-96.

10. MDS, "Comments on MACSOG's Operations and Intelligence," interview with Col. Donald D. Blackburn, Chief of SOG, June 1965–May 1966, p. B-n-22.

11. MDS, "Comments on MACSOG's Operations and Intelligence," interview with Col. Russell, p. B-n-5.

12. MDS, "Operations Against North Vietnam," p. C-9.

13. MDS, "Comments on MACSOG's Operations and Intelligence," interview with Col. Robert C. McLane, Chief, SOG Airborne Operations, May 1966–May 1967, p. B-n-50.

14. Ibid., interview with Lt. Col. David H. Arno, Staff Officer, SOG Air Operations, January 1964–March 1964, pp. B-n-13–B-n-18.

15. Ibid., interview with Col. John K. Singlaub, Chief of SOG, May 1966–August 1968, p. B-n-57.

16. Ibid., interview with Col. John T. Moore, Deputy Chief, SOG Operations Branch, June 1965–June 1966, pp. B-n-32–B-n-33.

17. Ibid., interview with Col. Singlaub, pp. B-n-54–B-n-57. In hindsight, Singlaub cast doubt on the ability to raise an effective resistance: "The problem with 34A was that it was a victim of earlier U.S. policy that emphasized compassion over intelligence. In 1954, we announced that we would lift out anybody that wanted to go south. The Catholics sent out the word that no good Catholic would live under communism, and the exodus

began. In effect, while acting under a humanitarian label, we purified North Vietnamese society for their security services. There was no framework that was left behind that 34A could build on. Nobody that wanted to remain behind dared cooperate with us, because they knew there would be retribution." Interview with John Singlaub, 27 February 1997.

18. MDS, "Psychological Operations," p. C-a-9.

19. MDS, "Comments on MACSOG's Operations and Intelligence," interview with Col. Singlaub, pp. B-n-54–B-n-57; interview with Col. Blackburn, pp. B-n-22–B-n-23.

20. Information on Blackburn's front concept comes from interview with Larry Trapp, Chief, Airborne Operations Section (SHINING BRASS), 9 June 1997. A copy of the concept is found in MDS, "Psychological Operations," pp. C-a-137–C-a-149.

21. Ibid.; interview with Donald Blackburn, 2 May 1997.

22. EASY was an odd exception to the resistance prohibition. During the second half of 1964, a dozen more agents parachuted into North Vietnam to reinforce EASY, joining five others who had been dropped in May. One of the agents allegedly died of sickness in 1965, leaving the team with a total of thirty commandos.

23. MDS, "Comments on MACSOG's Operations and Intelligence," interview with Col. Russell, pp. B-n-4–B-n-8.

24. Raymond Muelle and Eric Deroo, *Services Speciaux* (Paris: Editions Crepin-Leblond, 1992), p. 38.

25. MDS, "Comments on MACSOG's Operations and Intelligence," interview with Col. Blackburn, p. B-n-23.

26. Ibid., interview with Col. Russell, pp. B-n-5–B-n-6. For Lodge's approval, see ibid., interview with Col. Blackburn, p. B-n-23.

27. Ibid., interview with Col. Blackburn, p. B-n-23; MDS, "Psychological Operations," p. C-a-11. Blackburn claims CINCPAC opposed his scheme because he misunderstood the front concept and thought it was tied to the Saigon government.

28. For Blackburn's views on Sullivan's opposition, see *Conduct of the War: A Study of Strategic Lessons Learned in Vietnam,* vol. 6, book 1, pp. 8-21–8-24. For Sullivan's statement, see Department of State telegram, CIA to SecState, 15 July 1965, DDRS 1986-2773. In this message, Sullivan says operations into territory controlled by North Vietnam are "beyond our capability and of questionable desirability at this time." He then took a swipe at SOG-type agent operations: "It is no longer necessary to conduct ground operations . . . such as to interdict Route 7 in North Vietnam" because it is "being accomplished in effect by Rolling Thunder."

29. For opposition from Sullivan and the CIA, see MDS, "Psychological

Operations," p. C-a- 9. Douglas Blaufarb, the CIA station chief in Laos during 1964–65, does not remember any concrete SOG proposal making its way to Vientiane for comment. Had one come, Blaufarb says that both he and Ambassador Sullivan would have strongly objected. Correspondence with Douglas Blaufard, 9 December 1995.

30. Interview with Brig. Gen. Donald D. Blackburn, March 1983, Senior Officers Oral History Program, pp. 340–342.

31. Ilya V. Gaiduk, *The Soviet Union and the Vietnam War* (New York: Ivan R. Dee, 1996), p. 59. On 24 July, the first surface-to-air missiles were fired at U.S. planes, downing one of four F-4Cs on their way to a target northwest of Hanoi.

32. MDS, "Operations Against North Vietnam," pp. C-17, C-19, C-44; MACSOG 1965 Command History, p. IIA-1.

33. MACSOG 1965 Command History, p. IIA-2.

34. MDS, "Comments on MACSOG's Operations and Intelligence," interview with Col. Singlaub, p. B-n-55.

35. Ibid., interview with Col. Robert C. Kendrick, Chief, Special Operations Branch, Office of the Asst. Chief of Staff for Operations, (J-3) Hq. PACOM, December 1966–July 1969, p. B-n-105.

36. Ibid., interview with Col. Robert C. McLane, Chief, Airborne Operations Section, June 1966–May 1967, pp. B-n-50–B-n-52.

37. Ibid., interview with Col. Singlaub, p. B-n-57.

38. Interview with Nguyen Van Hanh, ROMEO radio operator, 3 November 1996.

39. MDS, "Airborne Operations," p. C-b-3.

40. MACSOG 1964 Command History, p. II-I-1.

41. Interview with Nguyen Quy An, a South Vietnamese air force H-34 pilot who flew SHINING BRASS missions, 28 March 1995.

42. Interview with Nguyen Van Hanh, 18 September 1994; interview with Nguyen Quy An. The other two choppers were piloted by Ho Bao Dinh (Spider) and Tran Van Luan (Cowboy).

Chapter 15. Premonitions

1. MACSOG 1966 Command History, pp. 59, 63.

2. MDS, "Operations Against North Vietnam," p. C-19.

3. Ibid., p. C-18.

4. MDS, "Comments on MACSOG's Operations and Intelligence," interview with Col. Robert C. MacLane, Chief, SOG Airborne Operations Section, May 1966–May 1967, p. B-n-51.

5. MDS, "Airborne Operations," p. C-b-93.

6. Interview with La Van Hoang, EAGLE team member, 26 July 1995.

7. The declassified version of the document has the pilots' nationality deleted, but it obviously refers to the Chinese. MDS, "Comments on Personnel and Training," interview with Col. Leroy V. Grossheusch, Chief, SOG Air Section, July 1964–July 1965, p. B-q-15.

8. MDS, "Airborne Operations," p. C-b-93.

9. MDS, "Comments on Personnel and Training," interview with Col. Grossheusch, pp. B-q-13–B-q-16.

10. Ray L. Bowers, *Tactical Airlift* (Washington, D.C.: Office of Air Force History, 1983), p. 430.

11. MDS, "Comments on MACSOG's Operations and Intelligence," interview with Col. John T. Moore, Dep. Chief, SOG Operations Branch, June 1965–June 1966, p. B-n-26.

12. If downed, the SOG C-130 crews would claim that they were transporting troops to a forward base in South Vietnam and got lost. Ibid., pp. B-n-26–B-n-28.

13. To set a precedent for MC-130 operations over North Vietnam, USAF C-123 crews assigned to SOG performed two leaflet drops over the north during the summer of 1966. Interview with Owen Hitchings, C-123 aircraft commander, 6 December 1995; interview with Tom Stiles, MC-130 navigator, 2 December 1996.

14. Interview with Leon Franklin, MC-130 aircraft commander, 20 June 1996.

15. MACSOG 1965 Command History, p. II-C-11.

16. For a history of the 20th Helicopter Squadron, see Project CHECO report, *The USAF Helicopter in Southeast Asia,* 4 December 1968.

17. Future EWOT plans called for teams to get a third increment of agents to provide them with a limited strike capability. See MDS, "Airborne Operations," p. C-b-4.

18. All ten Op 34A teams training at Long Thanh in 1966 were composed in whole or in part by lowland Vietnamese. Ibid., p. C-b-25.

19. Interview with Dang Dinh Thuy, team leader of HECTOR B, 11 February 1995.

20. Interview with La Van Tinh, SAMSON team member, 11 April 1995.

21. Interview with Nguyen The Khoa, HADLEY team member, 11 April 1995.

22. MACSOG 1968 Command History, p. F-III-4-C-3.

23. CIA Intelligence Memorandum, subj: Pathet Lao prison in Khammouane Province, 6 September 1967, U.S. Defense Intelligence Agency's

"Uncorrelated Documents on POW/MIAs in Southeast Asia," vol. 13. p. 483.

24. That VOI was unable to make even a single radio transmission hints it was engaged almost immediately upon landing. Only two of the four agents, Bach Moui and Hoang The Bao, were later seen in a Hanoi prison, suggesting the team suffered fatalities during capture. Both agents died in captivity before they could describe the circumstances of their arrest to fellow Op 34A prisoners. Interview with Nguyen Huu Tan, RED DRAGON team member, 11 April 1995.

Chapter 16. Suspicious Minds

1. Interview with Aaron Dorough, 15 July 1994

2. MDS, "Airborne Operations," p. C-b-65. ROMEO, in fact, had been captured in January 1966 and forced to transmit under duress. Interview with Nguyen Van Hanh, ROMEO radio operator.

3. In 1961, the CIA suspected—correctly, in retrospect—that two teams, DIDO and ECHO, were doubled and forced to transmit under hostile control. In both cases, the teams soon went silent, and their fates were unknown at the time. In 1962, another team, EROS, was incorrectly suspected of being doubled. The EROS agents were ultimately captured and publicly exposed by Hanoi in November 1964. Not until ROMEO's October 1966 message did SOG have irrefutable evidence that an agent transmission was coerced.

4. In June 1967, SOG toyed with a plan to forcibly exfiltrate ROMEO. CINCPAC vetoed the hazardous proposal. See MDS, "Airborne Operations," p. C-b-94. Continuing radio play, SOG in the summer of 1968 ordered ROMEO to conduct a reconnaissance foray into a heavily forested area where little or no intelligence information could be gathered. Perhaps realizing the game was up, the North Vietnamese security services ceased further transmissions from ROMEO on 5 August. See MACSOG 1968 Command History, p. F-III-4-C-4.

5. KERN was captured in May and transmitted under duress for four months before the North Vietnamese decided to terminate contact. SOG never suspected that the team was turned. See *Chien Si Bien Phong*, 2:136 for Hanoi's account of KERN's capture.

6. SAMSON infiltrated near Dien Bien Phu in October 1966. The team managed to avoid capture for two months but had come into contact with North Vietnamese security forces on 2 December after receiving an aerial resupply. Three were killed in the ensuing firefight. The team never transmitted under duress. Interview with La Van Tinh.

7. For the HECTOR spy trial, see FBIS, Asia and Pacific edition, 26 June 1967, p JJJ1. HECTOR A was captured soon after infiltration in June 1966. As a result, when HECTOR B inserted in September, North Vietnamese security forces waiting in ambush attacked the team fifteen minutes after the helicopters departed the landing zone. The team members fled in all directions. Four of them were able to evade into the Lao border, only to be captured on 8 October. Interview with Dang Dinh Thuy.

8. MDS, "Airborne Operations," p. C-b-19.

9. SOG Financial Records, Memo from Capt. NICK to LTC McCune, Chief, SOG logistics, 15 Nov 66, box 6, folder STS Accounting 1–30 Nov 66; James Morrison interview with George Lawton, 1 April 1993; MDS, "Airborne Operations," p. C-b-92.

10. MDS, "Airborne Operations," p. C-b-63.

11. Because TOURBILLON had long been turned, North Vietnamese security forces were able to easily apprehend VERSE at the drop zone. VERSE's doubled radioman later told Saigon two members were killed on the jump and TOURBILLON had transferred some of its members to flesh out the depleted reinforcement team.

12. VERSE's excuse: an RF-101 downed over Moc Chau district on 21 June had resulted in an influx of North Vietnamese troops that made exfiltration too risky.

13. FBIS, Asia and Pacific edition, 29 August 67, p. JJJ6.

14. Information on BELL's capture from interview with Lu The Toan, BELL team member, 22 December 1995 (via Nguyen Van Anh).

15. *Phong Khong Khong Quan, Ky Su* [Air and Air Defense Forces, Memoir], vol. 1 (Hanoi People's Army Publishing House, 1978), pp. 44–60.

16. By 1965, it was standard practice for teams to receive final word of an impending resupply from one to three hours in advance of the drop. See MDS, "Airborne Operations," p. C-b-34.

17. "25 Nam Chien Dau Va Truong Thanh Cua Bo Doi Ra-Da Trinh Sat Tren Khong" ["25 Years of Combat and Development of the Air Surveillance Radar Troops"], *Chien Si Phong Khong* [Air Defense Soldier Magazine], Hanoi, 1984, pp. 22–23.

18. "Gap Nhung Phi Cong Trong Tran Khong Chien 30 Nam Truoc" ["A Conversation with Pilots from an Air Battle 30 Years in the Past"], *Hang Khong Viet Nam* [Vietnam Aviation Magazine], July 1995, pp. 13–14.

19. Hanoi continued to insist the SOG C-123 was shot down, even after knowing otherwise from the interrogation of subsequent Op 34A teams. See *Vietnam Courier*, November 1984, p. 23.

20. Interview with Tien-tsung Chen; interview with Chuang-wen Yu, commander, 34th Squadron, Chinese Air Force, 28 November 1996.

21. Correspondence with Deo Van Kien.

22. SOG Financial Records, Travel Allowances, 25 May 1965, box 6, folder STS June 1965.

23. MDS, "Airborne Operations," p. C-b-93.

24. Interview with Austin Wilgus, 27 June 1995.

25. A brief account of the operation is found on "Citation for Award of Air Medal to Alton R. Deviney."

26. For an account of the BELL spy trial, see FBIS, Asia and Pacific edition, 3 July 67, p. JJJ2.

Chapter 17. STRATA

1. MDS, "Counterpart Relationships," p. B-t-5. Beginning in 1967, SOG added several new code names to already existing operations. FOOT-BOY became the overall name for secret missions into North Vietnam; within that was TIMBERWORK—long-term agent teams; PLOWMAN—maritime operations (it was changed to PARBOIL in 1970); HUMIDOR—psychological operations; and FORAE—diversionary operations.

2. Interview with Xuan Le, one of the original SAAT members, 10 July 1995.

3. From 1965 until 1968, SOG's twelve-man reconnaissance units used in Laos were officially known as Spike Teams.

4. The 1966 Command History lists bad weather as the reason for the delay, but according to another account, SOG needed Washington's approval to send in the rescue team because it included Americans. George J. Veith, *Codename Bright Light: The Untold Story of U.S. POW Rescue Efforts During the Vietnam War* (New York: Free Press, 1998), p. 110.

5. Interview with Richard Meadows, 22 November 1994.

6. MACSOG 1966 Command History, pp. 105–106.

7. Interview with Charles Kerns, 7 December 1994.

8. Morrison interview with Frank Jaks, 24 April 1994.

9. Msg, COMUSMACV to CINCPAC, subj: Bright Light Report, 14 December 1966.

10. According to the MACSOG 1966 Command History, p. 103, a total of six SAAT teams were operational by year's end, with another four awaiting training. Only four SAAT teams, numbered 111 through 114, were ever operational. Interview with Xuan Le; interview with Nguyen Van Huan, SAAT member, 17 February 1993; interview with Ngo Phong Hai, SAAT member, 26 November 1992.

11. The Joint Chiefs proposed "PRAIRIE FIRE–type operations into

North Vietnam to a depth of [24 kilometers] designed to locate North Vietnamese installations and facilities for attacks by tactical aircraft." See JCS Study, subj: Alternate Courses of Action for Southeast Asia, Annex A, Part III: Military Actions Outside South Vietnam, 22 May 1967.

12. Interview with Austin Wilgus, 18 October 1995; correspondence with Thien Van Bui, STRATA 111 team leader, 16 March 1992.

13. Interview with Ngo Phong Hai, STRATA 112 member, 26 November 1992; interview with Nguyen Van Huan, STRATA 112 member, 17 February 1993.

14. SOG took great pains to make sure the captured uniforms used by STRATA were authentic. Remembers Wilgus: "[SOG Chief] Singlaub even asked me if the buttons were the same as those used by North Vietnamese troops moving down the Ho Chi Minh Trail." Interview with Austin Wilgus.

15. U.S. military maps designated Route 101 as a feeder road that merges with Route 15; North Vietnamese maps made no such distinction and used the designation Route 15 in reference to the entire length.

16. Correspondence with Alton Deviney, 21 October 1992.

17. MDS, "Airborne Operations," p. C-b-67.

18. Correspondence with James Villotti, 1 October 1992.

19. Ltr, General Westmoreland to Commander, 7th Air Force, dated 5 November 1967.

20. Interview with Ngo Phong Hai.

21. *Chien Si Bien Phong,* 2:155–156.

22. Interview with Ngo Phong Hai.

23. Interview with Victor Calderon, 11 June 1992.

Chapter 18. RED DRAGON

1. On the last of these forays in March 1953, three Caucasian advisers, believed hired by the CIA and attached to Republic of China guerrilla forces, were killed in Burma. See *Far Eastern Economic Review,* 16 September 1993, p. 56.

2. Department of State message from U.S. Embassy (Taipei) to Secretary of State, 10 September 1958, DDRS 1992-1442.

3. Ibid.

4. Interview with Jack Shirley, CIA case officer for the team, September 1995.

5. Airborne insertions peaked in the summer of 1963 before dropping off almost entirely. According to Beijing, nine groups of Chinese agents parachuted

onto the mainland between July and October 1963. See Vietnam News Agency broadcast in FBIS, East Asia edition, 14 November 1963.

6. Jay Miller, *Lockheed's Skunk Works* (Arlington, Tex: Aerofax, 1993), p. 58. The last RB-69 to be downed had been outfitted with Sidewinder missiles to protect itself against MiG fighters. Wreckage photographed by the Chinese media showed the missiles still affixed to the wings.

7. *Chien Si Bien Phong,* 1:286, 397. Eleven surviving Chinese commandos were eventually released in 1988; of them, half resettled in Hong Kong, and the remainder returned to Taiwan. Interview with Ha Van Son, a SOG commando who was held prisoner with the Chinese, 27 November 1992.

8. *Chien Si Bien Phong,* 1:377.

9. Interview with Ngo The Linh.

10. Eclipsed by the expanding Vietnam War, Father Hoa in April 1965 asked for U.S. support in recruiting up to three thousand Hong Kong Chinese and bringing them to South Vietnam to fight under U.S. control. The U.S. embassy rejected his proposal. See U.S. embassy (Saigon) Memo of Conversation, 23 April 1965, DDRS 1988-1646.

11. CIA report, 24 June 1965, DDRS 1987-1310.

12. CIA report, 8 September 1965, DDRS 1987-1318.

13. Interview with Ngo The Linh; CIA report, 22 September 1965, DDRS 1987-1321.

14. CIA report, 6 October 1965, DDRS 1995-1824.

15. "The understanding of the people living in border areas was still poor . . . and there [were] still a great deal of Chinese spies." See *Resolution of the Second Conference of the Border Defense Police* (Hanoi, 1955), p. 17.

16. State Dept. Report, subj: Compilation of Statements of Support for U.S. Policy in Vietnam by Asian Leaders, 31 August 1967, p. 11, DDRS 2103-1997.

17. White House memorandum from George Ball to President Johnson, subj: Meeting with Defense Minister Chiang Ching-kuo, 21 September 1965, DDRS 1996-3249.

18. White House background paper, subj: Visit of Chinese Minister of Defense Chiang Ching-kuo, 17 September 1965, DDRS 1996-3252.

19. MACSOG 1968 Command History, p. F-III-4-C-3.

20. For notification of the Secretary of Defense, see Memo, Chairman of the JCS to SecDef, subj: CHINAT Agents for Oplan 34A Teams, 10 November 1966, as noted in MDS, "Airborne Operations," p. C-b-5 (footnote).

21. MACSOG Financial Records, "STS Accounting, 1–28 Feb 67," Entry 69-227, Box 9; "SOG Finance Records FY 68, 130 September 1967," Entry 69-A-205, Box 3.

22. Correspondence with Nguyen Thai Kien, RED DRAGON team leader, 18 July 1995.

23. Interview with Le Trung Tin, 7 September 1994.

24. Interview with Nguyen Phan Tuu, the South Vietnamese jumpmaster on the mission, 19 January 1997.

25. Interview with Nguyen Huu Tan, 7 September 1994.

26. While relations between China and North Vietnam were strained, Hanoi allowed Beijing to station air defense units inside North Vietnam through most of the Vietnam War.

27. Interview with Le Trung Tin; interview with Nguyen Huu Tan.

28. Interview with Vu Su, intelligence agent, RED DRAGON, 6 March 1995; interview with Pham Ngoc Khanh, demolitions expert, RED DRAGON, 7 September 1994.

29. MACSOG 1967 Command History, p. G-III-2-B-1.

30. *Air America Log,* vol. 11, no. 2, p. 3 (quarterly newsletter published by the Air America Association).

31. Pope, a highly regarded pilot seconded from Civil Air Transport, had been captured in May 1958 when his B-26 was shot down while supporting CIA-backed Sulawesi rebels battling the Sukarno government in Indonesia and was held in a Jakarta prison. The CIA explored ways of bribing prison guards in order to get a Fulton harness to Pope. Because the cooperation of the guards could never be confirmed, the plan was dropped. Pope, who remains convinced that the Skyhook plan could have worked, was eventually released in August 1962 following a goodwill visit by U.S. Attorney General Robert Kennedy. Phone conversation with Allen Pope, 1 November 1996.

32. North Vietnamese militiamen searching for Goodrich later found the Fulton canister on the forest floor. According to interviews conducted by Pentagon investigators in 1994, the militia reeled in shock when they accidentally activated the helium tank.

33. Interview with Do Van Tam, one of the two REMUS reinforcement agents, 19 November 1992.

34. Interview with Nguyen Van Vinh; MDS, "Airborne Operations," p. C-b-94.

35. Interview with Jonathan Carney, 7 June 1993; interview with Roland Dutton, 9 April 1992.

36. In January 1965, SOG's South Vietnamese counterpart, the SES, was renamed the Strategic Technical Service (STS). The more obscure title lent the organization better cover, but the unit's size and mission remained unchanged. In November 1967, the STS was redesignated the Strategic Technical Directorate (STD). This time, the change was significant. Keeping pace with SOG's expanding role, the STD was now responsible not only for

North Vietnam operations but also for cross-border ventures into Laos and Cambodia.

37. In late 1963, the Presidential Survey Office had plans to establish intelligence posts in Hong Kong and Tokyo. In the turmoil after Diem's assassination, however, these plans were shelved. Not until 1967 was the idea resurrected when Captain Du Quoc Luong, a South Vietnamese air force officer who had administered STD air assets, was briefly assigned to the staff of the South Vietnamese consulate in Hong Kong. Mathieu, who replaced him in 1968, went disguised as a civilian with no official standing in the consulate. After Mathieu's disappearance, the post remained vacant. According to senior STD officers, the Hong Kong post was a complete failure. Interview with Ngo The Linh; interview with Nguyen Van Vinh.

Chapter 19. Short-Term Targets

1. "SOG Finance Records, 1–30 April 1968," Entry 71-79, Box 8.

2. MDS, "Operations Against North Vietnam," p. C-70.

3. For the first half of 1968, STRATA used the radio at the neighboring Naval Advisory Detachment facility on the Son Tra peninsula; beginning in July, the project got a radio base set at its own compound. The STRATA program received some of the first PRC-74 radios supplied to SOG. See MACSOG 1967 Command History, pp. G-VIII-1, G-VIII-3.

4. MDS, "Comments on MACSOG's Operations and Intelligence," interview with Staff Sergeant Russell D. Allen, Adviser, Op-34 Reconnaissance Teams, August 1967–December 1968, p. B-n-128.

5. Ibid.

6. MDS, "Airborne Operations," p. C-b-78.

7. Because STRATA radiomen had only rudimentary English skills, SOG's communications section, along with the National Security Agency, designed a simple STRATA code for voice communication with FAC aircraft. See MACSOG 1967 Command History, p. G-VIII-5.

8. Interview with Kyron Hall, 3 February 1994.

9. MDS, "Airborne Operations," p. C-b-68.

10. Morrison interview with Stanley Olchovik, senior officer, Nakhon Phanom launch site, 7 July 1997.

11. MDS, "Comments on MACSOG's Operations and Intelligence," interview with Sgt. Allen, p. B-n-127.

12. Ibid.

13. MDS, "Airborne Operations," p. C-b-70.

14. Interview with Nguyen Nhu Anh, 1 December 1995.

15. Interview with Chuong Dinh Vu, member of STRATA 122, 8 November 1992.

16. MDS, "Airborne Operations," p. C-b-69.

17. Interview with Huong Van De, STRATA 114 member, 27 November 1992; interview with Hoang Van Chuong, STRATA 114 member, 27 November 1992.

18. Interview with George Gaspard, 11 June 1992.

19. MDS, "Airborne Operations," p. C-b-71.

20. Ibid., p. C-b-17A; MACSOG 1967 Command History, p. G-VIII-5.

21. Interview with Do Van Tien, 25 April 1996.

22. Interview with Son Sone, member of STRATA 115, 5 June 1997.

23. Interview with Lo Van Thong, 2 March 1996; Destatte interview with Lo Van On, 23 May 1996.

24. Interview with Floyd Payne, STRATA adviser, 6 December 1994.

25. Interview with Lo Van Thong.

Chapter 20. Denouement

1. MACSOG 1968 Command History, p. F-III-4-2.

2. *Chien Si Bien Phong*, 1:264–269.

3. Ibid., p. 273.

4. While reconnaissance aircraft were able to see cracks in the bridge, SOG had failed to take presabotage photos. There was no way, therefore, to confirm if the damage actually predated the alleged REMUS attack. See MDS, "Comments on MACSOG's Operations and Intelligence," interview with Lt. Col. Ernest T. Hayes Jr., STD Liaison Officer, September 1968–June 1969, p. B-n-41.

5. *Chien Si Bien Phong*, 1:273.

6. Nguyen Van Vinh viewed the photographs in the REMUS file folder when he assumed control over the team in May 1965. Interview with Nguyen Van Vinh.

7. Interview with Nguyen Van Vinh.

8. Dien Bien Phu airfield was bombed on 6 and 11 February 1966. See CIA Intelligence Memorandum, subj: Effectiveness of the Air Campaign Against North Vietnam, December 1966, DDRS 1258-1986.

9. Interview with Nguyen Van Vinh.

10. From the beginning, SOG had been giving its teams ground beacons to mark drop zones for resupply aircraft. However, the signal from the beacons was found to be too weak in practice. As a result, flame pots remained in use through 1967.

11. Interview with Do Van Tam, 9 November 1992.

12. MDS, "Airborne Operations," p. C-b-94. Hanoi later sent the captured communications gear to South Vietnam for use against allied forces. See *Cong An Nhan Dan Viet Nam*, p. 221.

13. Interview with Nguyen Van Vinh.

14. MDS, "Comments on MACSOG's Operations and Intelligence," interview with Lt. Col. Hayes, p. B-n-39. Had any of the SOG case officers been given access to earlier CIA records, they would have seen nearly identical radio problems in Albania during the early 1950s. In that CIA operation, Soviet intelligence advisers helped manipulate radio play and penetrate the entire guerrilla network, culminating in an embarrassing show trial in 1954. See Nicholas Bethell, *The Great Betrayal* (London: Hodder and Stoughton, 1984), p. 191.

15. MACSOG 1968 Command History, p. F-III-4-C-4; interview with Nguyen Van Vinh.

16. Besides REMUS, two other teams were exposed by unburied garbage: EROS in May 1962, and HELEN, an intelligence team that unsuccessfully tried to cross the Demilitarized Zone on foot the same month. See *Chien Si Bien Phong*, 1:143.

17. Interview with Nguyen Van Vinh.

18. Major Oanh, alias Antoine, was named commander of Group 68, the STD section responsible for long-term agent operations.

19. FBIS, Asia and Pacific edition, 13 May 1968, p. K7. Significantly, Hanoi said that members of REMUS would receive "lenient treatment" because they were "repentant agents"—a reference to the fact that they had proved highly cooperative in captivity. The North Vietnamese referred to only one other Op 34A team in these terms: BOONE, the agents who in July 1964 came out of the forest and surrendered even before security forces had started their search.

20. MDS, "Comments on MACSOG's Operations and Intelligence," interview with Col. Robert C. Kingston, Chief, Op-34, March 1967–August 1969, p. B-n-113.

21. MDS, "Comments on Personnel and Training," interview with Lt. Col. William C. Carper, Senior Adviser, Camp Long Thanh, November 1964–August 1965, pp. B-q-22–B-q-24.

22. MDS, "Comments on MACSOG's Operations and Intelligence," interview with Lt. Col. Vincent W. Lang, Chief, Plans and Senior Adviser, Camp Long Thanh, December 1965–November 1966, p. B-n-49.

23. Ibid., interview with Col. Kingston, p. B-n-115.

24. The first team to be uncovered largely by direction-finding equipment was ROMEO. Four days after it was inserted in November 1965,

North Vietnamese security forces picked up a message to the agents from Saigon. From this and subsequent transmissions, Hanoi was able to focus its search in southern Quang Binh Province. See *Chien Si Bien Phong*, 1:133–134.

25. Interview with Nguyen Van Vinh; interview with Roland Dutton, the senior U.S. Army Special Forces adviser at Long Thanh in 1967, 6 June 1992.

26. Interview with Austin Wilgus, case officer for ARES during 1966–67.

27. Interview with Nguyen Van Vinh.

28. MACSOG 1968 Command History, p. F-III-4-C-1.

29. Ibid., pp. F-III-4-2–F-III-4-3. But these security reviews were by no means consistent, and it is unlikely that SOG officials formed a clear picture of agent team status from any of them. For example, a CIA review in July 1967 listed REMUS, EASY, EASY ALFA, and VERSE as "probably not under hostile control." See MDS, "Airborne Operations, p. C-b-94.

30. *Cong An Nhan Dan Viet Nam*, p. 256.

31. MDS, "Airborne Operations," p. C-b-36.

32. Just as with REMUS, Hanoi took pains to prove EASY's bona fides, to include staging fake bridge damage and a mock vehicle ambush. See *Cong An Nhan Dan Viet Nam*, p. 256.

33. FBIS, Asia and Pacific edition, 7 August 68, p. K1.

34. MDS, "MACSOG and the Strategic Technical Directorate: Inception, Organization, Evolution," pp. B-340–B-343.

35. Thomas, *The Very Best Men*, p. 328.

Chapter 21. Guerrillas in Their Midst

1. MDS, "Psychological Operations," p. C-a-2.

2. On 16 June 1961, prior to dropping Team DIDO near Dien Bien Phu, the VIAT crew dispersed leaflets near the Tinh Tuc tin mine in Cao Bang Province. See *Chien Si Bien Phong*, 1:239. VIAT aircraft also dropped leaflets written in the Vietnamese, Tay, and Meo languages on six occasions during 1961. See *Tay Bac, Lich Su Khang Chien Chong My, Cuu Nuoc*, p. 130.

3. *Conduct of the War: A Study of Strategic Lessons Learned in Vietnam*, vol. 6, book 1, p. 8-26.

4. As a quid pro quo for use of its pilots, Taipei was allowed to use a SOG C-123 for a drop of leaflets and gift kits over Hainan Island on 8 June 1964. The gift kits included fake Chinese food vouchers, travel permits,

money, rice, and toothpaste. The plane, using an extra belly fuel tank, took off and landed in Taiwan. Interview with Tien-tsung Chen, the pilot on this mission; *Chinese Air Force in Action,* Series 3, p. 243.

5. Log entries of Tien-tsung Chen.

6. By the following year, letters were also posted from Bangkok, Paris, Singapore, and Tokyo. MDS, "Psychological Operations," pp. C-a-58, C-a-69.

7. *NYT Pentagon Papers,* pp. 301–304. While its content was obviously dictated by Washington and Saigon, VOF was classified as a gray station because it never publicly revealed its broadcasting location or its sponsors.

8. During 1966, nine CIA officers were assigned to SOG, nearly all of them in the Psychological Operations Group. Interview with John Singlaub, 27 February 1997.

9. MACSOG 1966 Command History, p. 56.

10. Interview with Vu Quang Ninh, Director, VOF, 28 October 1995; MACSOG 1966 Command History, p. 51.

11. Ibid.

12. Interview with J. H. "Pat" Carothers Jr., the NAD Chief of Operations and Training, 2 May 1994.

13. During April 1966 alone, more than fifteen million leaflets were dropped urging North Vietnamese troops to defect once they went south. See Department of State memo, JUSPAO Weekly Account, 7 May 1966, DDRS 1996-1644.

14. MDS, "Comments on Personnel and Training," inteview with Col. John K. Singlaub, Chief, SOG, May 1966–August 1968, p. B-q-47. Beginning in 1967, psychological operations in North Vietnam were code-named HUMIDOR.

15. Later in the year, these Vietnamese refugees in Thailand were exploited as an intelligence source by having their letters from North Vietnam secretly opened and read. From these, U.S. intelligence was able to glean sporadic references to the effects of its bombing campaign. See CIA Intelligence Memorandum, subj: The Effectiveness of the Air Campaign Against North Vietnam, December 1966, p. B-37, DDRS 1986-1258. In December 1967, SOG began exploring the possibility of establishing an SSPL "cell" among the Vietnamese refugees in northeastern Thailand. See MDS, "Psychological Operations," p. C-a-19.

16. Brig. Gen. Joseph A. McChristian, Assistant Chief of Staff, J-2, MACV, briefing notes for General Harold K. Johnson, Chief of Staff, U.S. Army, 30 July 1966.

17. White House briefing paper, "Military Pressures on North Vietnam," 17 March 1967, on file at the Lyndon B. Johnson Library.

18. MDS, "Operations Against North Vietnam," p. C-60.

19. Ibid., pp. C-65–C-66.

20. Interview with Jonathon Carney, 7 June 1993; MDS, "Comments on Personnel and Training," interview with Lt. Col. Jonathon D. Carney, pp. B-q-65–B-q-66.

21. MDS, "Psychological Operations," p. C-a-16.

22. Interview with Jonathon Carney.

23. Interview with David Kriskovitch, member of the Long Thanh advisory detachment, 11 May 1992.

24. In September 1993, a joint U.S.–Vietnamese search team located the MC-130 wreck on the side of a sheer karst cliff sixty kilometers southeast of the Lai Chau provincial capital. Of the eleven crewmen who perished on the plane, eight sets of remains were recovered. Interview with Col. John Donovan, commander of the search team, 20 June 1997.

25. MDS, "Comments on MACSOG's Mission," interview with Capt. Bruce B. Dunning, USN Special Operations Division, SACSA, August 1966–November 1967, pp. B-i-11–B-i-12.

26. MDS, "Psychological Operations," p. C-a-129. Although the study bolstered the conclusion that psychological operations were the best way to unnerve Hanoi, at least one participant said that the attempt was "a rather amateurish one. We had tried to get DIA to do it," he said, "but they fell flat on their face." See MDS, "Comments on MACSOG's Mission," interview with Capt. Dunning, p. B-i-11.

27. MDS, "Operations Against North Vietnam," pp. C-70, C-81; MDS, "Psychological Operations," pp. C-a-113–C-a-119.

28. MDS, "Psychological Operations," pp. C-a-18–C-a-19.

29. MDS, "Comments on MACSOG's Mission," interview with Capt. Dunning, p. B-i-13.

30. MDS, "Comments on MACSOG's Operations and Intelligence," interview with Capt. Dunning, p. B-n-86. The two North Vietnamese infantry colonels had found Russian girlfriends and refused to go home after attending an officer's training course. Interview with Ta Duy Huyen, a Vietnamese colonel who knew the two officers, 6 April 1995.

31. MDS, "Psychological Operations," pp. C-a-104–C-a-105.

32. MDS, "Comments on MACSOG's Mission," interview with Capt. Dunning, p. B-i-13.

33. Although Hanoi's demands that the United States cease psychological operations in North Vietnam show that they were having an impact, it would be a mistake to assume that they were crucial to bringing the communists to the negotiating table. Hanoi's communist leaders, after all, demanded hundreds of concessions in exchange for their cooperation, and

these were far down the list. See MDS, "Psychological Operations," p. C-a-110.

34. Other black SOG stations included the ongoing Radio Red Flag, Red Star Radio (allegedly run by communist dissidents in South Vietnam), and MIMIC. Started in October 1967, MIMIC was a subtly corrupted version of the underground Viet Cong radio station meant to confuse listeners. See MDS, "Psychological Operations," pp. C-a-66–C-a-67.

35. Ibid., p. C-a-124.

36. Interview with Phan Trong Sinh, the South Vietnamese officer who headed the black letter project, 14 February 1995; MDS, "Psychological Operations," p. C-a-90.

37. MDS, "Psychological Operations," p. C-a-90.

38. Interview with Nguyen Van Vinh.

39. Interview with David Faughnan, 2 February 1997.

40. Interview with Bert Spivy, 18 March 1992.

41. Copy of letter provided by Captain David Kriskovitch, an adviser with the Long Thanh training detachment who participated in BORDEN recruitment.

42. MDS, "Airborne Operations," p. C-b-17a.

43. Interview with John Mullins, 13 February 1997.

44. Morrison interview with Stanley Olchovik, 3 July 1997.

45. Interview with John Mullins.

46. Interview with David Faughnan, 14 February 1997.

47. Interview with Nguyen Tuu Phan, the senior South Vietnamese case officer for BORDEN; interview with David Faughnan. This ploy was repeated in 1969 when a BORDEN agent believed he was part of a reinforcement team intended for a mountaintop radio relay site in Laos. Thinking he had been separated from the rest of the team during the parachute insertion, the agent made his way to South Vietnam and eventually rallied to American forces. Interview with Robert Destatte, the U.S. Army linguist who interrogated the agent, 2 April 1995.

48. Interview with David Faughnan.

49. A transcript of KILO's interrogation was reportedly intercepted by American intelligence. Interview with John Mullins; interview with David Faughnan; interview with Bert Spivy.

Chapter 22. Urgency

1. MDS, "Maritime Operations," p. C-d-48.

2. Ibid., p. C-d-50; MACSOG 1967 Command History, p. G-II-7.

3. From five action teams in late 1965, ATHENA had been dissolved in 1966 and CUMULUS disbanded in mid-1967 following a heavy firefight at sea. See MACSOG Financial Records, "Accounting Report of CSS, Aug 67," RG 472, 69-A-205, Box 2 (55). This left just NIMBUS, ROMULUS, and VEGA on the books.

4. Interview with Robert Zweiner, NAD adviser, 1 July 1997.

5. Interview with Charles Duncan, 21 June 1997.

6. Ibid.

7. MDS, "Maritime Operations," p. C-d-57; interview with W. H. Rice, 28 July 1997.

8. MDS, "Psychological Operations," p. C-a-125.

9. Interview with Chong Dinh Vu, a former STRATA commando who later served as a radio operator on Paradise Island.

10. MDS, "Comments on MACSOG's Operations and Intelligence," interview with Capt. Dunning, p. B-n-83.

11. Ibid., interview with Col. Singlaub, p. B-n-68.

12. Ibid.; *Conduct of the War: A Study of Strategic Lessons Learned in Vietnam*, vol. 6, book 1, p. 8-26.

13. MDS, "Psychological Operations," pp. C-a-165, C-a-167.

14. FBIS, East Asia edition, 25 March 1968, p. JJJ1.

15. MDS, "Comments on MACSOG's Mission," interview with Capt. Dunning, pp. B-i-15, B-i-10.

16. MDS, "Airborne Operations," p. C-b-83.

17. MACSOG 1968 Command History, p. F-III-1-2.

18. MDS, "Psychological Operations," pp. C-a-75–C-a-76, C-a-120.

19. Ibid., pp. C-a-90, C-a-120.

20. Interview with Larry Trapp, SOG officer, 21 November 1996.

21. MDS, "Psychological Operations," p. C-a-74.

22. The North Vietnamese account of the 17 August incident is taken from *Mot so Tran danh cua Hai Quan (1965–1979), Tap II* [Several Naval Battles (1965–1979), vol. 2] (Hanoi: People's Army Publishing House, 1996), pp. 29–38, translated by Robert Destatte. The North Vietnamese fail to mention that nine members of the junks were captured and taken to Paradise Island. There, in the second such "trial" (the first was held in November 1967), the prisoners were sentenced to death—and then given clemency, because the "SSPL was an organization of peace, not death, and that the subjects had been forced to join the armed junk squad against their desires." Their confessions denouncing communism were aired over the Voice of the SSPL, and letters to their family members were carried home by other detainees. The men were later returned to the "tender mercies of [the] DRV." See MDS, "Psychological Operations," pp. C-a-17, C-a-74.

23. Msg, Gen. Creighton Abrams, COMUSMACV, to Gen. Earle Wheeler, CJCS, 23 Oct 1968.

Chapter 23. Closing the Gate

1. Ronald H. Spector, *After Tet: The Bloodiest Year in Vietnam* (New York: Free Press, 1993), pp. 304–305.
2. Msg, Adm. McCain, CINCPAC, to Gen. Wheeler, CJCS, 21 September 1968; Msg, Abrams to Wheeler, subj: Cease-fire Counter Proposals and Alternatives, 11 October 1968.
3. Quoted in Spector, *After Tet,* p. 305.
4. Lyndon B. Johnson, *The Vantage Point: Perspectives of the Presidency* (New York: Holt, Rinehart and Winston, 1971), p. 258.
5. Msg, Abrams to Gen. Thomas W Brown, Commander, 7th Air Force et al., subj: Special Guidance for General Officers Commanding, 1 November 1968.
6. MDS, "Comments on MACSOG's Operations and Intelligence," interview with Col. Blackburn, p. B-n-23.
7. Ibid., interview with Col. Singlaub, p. B-n-60.
8. Ibid., interview with Col. Robert L. Gleason, Deputy Chief, MACSOG, March 1968–March 1969, pp. B-n-133–B-n-134.
9. MDS, "Airborne Operations," p C-b-76; Msg, Gen. Abrams to Gen. Wheeler, 23 October 1968.
10. In 1967, SOG expanded its cross-border coverage to Cambodia under the code name DANIEL BOONE, later renamed SALEM HOUSE.
11. MDS, "Operations Against North Vietnam," p. C-72.
12. Regarding accomplishments of the maritime teams, McCain specifically noted the anecdotal data collected the effect of the Mk-36 destructor, a self-sterilizing mine dropped around the mouths of eight North Vietnamese rivers beginning in February 1967. See ibid., p. C-73.
13. MACSOG 1969 Command History, p. F-III-3-4.
14. *Conduct of the War: A Study of Strategic Lessons Learned in Vietnam,* vol. 6, book 1, p. 8-25.
15. MACSOG 1969 Command History, p. F-IX-4; MDS, "Airborne Operations," p. C-b-87.
16. MACSOG 1969 Command History, p. F-III-4-2.
17. MDS, "Airborne Operations," p. C-b-65.
18. Morrison interview with Stanley Olchovik.
19. MDS, "Airborne Operations," pp. C-b-21, C-b-62.
20. Ibid., p. C-b-83.

21. Ibid., pp. C-b-84–C-b-85.

22. Interview with Nguyen Van Vinh.

23. Ibid.

24. The two crew members, Hal Castle and Michael Shafernocker, were on a U.S. Navy UH-1B downed along the Cambodian border on 28 April 1969. The remains of the pilot, Richard Reardon, were never found.

25. Interview with Roy Meeks, 3 June 1994.

26. MDS, "Comments on MACSOG's Operations and Intelligence," interview with Lt. Col. Ernest T. Hayes Jr., STD Liaison Officer, MACSOG, September 1968–June 1969, p. B-n-48.

27. Joe Garner and Avrum M. Fine, *Code Name: Copperhead* (New York: Pocket Books, 1996), p. 84.

28. MACSOG 1969 Command History, p. F-IX-F-1.

29. Interview with Richard Meadows.

30. Interview with Jack Isler, the SOG commander at Danang, 1 June 1994; interview with Bill O'Roarke, commander of 1 Company, Ban Me Thuot, 10 June 1994.

31. Interview with Richard Meadows.

32. MACSOG 1969 Command History, p. F-IX-4.

33. Msg, Gen. Wheeler, CJCS, to Gen. Abrams, COMUSMACV, 2 February 1969.

34. MDS, "Comments on MACSOG's Operations and Intelligence," interview with Capt. Dunning, p. B-m-23.

35. Interview with John Mullins.

36. Interview with Warren Williams, THUNDERCLOUD case officer, 16 October 1993.

37. MDS, "MACSOG and the Strategic Technical Directorate: Inception, Organization, Evolution," interview with Lt. Col. Jefferson C. Seay, p. B-330.

38. Interview with Nguyen Huong Rinh, South Vietnamese commander for the THUNDERCLOUD program, 1 October 1993.

39. MDS, "Comments on MACSOG's Operations and Intelligence," interview with Lt. Col. Jefferson Seay, III, STD Liaison Officer, MACSOG, January 1968–September 1968, pp. B-n-131–B-n-132; interview with Larry Trimble, Recon Team ASP, 4 April 1993.

40. MACSOG 1969 Command History, p. F-IX-4.

41. Interview with Kieu Ha, South Vietnamese case officer for the EARTH ANGEL program, 8 November 1994.

42. MACSOG 1969 Command History, p. F-IX-4.

43. Interview with Le Thanh Nam, 6 September 1994.

44. Interview with Nguyen Dang Vieng, 29 December 1994 (via Nguyen Van Vinh).

45. MACSOG 1969 Command History, p. F-XII-B-1.

46. Shepard was an observer on an OH-6A light helicopter downed near Duc Lap on 2 November. His pilot, badly burned in the crash, later died. Peterson was in one of two choppers shot down the same day trying to rescue the crew of the OH-6A. Of the other three crew members in these two rescue aircraft, one managed to evade, and the remaining two were captured and released in 1973.

47. Interview with Le Thanh Nam.

24. Backdoor

1. SOG later used this same argument against the CIA. According to one Op 34 commander, Lieutenant Colonel Robert Kingston, the original STRATA team inserted into North Vietnam during September 1967 might have been "bugged by the presence of a friendly team operating from the Laotian side of the border into the area." See MDS, "Comments on Command and Control," interview with Col. Robert C. Kingston, Chief, Op-34, March 1967–August 1969, p. B-m-27.

2. DDRS 1992-3347; Conboy and Morrison, *Shadow War*, p. 143.

3. Conboy and Morrison, *Shadow War*, pp. 130, 138 n. 38.

4. Interview with John Singlaub, 9 May 1991.

5. Interview with Nhia Koua Xiong, NANSEN team member, 4 August 1991; MDS, "Airborne Operations," p. C-b-16.

6. According to the team's SOG case officer, Captain Fred Caristo, NANSEN was a play on the name of his girlfriend. Phone conversation with Fred Caristo, 2 October 1993.

7. MDS, "Comments on Personnel and Training," interview with Lt. Col. Vincent W. Lang, Chief, Plans and Senior Adviser, Camp Long Thanh, November 1965–November 1966, pp. B-q-44–B-q-45.

8. Interview with Nguyen Nhu Anh.

9. Interview with Lu Trieu Khanh, NANSEN case officer, 7 January 1997.

10. These four ex-NANSEN members were later converted into STRATA 122. Interview with Chuong Dinh Vu, NANSEN radio operator, 3 November 1995.

11. SOG recruiting efforts in Laos were officially discontinued in September 1968, in part because the North Vietnamese embassy in Vientiane was monitoring the activity. See MDS, "Airborne Operations," p. C-b-17.

12. Conboy and Morrison, *Shadow War*, p. 173.

13. *The U.S. Government and the Vietnam War: Executive and Legislative*

Roles and Relationships, pt. 4 (Washington, D.C.: Government Printing Office, 1994), p. 927.

14. Interview with Xieng Phoui, one of the two surviving team members, 27 July 1995; *Chien Si Bien Phong,* 2:148.

15. Correspondence with Somphonphakdy Phayloth, guerrilla officer in Luang Prabang, 27 November 1995; correspondence with Houmphanh Boungnasiri, guerrilla officer in Luang Prabang, 8 December 1995; *Chien Si Bien Phong,* 2:160; flight log entry of Kyron Hall.

16. *Chien Si Bien Phong,* 2:163.

17. Morrison interview with James Atkins, the team's CIA case officer, 14 January 1997.

18. On the return from the infiltration, one of the A-1E fighter escorts was shot down. Lieutenant Colonel Shirrel Martin, the CH-3 mission commander, rescued the pilot with a hoist. See Silver Star citation for Lieutenant Colonel Shirrel G. Martin, copy in author's collection.

19. Morrison interview with CIA case officer, 8 July 1995.

20. For example, a reconnaissance team was inserted near Dien Bien Phu on 9 August. North Vietnamese forces overran this unit on 5 September. See *Chien Si Bien Phong,* 2:164.

21. Interview with former CIA official, 12 August 1995.

22. Conboy and Morrison, *Shadow War,* p. 241.

23. Ibid., p. 244.

24. Ibid.

Chapter 25. Exceptions to the Rule

1. *Cong An Nhan Dan Viet Nam,* p. 152.

2. MACSOG 1970 Command History, pp. B-III-8, B-III-26, B-IV-3.

3. Msg, Adm. McCain, CINCPAC, to Gen. Wheeler, CJCS, subj: Cambodian Overview II, 4 May 1970

4. MACSOG 1970 Command History, p. B-1.

5. Ibid., p. B-12.

6. Interview with Richard Meadows; MACSOG 1970 Command History, p. B-IX-5.

7. Op 36B advisers stopped accompanying STRATA teams into the field after March 1969. Interview with Roy Meeks.

8. Op 36B peaked in early 1971 at twenty-five Americans. Interview with Bruce Pross, STRATA adviser, 11 January 1995.

9. MACSOG 1970 Command History, p. B-IX-5.

10. Ibid., p. B-69.

11. Among the new projects were PIKE HILL and CEDAR WALK, both of which involved ethnic Khmer agents operating in eastern Cambodia.

12. Interview with Michael Eiland, Op 36A commander (1971), 4 June 1991.

13. Interview with G. H. "Wick" Zimmer, Op 36A commander (1970), 6 October 1994.

14. Ibid.

15. *Conduct of the War: A Study of Strategic Lessons Learned in Vietnam,* vol. 6, book 1, p. 8-29.

16. One author raised the possibility that during the week preceding the raid the CIA had inserted an agent somewhere in the vicinity of Son Tay, and that his presence might have compromised the mission. Considering the CIA's dismal record in agent insertions before 1964, it seems unlikely that it could suddenly place someone on the ground in 1970. See Benjamin F. Schemmer, *The Raid* (New York: Harper and Row, 1976), pp. 82, 117–118, 219.

17. Author Greg Walker alternately claims that an EARTH ANGEL team or an American-led PRAIRIE FIRE recon team was inserted by helicopter near Son Tay in the week before the raid. See Greg Walker, *At the Hurricane's Eye* (New York: Ivy Books, 1994), p. 63; Greg Walker, "Son Tay—Story of Success," *Behind the Lines,* September 1997, pp. 37–44. He does not cite documentary proof; his claim relies solely on the testimony of a single "participant." However, many SOG officers and team leaders discount this as pure fantasy. Major Wick Zimmer, the Op 36A commander who oversaw EARTH ANGEL operations, denies there was any such mission. Mark Gentry, an EARTH ANGEL adviser who Walker initially claimed was involved in the operation, says nothing of the sort took place. Michael Taylor, a SOG liaison officer at Nakhon Phanom air base, discounts such claims despite the fact that Walker alleges the operation was staged out of the air base. Eldon Bargewell, a highly regarded SOG recon team leader, says there was no such raid. Most telling, General Blackburn, one of the most knowledgeable participants, called the story "rubbish." Interview with Donald Blackburn, 29 September 1998.

18. MACSOG 1971–72 Command History, pp. B-13-6–B-13-7.

19. During 1971, SOG sent 1,536 propaganda letters through third-country post offices in Paris, Tokyo, Hong Kong, and Bangkok. Ibid., p. B-13-6.

20. Msg, Gen. Abrams, COMUSMACV, to Adm. McCain, CINCPAC, subj: Covert Operations, 14 December 1970.

21. Interview with Gary Swartzbaugh, STRATA adviser, 27 October 1997; interview with Fred Smith, STRATA adviser, 1 May 1995.

22. MACSOG 1970 Command History, p. B-V-1.

23. The SMS, headquartered at Nha Trang, was subordinate to the SOG's direct counterpart, the STD. Long-range plans called for the SMS to be composed of five groups: three of them created especially for the new unit, plus the STRATA teams at Monkey Mountain and the agent teams at Long Thanh. From the start, however, there was strong resistance from the agents, and to a less extent STRATA, to being placed under the SMS. Interview with Ngo The Linh; MACSOG 1970 Command History, p. B-XVI-5.

24. On 8 February 1971, the U.S. Congress passed a resolution forbidding American military personnel from participating in ground operations in Laos. It was meant to prevent the Nixon administration from mounting an incursion in Laos as it had the previous year in Cambodia, but it also applied to SOG. The only exemptions were Americans performing "personnel recovery missions and crash site inspections." See MACSOG 1971–72 Command History, p. B-1.

25. Ibid., p. B-3-4.

26. Ibid., p. B-46.

27. There is some debate on the mission results. SOG claimed victory and mentioned only minor damage to the Nastys in its report. See ibid., pp. B-3-4, B-11-8–B-11-9. But the North Vietnamese said the freighter SOG claimed to have sunk on 10 February was not hit. Hanoi did admit to the loss of its gunboats on 19 February. For a complete North Vietnamese account of both engagements, see *Mot so Tran danh cua Hai Quan,* 2:54–62.

28. MACSOG 1971–72 Command History, p. B-11-8.

29. Ibid.

30. Ibid. p. B-52. On 26 December, following blatant North Vietnamese road construction in the Demilitarized Zone and a rocket attack on Saigon the week before, the Joint Chiefs authorized SOG to launch a rocket-boat attack against Quang Khe. Four Nastys left Danang but were forced to call a weather abort short of their target. The next night, three Nastys headed north but had to turn back after encountering North Vietnamese naval vessels. No further attempts were mounted.

Chapter 26. The Quiet One

1. The abbreviation PS, short for Pakse Site, was used by the CIA and contract aircrews for STOL landing strips in southernmost Laos.

2. Interview with James Glerum.

3. Interview with Chuang-wen Yu, commander, 34th Squadron, 14 May 1997.

4. Morrison interview with Tom Poole, 2 June 1994.

5. Taps that transmitted to airplanes were code-named LEFT TWIST; those that were used with helicopters were called LEFT BANK. Interview with CIA case officer, 3 August 1995.

6. "Design Requirements for a Quiet Helicopter," presented at the Twenty-eighth Annual National Forum of the American Helicopter Society, May 1972.

7. Press release, Hughes Tool Company, 8 April 1971.

8. In early 1971, Air America began S-58T upgrades for five of its H-34s. The first was completed in March, the last in July. See Conboy and Morrison, *Shadow War,* p. 379.

9. The Quiet One went by several unofficial names. Hughes coined the term "500P" when it prepared a short maintenance pamphlet for the experimental chopper. The Taiwanese pilots, by contrast, called it the "Hughes 600." Interview with Wayne Knight, Air America pilot, 19 November 1993; interview with Chuang-wen Yu.

10. Interview with Henry Lu, 17 December 1998.

11. Interview with An Liang, Hughes 500P pilot, 17 January 1997.

12. PS 44 was once hit by a small communist patrol, but the bulk of U.S. personnel were on weekend leave at the time. On that occasion, the on-site Commando Raider team was easily able to beat back the attackers. Interview with James Glerum.

13. Ibid.

14. Ibid.

15. Interview with Dan Smith, 6 February 1991.

16. Interview with James Glerum.

17. Ibid; FBIS, East Asia and Pacific edition, 8 December 1972, p. K-2.

18. For the original account of the mission, see Conboy and Morrison, *Shadow War,* pp. 382–384.

Chapter 27. Last Missions

1. Interview with Tran The Hong, EARTH ANGEL airborne team commander, 26 February 1995. In late December 1971, Op 36A began airborne training for all of its agent teams because helicopter assets were slated to be greatly reduced in the near future. Interview with Michael Eiland.

2. MACSOG 1971–72 Command History, p. B-72.

3. Ibid., p. B-86; interview with Bruce Pross, STRATA adviser, 11 January 1995; interview with Fred Smith, STRATA adviser, 5 January 1995;

interview with Roger Pezzelle, SOG Ground Studies Group commander, 13 February 1995.

4. MACSOG 1971–72 Command History, pp. B-16-1, B-17-13.

5. Ibid., p. B-3-15.

6. Ibid., p. B-9-1. Interview with Rolf Utegaard, Op 36 Commander, 8 April 1995.

7. By 1971, the Long Thanh training complex, originally named Camp Quyet Thanh, had been redesignated Camp Yen The, in honor of the mountain redoubt near Hanoi used by the anti-French guerrilla leader De Tham earlier in the century.

8. MACSOG 1971–72 Command History, p. B-16-6.

9. Msg, Col. John Sadler, Chief SOG to USARV HQ, Saigon, subj: Termination of MACV SOG Activities, 1030Z 30 March 1972.

10. Interview with Tran Viet Hue, STRATA team leader, 19 May 1997; interview with Tran The Hung, STRATA team leader, 25 February 1995; interview with SOD senior adviser, 4 June 1991.

11. Interview with Nguyen Phan Tuu.

12. Interview with SOD senior adviser; Ewen Montagu, *The Man Who Never Was* (Philadelphia: Lippincott, 1954). In the World War II operation, the British dressed a dead body in a British Royal Marine uniform with a briefcase full of documents handcuffed to his wrist. Supposedly the man had died in a plane crash at sea and his body floated to shore. In reality he had been delivered to the Spanish coast aboard a British submarine. The Germans recovered the body, examined the documents, and decided they were real. Hitler then shifted his main defenses away from Sicily to Greece.

13. Interview with Luan Nguyen, Vietnamese air force C-47 pilot, 31 May 1995.

14. MACV Intelligence Summary, "Cover and Deceptions," 10 September 1973; Msg, Gen. Abrams, COMUSMACV, to Maj. Gen. Frederick Kroesen, Senior Adviser, FRAC, subj: Quang Tri Operations, 21 May 1972; Dale Andradé, *Trial by Fire: The 1972 Easter Offensive* (New York: Hippocrene Books, 1995), pp. 207–208.

15. Strategic Technical Directorate Advisory Team 158 Command History, May 1972–March 1973, pp. 36–37. Hereafter referred to as STD Advisory Team 158 Command History.

16. On 5 June, planning for CONPLAN 5108 suffered a blow when a China Airlines C-46, on contract with Team 158, crashed during poor weather in the Central Highlands. Ten team members were killed, including Major Calvin Gore, the Detachment B commander who was to have played a major role in the unfolding North Vietnam operation. STD Advisory Team 158 Command History, p. 102; interview with Michael Eiland.

17. Interview with Tran Viet Hue.

18. Diary entry of Senior Adviser, Special Operations Detachment.

19. Ibid.

20. Ibid.

21. STD Advisory Team 158 Command History, p. 93.

22. Correspondence with Bach Van Dong, one of the Subic graduates, 5 September 1995.

23. Interview with SOD senior adviser.

24. Interview with SOD officer, 3 November 1992.

25. Interview with SOD senior adviser.

26. STD Advisory Team 158 Command History, p. 96.

27. Ibid., p. 89.

28. One aspect of CONPLAN 5108—airdrops of counterfeit North Vietnamese money—was conducted by U.S. Air Force F-4 fighters during the fall of 1972. Interview with William Patton, an F-4 pilot, 15 December 1998.

29. Ibid., p. 37.

Chapter 28. Defeat

1. Andradé, *Trial by Fire*, pp. 522–523.

2. Defense Attaché Saigon, "RVNAF Quarterly Assessment, 4th Quarter FY 73," 24 July 1973.

3. Interview with Le Van Hanh, 6 June 1993.

4. STD Advisory Team 158 Command History, p. 10.

5. Some STD team members captured in Laos remained in prison through the 1980s. The reasoning behind their extended sentences is unclear, although it is most likely attributed to their stubborn refusal to submit to revolutionary reeducation.

6. Interview with Hong Tran, 23 February 1994.

7. Interview with Tran Viet Hue.

8. Interview with Dinh Huu Doan, STD launch site officer, 11 March 1997.

9. Interview with Nguyen Cong The, 6 June 1993.

10. Interview with Le Huu Minh, 8 October 1995.

11. William LeGro, *Vietnam from Ceasefire to Capitulation* (Washington, D.C.: U.S. Army Center of Military History, 1981), p. 171.

12. Interview with Truong Duy Tai.

13. Interview with Le Huu Minh.

14. Interview with Do Van Tien.

15. Fellow inmates state that François, succumbing to pressure during his

three years in prison, cooperated with communist interrogators in their attempts to compile a history of STD operations. For this, he was released after a relatively short term. Some authors have claimed François was a high-placed communist agent from the start and was largely responsible for SOG's poor record in conducting covert operations into North Vietnam. For example, during U.S. congressional testimony on 19 June 1996, Sedgwick Tourison, author of *Secret Army, Secret War* (Annapolis: Naval Institute Press, 1995), claimed François had admitted to operating in this role during an alleged interview on Vietnamese national television. François vehemently denies the charge, and the fact that he served almost three years in prison speaks against wartime duplicity. Hanoi has openly admitted to having spies in the ranks of the South Vietnamese army and has generously rewarded those who served in such a capacity. François was not one of them.

16. During his time in reeducation, Marc was repeatedly quizzed about ARES. "They wanted to know about his family relations and what he looked like," recalls the former SOG officer. By all accounts, ARES was captured soon after his insertion in 1961 and manipulated by North Vietnamese intelligence until 1970. Why Hanoi was interested in such details in 1975 remains a mystery. Interview with Nguyen Van Vinh.

17. Sedgwick Tourison was the first to compile a reasonably accurate list of the commandos captured and killed in North Vietnam. See *Secret Army, Secret War*, Appendix 10.

18. John L. Plaster, *SOG: The Secret Wars of America's Commandos in Vietnam* (New York: Simon and Schuster, 1997), p. 221. Tourison also subscribes to this theory in *Secret Army, Secret War*.

19. William C. Westmoreland, *A Soldier Reports* (New York: Doubleday, 1976), p. 130.

Epilogue

1. "Once Commandos for U.S., Vietnamese Are Now Barred," *New York Times*, 14 April 1995.

2. MDS, "Comments on Counterpart Relationships—The STD," p. B-u-3.

3. Dale Andradé, "Paying Our Dues," *The Retired Officer*, January 1997, pp. 40–44.

4. Ibid.

5. Ibid.

A NOTE ON SOURCES

Researching covert operations is never an easy task. That's why they were covert in the first place—to thwart prying eyes. But it was more than thirty years ago that the United States launched its secret war against North Vietnam, and today much of what was done then is coming to the surface. The material is out there, although it takes some digging to find it.

The Pentagon Papers are the oldest source on the covert program, especially for 1964, its first year under Defense Department control. In fact, since they were leaked to the *New York Times* in 1971, the Pentagon Papers were virtually the only mention of policy surrounding the secret operations into North Vietnam up to that time. Careful readers of the Pentagon Papers can glean much about the program, from early operations immediately following the partition of Vietnam in 1954 to the birth of Operation Plan 34A—the final stage of the covert war against North Vietnam—and the early consensus that, although such actions would probably not deter Hanoi from its aggression in South Vietnam, they were the best course of action considering Washington's unwillingness to commit American troops to Vietnam at that time.

For the policy making behind the operations, the best source is the *Foreign Relations of the United States* series for Vietnam and Southeast Asia, published by the U.S. Government Printing Office. This compilation of documents is particularly valuable for its high-level discussion of the decision to transfer the covert program from the CIA to the Defense Department.

However, the lion's share of the documentation comes from a voluminous work known as the Military Assistance Command Studies and Observations Group (MACSOG) Documentation Study. Researched and written in 1970, this work numbers in the thousands of pages, although about half remain classified. For many years the few existing copies of this study lay forgotten in a few safes in government offices. They came to light in 1992 when the U.S. Senate Select Committee on POW/MIA Affairs was looking for documentation on American servicemen still missing in Vietnam. After a quick declassification process (had the Senate not expressed an interest in the study, it would certainly have taken years to be declassified), about half of it was made public. Although often heavily censored, this useful document outlines the 34A program and gives details on missions. Three of the sections deal almost exclusively with missions into North Vietnam: "Maritime Operations," "Airborne Operations," and "Operations Against North Vietnam." Each one

333

provides background to the program, as well as data on the teams inserted into North Vietnam, their location, and SOG's impressions of their effectiveness. These three sections provide the chronological core for any research.

Also very useful within the documentation study are dozens of interviews with officers involved in all aspects of the program. Found in several sections of the study, these interviews were conducted in 1969 and 1970, while the operations were still fresh in mind, and they are, for the most part, completely candid. They show the officers' frustration with political constraints on the war, as well as their opinions on how the covert program could have been made more effective.

Another key source is the annual Military Assistance Command, Vietnam (MACV) Command Histories. MACV attached classified special operations annexes to its annual histories detailing progress in the SOG program for that year. These mirror the documentation study in many respects but include more operational detail for specific missions into North Vietnam. Ironically, the most recent command history (1971–72) is the least "sanitized" (the U.S. government's euphemism for blacking out "sensitive" portions), while the oldest (1964) is the most.

A surprising source comes from a large batch of documents only recently discovered in the National Archives in College Park, Maryland. In late 1995 archivists discovered some eighty boxes of financial records pertaining to SOG operations. Ledgers and balance sheets do not make for exciting history, but, for the discerning researcher, they confirm much of the data that might otherwise have been excised from the documentation study or the command histories. For example, one of the last teams to parachute into North Vietnam, code-named RED DRAGON, was to have a component of Nationalist Chinese commandos from Taiwan. Apparently this has been kept secret by the declassifiers, but their existence is confirmed by the rosters and pay vouchers, which list the commandos' Chinese names. These records are especially useful for researchers who already possess a sound background in the subject.

Hanoi has not been silent on the subject of covert operations. From the communist perspective, covert operations were not only a failure for Washington and Saigon but also a counterintelligence success for North Vietnam. With the capture of the earliest CIA agent teams, Hanoi began to piece together an effective method of "turning" (forcing) the radio operators into sending false messages back to their handlers in Saigon. These successes are chronicled in several official volumes written under the auspices of the Ministries of Defense and Interior. One of the most important is a two-volume work, *Lich Su Bo Doi Bien Phong* [History of the Border Defense Troops] (Hanoi: People's Public Security Publishing House, 1990). Along with two other works, *Chien Si Bien Phong* [The Border Defense Soldier] (Hanoi: People's Public Security Publishing House, 1984), and *Cong An Nhan Dan*

Viet Nam, 1954–1964 [Vietnam People's Public Security Force, 1954–1964] (Hanoi: Institute of Public Security Science, Ministry of Interior, 1994), they detail Hanoi's internal efforts to combat the commando teams. Several other Vietnamese volumes examine the covert war and Hanoi's response, and all are listed in the notes.

In many cases, Hanoi chose to announce its capture of agent and teams and place these individuals on public trial. North Vietnamese newspapers invariably carried these trials. The Foreign Broadcast Information Service (FBIS), the U.S. government organization that monitors and translates media reports worldwide, invariably carried these trials.

Although the U.S. government lacks a uniform system of declassifying documents and making them available to researchers, one collection, with a lot of searching, sometimes yields valuable sources. Called the Declassified Documents Reference System (DDRS), it is a quarterly compilation of newly declassified documents from all branches of government.

Clearly, the subject of Vietnam War covert operations is fertile ground, yet only a few authors have tried to tackle the subject. The only book devoted entirely to the secret war against North Vietnam is *Secret Army, Secret War* (Annapolis, Md.: Naval Institute Press, 1995) by Sedgwick D. Tourison. Another book, *SOG: The Secret Wars of America's Commandos in Vietnam* (New York: Simon and Schuster, 1997), by John L. Plaster, concentrates on American-led secret missions into Laos and Cambodia but gives only a cursory account of the operations into North Vietnam.

Other works focus on certain aspects of the program, especially the covert maritime operations leading up to the 1964 Tonkin Gulf incident. One of the most complete accounts is contained in the U.S. Navy's official history, *The United States Navy and the Vietnam Conflict: From Military Assistance to Combat, 1959–1965* (Washington, D.C.: U.S. Government Printing Office, 1986), by Edward J. Marolda and Oscar P. Fitzgerald. This is the second volume in the navy's Vietnam War series. A more recent book on the Tonkin Gulf incident, Edwin E. Moise's *Tonkin Gulf and the Escalation of the Vietnam War* (Chapel Hill: University of North Carolina Press, 1996), yields new documents on the 1964 covert raids on North Vietnam's coast that helped set in motion the Tonkin Gulf incident.

Other works, mostly memoirs, chronicle narrow aspects of the covert program. In the opening chapter of *Teammates: SEALs at War* (New York: Simon and Schuster, 1994), former Navy SEAL Barry W. Enoch writes about his experiences with the patrol boats used on maritime operations. Two other memoirs, *Code Name: Copperhead* (New York: Pocket Books, 1996), by Joe R. Garner and Avrum M. Fine, and *One Tough Marine* (New York: Ivy Books, 1994), by Donald N. Hamblen and Bruce H. Norton, provide unsubstantiated stories of derring-do in North Vietnam.

INDEX